TABLE OF CONTENTS

CW00822881

Camomile St. 271.0

WITHDRAWN

INTRODUCTION

This is a functional guide to territory largely neglected by the film-criticism establishment—encompassing tens of thousands of films. Most of the films discussed test the limits of contemporary (middle-class) cultural acceptability, mainly because in varying ways they don't meet certain "standards" utilized in evaluating direction, acting, dialogue, sets, continuity, technical cinematography, etc. Many of the films are overtly "lower-class" or "low-brow" in content and art direction. However, a high percentage of these works disdained by the would-be dictators of public opinion are sources of *pure enjoyment and delight,* despite improbable plots, "bad" acting, or ragged film technique. At issue is the notion of "good taste," which functions as a filter to block out entire areas of experience judged—and damned—as unworthy of investigation.

The concepts of "good taste" are intricately woven into society's control process and class structure. Aesthetics are not an objective body of laws suspended above us like Plato's supreme "Ideas"; they are rooted in the fundamental mechanics of how to control the population and maintain the status quo.

Our sophisticated, "democratic" Western civilization regulates the population's access to information, as well as its innermost attitudes, through *media*—particularly film and video. The power to literally create desire, fashion, consumer trends, opinions, aspirations and even one's very identity is expressed through film and video. This force—power through persuasion—reaches deep into the backbrain, rendering more brutal, physical control tactics obsolete.

Since the sixties, film has ceased being a popular creative medium. The whole sixties' avantgarde filmmaking, from Brakhage to Conner, was based on the cheap availability of 16mm film, cameras, etc; many of the films in this book were originally shot in 16mm. After this became too expensive, Super-8 became the medium of choice. Several years ago, the major manufacturers began de-emphasizing professional-quality Super-8 cameras, film stocks, etc, saying, "People don't really want it. Editing is too hard for most people, and everyone's switching to video, anyway." The result: the number of low-budget films being produced has dropped drastically.

The value of low-budget films is: they can be transcendent expressions of a single person's individual vision and quirky originality. When a corporation decides to invest $20 million in a film, a chain of command regulates each step, and no one person is allowed free rein. Meetings with lawyers, accountants, and corporate boards are what films in Hollywood are all about.

So what makes films like Herschell Gordon Lewis's *The Wizard of Gore* or Ray Dennis Steckler's *The Incredibly Strange Creatures Who Stopped Living and Became Mixed-Up Zombies* worthwhile? First of all: unfettered creativity. Often the films are eccentric—even *extreme*—presentations by individuals *freely expressing their imaginations,* who throughout the filmmaking process improvise creative solutions to problems posed either by circumstance or budget—mostly the latter. Secondly, they often present unpopular—even radical—views addressing social, political, racial or sexual inequities, hypocrisy in religion or government; or, in other ways they assault taboos related to the presentation of sexuality, violence, and other mores. (Cf. George Romero's *Dead* trilogy which features intelligent, problem-solving black heroes, or Russ Meyer's *Faster Pussycat, Kill! Kill!* which showcases tough girls outwitting—and even physically outdoing—sexist men.) Thirdly, occasionally films are made of such unique stature (Cf. *Daughter of Horror*) as to stand virtually outside any genre or classification, thus extending the boundaries of what has been done in the medium, as well as providing—at best—inexplicably marvelous experiences.

It is all too common—indeed, a cliche—for otherwise well-read, thoughtful people to deplore "violence" depicted in movies such as the ones discussed here. Yet there is no direct evidence that the mere viewing of a film causes crime; in fact, a film may well act as a "safety valve" *preventing* its occurrence. In any case, violence cannot be eliminated through repression of its representation; in fact, there is evidence we have a primal *need* to express ourselves violently, just as we do so—involuntarily—in our dreams. When there's an accident on the highway, our immediate, uncensored instinct is to stop and stare. But . . . there is a crucial difference between the artistic *representation* of violence and its willful commission against another person in actual life.

Balinese have for centuries enacted *extremely* violent dramas touching on primal social issues, yet historically they are among the most peaceful people on earth. Obviously these dramas have served a cathartic as well as poetic function. In Western civilization, the history of painting (from early medieval depictions of martyrs and the allegorical landscapes of Hieronymus Bosch up to Goya and Francis Bacon) is replete with tortures and bloody dismemberments. The Bible itself depicts almost every kind of atrocity and sex crime—yet does one go out and rape and kill after reading the Bible?

In our society, the conditions that create rapists and murderers do not stem from the creative interplay of our fantasies—for well-balanced people there is an enormous difference between a *fantasy* and *reality.* Murderous inclinations already in an individual are not triggered by viewing one film—that is far too easy an explanation. Film censorship is a simplistic, backwards approach to profound problems in our society; it is much easier to bandage the symptom than to cure the deep-rooted disease. The sickness of the rapist-murderer may stem from a number of causes—economic repression (ghettos), violence in the family, even biochemical imbalance. But whatever the causes, film censorship is not the cure.

This volume focuses on unhailed filmmakers whose work dates primarily from the sixties and seventies. Most of the films mentioned are classifiable into two genres: gore (violence) and sexploitation, although the best transcend such facile labeling. Certain sexploitation or gore filmmakers (such as David Cronenberg, who already has had two books written about him) are absent because of previous publicity or inaccessibility. Many wonderful, more mainstream filmmakers, such as Bunuel, Polanski, Keaton, Fritz Lang and Val Lewton—and even entire genres such as Surrealist/Dada films and *film noir*—are not detailed for similar reasons. This is not a completist's volume—many other American movies, plus a whole other world of films from Hong Kong, the Philippines, Mexico, Spain, etc. remain to be explored and experienced. Rather, it is a presentation of the continuing *creative dilemma,* with specific emphasis on the problems of artists counter to the status quo. Here the filmmakers themselves articulate their philosophies and histories while offering views and insights applicable to any creative medium. In the world of low-budget filmmaking, it is still possible for the imagination to reign supreme.

—V. Vale and Andrea Juno, San Francisco, 1985

INTERVIEWS

FRANK HENENLOTTER

To date New York filmmaker Frank Henenlotter has made one excellent horror feature, **Basket Case**. Undoubtedly he deserves funding to make many more, but at present he works as a graphic designer at an ad agency. He is included here not for the magnitude of his creative output, but for his **thought**. Henenlotter's views on the entire process of independent filmmaking include careful consideration of the moral aspects of presenting violence, gore, and sexual deviancy; his analysis of this prickly area of aesthetic ethics forms an important core of the following interview.

Additionally, Frank Henenlotter is a broadly knowledgeable film historian whose perspective on obscure movies provides some surprising correlations. He's also a film memorabilia collector, trivia expert and the possessor of an extremely quick, enthusiastic wit behind his low-key, unassuming facade. Besides other unusual interests, he collects antique surgical tools—even possessing an authentic violet ray machine, complete with scarce accessories . . .

Andrea Juno interviewed Frank Henenlotter in his East Village apartment, which was neatly decorated with movie posters, an impressive collection of books and videotapes, and the original **Basket Case** dummy sitting alone in a corner . . .

■ *AJ: When were you last in San Francisco?*
■ FH: About ten years ago—it's probably a totally different city—totally different *planet* now. I got off at the Greyhound bus terminal and the first thing I did was go to Market Street and—I can almost *smell* sleazo movie theaters—see *Battle Beneath the Earth, Cannibal Girls,* and *Raw Meat*. It was perfect—I'd never been in the city before.

It reminded me so much of 42nd Street (or what 42nd Street *used* to be—*now* they're getting rid of it). That's where I have my fondest memories of seeing oddball films at oddball hours. Like, I saw *Blackenstein* at 12:30 Saturday night during the height of a snowstorm. There were only a few other people in the theater and they went nuts seeing the film—the star had a square afro. Every time the monster appeared I thought the balcony was going to come down—people were just screaming!
■ *AJ: Do you see a lot of films?*
■ FH: I used to. I'm less of a junkie now, only because of the unavailability of so many of them. When I was growing up on Long Island there were *drive-ins*, still. And there used to be lots of sleaze theaters that played horror films. One of my favorite ones is now just hardcore porn. There were three in one town; now there's *none* in that town. I hate going back to Long Island because everything I used to love is *dead*.

The few drive-ins left in this country are playing Steven

Spielberg's latest. Double features are a thing of the past; it costs too much money to ship two films. And that used to be the joy of the '60s—when I was going to the movies you *always* saw *two* pictures. Even 42nd Street now is showing too much mainstream. The only excitement I get lately is from what's being released on videotape. Of course I'd much rather see something in a theater, but—now I'm buying videocassettes like crazy. Yesterday I bought *Orgy of the Dead* and *She Freak*. The week before I picked up Ted V. Mikels' *Corpse Grinders*.

But it's not like I can just go to a theater and see *Corpse Grinders*. I'd much rather see films in a movie theater with a group of people, especially in the kind of run-down fleabags that played them—somehow the more peeling paint, the

> It's a strange concept: all these obscure films that I would have risked injury and death to see (literally, in some of those theaters) are now available at your local clean video store!

more smell of urine, the more exciting it seemed to be! But I'll take it where I can get it. I'm certainly not going to bypass *Corpse Grinders* simply because it's on videotape!

I didn't want anything to do with videotape when it first came out; the only films available were *Sound of Music* and *Hello Dolly*—give me a break! But once you saw *Blood Feast* being sold, that's when you knew: uh-oh, here it comes. That's when everybody I knew had to rush out and buy a VCR. We never anticipated the amount of the stuff that was going to come out. For awhile I was getting a lot of bootleg tapes from people, but you don't need to anymore because it's *all* going to be released!

It's a strange concept: all these obscure films that I would have risked injury and death to see (literally, in some of those theaters) are now available at your local clean video store! It's a little unnerving. I'm wholeheartedly in support of this, but I'm still not used to the fact that these films that I spent my whole life trying to see are now *consumer items*.
■ *AJ: People who used to search for rare occult books get a similar sense of dismay when they become available in cheap paperback editions—*
■ FH: Sure. Now I can watch *Spider Baby* anytime I want. On the positive side, I love to show these films to people. I used to have a hard time dragging people to *those* theaters. Now, fine—I can sit here and run a tape for them. It's a lot easier!
■ *AJ: Although . . . I first saw Dario Argento's Suspiria on videotape—twice. But when I finally saw it in a theater, it was like seeing a completely different film—*
■ FH: —and *hearing* a different film—the soundtrack is outrageous.

■ *AJ: But there were also aspects relevant to the plot that were blocked out in the video—like a woman in the background of one scene whom I had never noticed before. Also, the color changes assume much greater significance on a large screen.*

■ FH: The video you saw may have been a bootleg, although that doesn't mean it'll be better when they officially release it. *Deep Red* (also an Argento film) is out, and the cropping of that film is quite poor, blowing a key scene at the beginning. I really dislike that sort of thing, especially with a director like Argento who makes full use of the screen.

I have Herschell Gordon Lewis's *Something Weird* which is in wide screen, and they letterboxed it—kept it wide screen, which is great. They also left in all the scratches and breaks and the dirt! If it's a wide screen let me see the whole picture—I can live with the top and bottom framed. And in the print I have they even discolored the top and bottom for the LSD scene!

■ *AJ: Can I look at your film collection?*

■ FH: Sure. Here's some of my collection; a lost genre—sex-hygiene films. One called *Tomorrow's Children* (from 1934) is *for* sterilization. The highlight of the film is where a guy's getting a vasectomy—he's a real lowlife, sneering and insulting the doctors as they're doing it. But that's the only way to have one!

■ *AJ: I love drivers' ed films like* Safetybelt for Susie *and* Red Asphalt, *and other types like* Safety in the Shop. *Some of them are so gory.*

■ FH: Anything that's dogmatic like that—I love watching. That's why those sex-hygiene films are so marvelous. Back then, the only way you could see a taboo subject—a naked woman's breast or legs, or see a film where a couple actually goes to bed together *off-screen*—was to suffer through all this morality and educational footage, and a doctor standing there with a pointer saying, "This will happen to you if . . . !" The only way you could see a woman's private parts was to see a baby in blood burst forth. What a nice twisted world it was!

■ *AJ: Guilt with titillation.*

■ FH: Exactly. One that's now available in videotape is *They Must Be Told,* which is marvelous. A girl sleeps with someone and then gives V.D. to her husband, who goes blind. And, the baby's probably going to be born dead. What a significant guilt trip for the audience, who sit there knowing that if they . . . they're going to go home with V.D. I imagine a lot of those films are lost now, but hopefully they're going to be found and put out on tape. Everybody's seen *Reefer Madness,* but there's plenty more like that out there, maybe not as funny or as wacky, but if they're morbid and depressing that's fine with me!

I can't imagine what it was like in the '30s and '40s when

> **Anything that's dogmatic . . . I love watching. That's why those sex-hygiene films are so marvelous. Back then, the only way you could see a taboo subject—a naked woman's breast or legs, or see a film where a couple actually go to bed together off-screen—was to suffer through all this morality and educational footage.**

they would segregate the audience. I've got this great pressbook for something called *Sins of the Father.* Like many other films (e.g., *Mom and Dad*) they would segregate the audience: women only at 7:30, men only at 9:00. They would go into these small towns, and if the town didn't have a theater they'd set up a tent. Think of the anticipation of

Belial (from **Basket Case**) in Henenlotter's New York apartment.

people imagining what they might see! And the promoters would clean up. Of course, you could only have two shows, because once word of mouth got out about what a dog the film was, you'd be long gone to the next town.

Allegedly, the promoters would have a reel of nudity they would show if they could get away with it; if they realized there were no authorities in the place. But the birth-of-the-baby footage was the nice big shocker. And many of these films had a short running time because they had a person in attendance (like, a woman dressed as a nurse) selling books like *The Facts of Life* or a little illustrated V.D. pamphlet which you would take home and then go, "Wow!" All that's lost today. But the films aren't lost, I hope.

■ *AJ: You know a lot about obscure films and directors—*

■ FH: Just as a hobby. Usually they *all* live up to their reputations. Seeing *Orgy of the Dead* was a delight after hearing about it for so many years, owning the pressbook, and finally, not being disappointed when I saw it. It was written by Edward D. Wood, Jr. It's just a terrible nudie film with a bunch of girls dancing (supposedly "interpretative" dancing, but it's really awful, which only adds to it). Poor Criswell plays Bela Lugosi who was long dead by then, but it's all wonderful . . . There's terrible dancing which finally stops for great Ed Wood dialogue which goes on and on and on, without any plot or beginning or middle or end. You know it's going to continue like this until they run out of film, and then it'll have a fast finish.

■ *AJ: Did you ever meet Ed Wood?*
■ FH: I met Herschell Gordon Lewis—he once sat where you are and sang the theme song to *Two Thousand Maniacs* one night. I had Edward D. Wood, Jr.'s phone number and address. A friend went to see him and said, "There's a guy in New York who really wants to meet you." Ed by then was quite an alcoholic but dying for any attention, and he said, "Really? He knows my films?" But by the time my friend returned and I had made the call, he was already dead. I missed the man 'live' by a couple of weeks.
■ *AJ: Sometimes these directors don't really understand that on a true level we could like and actually love their films.*
■ FH: Sometimes they think the films aren't very good and wonder if *you're* the one that's bent—I mean, does it count if your IQ is zero and you like their film!?!

Hopefully, with the way videotape is making money, maybe *everything* will come to the surface. They're actually running out of "product," so they're going to have to dig deeper and deeper, and maybe the exploitation films will be re-released. For me, there's only a few horror films left that I haven't seen, but there's absolutely *no* source where I can get sexploitation films from the '50s and '60s, and I love them.

Unfortunately, with porn the big seller, why would a company release some cute little thing that shows you nothing, especially in black-and-white, etc? But hopefully they'll market them for film buffs, rather than as sex films. Then we can all sit around and wallow in that filth and to me they're a lot dirtier than any porno is today, because they had such unhealthy overtones, plus usually very ugly people, too. I have one trailer with a beautiful girl next to a hideous fat man with hair all over his shoulders and back (he's also probably one of the backers of the film).

I'd love to see more nudist camp films, too—another *dead art*. In the one I saw, all the strategic areas were covered by convenient bushes. It had a very artificial look as everybody was very obviously *posed*. When they walked they only walked 2 or 3 feet, because that's where the bushes stopped. Lots of tush, but even when somebody bent down they had to bend down *very carefully*. And again, there were some astonishingly ugly people (maybe those were the only people who would take off their clothes in those days). But that's part of the delight—you're seeing naked people you would *never* want to see with their clothes off if you saw them in the street. It's like Catholic guilt—if you're going to see *these* people naked, then you're going to be *instantly* punished!

Did you see *Mesa of Lost Women*? It's one of those films during which you're constantly convinced you're hallucinating, *or*, you must have fallen asleep for a long stretch and missed some important plot devices, because it's a different film from 10 minutes ago. It's very confusing and great.

The Tingler should be required viewing in biology classes—just put a little educational footage in front.

■ *AJ: Who are your favorite directors?*
■ FH: I don't have favorite directors, I just have favorite films, and I don't have *one* favorite. I like *The Tingler* and *Circus of Horrors*—god knows why, I don't know how to defend either one of them. They're just so loony; such untypical horror films. They're slick—they're not the kind of films we've been talking about—not obscure. But some of the wackiest plotting—a mad plastic surgeon's hiding from authority, so how does he hide? By running a circus. What!?! "Wow, what a great cover! Nobody'll ever suspect!" And *The Tingler's* the first LSD movie. The *Tingler* should be required

The Tingler.

viewing in biology classes—just put a little educational footage in front. And both of those films I saw when I was about 9 (usually your favorite films are ones you saw as a child) and I'm sure both of them severely traumatized me.

When I saw *The Tingler* I went to a showing where they had the buzzers under the seat. My seat did not vibrate, thankfully, or I would be dead now. I was petrified; I accepted every moment of that film; from the beginning until the end I never laughed. I figured what Vincent Price was telling us was the truth, no doubt about it. At that time my parents were telling me they didn't want me seeing this kind of "crap," so seeing one—actually going into a theater— really meant a lot. Seeing adults actually leaping up from their seats when the vibration was triggered and laughing while I was convinced my life was going to be taken any second—I came out of there a drained nine-year-old child who couldn't wait to see more . . . and shortly thereafter saw *Circus of Horrors*, too. But, those are favorites of mine that I just wallow in; I can't defend them.

You might say the films I'm attracted to most are ones I haven't seen yet! Like, I have a pile of lobby cards from women's prison pictures, oddball items (all from the '40s).

I'll never be satisfied until I see every sleazy film ever made—as long as it's different, as long as it's breaking a taboo (whether deliberately or by misdirection). There's a thousand reasons to like these films. A film can be exciting because it deals with an impolite subject, whether it's a severe taboo or a mild one. In most horror films—just *killing someone* is an impolite enough thing to do. Often, through bad direction, misdirection, inept direction, a film starts assuming surrealistic overtones, taking a dreadfully clichéd story into new frontiers —you're sitting there shaking your

10

head, totally excited, totally unable to guess where this is going to head next, or what the next loony line out of somebody's mouth is going to be. Just as long as it isn't the stuff you regularly see . . .

I won't see *any* film that's a major release anymore. I won't see any film that Stephen King's name is attached to. I don't want to see *Firestarter,* I don't want to see *Gremlins,* I just don't care about them. I'm sure I'm not missing *anything.* I've seen too many, I don't want to *go back.* But promise me some obscure nudist film from the '50s and I'll go way out of my way to catch it.

■ *AJ: Recent films like* Terms of Endearment *and* Back to the Future *are saturated with phony verisimilitude, with "ordinary" people's "real" lives expressing new depths of fake emotion. Whatever individuality or creativity the director or writer presumably once had can effortlessly be obscured in these megabuck corporate productions—*

■ FH: Of course! That's why your video store's selling *She-Devils on Wheels!* With the first frame of that film you knew Herschell was behind the camera. You knew that girl would leave the house, get into that car, close the car door, start the car and the car would drive around the block, all in one long continuous shot—you knew that. And where else could you get such a theme song? I sit there with a big grin enjoying every moment of that. I certainly would not be having a good time seeing *Cat's Eye*—it was boring just watching the *trailer* for that.

> **I'll never be satisfied until I see every sleazy film ever made—as long as it's different, as long as it's breaking a taboo (whether deliberately or by misdirection). There's a thousand reasons to like these films. A film can be exciting because it deals with an impolite subject. In most horror films—just killing someone is an impolite enough thing to do.**

■ *AJ: What do you think about Larry Cohen?*
■ FH: He's an independent director but at least his films have been released by mainstream companies. His originality and his own vision does shine through. I *love* his stuff.
■ *AJ:* God Told Me To *knocked us out.*
■ FH: Absolutely. In one shot Andy Kaufman plays a *cop.* And where else would you find Sandy Dennis (whom I love) in a horror film? The economics of the industry are such that they can't take chances; that's why Spielberg is a god. Herschell Gordon Lewis couldn't make films today, because he couldn't afford to. Film costs (lab costs, film stock) have escalated *severely,* and he couldn't get the distribution. The same avenues aren't open for him; the traditional way he would distribute the film—those theaters are gone now or they've changed to a whole different market. So it's not the same anymore. Nowadays you have newspapers that will not run an ad for your film if it doesn't have a rating on it.
■ *AJ: Why not?*
■ FH: I think they're afraid of offending people's sensibilities. Now they equate "X" with sex. When the rating code first came out, X meant an adult film (but not exclusively a *sexually explicit* film). *If* was X, *Medium Cool* was X, *Midnight Cowboy* was X, and these were mainstream films that weren't junk. They've all been re-rated "R" now. I don't know why horror films fall into that category; it's quite obvious you're showing blood and gore, not sex. I don't understand what they're *preventing.*

The pendulum's swinging the other way now to where sex is good but blood and gore is unhealthy. Internationally, what's happened is: England and Germany (Germany—the most barbaric country on earth) are now saying horror films are bad! Obviously, World War II started because someone must have seen *The Wolfman* and said, "I just saw a horror film; let's go persecute Jews now." So in Germany now there's an index; films are put on a list, and if a store wants to sell porno or horror films, no one under 17's allowed *into* the store! It's not a question of renting it or buying it—they're not allowed into the store. This is creating a whole red-light district in the industry. And in England there were police officers literally confiscating copies of *Evil Dead.*
■ *AJ: But that's such a silly film!*
■ FH: Yes, the police were protecting young people and old people from seeing such an offensive, morals-destroying film. That's not an issue yet in this country, but I'm sure it will be! The distributor of my film *Basket Case* gives out free surgical masks. It's on the radio spots: "Free surgical masks—to keep the blood off your face!" And there are stations that won't play it! I mean, *come on, folks*—who are they protecting? This is what kids love! The only ones to be offended are the people who won't go see this film anyway.
■ *AJ: And they're not banning* Miami Vice *or* Dynasty—
■ FH: Is there anything more corrupting than those!?!
■ *AJ: Or the* Friday the 13th *series.*
■ FH: It's an easy solution: why are we having socio-economic problems? Obviously it's because of what's on TV or what's in the movies, or it's the books people read or the music they listen to! I'm not surprised Germany's having this problem, given their past. If in the past they blamed everything on the Jews, why not now on horror films? I guess horror films made by Jews would *really* be a problem, folks!

When Palace Video bought *Basket Case* they wanted a gorier version, with even more blood than we had. They asked if we had *outtakes* of blood and gore they could put in the film! Six months later, they said, "Guys, we're in a lot of trouble. We're going to have to send the film to a censor, and we're going to have to release it cut." So, I don't know what version's playing in England—which bothers me because it was a best-seller and I don't know what's missing. I don't *want* to watch it to find out.
■ *AJ: What about the version available in the USA?*
■ FH: It's all been restored. It's all there in the videotape and the ones playing the theaters. I mean, there are prints missing scenes because collectors take them, but . . . We had a print which clearly revealed a projectionist with a fetish, because he had taken one or two frames—it couldn't have been much more—out of all the nude stuff at the end. Every time there was a naked breast, there were two frames missing. It was very nicely spliced—of course it made mincemeat out of the soundtrack, but—I wonder what he did with these frames? Did he sit there at night with a little flashlight holding them up to his eye, going . . . I don't know, but I don't really want to find out, either!

Hopefully (I don't know the economics of it), but what may happen is: a lot of the low-budget and gore films may start to be made directly for videotape. I don't know if that's feasible now. I do know that the *quality* of videotape is really piss-poor compared to film, but . . . If I were to make strictly a Herschell Lewis type of gore film now—call it *Gore Film* and just pull arms and legs off ladies—I would shoot just for videotape, because there would be no theatrical market. But, I don't like working in videotape—yet. I'm sure it will change!
■ *AJ: What's your film background?*
■ FH: I started doing 8mm films with magnetic soundtracks. You dub everything in later on, which you also have to mix at the same time. If you were doing music you'd have one hand on the record needle ready to spin and have everybody hovering around this chintzy little microphone. My films were all at least an hour long and all very heavily plotted. To me they were "movie" movies—sick mixtures of comedy and

horror; you were never quite sure what. I'd sit and write what I thought was really funny comedy, but everybody would think it was just really morbid . . .

I like a gag next to a bloodshed—it keeps everybody unnerved; you get the sense that the film is desperately out of control. And—if you miscalculate, *so what?* I mean, half the time I didn't know how an audience would react . . . but who cares? You still get a reaction. You're doing a film low-budget enough so you've made your market anyway; the weight of the film doesn't rest on whether this gag gets a laugh or a scream. So what the hell?

I've got films dating from 1964. There's a lot of folks in them who are now dead, which is pretty creepy. I've put them all on videotape—it's such a drag setting up the projector and screen and all that. I don't show them, but I also don't want to part with them.

> **Often, through bad direction, misdirection, inept direction, a film starts assuming surrealistic overtones, taking a dreadfully clichéd story into new frontiers—you're sitting there shaking your head, totally excited, totally unable to guess where this is going to head next.**

■ *AJ: How did you get the money to shoot your early films?*
■ FH: When I was shooting 8mm it didn't matter. 16mm was another problem—you had to be very cautious. With *Basket Case* it was insane—I didn't have the footage to worry about the acting being more believable or more sincere. We'd begin a day and it was never a question of "What scenes do we shoot today?", it was: "How much film do we have for what we *have* to shoot?" We had to do a lot of fast rewriting; scurrying around and cramming things in: "One take—right, folks?"

The costs started doubling while we were making the film. We shot it in 16mm and blew it up to 35mm. I was real dissatisfied with the blow-up—it came out very dark. On the other hand, when I was resplicing all the gore *back* into the film (after that sleaze outfit that first had it went under), all the gore footage had been printed in England and it was beautiful; all the light and color was back and it wasn't dark at all. But, I would not do that again.

The cost of the blow-up is comparable to shooting it *all* in 35mm. Except, you have to rent the 35mm equipment which is *really* expensive, and you have to deal with ugly things like unions and teamsters. Younger people I know who are starting in film always say, "Do it in 16mm, because you always know someone who owns the equipment!" It's still cheap to edit in 16mm; you can edit in your bedroom, and everybody knows *someone* with a 16mm camera. 35mm is a whole different problem, but that's the only way *I* would go next: I just want a better image—same rotten stories, but a better technical gloss! I would like to be able to move the camera around, too. We had to create pace in the editing—an old Russ Meyer trick, but I would have liked to have moved the camera *just a little bit, folks* . . .
■ *AJ:* Basket Case *did okay?*
■ FH: It made more money than it had any right to make! While it's not exactly a household word, it's gotten more comment than I would ever have expected.

I have no sense or concept of money, but you have to have common sense. If I only have this much film and I have all these people here, I don't want to look like a damn fool and not get around to their scenes. Now, it's a pleasure to be able to pay to have decent monsters made. I don't even care what

they look like as long as we're having a good time playing with them!
■ *AJ: Are you working on a film now?*
■ FH: The monsters are being made now. A guy upstate named Dave Kindling, who started as a make-up artist but got detoured, makes fabulous mechanical parts; he's making these radio-controlled eels. The stuff he can create is scary as hell. He's asking me, "Do you want the eyes to do this, and the mouth to do that?" and I'm saying, "Yeah, sure, great!" Strange vocation.
■ *AJ: So you've got the script and the funding?*
■ FH: The whole thing, of course, is getting the money. That's all that matters anymore: *where do you get the money?* It used to be different when there were tax shelters and you could ask your local dentist for money. I have no stomach for sitting down with people who have access to rich folks, so . . . Luckily, the distributor of *Basket Case,* Roger Grod, sent the script to some video companies who are offering ridiculous sums of money—*good* ridiculous sums. It's still mind-boggling to me that people can raise $800,000 and make a monster movie out of it. But, of course this is the real world where they make them for $12 million, so what am I talking about!?!

I don't want to do another *Basket Case,* meaning, I don't want to do another film *that* technically crude. There were just too many compromises. I'm not anxious to crank out films. I have no interest in *just* directing; I'd rather direct *my own* bad scripts than somebody else's. People occasionally call me up on the phone with this "real exciting" slasher plot, and I think, "Get out of here." I have nothing against slasher films—certainly nothing against killing teenagers, or gratuitous violence—certainly nothing whatsoever against blood and gore. *But,* I certainly don't want to do another formula work: "Ten years ago, these babysitters were . . ." and then flash to a summer camp. You sit there bored to death for 89 of its 90 minutes just to see a total combination of maybe one minute of R-rated gore-effects that have been severely cut. I mean, what kind of a movie is that?

One producer brought me a very boring script which she wanted me to rewrite. She admitted it was too much of a formula plot, but she liked the characters. Instead of rewriting the script—I wasn't going to waste time—I started

Henenlotter's collection of early Super-8 movies transferred to video. He also designed the covers.

writing treatments of it—you know, a thousand different ways to go with the story. Every one was getting rejected. Why? Because I was changing too much from the formula. What it came down to was—what she really wanted was funny dialogue—giving the characters funny names and having them say witty things. But how many times can you have a teenager wittily say, "Let's get laid! (and fast, because we're gonna get killed)!" So, I have no desire to make a film just for the sake of making a film.

> **I'd love to see more nudist camp films, too—another dead art. In the one I saw, all the strategic areas were covered by convenient bushes. And again, there were some astonishingly ugly people. It's like Catholic guilt—if you're going to see these people naked, then you're going to be instantly punished!**

The irony is: the script we are going to do is certainly the most outrageous one I've written. When I was writing it, at that point I didn't see any hope of making another film, so I didn't care what I was writing and it really flowed and it was funny—I was sitting there typing and cackling. But it looks like we have funding now.

■ *AJ: How much did* Basket Case *cost?*

■ FH: The total must have come to $160,000. But the film had to be shot for less than $50,000. We didn't have any money when we were shooting it. All the money came in later in post-production, so I was able to edit the film with decent equipment and put decent sound into it. Shooting it was: no money available for anything! I would have loved to walk into it with $160,000, instead of walking into it with $7,000 and saying, "Well, I hope we get another couple of hundred next week!"

■ *AJ: Was this your first film?*

■ FH: My first commercial one. But I had done lots of things before in 16mm. All I'd intended to do was another film in 16mm, but it just got larger and larger. I never thought it would have any significant commercial release; videotape had never occurred to me as a market. I just figured that if we could get it playing on 42nd Street someday, that would be a kick. And it still hasn't played there. [laughs] Probably by the time it'll be ready to open there they'll be tearing the last theater down . . .

■ *AJ: Do you do commercial film jobs like script rewriting or editing?*

■ FH: No. But it's such a small community in New York that you get to know people, and people ask you for favors, and you end up working on a film or helping out, etc.

I don't want to make a movie to pay the rent. I don't mind if it *does* later on, but I don't want to say, "Jesus, I've gotta go out and make a movie today because I need some money." Because then, what do you have? I do not want to make a career out of directing or making films, unless they're *my own* films. (As dubious a career as that might be, that's fine with me!)

■ *AJ: How do you support yourself?*

■ FH: Unfortunately, in advertising. To talk about it any further would just bore us both to tears! The only thing to come out of it was that I was able to slap a poster together *very fast!* And I did all the newspaper ads overnight.

But, once I look at film as a 9-5 job, the magic is over—forget it, I'll do something else. That's why when I'm asked to cut a trailer for somebody, usually the answer is *no.* But also, nobody's ever come to me with a good film and said, "Hey, you want to help out?" It's always been just terrible, and not

"fun"-terrible, "terrible"-terrible. It's *pain* to actually be associated with films like that.

Unfortunately, the majority of people would still rather see *Christine* or any new Stephen King film than *The Corpse Grinders.* But I think there's enough people bored with mainstream so that when something comes out that's a little offbeat, they'll stroll to see it. But the economics of how *Corpse Grinders* could play all those drive-ins just doesn't exist today.

■ *AJ: That's the sad thing—it's almost as if this were a lost art—*

■ FH: It won't be lost as long as people talk about it, write about it, and as long as it's on a videotape.

■ *AJ: But how can this be replenished?*

■ FH: Anybody who comes in here, if I end up getting friendly with them, and sit them in front of a TV set and put *Corpse Grinders* or *Ilsa, Harem Keeper of the Oil Sheiks* or *Wanda the Wicked Warden* or half a dozen of these others in front of them, is going to end up getting turned on and then turn somebody else on to them.

■ *AJ: Yes. But sadly, how many of these offbeat films will come out in 1985 or 1986? That's why it's very encouraging to hear your story—how you just went out and got a camera and did it.*

■ FH: It's also encouraging that we have two major video companies who want to put up the money for this next one. It's mind-boggling because: the script reads as an X; in both cases I have to be held to an R rating. But what's interesting is, both video companies said, "Still, go ahead and make an un-rated X," because they may want to release *both* versions on tape. They want theatrical R so it will make enough money at the box office to make their investment worthwhile on videotape.

One problem is: how do you give out sleazy, shlocky gimmicks on videotape? I wish I could cram a surgical mask into every box of *Basket Case.* I wrote a great 3-D film I wanted to do, but again, the economics of doing a 3-D film proved unworkable—there's no ancillary rights, no one will put up the money to do one, etc.

I wanted to do a film that was partial 3-D and partial flat, so whenever we switched to 3-D I wanted everybody in the film to put on 3-D glasses. Because I have a hard time with 3-D anyway—it's hard on the eyes, so give me half and half. That reminds me—I have *Paradisio* on tape! It's an early nudie 3-D movie; when the guy puts his glasses on it switches to *bad*-bad 3-D and nude girls. And the big gag in the film was: when he gets drunk, a girl sits down, and she has 3 breasts . . .

■ *AJ: I love gimmicks like that . . . How will you handle the X/R rating problem on your next film?*

■ FH: I'll send the goriest version I have to the MPAA anyway, because they're totally against any independent, totally against any horror film. They saw *Basket Case,* they gave me an X.

> **The pendulum's swinging the other way now to where sex is good but blood and gore is unhealthy.**

■ *AJ: Why?*

■ FH: That never should have been an X—they were pissed off that it had been playing midnight movies and they hadn't been consulted; that we'd already *had* a theatrical release. So, the best thing to do is to give them hours of footage; give them a 4-hour version with nothing but blood and gore; throw in autopsy footage, slaughterhouse footage, and keep cutting until you get your R. And they *charge* you $1000 or so to do this each time. You have to pay them for the honor of hearing them say, "We hated your film, by the way. We just

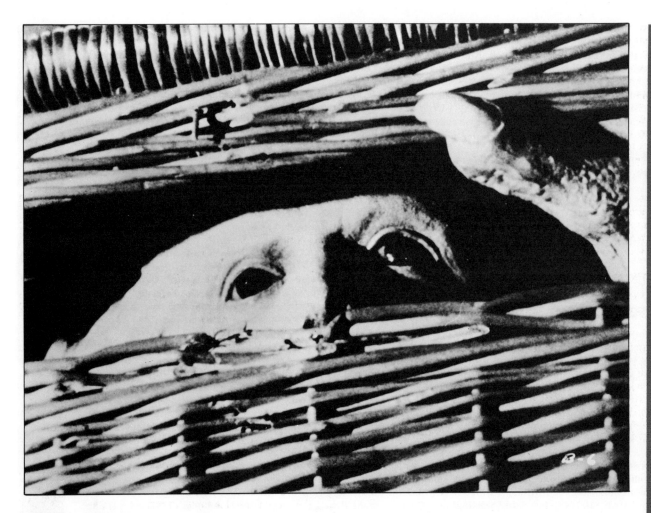

Scene from **Basket Case.**

want to let you know that even though it got an R, we really thought it was terrible." But you need that little R. The newspapers will say to you, "We're not allowed to advertise any un-rated films. Do you mind if we put an R on it?" You say, "No, we don't mind, as long as we don't know about it." It's all bullshit, it's all nonsense. Theatrical distribution is still a carnival sideshow, with all the cheap petty criminals and thieves tearing at your pockets.

■ *AJ: Do you ever write fiction or non-fiction?*

■ FH: I just sit and write scripts. I'm really into that now to the point that when I start writing, I really enjoy it; I look forward to it. I can't write 9-5 because I'm working, but I make sure I sit at the typewriter at least an hour every night. I actually look forward to weekends, not for going out or seeing friends, but to sit at the typewriter.

■ *AJ: How do you write?*

■ FH: It's like solving a jigsaw puzzle where you're putting all the pieces in and you're making it all work. I love figuring out ways to get out of plot problems and figuring out how to get out of this and that. I always carry paper and pencil with me because I'll be sitting on the subway and all of a sudden the solution hits, and if you're not ready for it—well, you have to be ready real fast to write it down! Or, I'll be watching another film which has nothing to do with it *whatsoever,* and—I don't know what triggers it, but all of a sudden I'll have to write it down, write all the notes and that stuff.

■ *AJ: Do your dreams ever provide solutions?*

■ FH: No. I constantly dream but I've never been able to turn a dream into a visual. But, solutions come at unexpected

moments. When it flows it's like stream-of-consciousness— just spewing out, and you have no control over when that's going to happen! Afterwards I spend the next couple of weeks trying to put what I just scribbled out into the English language, grammatically correct. When I sit down at the typewriter I'm usually in re-writing.

> **Anything that makes you think can't be bad! If you watch a cat being mutilated and react to it, you're going to think about why you are reacting to it. No one's going to sit there and just get off on it (if you are, you're such a sick fuck that it doesn't matter whether they put it on tape or not— you're a jerk anyway).**

■ *AJ: How long does it take to do a script?*

■ FH: It takes me about a year to turn a vision of a demented horror film into a script that an ordinary person could sit down and cackle over. But, I still don't understand how scripts ever came about, because *how can you write a script first?* It's like going to a painter and saying, "We won't buy you the canvas or the paints until you first tell us what your painting will be, in a 75-page essay. We'll read it first and see if the painting should be that, and then . . ."

14

In other words, you have to go through the process of telling your story in two totally different, separate mediums. On white paper it has to average about a minute a page; there's a certain format it's got to be in, etc. The trick it's taken me awhile to learn is how to write a script that reads like a script without me being around. So that somebody who doesn't even know me can chuckle and say, "Hey, this is funny. This is gory."

In a way you're lying to them, because you're convincing them they're being let in on this great little story, even though—how can you describe blood and gore on paper? *I* don't know. You allude to it, but you can't disgust them with it. You don't use words like "entrails" or "bloody stump," you try to write so that anybody could pick it up and read it and think it's great. I'm not crying, because if anybody gives you $800,000 to make a horror film, that's totally ludicrous to begin with. So, I'm sitting there cackling as I'm typing: "If I get money out of *this* one, *wow!*"

> **But as a ten-year-old kid I knew the difference between a real gun and a make-believe gun. Children especially are the first ones to know the difference. So, I don't know who people are protecting when they censor films. They're not protecting the children; I think they're protecting their own narrow thinking, now.**

When you finish the film and send it to the company they say, "Godalmighty, look what we have to put out on videotape; this is just hideous. But it'll probably sell at least 25,000 units right off the bat." So, it's all a con job, right? Just to get everybody interested, they put bloody advertising on horror films that have no blood in them. But that's the appeal of like, *Dr. Butcher*—a totally pointless film that offers you nothing but loads and loads of lovely, gratuitous violence. Not very convincing, but who cares—it's great.

A totally different approach was on this videotape, *Despair,* done by a British music group, *SPK.*

■ *AJ: Yes, that shows footage of an actual autopsy set to music.*

■ FH: When I saw the video I thought, "What a fabulous thing; what a strange way of using music. *Who* would make a *music video* to such horror—with actual severed heads . . .

■ *AJ: Did seeing that autopsy footage repulse you?*

■ FH: That autopsy absolutely repulsed me. If you were stoned, that video could do damage to you! But, whether I like it or not is beside the point—I was *excited* by it.

I *like* being in touch with things that repulse me. That's why I used to search for snuff films, too. When Roberta Findlay's *Snuff* appeared in the late '70s, 42nd Street then burst forth with a lot of "authentic" snuff films in peep shows. None of them were real, but if there *were* a real one I'm sure it would be out there selling like hotcakes.

Faces of Death is now a big seller; basically it's a snuff documentary about how we deal with death. Almost all the scenes are obviously faked, but that doesn't negate the sick beauty of a film that is a fake snuff documentary! There is some real video footage of a woman commiting suicide at a distance, of a plane crash with pieces of bodies lying all over the street. There is some obviously faked (though enjoyably sick) footage of somebody getting the electric chair, eyeballs bleeding and bubbling out. . .

I have no trouble watching the execution of human beings. But I really can't watch the killing of animals—some poor little guinea pig or cat or baby seal, *forget it.* I'll be depressed

for weeks after! Nevertheless, horror films should be at that frontier.

There should be films that combine hardcore porn with the most repulsive images of death, using music, plot, everything. That's what I would like to see, although that may not be what I'd like to *do.* I was hoping *Caligula* would be a hit, because I liked the idea of a legit film with porno throwaways, mixed with blood and violence. What I'm talking about here is defeating all the formulas and traditions, which is not going to happen—why kid myself? But that's what I would like to see. Maybe a film that totally defied *every* taboo could be made for video so you wouldn't have the usual commercial hassles.

■ *AJ: Still, there's that problem of distribution.*

■ FH: Yes, I had to send away to Kansas for that *SPK* tape. [address: Fresh Sounds, PO Box 36, Lawrence, KS 66044] What I liked about the *SPK* tape was: there was no heavy pompous narration like in *Faces of Death.* They didn't offer any good, bad or whatever, just "here's a visual of this. If you can't take it, leave the room or speed it up." They didn't say whether they embraced it, or were commenting against it; they weren't saying, "Oh, look at these horrible things in the world," or "look at these great things in the world." That was the brilliance of the video, and that's where horror films should be. Films should be able to *push* our responses to violence, our responses to death.

Why are we fascinated by death, blood and gore? Do we like only fake blood and gore (like me)? Or can we deal with real blood and gore? Is knowing it's fake the difference? Why was I repulsed by those severed heads? They looked fake, but I knew they were real. But how did I know they were real—they didn't tell me they were real. Why is autopsy footage so repulsive to me; why is it repulsive to anybody?

■ *AJ: Would you ever use real footage in your own films just to push your own boundaries?*

■ FH: I don't see how I could, commercially. I wouldn't do a film that called for a prolonged autopsy; I wouldn't want to kill somebody and then start pulling things out. But, I'm more interested in having a good time. I'm not saying I wouldn't do it, but at this point I have far too many problems I can't cope with to burden myself with more. Because *I* have to lick those problems first: deciding what bothers me, what repulses me, and why. *Despair* is not a tape I casually watch; I certainly have never sat through all of the cat mutilation [even though

Henenlotter's apartment.

the cat was already dead], and I probably never will!

Anyway, if they are selling hardcore pornography to housewives in this country; if the average family is taking hardcore porno into their homes; if it's now socially acceptable for a

> **I have no trouble watching the execution of human beings. But I really can't watch the killing of animals—some poor little guinea pig or cat or baby seal, forget it. I'll be depressed for weeks after!**

woman to walk into a video store and say, "I'd like to rent *Talk Dirty to Me, Part Two,* then maybe we can push the boundaries of horror like that—take all that horrifying stuff and *expand* upon it.

■ *AJ: What do you think about the effects of horror?*

■ FH: Anything that makes you *think* can't be bad! If you watch a cat being mutilated and react to it, you're going to think about why you are reacting to it. No one's going to sit there and just get off on it (if you are, you're such a sick fuck that it doesn't matter whether they put it on tape or not, you're a jerk anyway). If it's upsetting you, you're gonna wonder why you're getting upset.

I get upset, especially at real life violence—who could possibly cope with real life violence? I once had a gun put to my head. In the aftermath it was exhilarating, because I thought in terms I'd never thought before! But as a ten-year-old kid I knew the difference between a real gun and a make-believe gun; I knew that the girl in *Circus of Horrors* who got stabbed in the throat didn't really die. Children especially are the first ones to know the difference. That's why you loved the Three Stooges—you knew damn well they weren't getting hit on the head with a hammer. So, I don't know *who* people are protecting when they censor films. They're not protecting the children; I think they're protecting their own narrow thinking, *now.*

So, I like things that upset my thinking. I like things that really screw me up, that I can't come to terms with. It's not a comfortable feeling, but—boy, it shakes you up and it's very exciting.

When I saw those snuff films in the peep shows, they weren't real but it didn't matter. There was something unclean about me making this obsessive search to see a snuff film, especially since I wasn't sure how I would deal with a *real* snuff film. I figured I'd deal with that when I actually saw one, but how do you *really* deal with it? You're just looking at shadows of light, but can that make you an accomplice to murder?

Real life horror, like taking a child and murdering it while filming it, is not a horror that any of us want to deal with. I certainly wouldn't buy that on videotape. So there *are* boundaries. I will not watch concentration camp footage—I can't cope with that and I never will. So right away there's a problem: push it, but don't push it too far. I'm not the one to solve these questions.

■ *AJ: From earliest times our creative imaginations have unleashed raw, violent imagery, just as our dreams do. Balinese, who are a very peaceful people, have for centuries traditionally enacted dances and trance rituals that are very violent. Early recorded visual art like the Lascaux caves or Pompeii murals document raw, violent (and sometimes blatantly sexual) imagery. So there's a whole level of artistic expression and drama that has functioned in society as catharsis. Anyway, society cannot police the imagination; imagine censoring Bosch or Goya or Francis Bacon. Basically, no one has been able to prove a causal connection between artistic expression and "actual" violence.*

> **That autopsy absolutely repulsed me. If you were stoned, that video could do damage to you! But, whether I like it or not is beside the point—I was excited by it. I like being in touch with things that repulse me.**

■ FH: As long as we know it's in control, or it's imaginary, it's okay. The real stuff I'm always attracted to, but I don't want it dropped in my lap! I really wouldn't know what to do with a videotape of a real murder ... but I bet I'd watch it ...

What we're really talking about is: *being responsible for your imagery.* I'd rather be irresponsible about it. I'd rather just have blood and gore and have a good time. That may be corrupt and wrong, but I don't care. Having the police confiscate copies of *Evil Dead* was a wonderful tribute to Sam Raimi; he should be proud of that, even though he probably lost a lot of money ...

Today, with the cheapness of videotape, it would be nice to see what we liked in films pushed to boundaries that would

Henenlotter's apartment.

Henenlotter's refrigerator.

bother us. Not that it has to be real, but push it to the boundaries. Whether it's a rock band or a bunch of artists or some weird Ed Gein character, *somebody* should do it. The irony is that half the films we talk about *already* disturb the normal person . . .

■ *AJ: But it's an odd process, in that what was "X" 10 years ago is now "R" today . . .*

> I have nothing against slasher films—certainly nothing against killing teenagers, or gratuitous violence—certainly nothing whatsoever against blood and gore. But, I certainly don't want to do another formula work: "Ten years ago, these babysitters were . . ."

■ FH: Have you seen Herschell Gordon Lewis's *The Gore Gore Girls?* It's a good example of something that's blatantly phony, yet very effective. Didn't that go a lot further than you expected it to? Sticking a fork in an empty eye socket—you know what I mean? Cutting off nipples . . . the fact that it was blatantly phony helped you enjoy it. That was done in '72, but today no one comes close to that amount of viciousness . . .

Herschell's a delight. Before I had met him, I figured (just on the basis of films) the poor guy's probably a poverty-struck old man living above a deli somewhere. I didn't think

he would display such intelligence *and* affluence. All the fraud charges that were attributed to him he claims are untrue, yet I secretly hope they *were* true! I hope someday he'll come out and say, "Hey, folks, I really did do all that."

I asked Herschell where he was going to *take* horror, because the market was catching up to him. *Gore Gore Girls* was such an astonishing film because he had never combined nudity with horror before, let alone with that level of *prolonged* on-camera viciousness, although what he did was no worse than cutting off somebody's leg or tongue.

■ *AJ: What did he say?*

■ FH: Well, he didn't have an answer . . .

■ *AJ: Your film* Basket Case *is a minor classic. You're a filmmaker who on one level, achieved—*

■ FH: Stress what a *small, insignificant* level it is, because I'm really embarrassed by the amount of hype *Basket Case* has gotten. It's not an important film—

■ *AJ: But it's representative that a film can be made now with a kind of genuineness.*

■ FH: But that was four years ago—it was made in '81 and released in '82. You should interview Sam Raimi, because he made *Evil Dead* which was an important, independent gore film as well as a monster hit. Even magazines like *Film Comment* said nice things about *Evil Dead.* (I'm sure that depressed him, but . . .) He got the money to immediately make a second film, *Crime Wave,* which hasn't been released yet. They're hyping *Evil Dead II . . . He's* the one who's made an important, independent gore film. *I* should be a footnote with an asterisk! ■

Self-described as "the guru of gore—the first director to show people dying with their eyes open," Herschell Gordon Lewis invented the genre of **intensive gore films** in 1963 with **Blood Feast**. It featured a Playboy brunette whose brains were scooped from her skull, a blonde whose tongue was pulled out while still alive, and other memorable dismemberments filmed in "Blood Color." The film was instantly successful—causing a traffic jam—and Lewis went on to make other gore classics including **2000 Maniacs**, the artistic **Color Me Blood Red**, **The Gruesome Twosome**, **She-Devils on Wheels**, the philosophical **Wizard of Gore** and lastly, in 1972, **The Gore Gore Girls**—a satire on the genre. (Interspersed throughout the making of the gore films were other nudies including **Linda and Abilene**, a nudie western filmed in 1969 at the Spahn Ranch just a few months before it became famous for hosting the Manson family.) Then, disgusted by the financial chicaneries inherent in the film business, he became a successful direct-mail marketing consultant—which he remains to this day.

Born June 15, 1926, Lewis was an English professor with a Ph.D before being lured to filmmaking. In the late '50s he teamed up with Chicago producer David Friedman and made **The Prime Time**, a nudie-cutie featuring teenage girls in bikinis, juvenile delinquents and a beatnik artist. He made several more nudies before stumbling upon the gore formula. As he put it, "**Blood Feast** is an accident of history. We didn't deliberately set out to establish a new genre of motion pictures; rather, we were escaping from an old one."

These days Herschell Gordon Lewis lives near Fort Lauderdale, Florida in a modern stucco house on the edge of a lake. He owns four cars including a DeLorean and a white, right-hand drive Rolls Royce. There are rumors that he might return to film with projects such as **Blood Feast II** or **Galaxy Girls**, but for now he seems more than content to enjoy his leisurely life.

In the following interviews, initially Boyd Rice talked with Herschell Gordon Lewis on the telephone. Subsequently Andrea Juno and Mark Pauline visited the Godfather of Gore himself in his lush Florida paradise, just before his afternoon tennis game . . .

■ *ANDREA JUNO: How did you start filmmaking? I read that you had an academic background—*
■ HERSCHELL GORDON LEWIS: —Which, as you probably know, is of no value in trying to earn a living! Years ago, going back to the year 1831 [laughs], I was a teacher. I taught English and the humanities at Mississippi State which is not one of our major centers of culture. But, it was stimulating; I was reading Robert Browning and leading what I thought was the good life. One day somebody offered me a job in advertising. As you may know, most academicians have a profound contempt for anybody who works for a living—*I* did! I felt the peculiar sense of dedication you have when you have less responsibilities than you'll ever again have in your life, because the one marvelous thing about teaching school is that you teach school, and the next year you come back and look at your lecture notes and teach it again. Whereas in the world of commerce you live on your wits!

I got into radio and then television in the early days of TV. I became a producer at WKYY at Oklahoma City, pushing buttons and playing God—you push a button and screens change in tens of thousands of homes, and you feel you have a sense of cosmic destiny! From there I went back to Chicago as the television director of an advertising agency. When I had been at Oklahoma City we'd produced some TV shows which I had thought were worthy of syndication called the "Chuck Wagon Boys." They simply sang and played guitars and string bass. When I got back to Chicago I got the notion of using those same fellows. We made a bunch of television shorts together. In the course of production I became friendly with the fellow who owned the film studio. His partner had left for greener fields, so he was casting about for another partner.
■ *AJ: Was this Dave Friedman?*
■ HGL: No, this was a guy named Marty Schmidhofer. We formed a company called "Lewis & Martin Films"; "Lewis & Schmidhofer" would not have fit on the building! This was long before Dave Friedman. So, I got into the commercial end of the film business. I was shooting television commercials, business films, government films—the usual flotsam and jetsam that the typical commercial studio makes.
■ *MARK PAULINE: What year was that?*
■ HGL: Oh, we started that in 1952 or 1953. One day (I'd been doing this for 6 or 7 years, because in 1959 we made *The Prime Time*) somebody asked me, "How do you make any money in your business?" (I had been complaining [as I usually did] about the company overhead, the cost of equipment, the failure to make payroll, or whatever happens to people in that business.) I said, "The only way to make money in the film business is to shoot features." He said, "Why don't you shoot a feature?"

I really had no answer for him. That it didn't make sense to shoot features didn't occur to me; that I had no background in distribution didn't occur to me, because again, in the happy ignorance that you have not knowing what's going on in the world, you have what is called the Horatio Alger syndrome: "I'll do something brilliant and everyone will notice it! Some multi-millionaire will stop me on the street and say, 'You're a bright young man and I must have you! Whatever you want, it's yours!' " Unfortunately, life doesn't run along such straight lines. But fortunately, sometimes one can emerge from this cauldron with scar tissue, but without being killed! It's really a crap game; sometimes you get killed, sometimes you just get wounded. As you may know, where you have scars the skin is stronger than where you just have

Scum of the Earth.

ordinary skin. (I'm getting deep into allegory!)

Anyway, I started to make features, and I shot two of them. The first was called *The Prime Time;* the second was called *Living Venus.* In the case of *The Prime Time* I made the typical, classic mistake that everyone makes when he is more concerned with his image than with making money. This, again, is where scar tissue becomes helpful, because later on you don't feel you're losing face by helping the crew sweep up at the end of a shoot. This business of sitting in the

director's chair yelling, "Roll it!" and "Cut!"—that's a lot of malarkey! It's a positive way to waste money, and many people do it: waste money. And half of the time their films don't even get *finished.*

On the first film I made I was the producer, not the director. I went to a studio in Chicago named Fred Niles [sic] and they really took me for a ride! I was *unioned to death.* I hired a guy named Gordon Weisenborn to direct; he got his jollies directing this film. And we produced a film in glorious

FIENDISH IS THE WORD FOR IT!

NOT FOR THE EYES AND EARS OF ANYONE UNDER 16 YEARS!

COLOR ME BLOOD RED

Drenched in CRIMSON COLOR

A BLOOD SPATTERED STUDY IN THE MACABRE

black and white that was largely unplayable. But one thing I learned from that experience was that a powerful campaign can make up for an imperfect picture.

■ *AJ: What kind of picture was it?*

■ HGL: I can best describe it as a *nothing* picture! Fred Niles had a friend who claimed to be a screenwriter named Robert Abel. (Later, it turned out that Robert Abel had no screen credits, but Fred Niles *believed* he was a screenwriter.) He wrote this screenplay about a young girl who is wild, looking for thrills and kicks. In today's marketplace the picture doesn't have anything in it that would even cause it to rate a *PG*, except that somebody gets shot. It's closer to a *G*. But project yourself back in time 25 years. There was nothing about it that had any box-office appeal. One of the things you learn when you cease being an "auteur" and become a commercial filmmaker, is that you care less for impressing your cronies in the screening room than for impressing the yahoos out there in the theater!

■ *AJ: So that's more what you had in mind when you were making these films: how to make the maximum amount of money?*

■ HGL: Well, what happens is an evolutionary process. With the first film, I had no idea what I was doing. It's easy to say that I was at the mercy of forces larger than myself—I had a film distributor, I had a film studio, I had people pushing and shoving, each of whom had a vested interest which was peripheral to the commercial success of the picture. I learned that only after I made the second picture, *Living Venus,* a much more hard-boiled picture which I directed *myself*. From that point forward, I directed all the films. I found that being producer on the independent production level is a meaningless piece of title-passing. I laugh sometimes looking at film credits and seeing something like "Unit Manager"—what in the heck is a *Unit Manager?!* And after a while, just to give somebody who worked on the crew a credit, we'd call him a "Unit Manager"—he wouldn't be quite sure what he had done! Or, "Production Designed by"—that always appeals to me! What does that mean: "Production designed by"?!

■ *AJ: Did you write your own films, too?*

■ HGL: Many of them, yes. With *Living Venus,* I bought a half-finished screenplay from a guy named Jim McGuinn, and

> I don't think our films suffered from lack of polish. It was almost the crude power of a play by Aeschylus as opposed to a polished play by Sophocles.

then finished it. I wrote many—I wrote *2000 Maniacs,* I wrote *Color Me Blood Red.* I'm making it sound more impromptu than it really was. With *Blood Feast,* for example, which was our biggest winner of all, we gave somebody on the crew credit for writing that film because I didn't feel it looked good to usurp all the credits—that makes it look like a home-movie!

I still object to that when I see other people doing it: "Produced by Joe Glutz! Directed by Joe Glutz! Music by Joe

20

Glutz! Director of Cinematography: Joe Glutz! Starring Joe Glutz!" Well, if the film is successful, it's a miracle because Joe Glutz, like Woody Allen, often loses his viewpoint altogether and begins to appeal to a coterie. Woody Allen got away with it because he has a *large* coterie, but he has made some rotten films that are beyond human understanding. And that wouldn't have happened if he'd had someone there with a set of brains saying, "Hold it! The people in the audience will not understand this dark symbolism you are suddenly inject-

> Gradually I learned that there are trigger mechanisms that work on a motion picture audience. You can literally force the rats through the maze.

ing into what is supposed to be a comedy!"

In my case, what happened was: the distributor of those first two films went bust. Oddly, those films would not have been a commercial disaster if he hadn't gone bust. But because he owed the production about $100,000 at the time he went under, and that was about what we had in them, we weren't (on paper) in terrible shape. In reality, the company then folded and I was left to my own devices, realizing, like the Ancient Mariner, "a sadder and a wiser man he rose the following morning." Sadder and wiser, I went back into the arena, like the fellow who wrestles alligators and has just lost his left arm but still has his right arm, so back he goes the next day—it's only a *flesh wound.*

Gradually I learned that there are trigger mechanisms that work on a motion picture audience. You can literally force the rats through the maze. What are the limitations? Number one, I had no budget. Not ever did I have a budget. Once I was through with those first two pictures I never shot another film with a union crew, which is one reason we were able to compress so much into a film without spending a lot of money. I remember screening *Moonshine Mountain* for AVCO Embassy, and the fellow said to me, "What do you have in this film." I said, "Under $400,000" and he said, "Oh yes, uh huh." They don't know! I didn't have 1/10th of $400,000 in that picture, but even at $400,000 it's still embarrassingly cheap for AVCO Embassy!

■ *AJ: How much was* Blood Feast?

■ HGL: What did it cost to make? You're immortalizing these things, aren't you!

■ *AJ: Actually, there's an inverse pride in how much these*

The sacrifice of Ishtar in **Blood Feast.**

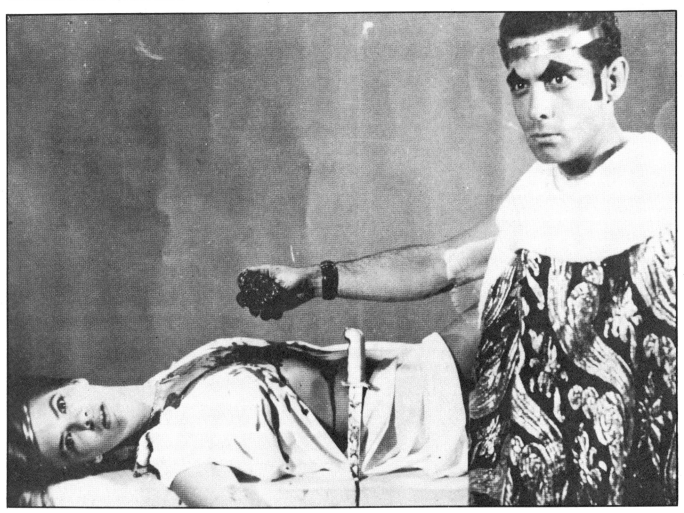

pictures cost!

■ HGL: Don't gauge anything by *Blood Feast.* It cost $24,000 to make and it was shot in 35mm color. And that's not much money considering we shot in 35mm color. The reason we were able to do it is: neither then, nor ever, did we shoot a rehearsal. I see people in the industry today talking about *take 24.* What is the logic behind *having* take 24 other than salving somebody's ego? *Why would you need 24 takes?* It means that for the first 23 takes the actors weren't well-rehearsed.

Actors are very shrewd. If they don't like a take they'll start to swear and then you *must* yell, "Cut!" Sometimes they do it quite deliberately to force you to yell "Cut!" so you won't use a take they don't like, but not on my pictures they didn't! That's because we work as a team, and we would end the take where we had to and pick it up with a close-up on somebody else if we were that deep into it. But in a typical picture, if you have a take of 45 seconds and 40 seconds in they blow the take, they'll start again from ground zero. We never did that, but that's a technical refinement.

The point is, that for a film that ran between 7-8,000 feet at 90 feet-per-minute (so a 90-minute picture is 8,100 feet), we would only buy 15-17,000 feet of film. Seldom was it over a 2:1 ratio. And we'd use part of that for trailers; sometimes we outblocked ourselves. *Lucky Pierre,* which was our first hit, ran exactly 70 minutes, because in those days, if you were under 70 minutes you had trouble getting a theater to book you as a top feature—it would be regarded as a *featurette.* So it had to run 70 minutes, which is 6,300 feet. We only bought 8,000 feet of film. We cut the slates off and there wasn't enough to fill a little 400-ft can! In fact, we had to go out and *duplicate* footage to make a trailer.

I don't want to *overstate* the commercial aspects of film-making, nor am I trying to justify making films for almost no money. I read your *William Burroughs Re/Search* and it seemed to be a thoughtful and literate piece of journalism which one doesn't often find, so I suspect that some of the finer philosophical points will not be lost on you, as they would be on a more *crass-mass* level. There are a couple of problems that pertain to independent film production, and unless you face and dispose of those problems, *sine qua non,* there is nothing else. One is, I was self-financed. I didn't have some main office I could call to say, "Well, I need another $1,000,000 to finish the picture!" I didn't have any angel; I didn't have any sugar-daddy. I had hard-boiled partners in some cases; I had *no* partners in others. In every case, the success of the film was directly related to my ongoing life-style, or lack thereof. That's an overriding factor.

There's a big difference between a couple of hoodlums who hold up a gas station because it gives them a thrill, and a fellow whose baby is starving and he has to have a loaf of bread and he takes it all to the grocery store. In making independent films, I was not about to ignore the lessons I had learned so hard, so bitterly, and so expensively. Those lessons being: 1) there is a way to get people in the theater; 2) there is a way of shortening the odds; 3) the ability to *cram* production value into a low-budget picture is a peculiar talent I happen to have, and I might as well exploit it!

Let us suppose that in the middle of all this, somebody from one of the Hollywood major companies had noticed what was going on, because our films *were* making money. (Invariably they were making money, invariably they were commanding playing-time.) They were never in trouble because the investment in them was so low. I think that the most I ever spent on a film was between $60,000-$70,000. Suppose someone had said, "Hey fella, you seem like a bright young man. Here's $1,000,000. By our standards, that's nick-els and dimes; by your standards it's a *Croesus'* fortune. Spend this money wisely, my son. Go forth into the world and make a picture with good production values." Now what would I have done? What I would have done is: 1) *perhaps,* hired less inept actors.

■ *AJ: Weren't most of them your friends?*

■ HGL: *Oh, no.* On occasion someone would say, "Why don't you put me in one of your pictures," and I'd say, "All right," but I wouldn't give them a lead. This myth—that our films were badly acted—in my opinion is just that: a *myth*. Because I have seen the *Halloweens* and the *Friday the 13ths* of this world, and their acting isn't any good either. What they have is *polish*.

I don't think our films suffered from lack of polish. It was almost the crude power of a play by Aeschylus as opposed to a polished play by Sophocles. The audience *knew* that whatever happened was going to be brutal, because that's the way these films were shot. But the acting levels generally were reasonably adequate. The reason they sometimes had the look of half-baked was because we would settle *knowingly* for imperfect takes. Somebody quoted me in print once as saying, "Nobody ever walked out of the theater because of a ragged pan," and that quotation was accurate; I firmly believe it.

What happens is, you're panning the camera, and—yeah, we shot in 35mm; I had a Mitchell NC with a blimp that weighed roughly 2,000,000 pounds. Alex Ameripoor, my assistant cameraman, and I were the only two people who could lift that camera on any crew we ever had. And in the blimp it took the two of us together, grunting and heaving, and if we tried to put it on a wooden tripod it would crack the tripod legs regularly. Even in our times the technology had gone beyond it, but *that was the equipment we had*. If our sound recorder developed a hum we'd wrap it in Reynolds Wrap, which would tend to insulate against line-bleed, but it really wasn't solving a problem; it was putting a bandaid over it. Professional filmmakers laugh at this procedure.

■ *AJ: What would you have done if you had been given an unlimited amount of money?*

■ HGL: Well, if I had had more money, I would have made the same *kind* of picture, but perhaps on a more *extensive* basis rather than on an *intensive* basis. And the difference would not have justified the additional expense; rather, I would have preferred to take that money and form a permanent production company which would have put a floor under what we did and enable us to own equipment of a better technical level—to have had film editors, for example, full-time, instead of saying, "Who's available to cut this picture?" (forcing us to begin our own educational process time after time). I would have used the money simply to stabilize the operation. Because spending 20 times as much on a film does not mean you're going to get 20 times as much money in; nor does it mean you're going to have 20 times the impact on the people out there.

> **Sometimes one can emerge from this cauldron with scar tissue, but without being killed! It's really a crap game; sometimes you get killed, sometimes you just get wounded. As you may know, where you have scars the skin is stronger . . .**

■ *MP: In view of the fact that your films clearly were successful in terms of making money, and over a long period of time, too (it wasn't like an "underground" thing, it was* out there *and the public was* seeing *it), why didn't a major company come and offer you a deal? It seems unusual that it didn't happen.*

■ HGL: As far as they were concerned, I *was* an underground filmmaker—*I assume*. I don't know the answer to that question. I have never discussed it with anyone: "Why didn't you call me?" Number one, I wasn't knocking on doors.

Number two, I was not on the West Coast.

■ *AJ: You made your films here in Florida.*

■ HGL: I made 70% of them here in Florida. I made some in Chicago and 4 or 5 in California. But most of them were made here in Florida, yes.

■ *AJ: Do you have any other favorite filmmakers or any filmic foundation for your work?*

■ HGL: No, I'm not a student of film. The guy to talk to about all that is out in California, Alex Ameripoor, who cut a number of films, and he was Assistant Cameraman on a number of films. He lives in Tarzana. Alex was a perpetual

> **Gore was easy, because it was obviously the kind of subject that could be handled intensively rather than extensively.**

student of film. He could tell you every cut in every John Huston film ever made! I took a more *calloused,* casual view of the medium. So the answer to your question is: I don't have any favorites of that type.

I startled someone by saying that I thought that *War Games* was a well-made film. He said, "WHAT! The potboiler!" I don't understand that reaction. Is it necessary, in order for a film to be considered first-rate, that it be a) not entertaining, and b) obscure? This *cult,* that seems to be growing in the land like the creeping blight, says that a film that is easily understood can't be any good. What happens in film, as in fine art, is that these people spawn others who have the same arrogant condescension toward the rest of us that *they* have. So they will give awards to films that if they're hand-held and shot with existing light, they're 2/3 of the way there to winning an award! You see, my films fell in the *in between*. We used lights, and they weren't hand-held. So they didn't *qualify*.

And, we used *actors,* we didn't use *friends,* so we didn't qualify there. And we shot them in 35mm, not 16mm, so we didn't qualify there. So instead of being the extension of somebody's personal ego, they were the *bottom end* of the commercial film world, and that may be another reason why nobody grabbed me off the street. But another problem was that I really was not looking to be grabbed. I wasn't haunting people's offices saying, *"Please hire me,"* which is what you do if that is your goal. You see, I always had a great good time making these films, and I never felt that this was, as apparently will happen, what they would put on my epitaph, so the joke is ultimately on me!

■ *AJ: How did you get into the violence? You did* Blood Feast *in 1963*—

■ HGL: Dave Friedman had worked for the film distributor, Irwin Joseph (Modern Film Distributors), who went bust. His background was that he had been a publicist, I think with Paramount. He and I became quite friendly. I felt that Dave was a *master* of campaigns. Dave and I literally taught each other the business, because I had *no fear* of the technical aspect of filmmaking. Nothing puzzled me; if a camera quit running, I'd take it apart and make it run. If we needed a wipe and didn't want to pay a laboratory $800 to do a wipe, we'd do it with a shirtboard. The dissolve mechanism on the back of the Mitchell camera was 30 years out of date, but I used it in every film 20 times over, usually with good luck. If a light meter didn't work, we'd guess at the exposure and it'd usually be within a half a stop. Nothing bothered me in the shooting of films.

In the *campaigning* of films, although my background had been in advertising, it hadn't been in that kind of *hard-boiled rock-em sock-em slam-bang* advertising, as Dave's had. So Dave taught me campaigning, I taught him how to technically make a film, and the marriage worked out very well.

■ *AJ: What do you mean by campaigning: the distribution?*
■ HGL: No, the I mean the *one-sheets* and the posters, and the advertising impedimenta that goes with a film, and later on I did it all myself because Dave moved out to California. He and I made a couple of films almost on contract. *Lucky Pierre* was one. People came to us because *we were able to make films cheap.* So if somebody wanted to make a film, and didn't know how or what, but he knew that *Lewis and Friedman* could make film at a fraction of the cost of anybody else, including himself . . . .

So we made a bunch of harmless, we used to call them *nudies,* but again, in today's marketplace they weren't nudies at all because nothing was bared below the top half, and they were completely innocuous, although in context there was a certain amount of daring to them.

Lucky Pierre was the first one of these things shot in 35mm. There had been two or three before, but they were shot in 16mm. Gradually we became aware (the market told us, if nothing else), that one of two things was going to happen: we either were going to have to *strengthen* the kinds of films we were making, making them less and less "socially acceptable," or do something else.

And we sat down one Saturday afternoon, because it was getting cold in Chicago (which meant it was time to shoot a film). That was part of our motivation. I don't have that down here any more, but in Chicago in January or February, you can think of a thousand reasons to come to Florida and shoot a film! We sat down and made up a list of the *kinds* of films the major companies either could not make, or *would not* make. And on the list, staring us in the teeth, was *gore.*

Gore was *easy,* because it was obviously the kind of subject that could be handled *intensively* rather than *extensively.* If I'm going to shoot *The Life of Marco Polo* (god help me), I need costumes, I need Venice in the 14th Century, I need props I could never possibly get. (But I *don't* need scholarship; that's a mistake a lot of people make when dealing with historical subjects! They say, "I am *dealing* with an historical subject, ergo, I am a scholar." *Bull!* Let them have their little fantasies.) But with *gore,* you need one person, and you get in close on that person, so you don't need a whole battery of lights. For the independent filmmaker, scrambling for his life like a bunch of women mud-wrestling (the last one left is the winner), or a demolition derby may be a better way of describing it; for us, it was quite a logical conclusion.

Right at that time, a fellow named Leroy Griffith who owned a theater here in Miami, and another man named Eli Jackson who lived in Cincinnati, decided to make a film. They were going to make a nudie starring Eli Jackson's wife—a woman who had, so help me (or so advertised), a 48-inch bosom. And that's *all* she had. I felt that Virginia Bell was a *freak,* but freaks also are a reason for making films. She was some kind of a burlesque star, but again, that's an area that I don't pry into or care about. If Eli Jackson felt that her name on the marquee would sell some tickets, god bless Eli Jackson. I'm the hired Hessian; I come in and kill and then go on to the next war, assuming I'm still alive myself!

So, we came down to Miami to shoot this film for Eli Jackson and Leroy Griffith (Leroy lived in Miami), and we decided to shoot *Blood Feast* while we were here. (I say "here" as though Miami and Ft. Lauderdale were one com-

Two Thousand Maniacs.

munity, which obviously they aren't, but they're both here in South Florida.) We had no time to cast the picture, so half the cast of *Blood Feast* were the same people who were in the cast of Leroy Griffith's picture (I don't remember the name— oh yes I do!) *Bell, Bare and Beautiful*—"Bell" for Virginia Bell! It turned out, by the way, that we had to shoot the picture in a hurry, because Virginia Bell was pregnant. I said, "My gosh, a woman with that pectoral achievement being pregnant! It's like shooting a game of bumper pool!" So we had to shoot it in a hurry before she showed too much. A lunatic notion! Again, that's why I say much of what we did was done with high good humor.

> This cult . . . says that a film that is easily understood can't be any good. What happens in film, as in fine art, is that these people spawn others who have the same arrogant condescension toward the rest of us that they have.

Those people (e e cummings, the poet, had a marvelous word, *those people*) don't understand how you can have a good time and still make a film, because they regard film as something that should be treated with reverence, *deadly serious*. Unfortunately, I don't march to that tune—never did, and now that I am in my dotage (!) probably never will.

■ *AJ: Right now the French are taking an academic interest in your films, writing long, semiological, serious exegeses. What do you think of this new interest?*

■ HGL: Well, I'm delighted to gradually find out what I *really meant to do*. It's odd when the analysts start to take over. T.S. Elliot once made the remark, when someone was analyzing one of his poems, "I'm very interested to find out what I really meant by that!" To be worthy of further study, like some loathsome disease, is, I guess, an honor. But very few of these people bother to ask *me*, as you are doing. They just draw a conclusion. Why do they draw the conclusion? Well, they draw the conclusion because this happened, it was the first time it happened, therefore it is a matter of great historic moment. They don't want something to get past them. Whoever invented the wheel is lost in history. I'm *not*. They don't want this to happen again! And just in case this is a *wheel*, they want to make certain it's thoroughly documented. Dan Krogh wrote a book, *The Amazing Herschell Gordon Lewis*—

■ *AJ: What did you think of that book?*

■ HGL: Ha ha! An interesting work of fiction (I shouldn't say that)! Dan means well, and John McCarty, his co-author, is well-versed in film. I'll tell you my opinion which may not please you; I think it was *too reverent* a piece of work. That is, *I* like it, *because* it puts me on a pedestal. But for someone who's truly interested in *what went on*, it lacks that slight *cold-blooded* reportorial approach that might have made that difference. I may be stating this poorly because I do *like* it. I was pleasantly surprised by everything except the cover; the cover was designed to sell a few books, so I can't disclaim the thing. And I admire what he's done. Dan remembered things I'd long since forgotten, so I must hand it to him there.

Anyway, going back to *Blood Feast,* we used half the cast, the same crew, and I think we started shooting it within three days after we had finished shooting the other picture. In fact, *because of them,* we shot *Blood Feast*. We were staying at the Suez Motel at 182nd St. & Collins Avenue in North Miami Beach. The Suez Motel was typical of a whole string of motels that line that north beach. It's a so-so kind of place: not particularly fashionable, but it's not a fleabag. *But,* outside the Suez Motel, in all its glory, standing about 5 or 6 feet high,

is a pyramid and a sphinx! Which is why they call it the "Suez Motel." If it were called the "Gotham," they'd probably have a fake Empire State Building. If it were called the "L.A. Special," they'd probably have hop-heads sitting on the curb—I don't know! Or if it were the "Chicago" they'd have a replica of Al Capone smoking a cigar!

■ *AJ: Just by being inspired by the decor, you made up the story?*

■ HGL: Yes; driving into the motel, trying to think of what would *seize* an audience as being weird. In fact, the title I gave that film was *Something Weird;* I loved the title *Something Weird* and later on (I guess it was five years later), I *used* that title on another picture; we called a picture *Something Weird*. But because *Blood Feast* was so obviously superior a title to *Something Weird*, we used that.

The film opens with a shot of that fake sphinx outside the Suez Motel. And then we start pouring blood all over the place. There again I proposed to do that with an optical effect, and every optical house in the business said, "You can't do that. If you're going to have an optical in color, you have to shoot it against a blue background." I said, *"Not true!* If you make a mask, the mask will be black; therefore I'll give you the mask for it." And we did it, and it was perfect— accidentally, perhaps, but *it turned out* that way.

■ *MP: To create a broader base of appeal to your audience, did you think it was necessary to temper the hardness of pure violence with some kind of humor?*

■ HGL: Most astute question! Actually, as you know, we began to parody ourselves in the later films. *The Gore Gore Girls* is a *joke*, although it's full of violence. I think part of it was because I refuse to take the whole *genre* seriously. In *Blood Feast*, which was our first, there is no humor—well, there *is*, really, because we treated it with *broad* strokes. Fuad Ramses drags one leg. It's really funny, because there's a chase scene at the end. These police are chasing him, and he's dragging one leg, and they're never the right distance. They passed him once because they didn't get the instructions straight!

■ *AJ: So it's* inadvertently *funny, in retrospect?*

■ HGL: I don't share that view. The reason I don't is this: I'm not a film historian. I'm the kind of jerk who sits in the theater watching the audience, and if they react, that's all I care about. I don't care about someone who is writing *l'histoire du cinema*, attributing motivations that aren't there.

■ *MP: Don't you think that when people saw* Blood Feast, *they thought it was a funny film?*

■ HGL: The *hell* they—well they certainly did *not*. I quote you Charlie Cooper from the Englewood Theater in Chicago, which was in the middle of a black section, 63rd & Halsted. He played *Blood Feast* and he said, "The picture opens up,

> We had to shoot the picture in a hurry, because Virginia Bell was pregnant. I said, "My gosh, a woman with that pectoral achievement being pregnant! It's like shooting a game of bumper pool!"

and these guys are hootin' and hollerin' and slashing the seats, firing bullet holes at the screen, then on comes that "tongue" scene, and all you can see in that theater is a bunch of white eyeballs!"

We pull them up short, because just when they think they've got it, they *don't* have it. That's the thing about a gore film. I have seen enough of my own gore films, sitting nondescript in an audience, to know that, yes, there are those who feel that they must take a condescending point of view. Because there's never a question of this being an *expensive* film. I think *Return of the Jedi* is an inferior film. It's a *poor* Walt Disney film. *But,* they spent a lot of money . . . therefore, *reverence.* So you see, people tend to admire the *wrong thing,* or what I regard as the wrong thing.

In *2000 Maniacs,* you're never quite sure until that first thumb comes off, and from that moment, *we've got 'em!* That audience doesn't know what to do! We have them! How many films are there where the *production* keeps the audience in such an unsettled state that the audience literally doesn't know what to do. They're afraid to leave their seats because that's a sign of cowardice. They're afraid to watch because they're afraid of what they'll see. But the one thing that does happen is they leave the theater *not feeling cheated!*

■ *MP: Why don't people make films that really work, instead of spending money on something that looks like a film but doesn't really* work *like a film should work?*

■ *HGL: Beats me!* I read in this morning's paper about Sylvester Stallone, going to make *First Blood II.* That's the ultimate joke—*First Blood II.* It's like saying *old* New Mexico! It just doesn't work together. This will come right after *Rocky 34!*

■ *MP: Why do audiences even accept this now?*

■ HGL: Wait a minute—there's only one way to keep score in the film business: *it made money, it lost money.* Somebody made *Heaven's Gate.* Now, his name escapes me at the moment, but he spent $30-$40,000,000 for an unplayable picture. Did he do it alone? I don't think so—that's too much money for one person to control alone. Somebody saw some dailies. Somebody saw a screenplay. Someone went to a preview, and of course, the preview is what killed the picture. Someone, somewhere, in a system of checks and balances, should have said, "This will not work for *those people.* I tried vainly, on three occasions, to watch *Reds.* I once made it 35 minutes into the film, and I felt heroic, and then I said to myself, "What kind of test of will-power is this? Why are you doing this to yourself? The purpose of paying Home Box Office to deliver this picture to your home is so you'll be *entertained.*"

> Since I couldn't have exploding clothing and couldn't cleave somebody in half with a Japanese samurai sword . . . what I did instead was to dig into somebody and actually pull the stuff apart and fondle it and let the viscera drip.

If I want to test myself, I'll go jogging or bicycling or go to some health studio and see how many push-ups I can do. I won't see how long I can sit into a film before I become so restless that I say, *"Oh, please!"* In our films, that problem doesn't exist, but that isn't necessarily *generic* in that kind of film, either. Maybe it's a sixth sense that *we* developed after a while, because I've seen other films of that type where [the filmmakers] just thought, "Okay, we'll cut up a few people," and it didn't work. You've got to *lead the audience*—it's like the stations of the cross. Unless you're here, you can't go *there.*

■ *MP: It seems like the kind of success your films have is usually associated with a* strong *independent company where someone is definitely leading . . . where you* don't *have a lot of faceless decision-makers.*

■ HGL: I'll tell you what *else* we don't have—we don't have somebody who says, "I won't be in this picture unless my hairdresser comes with me!" We don't have someone who says, "Only shoot me from the left side." We don't have someone who says, "It's 5:00, therefore if I'm going to load that magazine, I'm going to do it very slowly so I'll be sure to

get that overtime!" That makes a difference. I grant you, I'm talking about the fiduciary aspects of filmmaking, but that enters into it. Because nobody's ego is on the line. That's why, in our productions, it was important that at the end of the day we'd all go down to the film lab and look at the rushes from the previous day. It made it a *family affair.* The other point of having no one's ego on the line (people feeling secure enough so they don't try to insulate themselves from the public, which is a terrible mistake in any theater) is that suggestions tend to come in, and you can pay attention to them. Many of the good things in our films, the *good things* being those which titillated the audiences, came from somebody on the crew or in the cast who said, "Why don't we . . ."

> When we opened **Blood Feast** we had vomit bags, and all that was printed on them was "You may need this when you see Blood Feast!" And people would come just to get the bags!

In a classic circumstance, that person is afraid to even make that suggestion. Or if he does, he'll make it to the Third Assistant Director, who will make it to the Second Assistant Director, who will squelch it before it gets to the First Assistant Director. But we operated on the basis of democracy. It was a necessary technique because that way, everybody would grab a handful of cables when we were through shooting, which you don't have when you have a hierarchy: [deep voice] "That's *his* job"!

■ *AJ: Were you a hypnotist also?*

■ HGL: I was a member of the Society for Clinical and Experimental Hypnosis, but I haven't been a member for years. I don't know where you heard that little tidbit; it has nothing to do with filmmaking!

■ *AJ: Well, what I was relating it to was the whole notion of* leading the audience; *in a sense, the whole force-psychology that you were talking about. I'd like to know if you've ever analyzed the processes in your films—how you push the buttons for* reaction, *and how you do go about "leading the audience," manipulating the audience to stay tantalized. I thought that maybe if you* were *a hypnotist, that it would help!*

■ HGL: It's the *Svengali syndrome,* but the audience refuses to play Trilby to your Svengali. It's really a tug-of-war, a battle of wits, and nobody is very well-armed in a battle of wits! I think that it is much more basic than most people accept as being basic.

What I always tried to do was to say to that faceless creature looking at the screen, "You're going to walk out of this theater *talking to yourself.*" That was the key. I maintain that any filmmaker who keeps that in mind won't wind up making a *Heaven's Gate.* What happens is, in order to be a seat-of-the-pants psychologist, you can't assume the road is paved with gold. It is not: *whatever I make, they'll accept.* You have to project yourself into the position of *the person watching.* You can't say, "Public be damned!" If you're going to say "Public be damned!", be a poet! Starve in a garret somewhere in Greenwich Village! Be at the window with a sponge, in impotent outrage at an unhappy world!

■ *AJ: You were talking about* campaign schemes *with Dave Friedman; did you ever hear of Ray Dennis Steckler and some of his campaign schemes? Like when he showed* Incredibly Strange Creatures, *he had monsters come out into the audience while the movie was being shown, dressed like in the movie and—*

■ HGL: When was this?

■ *AJ:: Around '66—*

A TOWN of MADMEN..CRAZED for CARNAGE!
BRUTAL..EVIL..GHASTLY BEYOND BELIEF!

GRUESOMELY STAINED IN BLOOD COLOR!

INADVISABLE FOR CHILDREN UNDER 16

Starring
CONNIE MASON
Playboy's Favorite Playmate
with **THOMAS WOOD**
JEFFREY ALLEN
Shelby Livingston—Jerome Eden

BOX OFFICE SPECTACULARS, Inc. Presents **TWO THOUSAND MANIACS!**
• Produced by DAVID F. FRIEDMAN
Directed by HERSCHELL G. LEWIS

■ *MP: —in the Los Angeles area.*

■ *AJ: He would do things on the level of the* Tingler *movie which had "tinglers" under certain theater seats.*

■ HGL: That was William Castle, wasn't it?

■ *AJ: William Castle did that; Ray Dennis Steckler did low budget gore movies, too. I was wondering if you had any marketing schemes like that?*

■ HGL: We often did. The idea of live monsters we had early on. We often had a casket, not in the lobby, but outside the theater. When we opened *Blood Feast* we had vomit bags, and all that was printed on them was "You may need this when you see *Blood Feast!*" And people would come just to get the bags! It's astounding what motivates people. So, yes, I regard all of that as showmanship, and I'm very much in favor of it, because it *preconditions* someone to accept what you're going to show him before he sees a foot of film.

■ *MP: Have people ever done live protests against your films?*

■ HGL: Somebody in San Diego once organized something. We got a flood of mail, and we knew it was *organized* because they all referred to us as "you wreckless men"! It reminded me of Woodrow Wilson; once he was approached by some labor leader who said, "Sir, I would never vote for you." Wilson said, "Sir, I would be highly outraged if you did!" The same thing is true—I don't want to be admired by someone who spells *wreckless* with a *w!*

But generally we didn't generate that white-hot kind of reaction. We did catch the world unawares. I saw that as the difference between *Blood Feast* and *2000 Maniacs. 2000 Maniacs,* in my opinion, is twice as good a film from every viewpoint—technical, acting, plotline (it was heavily scripted), where *Blood Feast* was more like, "Well, what are

we going to shoot today, fellas?" But it never did quite the business *Blood Feast* did, and one reason was the censor boards were waiting for us. With *Blood Feast* we caught them unawares; there was no sex in it. They were all geared for sex; they weren't geared for blood. By the time we came around the second time, they had amended their statutes and their attitudes. But of all the films I've made, I think the best was a picture called *A Taste of Blood,* a Dracula film. It seems to have vanished forever! Losing a film is like your children leaving home, and then you read in the paper that one of them was elected President of Andorra, but you never hear from them. That's the way I feel about *Taste of Blood.*

■ *AJ: What kind of movie would you make today, considering that there is a huge leap in the level of violence that people can accept right now, as opposed to what they could accept in 1963?*

■ HGL: I would probably get into some of these prosthetic devices that have become so popular; not because I'm an admirer of that particular technology, but because I revere *verisimilitude,* the appearance of truth. And it's certainly better than breaking off a mannequin's arm, which is obviously a stiff and unyielding piece of plaster. It would be better to have the fingers fluttering a little! Or when we take an eyeball out, it would be kinda nice to have some reactions in the tissue around it! So probably what I would do, is to *use* some of this technology.

The second thing I would do, would be to give myself the *pure luxury* of somebody bleeding on the carpet, instead of having a piece of plastic under them. We always shot on location, so protection of the location became paramount, sometimes to the detriment of the effect. *I would just let 'em bleed!* ■

27

■ *BOYD: When we started work on this book barely anyone was aware of your films; now you seem to be the most interviewed living director—*

■ HGL: Yeah, I'm a cult figure, if posthumously—I say that as a joke. Some people think I died years ago.

■ *BOYD: I'm glad you didn't.*

■ HGL: [laughs] Maybe at the box office, but not in person.

■ *BOYD: I first saw* Gruesome Twosome *about ten years ago and thought it was one of the best movies I'd ever seen.*

■ HGL: Good, good! Wish *I* could see *Gruesome Twosome* again—that one I can't seem to find. It apparently has vanished into the night, but I'm sure these films will all start surfacing again. About two months ago somebody sent me a videotape of *Just for the Hell of It,* which I thought had been lost forever, so it shows just how cloudy the crystal ball can be.

■ *BOYD: What happens to films?*

■ HGL: Negatives tend to vanish and then suddenly reappear. I have a film called *Moonshine Mountain* (not really a gore film, it's more country music; there are one or two gore effects, but not many because basically it's a family film), and the negative of that simply *disappeared.* It was not in the laboratory where it was supposed to be. About two or three months ago, a man in California named Jimmy Maslin was buying the rights to some of the old films (he now owns *Blood Feast* and *2,000 Maniacs*). He was going through somebody's vault in Chicago and came across the negative of *Moonshine Mountain.* The owner of the vault had never had *any* relationship to that picture, made no explanation as to how he got it, expressed some surprise that it was sitting there (though it was clearly labeled). Meanwhile I had been raising hell all over the country trying to *find* this negative. So, it merely proves that the film business is an odd business indeed.

> We had effects in there that I myself was literally afraid of: when we french-fried that girl's face . . . when we cut off the girl's nipples (and out of one came milk and out of the other chocolate milk). I felt that was the ultimate in black humor, but there were those in the audience who didn't understand . . .

■ *BOYD: How many of those films are gone forever?*

■ HGL: You want an opinion? They are *all* still *somewhere,* but I lost touch with them when I moved out of Chicago. I have no idea where they are. My proprietary interest in those films has long since ended, so I don't really care that much. It pleases me that *Blood Feast* has gone into re-release and that these films are coming out on videocassette. But it pleases me emotionally rather than financially, because there's nothing in it for me.

■ *BOYD: That's too bad.*

■ HGL: Oh well, these films owe me nothing!

■ *BOYD: How did you get interested in filmmaking?*

■ HGL: My initial interest in films was purely mercenary. I had a commercial film studio in Chicago doing television commercials, business films, films for the government . . .

■ *BOYD: Educational films?*

■ HGL: On occasion, but educational film companies are pretty specialized and are usually self-producers, like Encyclopaedia Brittanica Films or Coronet. The films I made would *on occasion* have some dramatic content, but they were basically films paid for by someone else. "Sponsored films," you might call them.

■ *BOYD: Did any of the exploitation pioneers have an impact on you? Did they influence your attitude toward filmmaking or inspire you?*

■ HGL: Not that I can recall. I'm not that easily inspired by other people's work. I'm a better critic, I think, than I am a [stops to rephrase his statement] . . . What I do best is criticize other people's creative work. This inspiration comes on a negative rather than a positive level. You see what somebody else did wrong and you say, "Hey, what if this were done *right?*" When I shot *Blood Feast* and we started making money with it, I said, "Wow! Look how rotten this picture is. What if we made a *good* one?" So we shot *2,000 Maniacs,* which from a production point of view is far superior (both technically and theatrically) and it never made the money *Blood Feast* did. This is all part of your professional education.

■ *BOYD: You did something nobody else had done. Did that just "happen"?*

■ HGL: That certainly was not accidental. That was an absolutely cold-blooded decision. We went through a whole list of possible topics and procedures that the major companies would not (or could not) make, and that's how we settled on *gore.*

■ *BOYD: Some of your achievements seem as yet unsurpassed, even though producers today budget millions for special effects. Why?*

■ HGL: Because they don't linger as I did. I went for *intensive* gore rather than *extensive* gore, and the rationale behind that is quite simple: I didn't have any budget. Since I couldn't have exploding clothing and couldn't cleave somebody in half with a Japanese samurai sword, and since I couldn't show an alien creature leaping out of somebody's chest cavity (any *one* of those effects would have cost more than my whole film cost), what I did instead was to dig into somebody and actually pull the stuff apart and fondle it and let the viscera drip. And that is where the impact came. Even today, no film producer I know of has the courage ("courage" is perhaps the wrong word; maybe "lack of taste?") to linger on the shots the way we did.

Recently Jimmy Maslin very graciously sent me a videotape of *Blood Feast* which I hadn't seen for a long, long time. (I had seen a bootleg video of it which was almost without color; it looked like it had been soaked in beer; half the effects had been chopped to pieces, and there was a heavy scratch through it.) So, to see this tape in pristine condition was like having my child reborn. We had just screened somebody else's film—*Halloween* or *Friday the Thirteenth Part 37,* or something like that—and the people in the room said, "God, their film is *nothing* compared to this!" So—proud parent, you know!

■ *BOYD: Do you think you're just more sincere than they, more clever, or both?*

■ HGL: No. Sincerity doesn't enter into it. It's more a matter of showmanship than sincerity. Do you think there's any sincerity *at all* in exploitation film production? I don't.

■ *BOYD: Well, some films seem more* personal *than others.*

Blood Feast.

It seems like a great deal of creativity went into your films.
■ HGL: That's because they were more *auteur*-oriented. But, when someone decides to be a one-man gang (produce, direct, perhaps write the film, and be on camera; even write part of the music—and I've done *all* of these), the problem often is: that individual begins to lose viewpoint and begins to make a *personal statement.* And that statement may well be, "Public be damned. If you want to appreciate me, come up to my level. I am telling you *my* position." Instead of saying, "Hey, I'm going to entertain you, or frighten you, or charm you"; instead of thinking in terms of audience reaction.

That's what's missing today: *no one thinks in terms of audience reaction.* They make films like *Heaven's Gate.* They choose impossible, *stupid* titles; the titles *alone* would keep people out of the theaters. They'll say, "Oh well, if it bombs at the box office, we'll still have videotape and cable and foreign sales." They don't think in terms of showmanship. Some of the campaigns I see look like they were written by half-wit oysters.

On Fridays, when films are advertised, you see a bunch of ads in any paper. Some of the ads attract you, some of the ads repel you. But some of the ads leave you saying, "Ehhh . . ." I have no quarrel with those that attract or repel you, but those that elicit "Ehhh" are often written by teams of people, each of whom makes $200,000 a year. This shows me (once again)

that these are *robots, automatons* at the typewriter. The same is true of the scripts and the direction of these films; the directors are often more concerned with the camera shot than with *the effect on the screen.*
■ *BOYD: Movies seem more and more like formulas—*
■ HGL: Well, they're coming out of U.C.L.A. film school and lord knows *what* they teach them there. I'm certain *I'm* not lionized in those quarters and that bothers me not at all, because I believe positively, absolutely, that a motion picture should appeal to the people in the theatre and not necessarily to the person who made it. People are making films for themselves rather than the people in the audience. But there are *bodies* out there!

You walk into a videotape store and there's shelf after shelf of titles. Some you won't even *look* at because the title sounds so dull. Some you'll watch for a few minutes and just can't *bear*—too slow-moving. And some films grab you and hold you. The ones that grab you and hold you are the ones that the producer, the director and the writer have thought about in terms of who's sitting there looking at it. Not who was in the screening room at Paramount, saying what a bright fellow you are . . .
■ *BOYD: Blood has played a very important role in your success as a filmmaker. Throughout history, blood's role in many of man's rituals was of key importance. In ancient Rome, bloodletting was almost a national pastime, and*

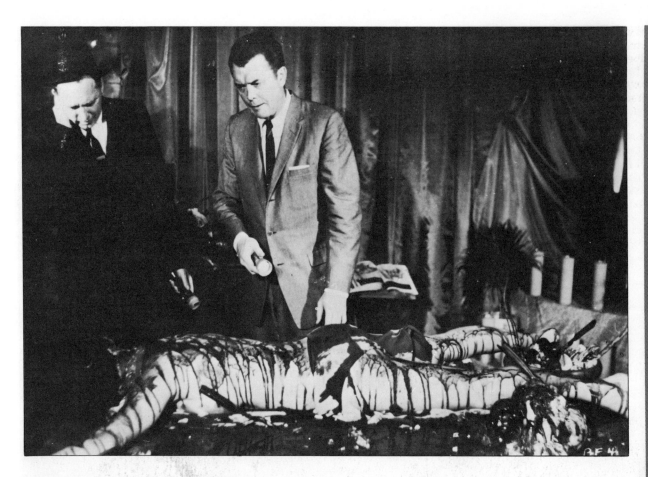

Leftovers from Fuad Ramses' feast (Blood Feast).

even today the most violent episodes in history exert the most profound fascination on people. What's the connection between your films and the bloodletting rituals of bygone days?

■ HGL: Well, as a matter of fact *Blood Feast* was a recapitulation of a bloodletting ritual of bygone days. Yes, blood is the ultimate symbol. It's the one symbol everyone understands. You squash a bug—if it happens to be a mosquito that has recently gorged itself, instead of being just a yellow mess there will be some blood in there and you'll recoil. There is *power* to blood. It has emotional impact unlike any other substance on earth.

■ *BOYD: Do you think the public is bloodthirsty?*

> **When I shot Blood Feast and we started making money with it, I said, "Wow! Look how rotten this picture is. What if we made a good one?"**

■ HGL: More and more, yes. We are devolving ... I think society is slowly going back to the jungle. Everybody has a gun. It's macho to wound somebody and to carve somebody—the term, in fact, is *waste* somebody. We have no regard at all for our fellow man; we are statistics. So if someone happens to squash a statistic, so what?

In these films, what I do (or did) was to *destatisticize* the circumstance. We didn't wipe out a row of people. One by one, *selectively,* blood spurted. *That* has much more impact than killing off a whole battalion of soldiers.

■ *BOYD: It's been said that horror and humor are the same thing. Do you agree?*

■ HGL: Who said that—am *I* quoted as saying that?

■ *BOYD: No.*

■ HGL: Okay, *good.* I would *never* say that.

■ *BOYD: But there* is *a strong connection between the two.*

■ HGL: There's a strong connection between shoelaces and peanut butter, but I don't know what! Other than they are both *items.* Horror and humor are allied in that one can spring from the other. *That,* I started to do. We were creating caricatures and parodies of our own films. In a picture such as *The Gore-Gore Girls,* horror and humor were intermixed, and that was done not only to confound the audience, but also to have them say, "Oh, this isn't real."

■ *BOYD: Why?*

■ HGL: Because we had effects in there that I *myself* was literally afraid of: when we french-fried that girl's face ... when we cut off the girl's nipples (and out of one came milk and out of the other chocolate milk). I felt that was the ultimate in black humor, but there were those in the audience who didn't understand, and didn't see—well, they *saw* what I intended, but they thought it was a desecration to have chocolate milk come out of a ... [laughter].

■ *BOYD: Your films seem to have a* great deal *of black humor.*

■ HGL: Oh, sure!

■ *BOYD: You called* Gruesome Twosome *the most barbaric humor since the guillotine went out of style.*

■ HGL: Yes, that's in the campaign.

■ *BOYD: Do you think your humor is at odds with the general public's?*

■ HGL: If, by "general public" you mean Jerry Falwell or the people who live in Sedalia, Missouri, the answer is "Yes!" If, by "general public" you mean people who are moderately literate and who have been exposed to many facets of our civilization, the answer is no. The other day I read a little booklet that someone quickly published following the screening of that TV movie, *The Day After*. Based on how to

30

live in a post-nuclear society, it's black humor from front to back. There will be those who are amused by it, and those who are disgusted. There's a paperback called *101 Uses for a Dead Cat* [laughs]; some people think that's funny, cat lovers won't. That's part of being in the marketplace—you position yourself. You cannot appeal to all the people all the time.

■ *BOYD: I loved* Gruesome Twosome, *although the rest of the people in the theatre didn't seem to find it very amusing.*

■ HGL: Well, they came in!

■ *BOYD: I really like all the soundtracks you've done. Did you have any musical training?*

■ HGL: Some. I played the violin when I was a child, like everyone else did. I still play the piano. I would not call myself a professional musician.

■ *BOYD: When you were younger, were you a joker?*

■ HGL: No, no. I was a serious student.

■ *BOYD: Many of your films deal with unusual philoso-*phies and ideas. For example, you're familiar with the dynamics of hypnotism—*

■ HGL: Yes, I am.

■ *BOYD: I was wondering how that shaped your films, where things are* not *what they appear to be—*

■ HGL: That's especially true in a film such as *The Wizard of Gore*. If so, it's subliminal, but you can raise an interesting point. I was, and am, and probably always will be interested in what I call *force communication* . . . which is causing the rats to go through the maze the way you want them to. And that understanding undoubtedly has to seep through (by osmosis, if nothing else) into the creative product.

■ *BOYD: Rats, eh?*

■ HGL: Of course, I don't mean rats as rats; I mean rats as people. [laughter]

■ *BOYD: Why did you choose to go into mail order marketing rather than continue as a filmmaker? Weren't you*

A woman admires the wares at a wig shop in The Gruesome Twosome, unaware she is about to join the display.

riding high financially with The Gore-Gore Girls?

■ HGL: Not necessarily. There are several conclusions I reached: one, there are more scoundrels per square inch in the film business ... people who swipe negatives, people who cheat you on box office receipts, people who cheat you on distribution receipts ... *I grew weary of the game.* For example, there was a time when I enjoyed arguing with car dealers over the price of a car. I don't enjoy that anymore; I'm tired of that kind of negotiation. Furthermore, in the mail order business (actually, I'm a consultant and writer rather than really being *in* the mail order business), I am making a tremendous amount of money and working less than I ever have before. I would be *foolish* to discard that in favor of a murderers' row of circumstance, in which I'm dealing with people who have the morality of a bunch of *siding salesmen.* So that really was the reason. I can still make a film; I'm talking to some people now ... not aggressively, but rather passively. When they're ready, I'm ready.

■ *BOYD: So you might make a film again?*

■ HGL: Yep. I could—like Dracula—rise from the grave!

■ *BOYD: A lot of people still believe the worst rumors about you—*

■ HGL: I myself have heard a few: that I was rotting away on a Georgia chain gang, that I had died and hadn't necessarily gone to heaven. Stories just *appear,* as though someone is *looking* for a controversial ploy, just as D. W. Griffith was accused of being a racist. But I'm alive and well, and I'm looking out over the water behind my house, and there's birds out there, and I'm going to play tennis this afternoon, and life is good.

■ *BOYD: Great ... some people imagine that your films were the product of a person much closer to his subject matter than, say, an Alfred Hitchcock movie—*

■ HGL: It's closer—if only because of the physical technique of making the films with a smaller crew.

■ *BOYD: In your films, you allow people to enjoy experiences normally deemed "horrible." And that's taboo in our culture: to be able to enjoy something that's horrible.*

■ HGL: That may have been true when we first started making films, but not anymore—today it's an accepted technique of filmmaking.

■ *BOYD: Yes, but it's altogether different with you. I see you as more of an alchemist. You take these different emotions—base emotions—and blend them together to create something else.*

■ HGL: I turn gold into lead!

■ *BOYD: I really do think you create a different* quality *of experience, where you take different emotions and blend them into one another. You get grotesqueness integrated with humor, and repulsion and enjoyment both at the same time.*

■ HGL: Good theory. I think you've hit it exactly dead center ... ■

Climactic scene from The Gruesome Twosome.

FILM PRESSBOOK SYNOPSIS

SHE DEVILS ON WHEELS

Karen, a quiet and reserved girl during the week, on weekends is a member of The Man-Eaters, a wild gang of female motorcycle riders headed by the beautiful and vicious Queen.

Each week The Man-Eaters stage a cycle race down the length of an abandoned airport runway. Queen, Karen, and the huge, tough Whitey are usually the top contenders. Winner of the race gets first pick of the "stud line"—a strange bunch of men who are The Man-Eaters' playthings for the weekend.

Karen wins the race. As Top Mama, she gets first pick, and as usual, picks Bill, a good-looking stud who is unusually clean-cut for his type.

Next day, Queen calls a meeting of The Man-Eaters, excluding Karen. At the meeting, all voice their resentment: Karen picks Bill week after week, in violation of The Man-Eaters' code. Honey-Pot, young mascot of the group, is dispatched to instruct Karen to be at the airstrip that night. Karen arrives to find the others waiting. They have brought Bill, tied and beaten, and Karen has a choice: she either drags him around the cement runway behind her cycle or will be forced out of the group. In tears, Karen nonetheless agrees; Bill, tied to a rope behind Karen's cycle, is dragged around the strip until he is literally in shreds.

A few nights later, Honey-Pot, the only one of the group regarded with affection by all, undergoes her initiation: all the "studs" are invited to participate, to Honey-Pot's delight. To celebrate, the gang rides through the town, spreading terror and destruction; but, because no one will testify, the police can only threaten.

Arriving at the strip the following weekend, the girls are outraged to find a bunch of hot-rodders using the runway for auto drag-races. A bloody fight ensues, with The Man-Eaters victorious; the boys' gang, headed by the mean and calculating Joe-Boy, is left gasping and bleeding on the ground.

Karen is called by Ted, the decent boy-friend whom she abandoned when she joined The Man-Eaters. Ted has heard about the fight. He also has had word that Joe-Boy's gang has sworn vengeance, and he warns Karen to leave the group before there is violence that will leave her permanently marked. She thanks him for his interest, but says that she is in too far and cannot leave The Man-Eaters.

When the girls return from the next race, Karen is horrified to see Ted in the stud-line. She chooses Ted, and he forces her to leave the building, which, he has learned, Joe-Boy's gang will attack that night.

However, Joe-Boy has another idea: he will destroy The Man-Eaters one by one, starting with Honey-Pot. His gang sneaks up on The Man-Eaters' house late at night and manages to kidnap Honey-Pot. It is done with stealth, and the others are unaware; Karen, returning late with Ted, sees nothing awry.

In the morning, Joe-Boy's gang returns Honey-Pot. She has been attacked and beaten, and a ring, jammed through her nose, holds a note carrying the threat of future similar acts against all The Man-Eaters.

Queen's rage leads to instant vengeance. She leads the gang to the bar at which Joe-Boy's gang usually hangs out; and only after she has beaten up the bartender with her belt—a motorcycle chain—does she agree that Joe-Boy is not hiding there. Ultimately the girls track down Joe-Boy's gang. In broad daylight, the fearless Whitey, along with another Man-Eater, approaches and slashes the tires of Joe-Boy's prized hot-rod. Spraying Joe-Boy's face with insecticide, the girls leap on Whitey's big motorcycle and ride off at top speed. Deliberately, they have left the other cycle. Joe-Boy jumps on it and follows them.

But the girls have strung a wire across the road, neck high. From just beyond it, they taunt Joe-Boy as he approaches. Too late, he sees the wire. It slashes through his neck, decapitating him. As the girls cluster around Joe-Boy's body, Queen inadvertently drops her chain-belt.

Back at their lair, the girls are about to ride off when Ted drives up. Ignoring Whitey's taunts and Queen's threats, he calls to Karen. She dismounts, and when she walks over to him, he pleads with her to quit the gang—to walk over and tell the others she is through. She kisses

She Devils On Wheels.

him tenderly, then walks over to the gang. One by one, they lock eyes with her. She walks to her cycle, and as she sits on it she realizes that she can't go back. The girls ride off, and Ted, alone in the field which surrounds their house, listens to the diminishing roar of the motorcycle.

The police have found Queen's belt, and as the girls return to the scene of Joe-Boy's death, they are arrested.

The end? Not for The Man-Eaters. The picture ends with the gang, free once again for lack of concrete evidence, tearing down the highway, cut-out mufflers belching an ear-splitting roar. Queen and Whitey tell the camera of their future plans and ride off into the distance.

HERSCHELL GORDON LEWIS
BIOGRAPHY
BY JIM MORTON

Herschell Gordon Lewis made films like no one else—filled with grisly violence and black humor, morally indefensible—which is probably why they are so good.

Lewis' background sheds little light on his originality as a filmmaker. He attended a midwestern university where he obtained a Ph.D, taught English at Mississippi State University, then switched to advertising and marketing. During the '50s, he made industrial films in Chicago.

With Chicago producer David Friedman, Lewis started Mid-Continent Films. Soon they released **The Prime Time** (which Lewis produced and Friedman publicized), the story of rebellious youths and a mad beatnik artist. Only moderately successful, the film is best remembered for featuring the first screen appearance by actress Karen Black.

Lewis and Friedman's next film, **Living Venus**, depicted the rise and fall of a girlie magazine. Though risqué, the film was devoid of frontal nudity. Court rulings on a nudist film called **Garden of Eden** made nudity less risky, so they next made **The Adventures of Lucky Pierre**, shortly after Russ Meyer released his box-office smash **The Immoral Mr. Teas**. Despite the fact it was little more than a series of vignettes featuring Chicago comedian Billy Falbo, **Lucky Pierre** made a big profit.

Next Friedman and Lewis improved upon the nudie genre by selecting attractive people to play the sun worshippers. **Daughter of the Sun** starred the delectable Rusty Allen as a woman who is summoned to defend her nudist practices. The film used the unusual device of showing the scenes outside the camp in black-and-white (the mundane world), while all the scenes inside the camp were in color. The film did well, so they followed up with **Nature's Playmates**, **Goldilocks and the Three Bares** and **Bell, Bare and Beautiful**.

Two standouts directed by Lewis during his "nudie" period were **BOIN-N-G!** and **Scum of the Earth**. **BOIN-N-G!** chronicled the exploits of would-be filmmakers trying to shoot a sex film, with their final product being just what their distributor wanted—an atrocity. **Scum of the Earth**, a mean little tale about women forced to pose for a pornographer, was one of the earliest examples of the "roughies"—films released during the '60s that mixed sex with violence.

When the demand for nudie films diminished, Lewis and Friedman sat down and made up a list of possible topics that would sell. They narrowed the list down to one: gore. Not your ordinary bloodletting, but buckets of blood, spilling from the mouth, running from the nose; exposed raw meat, bone and gristle ... eyes gouged from the sockets, limbs hacked off, faces pounded to mush.

The duo started their sanguinary experiment with **Blood Feast**, the story of an Egyptian named Fuad Ramses who runs a catering operation in Florida. When a woman asks for "something special" for her daughter's birthday, Ramses suggests an authentic replication of the "Feast of Ishtar" (a particularly bloodthirsty goddess of ancient Egypt). Unbe-

knownst to her, Ramses plans to use the feast as an invocation rite to bring the goddess Ishtar back to life. In the back room of his delicatessen stands a statue of Ishtar, which resembles a thrift store mannequin painted gold.

To invoke Ishtar, Ramses goes around town collecting body parts from various living women. One woman has her legs cut off, another loses her brains, and in one of the most memorable scenes Ramses breaks into the apartment of a woman and rips her tongue out with his bare hands.

Blood Feast was a hit. People queued up and all over the country there were seas of white eyeballs and open mouths. People stared, aghast at the onscreen carnage. Some fainted; some threw up. Some wondered why it was okay to portray extreme violence but not sex.

Realizing they were onto something, Lewis and Friedman quickly made **2000 Maniacs**, which, despite the fact that it didn't match the success of **Blood Feast**, remains Lewis' favorite film. A group of Northern tourists encounter a small Southern town celebrating the centennial of the Civil War. Eventually the tourists learn their role is to "help" the townspeople even the score with the "Yankees." One woman has a boulder dropped on her; another man is drawn and quartered and his remains barbequed that night. Another man is put in a barrel lined with nails and rolled down a hill. Between bloodlettings a bluegrass group, The Pleasant Valley Boys, sings rural folk songs.

Next Lewis and Friedman made **Color Me Blood Red**, about an egocentric artist striving to find the perfect shade of red for his paintings. During the filming the two parted ways, and Friedman ended up finishing the film and then returning to sexploitation. Lewis split the rest of his career between gore and sex.

Like other exploitation pioneers, Lewis built up his company by buying completed and uncompleted films and releasing them under new titles. He bought an incomplete **Terror at Halfday**, shot a few connecting scenes, added narration, and released it as **Monster A Go-Go!** Besides featuring an

Herschell Gordon Lewis at home holding up the sound track of **Blood Feast**.

outstanding theme song, the film starred Henry Hite ("the tallest man in the world") as an astronaut who returns to Earth a giant. Lewis also bought a British roadshow feature, added "birth of a baby" footage and released it as **Sin, Suffer, and Repent**.

In 1966, Lewis made a low budget rip-off of **I, A Woman** entitled **Alley Tramp**. It was produced by Thomas Dowd, owner of the Capri Theater in Chicago and sponsor of many of Lewis and Friedman's early ventures. During this same period Lewis released two of his most atypical films: **Jimmy, the Boy Wonder** and **(Santa Visits) The Magic Land of Mother Goose**.

1967 was a banner year for Herschell Gordon Lewis. He released three sexploitation films (**Suburban Roulette; The Girl, The Body, and The Pill**; and **Blast-Off Girls**), and three gore films (**Something Weird, A Taste of Blood** and **The Gruesome Twosome**). For its intense gore and goofy humor, **The Gruesome Twosome** is outstanding, chronicling the attempts of a demented old woman and her retarded son to keep their wig shop supplied with fresh scalps. After he finished editing it, Lewis found the movie too short, so he quickly shot a prologue featuring two styrofoam mannequins with faces painted cartoon-style. This addition was one of the most memorable scenes in the film.

A favorite genre of H. G. Lewis was the "Hillbilly Movie," which provided for him (and many other exploitation directors) an ideal context for varied sex and violence—usually more violence than sex. Besides, he liked the music. In **Moonshine Mountain** the hillbillies battle revenuers, dumping the bodies of dead federal agents into their still. In **This Stuff'll Kill Ya'**, two college girls are crucified and another woman is stoned to death.

When Biker Movies became fashionable, Lewis released **She Devils on Wheels**, about an all-female motorcycle gang called "The Maneaters." Only **Blood Feast** made more money than this one. In one scene, a man is dragged on the ground behind a speeding motorcycle driven by his **girlfriend!** In another scene a young woman is beaten to a bloody pulp and a ring put through her nose. Unlike most of his films, "goodness" did not win out in the end—the female bikers, arrested for cutting a man's head off, are set free for lack of evidence.

In 1969 Lewis opened a movie theater in Old Town, Chicago, called "The Blood Shed," which featured many of his gorier films and similar films made by others. The theater also staged live shows filled with gory moments a la Le Theatre du Grand Guignol. Sadly, The Blood Shed wasn't economically feasible, and closed within a few months. However, the little stage shows Lewis produced there provided the inspiration for his next gore film, **The Wizard of Gore**.

Of all his films, **The Wizard of Gore** may be—if not his best—the most purely H. G. Lewis of all his films. It tells the story of Montag, a magician who invites women from the audience to participate in his act. One is sawed in half, another has a spike pounded through her head from ear to ear, two more get swords rammed down their throats. After the acts are over, the women appear to be good as new—for about half an hour—whereupon they suddenly revert to the gory mess they were onstage.

Throughout the film Montag tosses off wonderful speeches concerning topics such as mankind's lust for violence and the question of illusion vs. reality. Much of the power of this film derives from scriptwriter Alison Louise Downe, Lewis' long-time cohort and author of many of his best films including **Blood Feast, The Gruesome Twosome,**

She-Devils on Wheels and **Just for the Hell of It.**

H. G. Lewis ended his filmmaking career with his goriest film ever: **The Gore Gore Girls**, about the murder of strippers who work for a nightclub owner (played by Henny Youngman). In one scene a woman's nipples are cut off; one breast squirts white milk while the other yields chocolate milk. In another, a woman is stabbed while blowing bubble gum; the bubble fills up with blood. Besides more violence the film featured more naked flesh, thanks to the strip joint locale of much of the movie.

At this point, Lewis suffered a series of business setbacks that forced him to close up shop in Chicago. Amidst various rumors he disappeared completely for awhile. Some said he left the country; others thought he was in jail.

In 1977 H. G. Lewis surfaced as the founder of Communi-Comp, a direct-mail marketing agency, and now he is considered one of the foremost authorities in this field—a long way from **Blood Feast**. Being happy, successful and prosperous, he has little desire to return to the uncertain financial realities of filmmaking. No matter; his position in the world of unique/extreme cinema is assured. ■

PARTIAL FILMOGRAPHY

AS DIRECTOR:
One Shocking Moment, 1965
The Prime Time, 1960
Living Venus, 1960
The Adventures of Lucky Pierre, 1961
Daughter of the Sun, 1962
Nature's Playmates, 1962
BOIN-N-G, 1963
Blood Feast, 1963
Goldilocks and the Three Bares, 1963
Bell, Bare and Beautiful, 1963
Scum of the Earth, 1963
2000 Maniacs, 1964
Moonshine Mountain, 1964
Color Me Blood Red, 1965
Monster A Go-Go, 1965
Sin, Suffer, and Repent, 1965
Jimmy, the Boy Wonder, 1966
Alley Tramp, 1966
An Eye for an Eye, 1966
(Santa Visits) The Magic Land of Mother Goose, 1967
Suburban Roulette, 1967
Something Weird, 1967
A Taste of Blood, 1967
The Gruesome Twosome, 1967
The Girl, the Body, and the Pill, 1967
Blast-Off Girls, 1967
She-Devils on Wheels, 1968
Just for the Hell of it, 1968
How to Make a Doll, 1968
The Psychic, 1968
The Ecstasies of Women, 1969
Linda and Abilene, 1969
Miss Nymphet's Zap-In, 1970
The Wizard of Gore, 1970
This Stuff'll Kill Ya!, 1971
Year of the Yahoo!, 1972
Black Love, 1972
The Gore-Gore Girls, 1972

Note: **An Homage to Herschell Gordon Lewis** (8mm film) is available from Daniel Krogh, 4-F Films, 520 North Lincoln Ave, Box 444, Chicago, IL 60614. (312) 929-4194.

RAY DENNIS STECKLER

Ray Dennis Steckler is a fast thinker and fast talker; he makes films quickly and efficiently—but with sardonic wit and inimitable style. Before the age of 24 he had produced, directed and starred in **The Incredibly Strange Creatures Who Stopped Living and Became Mixed-Up Zombies.** The first monster musical ever, **Zombies** was shot in only 11 days on a budget of $15,000 for lab costs, $6,000 for editing, $5,000 for cast, $5,000 for crew, $1,000 for score, and $6,000 for rentals. Ray often accompanied the film's premiere in different cities, playing one of the monsters that come out and attack the audience at a critical point in the film. Since then, he directed the psychopath-classic **The Thrill Killers,** the Batman-and-Robin-ish **Rat Pfink a Boo Boo,** the Bowery Boys-like **Lemon Grove Kids Meet the Monsters,** and diverse others—no two films alike.

Steckler once remarked, "When someone asks, 'How do you make movies, Ray?'—well, I just talk to the cast." Of all the directors in this book, Steckler may be the most extemporaneous. Musical director Andre Brummer, who has been with Ray from the beginning, once remarked, "[From the first film on] I began to admire Ray because he could take any situation and make it work. Ray is marvelous—he thinks very quickly and doesn't let anything become a problem. Once I was shooting with him on a beach scene and a heavy fog came in. I said, 'What will we do, Ray?' He said, 'We'll change the story.' So we changed the story to match the fog—Ray can do that very well."

Boyd Rice first interviewed Ray Dennis Steckler in Las Vegas; later a second interview took place with Ray and actress Carolyn Brandt. Steckler's most recent work-in-progress is **The Hollywood Strangler Goes to Las Vegas.**

■ *BOYD RICE: Are you an outsider in Hollywood?*
■ STECKLER: I don't think I'm *allowed* in Hollywood—I have to sneak in and out! I had a lot of opportunities, but I just did not *fit* here; I don't know why. It's the people in general—I don't get along with them. It's their attitudes . . .

I'm not saying I'm a great filmmaker or anything; I try to *just be different,* not to be like everybody else. That's all it is. It's so easy to copy someone else, and I just don't do that.

As I get older maybe I'll get more money to make better films; then I can do what I really want to do. In the meantime I believe: *get an idea, go make it.* Just do it. It's not easy to make *any* film. Even if you have 20 million dollars, you've got the same problems as some kid with $10,000. There's never enough money; you never get what you want. And the more money you have the more pressure you have. At least *that* kind of pressure I don't have!

So to me, I just don't get along with the people in this town. I'm not a coke freak, so already I'm eliminated from 95% of all the social parties here. And at the same time, if I come up with an idea of something I want to do, they think I'm nuts. So I'd rather just be on my own.

I've been in Vegas for 10 years. The funny part is—I'm well-known, but I'm unknown. I have everything anybody could ever want in Vegas: I've got 10 movieolas, 15 cameras, *everything.* And in Hollywood it's $5 a square inch just for space, with no parking! Hollywood is a situation where it really is *all money*—
■ *BOYD: And no content. It seems like the whole set-up in the movie industry is geared toward inhibiting creativity*—
■ STECKLER: You're trapped! In Hollywood you spend all your time trying to survive: 100%. You have to do all kinds of things you'd probably never even *think* of doing. In Las Vegas, at least, if I walk out my back door I've got nothing but desert. It's a good feeling to just get on a motorcycle and *go!* In Hollywood, you get on a motorcycle and you get smashed at Hollywood and Western!

I like the feeling of *independence.* Stanley Kubrick could never work in Hollywood; he had to get away. I don't feel

> I'm only rebellious around bullshit. I mean, I can conform to any situation, but when it gets to bullshit, I can't handle it, and there's too much of it in Hollywood. Nobody wants to just sit down and say, "Here's what we have to do and let's do it."

comfortable around so-called Hollywood people; never did and never will. It's always a big show, it's "Look at my new Mercedes!"

After I moved to Vegas I bought a brand new pickup truck. A producer I know said, "For the same money you could have bought a Cadillac to impress people." I said, "Yeah, but I can put my camera in the back of the pickup and shoot, and do all kinds of other things. I'm not in the Cadillac business, I'm in the movie business." End of short story. Tells the whole thing.

You should buy *tools* for your trade—for what you want to do. I buy cameras and all kinds of equipment. Those are important to me—not a new suit. (I've *got* new suits, but they're not important.) It's important to have film in the refrigerator (I always have 20 or 30,000 feet) and to be ready to *go* when I get an idea. So I don't change my mind, see?

Too many great filmmakers have gotten great ideas, started on them, then never got them together and never made them. They gave up because they didn't have *all* the elements to make a film. Obviously, they need great talent, but there's a lot of great talent that's never been exposed and never will. A lot of kids don't get breaks. (But look at some that do—they're on television every night! How did they ever get

"The INCREDIBLY STRANGE CREATURES
WHO STOPPED LIVING AND BECAME MIXED-UP ZOMBIES"

A MORGAN-STECKLER Production

STARRING
CASH FLAGG

INTRODUCING
CAROLYN BRANDT

EXECUTIVE PRODUCER
GEORGE J. MORGAN

PRODUCED AND DIRECTED BY RAY DENNIS STECKLER   A FAIRWAY INTERNATIONAL *SHOCK* RELEASE

Filmed in TERRORAMA and EASTMAN COLOR

in—how'd they even get on the *location?!* That's Hollywood!)

■ *BOYD: How did you get involved in filmmaking?*

■ STECKLER: I started making 8mm movies when I was 14 or 15 years old back in Reading, Pennsylvania. In fact I still have them and they're pretty awful. Kids in the neighborhood were my movie stars; we'd just make things up. We did a little pirate film; a little Western at a place called Daniel Boone's Homestead.

They were just fun things. Today, kids 14 or 15 are out with video cameras making epics, but in those days an 8mm camera was very expensive—just to shoot film was expensive. At that time, it was all fun and games for me.

Then I went into the army where I studied photography. I went to Korea and worked as a cameraman, then came back to New York City where I studied photography for a year. Then I got a call from an army friend who needed a cameraman for *Frenzy,* starring Timothy Carey. I shot for him, and that was my first move into the movie business out in California. I worked on many miscellaneous movies. I shot a movie called *Secret File: Hollywood,* but couldn't get screen credit on it because I wasn't in the union at the time. Then I was director of photography in *Drivers in Hell;* I also wrote part of the screenplay and had one of the lead roles. From that I directed *Wild Guitar,* and that's when I met George J. Morgan and we put together *The Incredibly Strange Creatures.*

The Creatures has now been re-released, and a couple other ones are starting to pop up, like *Blood Shack,* a little film about an old house out in Death Valley that was haunted by a mysterious killer (Ron Haydock). That one we made in about three days. *The Hollywood Strangler Meets the Skid Row Slasher* and *Revenge of the Ripper* will be out as well. These are all films made years ago; all of a sudden everyone wants to see them.

■ *BOYD: Were you in any of these?*

■ STECKLER: I was in *Revenge of the Ripper.* It was the last thing I did.

■ *BOYD: Were you the Ripper?*

■ STECKLER: You'll have to see that to find out! Oh, *Body Fever* is another one that's coming out on videotape. They're *all* coming around; I can't explain it. They're not really *great* films, but I never had any real money to make them with. The biggest budget was on *The Creatures:* $38,000.

■ *BOYD: But you had great actors with interesting faces.*

■ STECKLER: You see that in everything I do; I go for faces, etc. I should have been making movies in Europe; I think that's where I missed it. But now, all of a sudden my films are starting to show in Europe.

■ *BOYD: Why?*

■ STECKLER: Over in Europe, when they see a movie like *The Creatures* or even *The Lemon Grove Kids* they say, "Hey, that's really interesting, that's different," because their *atti-*

tudes are different. *The Lemon Grove Kids* was actually made for kids, but over there it has a "British" humor with the same kind of crazy stuff they do in England, only spicier.

There's a crazy short I did that people are *dying* to get—god, I must have had a hundred phone calls for it. It was the first thing I ever did in Hollywood, called *Goof on the Loose*. After 20 years I still think it's great. We did the whole thing at Echo Park in Hollywood; it's a little Buster Keaton/Charlie Chaplin-type short that runs about 8 minutes. It would have run 10 minutes, but we got chased out of the park!

■ *BOYD: Do you control all the videocassette releases?*

■ STECKLER: The only one I don't have control of yet is *Creatures;* George has to make the decision as to where he wants that to go. The rest I have control on. We're trying to get into the midnight movie circuit in L.A. now.

> As I get older maybe I'll get more money to make better films; then I can do what I really want to do. In the meantime I believe: get an idea, go make it. Just do it.

Rat Pfink is one picture that should play that circuit, 'cause they're always picking up offbeat films. I think we can do it; I just made a brand new 35mm print and did a lot of tinting which I think really enhances it a lot (it was originally shot in black-and-white). We did all the night scenes in blue, and the Rat Pfink scenes (when he shows up in his costume and

everything) in amber, and it really holds up—I'm amazed! . . . Where did you see *Creatures?*

■ *BOYD: At a theater in San Diego called the California, where they had the people in masks and—*

■ STECKLER: The whole gimmick?

■ *BOYD: Yeah. And I went back to the California to see* The Maniacs are Loose, *but I went to a matinee and they only had maniacs in the audience for the midnight show. But even that was great, because people were looking for maniacs and there weren't any.*

■ STECKLER: I traveled with it for a couple of months. There was a point when I would jump out of the screen with a girl just like in the movie, and we used to just *run 'em out* of the theaters. But one time near Sacramento someone shot me with a pellet gun—I think that's when I retired.

Steckler doing his Huntz Hall imitation in Lemon Grove Kids Meet the Monsters.

38

In Glendale we had a packed house. And 5 years ago on Hollywood Boulevard near Wilcox some *big* movie was playing and doing awful business. We put *The Creatures* on at midnight and had to run 2 shows; they were standing in line to see it. And applause! God, they applauded for 15 minutes after the movie. What I thought was great was: almost all the people in the audience were in the industry: actors, actresses, etc.

All my cameramen have gone on to the biggest movies in the business. They're all great guys, all of them. It's amazing how many people you work with go on to bigger and better things. But all these guys had great talent when they were working with me.

The whole key was: when I was making those films, we wanted to do it, we liked doing it, we weren't in it for the money, *it was fun.* You wanted to let everyone have a chance to come up with something. You'd tell the guy who was playing the hunchback, "Go make up your own wardrobe and then come out. Let's see what *you* can do." You'd tell the girl who was playing the gypsy (she was Susan Hayward's stand-in for years but never got a movie role during 15 years in Hollywood until I let her play the gypsy woman), "Just do what *you* can do; come up with something." She came out with a wart on her cheek (and this girl was a fox); she went in there and made herself look *weird.* Today—just ask Barbara Eden to put a wart on her cheek! But it was fun; really it was a lot of fun.

If you can't have any fun don't make a movie. It's hard work and if you don't like doing it, then . . . Movies today—if they didn't have special effects they'd die. I've never had one special effect in any film I've ever done. One reason why *Thrill Killers* did very well down South was because some critic said, "My god!"—he'd never seen such horrifying and scary scenes, yet practically everything was shot in the daytime. Every horror movie you see—it's always in the nightime.

I'll tell you what happened to one of those actors, Herbie Robins, who was the leader of the gang. He worked day and night with a group of strictly improvisational actors in improvisational scenes. Ten years in Hollywood and he had never done a movie. Two days before the movie was sup-

> It's not easy to make any film. Even if you have $20 million dollars, you've got the same problems as some kid with $10,000. There's never enough money; you never get what you want. And the more money you have the more pressure you have. At least that kind of pressure I don't have!

posed to start, Herbie was beaten up very badly and put in the hospital. His eye was all puffy and closed, and he was crying—not because he was beat up, but because he felt he couldn't do the movie (we were going to start the next morning). I said, "Why are you crying? What are you worried about?" He said, "I know I'm out of the film." I said, "You're not out of it. Use your eye the way it is." So the next time you watch that movie, watch his face. You can see the way his eye was, but it looks like a nervous disorder. I think he still has it to this day. Recently he played a small part in Tobe Hooper's *Funhouse.*
■ *BOYD: I didn't see that. I don't see many new films; they usually don't seem to have anything for me.*
■ STECKLER: I watch all the old films and I watch all the European films. I've seen all the Brazilian movies—that's my kick now. That's where I'm at, completely. You ever see Brazilian movies?
■ *BOYD: No, but—*

■ STECKLER: Boyd, go see the Brazilian movies! I've seen *Bye, Bye Brazil* 20 times. And go see Sonia Braga if you want to see something special—whew! There's one Brazilian film called *Xica;* catch it. It has the flavor of *The Incredibly Strange Creatures Who Stopped Living and Became Mixed-*

FILM PRESSBOOK SYNOPSIS
THE THRILL KILLERS

Dennis Kesdakian (ATLAS KING), a traveling salesman, is enroute to Los Angeles to close a business transaction when he hears over his car radio that three homicidal maniacs have escaped from a nearby insane asylum. He pays the broadcast little attention as he stops to pick up a hitchhiker, who turns out to be the notorious Mort "Mad Dog" Click (CASH FLAGG), brother of Herbie, one of the asylum escapees. Mad Dog brutally slays Dennis, steals the salesman's car and drives into Los Angeles.

That night, at the Brentwood home of would-be movie star Joe Saxon (BRICK BARDO) and his wife Liz (LIZ RENAY), a wild and riotous orgy is in full swing. Joe has thrown the girls-galore party to influence film producer George J. Morgan (HIMSELF) into giving him the lead role in Morgan's next picture.

Meanwhile, Mad Dog stalks the late night streets of downtown Los Angeles and meets a shapely young brunette named Erina (ERINA ENYO). They go up to her apartment. After making love to her, Mad Dog goes berserk, accusing Erina of being a shameless tramp. In his rage he seizes a pair of scissors and fiendishly murders her. He flees the bloody scene as neighbors react to Erina's screams and phone the police.

Joe and Liz Saxon have an argument the next day over all the money spent on the party—money they cannot afford—and Liz runs off to see her cousin Linda (LAURA BENEDICT), who operates a roadside cafe in Topanga Canyon. At the cafe are Ron and Carol (RON BURR and CAROLYN BRANDT), who plan to marry the next week. They go to look at an old house in the area which they are considering buying and fixing up.

At the house, while searching for the owner, they meet up with the three escaped maniacs, Herbie, Keith and Gary (HERB ROBINS, KEITH O'BRIEN and GARY KENT). The mad men maliciously assault Ron and Carol, finally lopping Ron's head off with an axe and dealing Carol a similar fate.

Joe Saxon and producer Morgan show up at the roadside cafe. Morgan tells Liz he's going to use Joe in his next production. The three maniacs burst into the cafe, assault Liz and Linda and terrorize Joe and Morgan. A free-swinging, axe-hurtling fight breaks out. Joe and Morgan subdue Keith as Linda poisons Herbie's coffee. Gary chases Liz up into the mountains, with Joe in pursuit.

Gary attacks Liz atop a mountain peak as Joe arrives on the scene. Joe and Gary engage in a hand-to-knife combat while Liz escapes, only to fall into the evil hands of Mad Dog Click, searching the area for his brother. Gary plunges a thousand feet to his death and Joe races off to rescue Liz from Mad Dog.

The police arrive to aid Joe. Liz breaks away from Mad Dog by a clever ruse and the police close in. Mad Dog encounters Officer Tracy (LONNIE LORD) and after using him as a hostage, puts a bullet in the valiant officer's brain.

Mad Dog kills an innocent rancher and steals his horse. The police cut off Mad Dog's avenue of escape but the kill-crazy lunatic charges through the blockade. Motorcycle policeman Frank West (TITUS MOEDE) is ordered to pursue the deranged Mad Dog. After a perilous, breathless chase between motorcycle and horse through treacherous Topanga mountain trails, Officer West captures Mad Dog. In a titanic kill-or-be-killed gun battle, Officer West is forced to shoot Mad Dog in the head, killing him and thereby bringing to a shock-charged ending the reign of terror incited by THE THRILL KILLERS and leaving producer Morgan free to cast Joe, Liz and Linda in his new movie.

up Zombies, the kind of thing I go for. Remember *Black Orpheus?* I looked at that film about a hundred times last month. Basically, *Black Orpheus* had a lot to do with *Creatures*—I probably wouldn't have admitted that in '63. I'm a fanatic about carnivals.

■ *BOYD: Me too!*

■ STECKLER: Whenever there's a carnival, I'm there. Whenever there's gypsies, I'm there. When I was a little kid I was always around them. Ferris wheels, anything like that—that's for me. So when I made *The Creatures* I had all those elements in it. I think I had a little bit of *Black Orpheus* in me, and I think I still do. We're all involved, at times, with some film in our mind. Even the guy who made *Orpheus* (Marcel Camus) had seen films where he *saw something.*

I'd always wanted to do a film with Sunset Carson, the cowboy star, and it just never happened. Last week I looked at five of his movies, and I was thinking about him. Yesterday I was at U.S.C. and everyone was talking about him; then I came back to my motel and he *called* me: "Hi, Ray, this is Sunset!" It was a great feeling!

We all have our idols, because we're in tune with something they did; they gave us an *impression* that inspires us to do other things somewhere down the line. Sunset Carson was 6'4"; he was young, clean-cut, manly; had everything going for him. Then in the '40s there were no more Westerns. The guy didn't make a movie for 30 years, but that doesn't mean he's washed up. I think he's in his prime now; he kept himself in shape and looks great—60 years old. Most guys at 60 are out to *here* [traces an imaginary pot belly]; done for. I think he always knew he'd get another turnaround. You've got to have that feeling; if I didn't feel that some day I could make the movies I *want* to make, I probably would have given up a long time ago. But the one thing you musn't lose is the energy. You lose the energy, you're *done for.*

■ *BOYD: What was it you always wanted to do? What fantasy?*

■ STECKLER: Well, when I was a kid I was affected immense-

Esmerelda and her hypno-wheel in **The Incredibly Strange Creatures.**

I just don't get along with the people in [Hollywood]. I'm not a coke freak, so already I'm eliminated from 95% of all the social parties here. And at the same time, if I come up with an idea of something I want to do, they think I'm nuts.

---

ly by Bogart's films. *Sahara* was one of my favorites—that desert. Now I'm a desert rat—I love the desert. I didn't live there when I first saw *Sahara,* I lived in Reading, Pennsylvania—there's no desert back there! But more than that, there was something about the situations and characters that Bogart always played. In almost every movie he's a rebel, a nonconformist. I was like that as a kid, so I identified with him. That went into my personality and my making of movies. If I could have made a movie with Bogart, that would have been great! But it's never going to happen unless I make one *up there* . . . [points toward heaven]

I like the love triangle in *Casablanca.* I still think it's the greatest—a real, honest, love triangle. Today it's all bullshit; they can't have a love triangle without the girl sitting on a toilet seat while the guy says, "Keep the door open while I watch."

The secret to a lot of movies is called *film chemistry.* You *know* if a film has chemistry—and *Casablanca* was the greatest film about chemistry that was ever done. I mean the *rapport* between people, cutting back and forth to each

other; without words—just what you see.

■ *BOYD: I liked the romantic plot of* Wild Guitar; *I especially liked Nancy Czar—*

■ STECKLER: You know the story about her, don't you?

■ *BOYD: What story?*

■ STECKLER: Do you remember when all those kids on the Olympic ice skating team were killed when they went to Europe and the plane went down? She was the girl who missed the plane.

■ *BOYD: Wow! How did you happen to find her?*

■ STECKLER: I had wanted to find a little extra "kicker" because I felt that Arch Hall, Jr. wasn't strong enough to carry the movie. I said, "It would be nice if we had a girl who had a talent we could *use* in the movie—something entertaining." I remembered that she had come in for an ice skating interview, so I said, "Let's use her."

When we were shooting *Wild Guitar,* there was a scene where 2 people were ice skating (with no one else in the skating rink) and I said, "Let's use the spotlight." The cameraman, Vilmos Szigmond, said, "You can't use the spotlight because there's no *source* for it." I said, "Listen, we're *going* to use the spotlight, and someday you're probably going to win an Academy Award for your lighting." Well, I had to fight to do it *then,* but now when you see the lighting in *Close Encounters* (when those spaceships come in), remember that *Wild Guitar* was the beginning of his use of spotlights and backlighting and everything. And sure as hell he won an Academy Award. But he was already a great cameraman; he was *born* to be a cameraman . . .

■ *BOYD: One of my favorite actors in the world is Atlas King—he had such an unusual accent. Whatever happened to him?*

■ STECKLER: I just . . . don't know. I don't know if he *ever* mastered the American language or not.

■ *BOYD: He was so sincere.*

■ STECKLER: He was okay. He was *super.* A very unusual person. One thing about Atlas I'll never forget: right in the middle of shooting *The Incredibly Strange Creatures* I was running short of money (every day, probably!) and I turned around and Atlas put $300 in my hand. I looked (I don't know *where* he got the $300; he probably sent to Greece for it) and he said, "That's for you. You don't owe me nothing, just keep going." And he walked away. That's never happened to me again. Never.

On the last day of shooting on the beach, I said to him, "Atlas, the movie's almost over. I can always add something; can you think of anything you want to do at this point?" And he said, "One time, let me run through the water!" You know that scene at the end where he runs through the water— *that's it*. He did it, and it was great, really super.

■ BOYD: *Why was Atlas King killed off so early in* Thrill Killers?

> I told the girl who was playing the gypsy "Just do what you can do; come up with something." She came out with a wart on her cheek (and this girl was a fox); she went in there and made herself look weird. Today—just ask Barbara Eden to put a wart on her cheek!

■ STECKLER: Let me think—why did I do that? I guess *somebody* had to be killed in the beginning, and King was just the person I picked! That was probably the only part I could slip him in. People didn't understand that he couldn't speak very good English; we had to teach his lines to him, then he would do 'em by ear. Just as, if you were in Japan acting in a movie and couldn't speak Japanese, you'd have to say the words from memory. You could never learn the language quickly enough.

■ BOYD: *What was his real name?*

■ STECKLER: Something like "Dennis Eusteckean"; a long Greek name.

■ BOYD: *Atlas King is such a great name. Always won-*

Atlas and Cash in The Incredibly Strange Creatures.

ATLAS KING is

MEMORABLE

EXCITING

FORCEFUL AND

PROTECTIVE to CAROLYN BRANDT

SENSITIVE

BRILLIANT

UNUSUAL

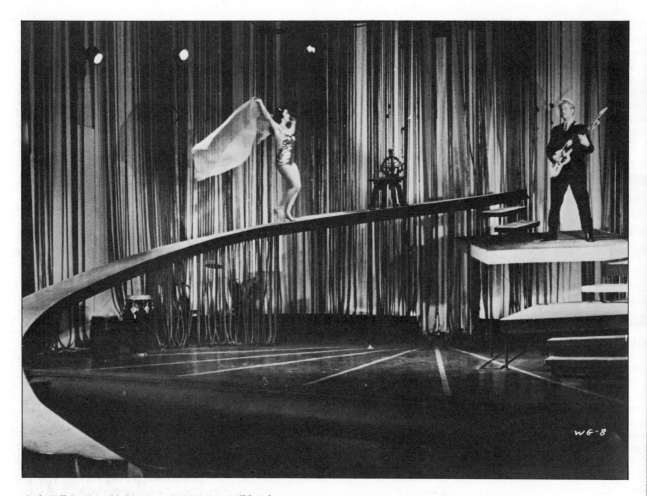

Arch Hall Jr. sings his hit song, "Vickie," in **Wild Guitar**. The dancer is Steckler's former wife, Carolyn Brandt.

dered about him ... Did you have any problems with the unions?

■ STECKLER: There was one union guy who chased me around for years; I'll never forget him. When we were shooting *Creatures* in Glendale, he somehow found out where we were. We were several floors up in this old temple. The place was loaded with people, extras, lights and sets—we had to hoist the sets up from the street and put them together in the temple (because that whole midway scene was just a set, you know). All these people driving by had been seeing these sets going up into the air. So, while we were filming we put

Rat Pfink a Boo Boo came out. The film was [originally] called Rat Pfink and Boo Boo, but the guy who did the titles misspelled it and I couldn't afford to have them redone, so I left it.

warning signs on the elevators, like, "Danger." "Out of Order." The union people showed up looking for us and couldn't find us. They didn't think anyone could go up in the elevators, so they left.

■ *BOYD: Those boots you wore in that movie were so distinctive-looking.*

■ STECKLER: In that last scene in *Creatures,* on the rocks where I fall off into the ocean, we had a dummy dressed like me so we'd be able to show the actual fall into the water.

Those boots I was wearing—my boots—were put on the dummy. We set it all up, had the dummy fall off the rocks, and it completely went to pieces and floated out to sea. So when we were setting up the next scene I asked, "Where's my boots?" and they said, "Oh, right, your *boots.* Well ... they're still on the dummy." I said, "Where's the dummy?" and they told me it was somewhere out in the ocean; it had never returned. We couldn't use the scene at all, and I had lost my boots besides!

So then we had to find another pair of boots like those before we could do another scene. We searched high and low, all over, until finally we managed to find an *almost* identical pair—in *Oxnard.*

They didn't fit—you'll notice I looked a little pigeon-toed in that scene on the rocks. They were a size-and-a-half too small. The thing I remember to this very day is how *cold* that water was—it was like ice. The cameraman, Old Joe Michelli (how the hell could he hear "Cut!" above the ocean?) just kept it running, and—

■ *BOYD: You stayed in the water so long I wondered ...*

■ STECKLER: If I had died, that would have given us an extra 40 seconds in the movie!

■ *BOYD: Do you have any more stories about the making of* Incredibly Strange Creatures?

■ STECKLER: Originally I had picked a girl named Bonita Jade to play the lead. She had a Spanish-Italian look to her. She was only 17 years old at the time; she couldn't even walk straight or anything. But I liked her face and saw some potential there, although I've never seen her since. (Actually, I saw her two years after the movie; she walked up and handed me a book on Antonioni, said, "Read it!" and walked away—I've never seen her since.)

Now . . . we had just shot all the dance numbers, and you know that scene where the girls come out one by one through all those doors? I had shot that and was getting ready to shoot the first scene with Bonita. I walked over to her and said, "Oh boy, you're on." And she said, "Uhh, could we do my scene tomorrow?" (This was the carnival set, with all the people on the midway—extras and everything.) I said, "Well, no, all the extras are here. Everybody's ready to go." She said, "But my boyfriend wants me to be with him tonight; he's got a gig, he's a drummer." I said, "*What?!* You're starring in a *movie,* Bonita, you've been waiting for 5 weeks to . . ." She whined, "I *know,* but *come on,* Ray, he'll be *awfully upset.*" I said, "You mean he can't drum without you?" She said, "Well . . . he *likes* me there." I said, "But you're starring in a *movie.*" (Everybody's standing there looking at

> The whole key was: when I was making those films, we wanted to do it, we liked doing it, we weren't in it for the money, it was fun.

us.) Just at that moment another actress, Sharon, walked by in her striped costume. And I went like this [reaches behind him without looking], grabbed her by the wrist and said, "I think you've got the part, Sharon." She said "*What* part? I just did the number." I said, "No, you're now going to play the part of the *star.*" She said, "But I can't do that; I just did the number!" I said, "Oh yes you can! Come on." We changed her hair and I said, "This is it." And Bonita stood there. I said, "Go to your drummer." She said, "Well, I can do it tomorrow." I said, "GO TO YOUR DRUMMER." To this day she hasn't done a movie! And that's how Sharon got the part.

■ *BOYD: When did you first meet Carolyn Brandt?*

■ STECKLER: You know, we've been married 16 years—we go *way back* . . . I had just finished photographing a movie for Timothy Carey called *Frenzy,* which was later released as *The World's Greatest Sinner.* Timothy Carey was in Stanley Kubrick's *The Killing;* he's the guy who shoots the horse at the race track. And in *Paths of Glory* he was one of the 3 guys they executed; he played the big guy who smashed cockroaches on a table or something—great scene. Anyway, he met me in New York, then gave me a call and asked if I'd like to shoot a film for him. I laughed (because I had just seen his movie) and said, "Well, you're too big for *me* to talk back to." I mean, he was a *monster.* I said, "What if you don't like what I say—you'll crush me like that cockroach." He said, "You're right!"

So I went to Long Beach to shoot this movie with 200 extras smashing up the Coliseum; it was wild, and we did some crazy things. (If you ever get to see the movie, you'll see.) But it was not a great movie by any means. Timothy Carey had some great ideas but he lacked technique; he didn't know how to put them together. But it was good experience, because I met other people and worked in the business from that point on.

He got the money from Mike Ripps, who had made *Poor White Trash.* Very successful film! Mike took a movie that nobody wanted, added 3 minutes of a girl running through a swamp semi-nude, and called it *Poor White Trash.* Three weeks later he released it and the theaters were packed! It just goes to show that if you have an *idea,* you can still pull it off.

■ *BOYD: What was the movie originally called?*

■ STECKLER: *The Bayou.* The leading actor was Peter Graves from *Mission Impossible;* Carey was in it, too. After Ripps renamed it *Poor White Trash,* for years it was like the

Deep Throat of horror movies! So Tim got the money to make his one and only movie—never could put another one together after *that.*

Tim and I got along real well because I was a rebel and he liked that. He and James Dean used to pal around a lot, too. He said James Dean wasn't from this planet anyway and just got called back early!

■ *BOYD: You still didn't say how you met Carolyn Brandt; was it through Timothy Carey?*

■ STECKLER: Oh, is that how we got here? *No.* There was a TV pilot, starring Tommy Rettig called *The Magic of Sinbad.* She was on the flying carpet with Tommy Rettig and I was on the set, and I met her. (She was actually one of the genii's maids or something.) Then I got her a part as a dancing girl in *Secret File: Hollywood,* a film I photographed. Then she was in *Wild Guitar,* on the dance ramp.

Carolyn and I got jobs as ushers at the Ivar theater. I talked the people there into letting me use the set, 'cause I was directing *Wild Guitar* and ushering at the same time. It was crazy. And while we were there the union came in; I'll never forget that. One guy took a roll of film right out of the can and threw it down the street—we lost a reel of film! We went after them but then dropped the case, it wasn't really worth it; they suspended the guy from work rather than have us sue. (You don't really want to make enemies.) The budget on *Wild Guitar* was something like $12,000. On *Rat Pfink* I think we put in maybe $8,000 on the whole movie.

■ *BOYD: Rat Pfink is an odd movie; there's such a contrast between the first part where the stars are such "heavy" characters, and the second part where all these "goofy" scenes happen.*

■ STECKLER: I know; I don't know if I did the right thing there or not. I just got halfway through the movie [starts to laugh] and . . . Ron was sitting in the chair with his guitar singing this song, and it was *so bad;* Titus was playing with the ice cubes, and I said [more laughter], "If you went in that closet and came out as Batman and Robin, I wonder what the audience would say."

Therefore, Batman and Robin (or Rat Pfink and Boo Boo) came out. The film was called *Rat Pfink and Boo Boo,* but the guy who did the titles misspelled it and I couldn't afford to have them redone, so I left it.

■ *BOYD: That's great! Such a perfect title:* Rat Pfink a Boo Boo.

■ STECKLER: He wanted another $50 to change it, so I said, "Never mind!" Two things I liked about *Rat Pfink* and *Wild Guitar* are those 2 numbers on the beach at the end. And we did 'em in like 2 hours each—both of them. We just went to the beach with no plans, no props, no money for anything, had a good time for 2 hours and left. And those 2 numbers, I think, can hold their own anywhere! Major studios make all kinds of preparations to go out and do beach party scenes, and they don't come up with anything better. Come to think of it, I ended *The Creatures* on the beach; and even *Thrill Killers* basically ended on the water, when I rolled down the hill and fell into the water.

■ *BOYD: That's right!*

■ STECKLER: The first time I rolled down the hill I said,

> **European filmmakers get out there; if they say to an actor, "Stand here" (it's raining), "and don't move until we get the shot," he stands there in the freezing rain until they get the shot. In Hollywood, you aren't going to see a star standing in the rain—none of them. They're all wet, anyway!**

"Let's do this again, I want to fall into the water." And they said, "There's no water here!" I said, "Well, we're going to *make* it." We went to a nearby Boy Scout camp and got buckets and buckets of water and Don Russell (he was the hunchback in *Creatures*) dug the ditch. And (I'll never forget) he said, "I'll get a hump for *sure* doing all this digging!" That's how we did it.

■ *BOYD: . . . At the beginning of several different films, you show Hollywood, the stars on the sidewalk, and the Capitol Records building—*

■ STECKLER: Yeah, I did that in *Wild Guitar, Rat Pfink* and *Thrill Killers.* Oh well . . .

I made a movie for some people in Texas that I can't get a print of anywhere. It was called *Sinthia: The Devil's Doll.* It really was an intriguing movie; then they made me add 3 scenes I didn't want to add. They were afraid it was too "European" for audiences, so they put in a psychiatrist to explain my movie! I got really pissed off, took my name off and put a phony name on it.

That film contained the best photography I ever did. It did pretty well for them, I understand. A girl who had lots of potential played the lead. Here was a typical Hollywood story; I've got to tell you this.

Her name was Bonnie Allison. A stage director named Ted Roter was to play the girl's father; he's Hungarian and was perfect for the part, even though he wasn't an actor. I asked him to come to my office. At this point I'd interviewed 200 girls for the lead and couldn't find one; I wanted a girl that had a little bit of innocence, because she's supposed to be a 12-year-old girl who grows up. (It's very hard to be 21 years old and play a 12-year-old, unless you do a "surrealistic" scene.) Anyway, he called me up and said his car broke down, but somebody's giving him a lift. Finally he walks in with Bonnie, a school teacher. As soon as I saw her I said, "Come in; I want to talk to you. You're just what I want, *exactly.* You'd be perfect for this movie." Ted said, "But she's a school

teacher, Ray!" Then she said, "Well, I have to tell you something. All my life I dreamed of being a movie star, but I never had the guts to go out and do it." I signed her on the spot. It was the only movie she ever did, but she was great. The movie was produced by a 65-year-old woman, Dorothy Sunny.

■ *BOYD: What was the plot?*

■ STECKLER: Basically your "girl who was in love with her father" story, but weird and complex, because I had a couple of very fine writers. One, Mort Fine (he wrote *The Pawnbroker*) came over to see it, and after he saw the film he grabbed me around the neck and said, "Nobody in America could make a film like that but you." He was overwhelmed. The film kept going into flash-forwards where she would get older, and go into the next stage, and the next stage. You'd have thought it was a low-budget Bergman film! It was horrifying, extremely horrifying, and yet fascinating at the same time. That was the word Mort used: *fascinating.* You couldn't take your eyes off the images. And the musical score was great. The same guy does all my music: Henry Price.

The only problem was: I had no control over the film because I didn't produce it; a sorry lesson I learned. I made a film I really cared about, yet they took it away from me and changed it. I swore I'd never do that again.

■ *BOYD: Are you working on any scripts now?*

■ STECKLER: I'm working on a script involving gypsies and a movie star who runs away from Hollywood (she can't handle it) up to Lone Pine, California. She rents a bungalow and she's *through* with Hollywood, you know. But this producer cons her into coming back to make *just one more film.* His wife doesn't want her coming back because *she* wants the part. The actress meets these gypsies who warn her what not to do, and you have these mind trips. She goes back, the producer has her stay in this house, but something's wrong because years ago something *happened* here. And she keeps getting all these flash-forwards, seeing herself in visions where she doesn't know what's what. In the meantime she's been taking a lot of 'ludes and she's not sure if she really is seeing what she sees, or if what's happening is happening. A supposed killer comes back to the house and so forth, but what people don't know is: there's another killer coming to the house to kill her besides the supposed killer: the wife, who's going to *kill* for the part, no matter what. That's my little tribute to Hollywood!

That's probably going to be my next film. The costumes for the gypsies are being made right now. I'm going to shoot in Death Valley; I'm going to Zabriskie Point for one shot. My tribute to Antonioni!

■ *BOYD: Were you shooting footage of Hollywood Boulevard for this film?*

■ STECKLER: For about 3 years I've been compiling footage for a little film called *Hollyweird,* putting different scenes aside. I want to dedicate it to Hollywood and wish 'em luck. Good title, huh? I see it every week in the *National Enquirer.*

You will really like Carolyn Brandt in *The Hollywood Strangler.* She doesn't say one word; in fact there's only about 5 lines of dialogue in the whole film. Everybody's screaming at me for not putting in any dialogue, but it just doesn't need it. I want to see if I can make a 72-minute, silent horror movie!

■ *BOYD: Do you always script out your movies?*

■ STECKLER: You have to, although I didn't write *Wild Guitar;* that was Arch Hall's script. I went pretty much with what he had, but I added the kidnappers and stuff like that for fun because I thought the script was kind of hokey. But I liked it; I liked Junior—he was a nice kid. He wasn't a great actor but he had a clean, wholesome personality. And we had nothing, no money, to make the movie. If we had pizza it was like going to heaven!

■ *BOYD: You were great as a "heavy" in that; did you enjoy playing that type of character?*

■ STECKLER: Well, this is a long story. I went to Los Angeles

City College and studied acting with a gigantic, fantastic, black actor. I don't know whatever happened to him, but his name is Eddie Rowey and I always wanted to work with him in a movie. I took Eddie to Arch Hall and said, "Arch, Eddie would be great to play the heavy, 'Stake.'" And he said, "All right." But at the last minute he chickened out because Eddie

> **You should buy tools for your trade—for what you want to do. I buy cameras and all kinds of equipment. Those are important to me—not a new suit.**

was black, and he was afraid he would lose all his bookings down South. (This was 1962; remember I got flak down south with *Rat Pfink* just for having the black guy get in the back of the truck.) So anyway, I said, "What are we going to do? We're shooting in the morning." He said, "Well, *you* play it." I didn't want to direct my first movie *and* act in it, so I said, "How can *I* play the part?" (Arch Hall outweighs me by 40 lbs, he's taller than me, and I've got a fight scene with him at the end; for Christ's sake, you don't want the hero beating up a little squirrel!) So I had to play him slimy so that no one, in my mind, would be offended at the leading man beating up a little guy at the end. Originally, Eddie Rowey was supposed

to play the character with a lot more class, but I made the character a little sneaky, deliberately … a little money-making guy protecting his boss's money. And that's when the name "Cash Flagg" came out.

I didn't make up the name "Cash Flagg," because at the time, in Hollywood, I had a little reputation that I wouldn't take checks from anybody. I would say, "Pay me in cash or don't pay me at all." So the nickname "Cash" started to come around, little by little. I would say, "Arch, if you don't have any money don't give me a bad check, just pay me cash." So the next thing was "Cash Flagg" (I'm not sure where the "Flagg" came from). When I made *The Creatures* I used that name. Arch and I were always kidding about this; until the day he died he was fascinated by the name "Cash Flagg."

Anyway, I used "Cash Flagg" in *Wild Guitar, Incredibly Strange Creatures,* and *Thrill Killers.* And I used it once more in *Revenge of the Ripper,* which will be coming out in another 6 to 8 months—*maybe.* I shot *Revenge* in '72, and I said I wasn't going to edit it for 10 years. Well, I just edited the first 2 reels last month. Not many people can do that: make a movie, put it on the shelf for 10 years, and not even edit it! I shot it at a festival in Santa Fe, New Mexico and I'm going to start out the movie saying, "The year was 1974 …" and people are going to say, "Wow! he sure did a lot of good research!"

The star of *Revenge of the Ripper* is great; he's *something else,* that guy. He's a little upset that I waited 10 years, though.

Cash Flagg (Ray Dennis Steckler) does the bidding of Esmerelda in this scene from **The Incredibly Strange Creatures.**

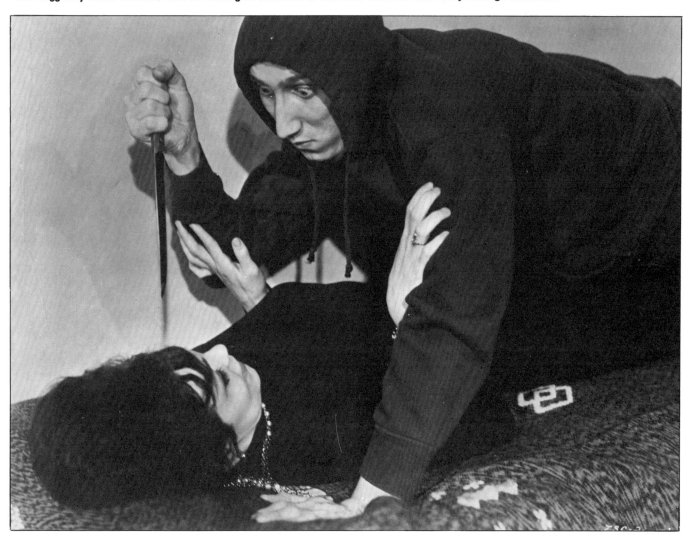

Carolyn Brandt relaxing in a scene from The Incredibly Strange Creatures.

I said to him, "I told you ahead of time that it was going to be 10 years until this picture gets out." I knew it right then and there, and I probably will do that in the future with some films.

I'm in another movie that I can't get a print of called *Drivers In Hell*, re-released as *Wild Ones on Wheels*. In *Wild Guitar* you can see the poster for it right on a table; the movie was made right before *Wild Guitar*. I loved making it; nice little film.

■ *BOYD: Is that about a gang that terrorizes a family*

driving through the desert?

■ STECKLER: Yes, they're in sports cars and they kidnap a guy and his wife in a jeep. For *Drivers In Hell* I was head cameraman; then they decided they wanted me to play a part in it as well. It's easy enough to act in a film when you're the director, but when you're supposed to *film* a movie as well as be in front of the camera playing a role about 50% of the time, that's some trick!

> **Originally I had picked a girl named Bonita Jade to play the lead. I saw her two years after the movie; she walked up and handed me a book on Antonioni, said, "Read it!" and walked away—I've never seen her since.**

■ BOYD: *What about some of these other films, like "the last original B movie"?*

■ STECKLER: Oh, *Body Fever*. That never saw the light of day anywhere, but I just sold it to England and they loved it. The guy called me and said it's being dubbed into Spanish; and he's got a deal for Ireland and all the Scandinavian countries. The reason being: *The Creatures* had been sold to England 7 or 8 months earlier, and all of a sudden everybody wanted to see movies I had made. So England took *Body Fever*, *The Lemon Grove Kids*, *Blood Shack* and *Hollywood Strangler*.

■ BOYD: *What's* Body Fever *about?*

■ STECKLER: I had my office at 9100 Sunset and I wanted to make a little detective movie but I didn't *really* want to make a detective movie but I *did* want to make a detective movie—you know what I mean? I had all these kids coming in, and this one guy had been bugging me for about a year (I won't mention his name) who said he really wanted to work for me. Finally I said, "I'm gonna take a chance and give you a role and do it." Third day into shooting, he started to tell everyone what to do. (The guy had never made a movie; I had sent him to Max Factor, got him a hairpiece, I got him everything.) Anyway, he said, "You've *got* to do it my way, because you've already shot for 3 days" (and we had spent a lot of money). I said, "What do you mean I have to do it your way?" He says, "You can't go back and re-shoot all those scenes." I said, "Oh yes, I can!" and grabbed the hairpiece off his head and put in on *my* head. I told the makeup woman, "We can make it fit," and said to him, "You're fired! Out!" To this day he hasn't done a film. And I made the movie. I may have made a mistake because I don't think I was right for the script, but I don't like *anybody* putting pressure on me! I *hate* that.

So now *I'm* playing the detective and all of a sudden I'm looking at the footage and saying, *"Uh oh."* And I thought, "Either start over with a new actor or just do it and get it over with." I checked the money I had and said, "Let's go with what we have; see what comes out of it, and do the best we can." In a way, I'm glad I did, because I look at it every 2 or 3 years and there are 2 or 3 scenes that are probably as good as anything ever done in the movie industry.

There's one scene in particular that was not in the script. We had finished the last day of shooting and Ron Haydock and I had gone to the Hollywood Ranch Market to get something to eat. When we came out we saw this guy lying in the gutter. I said, "That looks like Coleman Francis."

Now I don't know if you know Coleman Francis or not, but he was an old-time actor who did a lot of work. Coleman was in my *Lemon Grove Kids;* he played Mr. Miller, the old man

Carolyn Brandt with killers in The Thrill Killers.

Carolyn Brandt with Ron Haydock in Blood Shack.

who came out, chased the kids, and got hypnotized. I said, "What are you doing, Coleman?" (it was Saturday night, by the way, and I was so glad the movie was over). He said that he hadn't worked, and had no place to go. I offered him $20 and he said, "I don't want the money. I'm an actor; I want a job." And I'll tell you, my stomach and my heart . . . he was sitting there and it was *cold,* man. I said, "Well, how would you like to work tomorrow? We've got one more day left on this movie," and Ron looked at me (we had just been celebrating the *end* of the movie, and I knew I had made a dud to start with; no one was going to accept this picture). So I said, "Meet me, uh . . ." and I had to think fast because I didn't have any money to shoot. I remembered once shooting near this laundromat right around the corner at Sunset near the freeway, and I said, "Meet us at this laundromat."

Ron was *looking* at me, but—one thing I liked about him was, he never asked me questions in front of people; he'd wait until afterward. Then Ron said, *"What* are we going to do?" I said, "Let's shoot a scene down there because it's deserted; it won't cost us any money. If we shoot in the

morning, there will be enough light coming in . . ." He said, "All right." And I told Coleman (I had seen him and he's a derelict, right?), "Now this is just an advance," and I put $20 in his pocket. He said, "Thank you, Ray, that's *different.* I'll be there. What time do you want me?" I said, "9:30."

The next morning we got there about 8:30 and set everything up. 9:00 came; nothing. 9:15 came; nothing. And Ron said, "Well . . ." I had envisioned this scene about a derelict working in a laundromat, making it up as I was waiting. All of a sudden I see this guy coming across Sunset Boulevard— *"That's him!"* He was dressed in a sport coat, not new but clean; clean clothes, clean-shaven, his hair shaped up and everything. He'd used the $20 to go to a used clothing store or some place where they sell sport coats for 6 bucks . . . He said, "I wanted to be presentable." I hadn't told him what to wear; it was really my fault, but I'd assumed that because I had seen him in such terrible shape the night before, the next morning he would look the same. But I will never assume anything about an actor again. He came in ready to go to work, looking the best that he could look for $20. (He didn't

FILM PRESSBOOK SYNOPSIS
THE LEMON GROVE KIDS

To settle their differences, SLUG, GOPHER and THE LEMON GROVE KIDS agree to participate in a cross-country race with their neighborhood rivals, KILLER KRUMP and THE EAST LEMON GROVE KIDS. But DUKE MAZARATTI, formerly a member of Slug's gang and now working for BIG ED NARZAK, local bookie, has plans to make a lot of money on the race. He takes bets on Slug's gang to win the race while secretly placing his own money on Killer Krump's group, even though it is Slug's boys who are the better athletes of the two teams. Duke is confident of making a pile of money on the race because he has hired THE SABOTEUR, who can fix anything, to fix the race against Slug and The Lemon Grove Kids. It's a riotous race through city, beach and desert as the Lemon Grovers heroically overcome the many plots hatched against them by the notorious Saboteur and race to the finish line, neck in neck with Killer Krump's Kids.

take the $20 and buy himself a bottle; he took it and made himself look good.)

We improvised this scene in the laundromat, and Herb Robins (who was in *Thrill Killers*) came down to do the scene, too. I have to tell you: that scene is so good and he is so great in that part that, the few times we've screened the picture, it blows everybody's mind. It's very simple and yet tells the whole story about what we were trying to do in the movie.

You know, sometimes you don't do what you set out to do. Had I shot that scene first before I made the movie, it would have been a completely different movie. But that was the last scene. In a way, it's almost out of context in the picture and yet in another way I'm not sure. The only people who can judge it are people who look at it.

Coleman Francis was *great*. He passed away not too long after that. I just saw him in a movie opposite Rock Hudson, *Twilight for the Gods.*

It's amazing what Hollywood can do to someone. Coleman was a professional. He may have been drunk on his own time, but he wasn't drunk on my set—know what I'm trying to say? I found out later that a lot of people wouldn't touch him because he was drinking a lot. I said, "Yes, but does he drink while he's working?" That's the whole key: *does he drink while he's working?* There are great stars that drink too much and there are great stars who're on too much dope. But somehow they manage not to screw around when they're working; they stay away from it, or else they wouldn't work. Anyway, he was a fine actor; I'm glad he worked for me on 2 or 3 movies. In *Lemon Grove Kids* he was the head gangster, Big Ed Narzak . . .

■ *BOYD: Who else was in* Body Fever?
■ STECKLER: I had the creator of *Hogan's Heroes,* Bernie Fine, who was the big guy in the *Sgt. Bilko* shows. He asked me, "What name do I have in the film?" and I said, "Big Mac" (because at that point in this country the "Big Mac" had come out). He said, "Steckler, you're crazy!" I said, "You were great in *Sgt. Bilko,* so give me a break." Then I got the guy who strangled Steve McQueen in *Love with a Proper Stranger* (or one of those movies); he was the heavy. So I had these 2 gigantic guys—I mean *really big*—and I had some other weird faces I found around town. After I fired the actor playing the detective (who had looked good against these people), all of a sudden *I'm* playing the role, and it's like half a step above Woody Allen!

But the *last* thing I want is to be compared to Woody Allen. Yet people sometimes do—because of looks and everything. And my attitude is sort of crazy like his, I guess, or vice versa.

The difference is, he's so much into himself; he's *completely* into himself in all his films. Woody bases everything on some personal, exaggerated experiences, whereas I *make up* experiences and use them.

■ *BOYD: Were you actually in* Eegah!?
■ STECKLER: Yes. I was the cameraman and I made my acting debut. We were at this country club where they had this great pool and someone said, "Somebody should throw someone in the pool." I volunteered, so Richard Kiel threw us in. Richard Kiel, who plays "Jaws" in James Bond movies, played Eegah. At the time he was another starving actor and Arch actually wrote the screenplay for him because he used to rent a room from Arch and I guess he got behind in the rent, because Arch said, "I've got to make this up *somehow*" so he made the movie *Eegah!* That was a fun movie to make. I've got to tell you this story . . .

We were making *Eegah!* in the *hot* summer, 120 degrees in the Palm Desert. At that time Wilos Gapaniks, who's done a lot of big movies recently, was the director of photography. Arch Hall asked me if I wanted to assist him and I said, "Sure!" (I had just finished *World's Greatest Sinner;* I had met Wilos, and really liked him.) So, we went out there. In daytime you load film in a black changing bag; it was so hot that my hands were melting in the bag. In the heat the film got *very soft,* and I sweated a lot, so it wasn't easy to load in the magazine. And we had no air-conditioned vehicles or anything.

Arch had told us earlier that we were on private property, and if anybody came up to be careful about what we said, because he didn't want to spend any money to rent grounds or anything out there in the desert. While I was changing the film all of a sudden someone came up and said, "What are you doing?" I turned around and saw this guy with curly hair, about 70 years old. And I said, "Oh, we're just making a little educational film down there." He looked down there and asked, "What's that guy doing with the club?" I said something like, "Oh it's just a . . ." (I was reaching for words.) And he's smiling at me. (At this point I was a little naive about how you have to hustle to steal *everything* in the movie business.)

> I did a lot of tinting which I think really enhances it a lot (it was originally shot in black-and-white). We did all the night scenes in blue, and the Rat Pfink scenes in amber, and it really holds up—I'm amazed!

And he said, "You're making a horror movie or something, aren't you?" I said, "Well . . . yeah, sort of." He said, kind of politely, "That's my land, you know that?" I said, "Oh really?" He said, "I used to make a few movies myself once in a while. I know what you guys are doing. But it's okay; be my guest! Have fun, kid. Good luck in your career," and he got in his car and drove away. Arch came down because he saw him talking to me and asked, "What did he say?" and I said, "It's okay, Arch, everything's under control. He said it's okay; we can shoot here." Arch said, "You know who that was, don't you?" I said, "Well, he kind of *looked familiar;* he said he was in movies, but I couldn't place him. I didn't recognize the voice." He said, "Of course not—that was Harpo Marx!" It *was*—I'll be a son of a gun. I mean, my heart went . . .

I tell you, of all the guys that I as a kid loved—I couldn't believe I'd met Harpo Marx. He was putting me on all the way, he had me going and loved every second of it. 'Cause he'd have been the first on the hill making the movie if it had been the reverse situation, know what I mean? Those were the guys that had the energy! They *loved* their work. That day was really exciting. Anyway, that was my really great moment. And I think I've met everybody from Troy Donahue to Gardner MacKay.

■ *BOYD: I recently met Gardner MacKay.*
■ STECKLER: I met Gardner 20 years ago. I liked him, liked his personality. He's very nice to be with. I met him at a party and we had a great talk one night, after his series was finished. What's he doing now?
■ *BOYD: He's a playwright. He just went to the East Coast where a couple of his plays are being done on Broadway. After that he's going to Europe to get away from everything, and get some writing done.*
■ STECKLER: How's he look?
■ *BOYD: Great; he still has the same sort of boyish good looks.*
■ STECKLER: That's fantastic. He never did any more films after that series, did he?
■ *BOYD: He made a film called* I Sailed to Tahiti With An All-Girl Crew.
■ STECKLER: Right! That should be a classic little cult film somewhere. It's a man's dream to go across the ocean with a boatful of girls.

> **I made a movie for some people in Texas called Sinthia: The Devil's Doll. It really was an intriguing movie; then they made me add 3 scenes I didn't want to add. They were afraid it was too "European" for audiences, so they put in a psychiatrist to explain my movie! I got really pissed off, took my name off and put a phony name on it.**

Back in the late '60s I tried to put a couple of films together with Troy Donahue but I couldn't. I always thought Troy had a lot more talent than was expected of him in Hollywood. I thought he could have gone farther, but he was in *that system.* But without that system he wouldn't have been Troy Donahue, either, and he would never have gotten the break.

Another actor I like (believe it or not, he's so stereotyped now) is Dennis Cole. He's trapped by his good looks and everything, but I think he's got a lot more going for him than he's getting. At some point I hope he gets a break. Stuart Whitman's another actor; those are some of the guys I like. Of course I *met* them so I got to know them a little bit personally, just enough to feel that I'd like to work with them. I don't know how *anybody* can make a movie—be stuck with someone for 3 or 4 weeks—and not feel some sort of *rapport.* I mean it's hard to live with a person for *one day.* So anyway, I hope all 3 of them eventually grab something, somewhere.
■ *BOYD: I wanted to ask you: wasn't Liz Renay fresh out of jail when you cast her in* Thrill Killers?
■ STECKLER: Yes, I think she was in Chino. Joe Bardo, who played in *Thrill Killers,* had told me that she'd be getting out of jail soon and had to find some work *immediately.* I said, "Hell, let's shoot a movie with her. I'll put you both in it, let's do it." So she came over, I met her for the first time, and we started shooting the next morning (she had just gotten out of jail the day before.) And we made this movie. I told you the Herb Robins story, didn't I?
■ *BOYD: He was the guy who got beat up a few days before you started filming.*
■ STECKLER: Yeah. You'd find him a very fascinating guy. He directed and starred in a movie called *The Worm Eaters.*
■ *BOYD: Did he? I thought Ted V. Mikels did that.*
■ STECKLER: Ted *produced* it.
■ *BOYD: Do you know Mikels?*
■ STECKLER: I know him very well. Ted lives in a real castle here. And I tell you, it is *spooky* to go into that castle at night.

I went there once and I don't know if I want to go a second time. You've got to go through the dogs and up the mountain and into it. Once there you look around and he's got everything; it's another world. The world of T.V. Mikels.
■ *BOYD: That's amazing.*
■ STECKLER: The legend.
■ *BOYD: I've heard so many weird things about him.*
■ STECKLER: He's got about 8 wives, I know that.
■ *BOYD: At the same time?*
■ STECKLER: At the same time, living with him there.
■ *BOYD: ... Weren't soundtrack records from* Creatures *and* Rat Pfink *released? On what label?*
■ STECKLER: I can't remember—I think it was REL Records. I can't tell you where they are today; I have no idea whatsoever. One of them was out of Chicago, because Ron had a record out of one of the songs he sang in *Rat Pfink.*
■ *BOYD: Did he record under the name of Ron Haydock?*
■ STECKLER: He picked the name "Vin Saxon"; I don't know why. He made one record.
■ *BOYD: "Vin Saxon" and "Lonnie Lord"—*
■ STECKLER: Yeah, those were his names; he made them up. He was a writer, too; he wrote the original screenplay for *The Depraved.* It takes you right up to the point when we decided to go zonkers and had Rat Pfink come out of the closet.
■ *BOYD: So that was the original title of* Rat Pfink?
■ STECKLER: *The Depraved* [laughs]. To this day I don't know why I did it, and I don't really care! You just get an impulse: "If you came out of that closet as Batman and Robin ..." So we got an "R" and some long underwear; Titus had a Halloween costume with some lights that lit up ... only *we* could ever do it!
■ *BOYD: What films was Ron Haydock in?*
■ STECKLER: He played one of the cops that got killed in *Thrill Killers,* that was his debut. Then I starred him in *Rat Pfink,* and then in *Blood Shack.* He has a small scene in *Lemon Grove.*
■ *BOYD: Whatever happened to him?*
■ STECKLER: He was killed in an automobile accident about 5 years ago.
■ *BOYD: ... What was* Face of Evil?
■ STECKLER: *Face of Evil* was the original title, concept and screenplay for *The Creatures.* I didn't like it, but it wasn't a bad title, though.

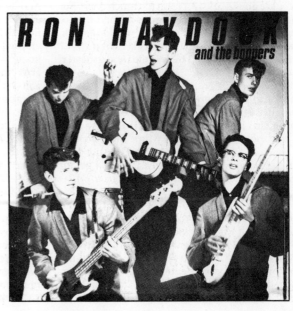

■ BOYD: *Didn't Columbia sue you when you switched the title to* Incredibly Strange Creatures?
■ STECKLER: [disgustedly] Oh, that was so crazy. Kubrick was making a movie called *Dr Strangelove Or Why I Stopped Worrying and Learned to Love the Bomb,* and I had advertised my picture as *The Incredibly Strange Creatures Or Why I Stopped Living and Became a Mixed Up Zombie.* But it had nothing to do with *his* picture. In fact the last thing I would have wanted to do was steal something from Kubrick, who I had met a few times; we had gotten along real well.

As I recall, he was still shooting *Dr Strangelove* after I had *already* shot my movie. I called Columbia and said, "What's the big problem? Can you get Kubrick on the other line so we can work this out?" And they got Kubrick on the other line, but not where I could talk to him—it was relayed. (Now remember, this litigation had been going on for months. But if all of a sudden you get everybody together, you can resolve something so quickly. And this is a town where they never get together.) I said, "You ask Mr Kubrick if I change my title from *The Incredibly Strange Creatures etc.* to *The Incredibly Strange Creatures Who Stopped Living and Became Mixed-Up Zombies,* would that be alright?" (Just remember: 5 minutes earlier they were going to sue me for $5 million. You can imagine how much the attorneys got paid on this; imagine how much money was being spent to prevent me from using that title on a picture that cost $38,000.) And Kubrick says, "Fine; that's good. Okay. Wrap it up. Back to work." End of story. In other words, once we made contact it was over in a flash.

But, I could have made 5 movies on what they probably spent trying to figure out how to stop me. I would have changed the title if they had just *asked* me politely. But it was the way they went about it: letters and subpoenas and all that crap—crazy. So there you are—big deal.

Scene from Blood Shack.

Col Waves Legal Stick; Indie Drops 'Mixed Up' Title

Variety article dated April 2, 1963.

After threatening legal action, Columbia has received assurance from Morgan-Steckler Prods. that title of latter's proposed indie, "The Incredibly Strange Creature: Or Why I Stopped Living And Became A Mixed-Up Zombie," would be changed, according to Col attorney Seymour P. Steinberg.

Studio contended "Creature" tag infringed on Stanley Kubrick's "Dr. Srangelove: Or How I Learned To Stop Worrying And Love The Bomb," now lensing in London for Col release.

It's probably better that I didn't use that title in the long run, 'cause (like I say) I wouldn't want anybody to think I stole that crazy title from him. What's crazy about having a long title? People thought I was nuts when I came up with it. They'll think I'm nuts someday when I make *Creatures Part II.*
■ BOYD: *You think you will?*
■ STECKLER: Yeah; just for fun I'll make it. I'll use the gypsy wardrobe that's left over from my next movie and start again. Just last week I found a girl who looks almost exactly like the original girl who played the gypsy, Bette O'Hara. She could be her daughter! I'm already looking for faces who resemble people.
■ BOYD: *Recently, at the plasma center in San Francisco, I saw a young Cash Flagg lookalike.*
■ STECKLER: Walking around? Did you know they sold Cash Flagg masks for years?
■ BOYD: *Ohmigod!*
■ STECKLER: Yeah, I had one, but recently I pulled it out of the box and the rubber had just deteriorated after all these years. See, we used them in the drive-ins. They would have guys running around looking like me. I got them from the same guy who did Bela Lugosi and all of them—Don Post. He's probably still got the mold. Do you think you were at the theater when I was there?

For Drivers In Hell I was head cameraman; then they decided they wanted me to play a part. It's easy enough to act in a film when you're the director, but when you're supposed to film a movie as well as be in front of the camera playing a role about 50% of the time, that's some trick!

■ BOYD: *I wish.*
■ STECKLER: Because I went with a lot of 'em. It was great. One time a woman collapsed and they had to take her to the hospital; it'd scared the shit out of her. At another theater they'd planned an afternoon showing and I asked, "We're going to do this at a *matinee?*" Well, a lot of little kids showed up; I jumped out, and 20 or 30 ran straight out to the street! Jesus! I didn't realize the effect it had in those days.
■ BOYD: *If you do* Creatures II, *where will you find an amusement park? Santa Cruz?*
■ STECKLER: I've already compiled a lot of great footage of

the ferris wheel, etc. I've been putting things aside. They have carnivals in Vegas once or twice a year; if I shoot at night it will look great. I've already got the gypsy motor home. I'm slowly putting it together; I haven't figured out *how* I'm going to do it or just *what*, yet. I can't find many members of the original cast; I don't even know where they are anymore, or where to begin to look. I tried but they're all gone; they disappeared. I have no idea where Atlas King went; I never saw him again after *The Thrill Killers*. (Oh, I did bump into him a year or two later, but I don't know what happened to him.) The hunchback? No idea. I know the kid who played Madison Clarke is a lighting technician who works here somewhere. I don't know where anybody is, to tell you the truth; after 20 years people go. But it would be interesting to get a few back. I figure that with a little publicity a few will call. I've already had about 10 calls, because they're running clips from it in *It Came From Hollywood*.

> To this day I don't know why I did it. You just get an impulse: "If you came out of that closet as Batman and Robin . . ." So we got an "R" and some long underwear; Titus had a Halloween costume with some lights that lit up . . . only we could ever do it!

■ *BOYD: What's that movie like?*
■ STECKLER: It's alright. I enjoyed it because I look at old movies and clips all the time, anyway. There were a couple of scenes I'd never seen before from Edward D. Wood, who was supposedly the "worst" filmmaker of all time. But maybe they should re-evaluate his work a little more, because I don't think they *see* all the underlying currents there.
■ *BOYD: Exactly. By letting superficial "judgments" and "standards" keep them (and their readers) away from certain films, most "film critics" have cheated themselves and others out of amazing experiences. They never really see the substance of what's really going on in a lot of films, especially lower budget films.*
■ STECKLER: Harry Medved, author of *The Golden Turkey Awards*, saw all my movies except for *Rat Pfink* and he was

"Zombies" on the loose in **The Incredibly Strange Creatures.**

fascinated. I said to him, "Why did you write about *Rat Pfink* if you'd never seen it?" He said, "Well, it was mainly the title." In his book he called it "the worst title of all time." But when he actually *saw* the film, his words to me were, "Ray, if I had seen this movie before I had written this book, the things I would have said in there would have been . . ." He really liked the picture, really got carried away with it.

But even so, how can you write about something you've never seen? It's not fair. Even if you write something good about a film you've never seen, you're still misleading the people you're writing for.
■ *BOYD: Rat Pfink a Boo Boo is a great title; it could mean anything. And it does convey a certain feeling. When people use terms like "bad" or "worst"—their criteria are always suspect.*
■ STECKLER: What do you think of Roger Corman's films?
■ *BOYD: I like Bucket of Blood and a few others, but I'm not crazy about him. I think he manages to achieve something interesting because he's a fast-buck artist doing things as fast as possible, and also because he doesn't think too much about some aspects of what's he's doing.*
■ STECKLER: He's a super-intelligent guy and I think he knows just what to do in order to get the job done. He did nice work in those Edgar Allan Poe films—*The Masque of the Red Death* was super. Finally, he tried to make a movie he felt was important: a horror movie with William Shatner about a bigot down South—the best thing Shatner ever did. It was originally called *The Intruder*. He got slammed down badly. After that he never tried to make another film. He didn't even try to *release* it; he gave it to someone else to release. You'd think American International Pictures would have jumped in and tried to help him out; I don't know what went wrong. But

the movie was great. They put some really terrible title on it. Talk about low-budget movies where somebody tried to do something really unusual—he did it. And got slammed down!

■ *BOYD: Have you seen the Mondo Cane films?*

■ STECKLER: I only saw the very first one, but I read an article about the filmmaker which said the reason he made it was because he and his girlfriend were in an automobile accident, and she was killed. He was so bitter at the world that he went out and made *Mondo Cane!* When he killed all the cows and showed that other [shocking] footage, he was taking it out on the attitude of the world. I think it was a drunk driver who hit him—you know, something that *never* should have happened. So he made that film.

Last night I went to Zuky's out in Santa Monica. It used to be the place where all the kids from the Santa Monica Theater hung out. It was late (close to midnight), and I wanted to get something to eat. And, I wanted to see how the place had changed since I'd been there 10 or 20 years ago. Guess who I opened the door for? Linda Blair. I said, "Aren't you that girl in those horror movies?" and she looked at me and just smiled and started to walk away. I said, "I *hate* people who make horror movies." She did a triple take with her girlfriend, like *What's with this guy?* The waitress said, "That was Linda Blair," and I said, "I know, I know. I was just putting her on . . ."

Once I worked at Universal as a grip on the *Alfred Hitchcock Presents* show. You know what A-frames are? They are big heavy A-frames that you clamp on flats that are 12′ long, with wheels on both sides, and you wheel them around. Anyway, I got this flat and they told me, "Get it out of here and take it over to the other set." And when you're working as a grip you move very fast. (I did; I don't know what they do today.) So I got this thing and started wheeling it [makes race car-like noises] rrrrrrr. Just as I got to a corner I missed Hitchcock by *that much!* And he was like this [Ray jumps to his feet and stands in profile assuming the classic Hitchcock pose, perfectly mimicking his posture and facial expression]. If I'd hit him I'd have knocked his head off! And he went over to this guy and whispered in his ear and *he* looked at me and *the guy* looked at me . . . I said, "Don't say it; I'll go get my card, *I know.*" And I walked over and punched out and went home. I knew I was going to get fired (and I was right) because I'd been going too fast. I thought, "What if I had killed Alfred Hitchcock?!" Of all people, you know? Ah, it was great!

> I had a Cash Flagg mask but recently I pulled it out of the box and the rubber had just deteriorated after all these years. See, we used them in the drive-ins. They would have guys running around looking like me.

■ *BOYD: When you make films do you improvise much?*

■ STECKLER: All the time, because when you work with amateurs you really have to be ready to get the best out of what you can get. Those kids weren't trained actors at all. I don't know how good *that* is: to get actors who have no ability. A lot of kids who study acting aren't worth shit, and are *never gonna* be worth anything! And just because you study doesn't make you good, either.

You might find a guy walking down the street who could have more impact than a professional actor—*if* he's used correctly. In Europe in the '20s (silent movies) they found all their actors in the streets. Nobody had to take acting lessons back then; that's why there were so many great *faces.* Because even if a guy couldn't act, they could make use of his face.

Today an actor has to talk, and if he talks he can blow the whole thing: "My, name, is, Harry." What do you do, Harry? "I, murdered, fifty, women, last, year; they, did, not, like, my, looks." Oh, okay, Harry. Now if you did a silent movie and Harry's face came on with a subtitle that said, "Harry murdered 50 women last year," *whoaaa* is what you'd think. Because you'd never know that when he opens his mouth he's a turkey.

■ *BOYD: I wanted to ask you if you have always been rebellious.*

■ STECKLER: I'm only rebellious around bullshit. I mean, I can conform to any situation, but when it gets to bullshit, I can't handle it, and there's too much of it in Hollywood. Nobody wants to just sit down and say, "Here's what we have to do and let's do it." They don't know those words. It's like, "Okay, let's figure out how we're going to do this, and how much money we can take and put in our pockets."

They hire production managers who are supposed to save money for the company, but all *they* do is get kickbacks everywhere they go. (Not *every* one of them—but too many of them.) In other words, everybody's out for their own benefit; nobody gives a shit about making a really good movie. European filmmakers get out there; if they say to an actor, "Stand here, it's raining, and don't move until we get the shot," he stands there in the freezing rain until they get the shot. In Hollywood, you aren't going to see a star standing in the rain—*none* of them. They're all wet, anyway! ■

■*BOYD RICE: You've been in nearly all of Ray's films, from* Wild Guitar *up to the latest—*

■ CAROLYN BRANDT: When we started out in films there was a joke among our friends that I was always either stabbed, abducted by an ape, or had my head cut off... Friends used to say, "Carol, Ray's trying to *tell you* something. Beware! Are you sure he *really* likes you?" But eventually (in films) I took the *other side* and turned bad—*I* started doing people in. It's fun! I figured I'd taken *enough* abuse and punishment—I'd give a little bit *back*.

■ *BOYD: In some films you seemed to get killed off early—*

■ RAY: I had to have *somebody* around to do the makeup; the sooner she was killed off the sooner she could...

■ CAROLYN: There was a scene in *Body Fever* where I'm sitting behind a desk. In between takes I was *also* keeping script; it was there in the drawer. In front of the camera it's not as easy to do that as on the sidelines. *That* was one of the most mini-crew films we worked on.

There were times when there'd be just the two of us working crew. When we were in Santa Fe doing *Bloody Jack* there was one time when Ray would set up the scene and tell me to push the button on the camera when he walked by. Now *that's* mini-crew!

■ *BOYD:* Bloody Jack?

■ CAROLYN: Ray, are you finishing that one up, dear?

■ RAY: That's the one where at the end they put me in jail. I've been waiting 12 or 14 years to shoot the additional scenes; in another year I'll shoot them, put it all together, and when I flashback they'll say, "What a makeup job! What a set! That *really* looks like 1972!" Nobody's ever done anything like that before...

> When we started out in films there was a joke among our friends that I was always either stabbed, abducted by an ape, or had my head cut off ... Friends used to say, "Carol, Ray's trying to tell you something. Beware!

■ *BOYD: How'd you two meet?*

■ CAROLYN: I was a harem girl in a thing called *The Magic of Sinbad*. Ray came in with a friend of his, probably to do some of the filming. He walked in, saw me, and chased me for 3 months. I finally agreed to go out with him. I don't know why I didn't before—I think I was being very "career-oriented." Finally I gave in and went out with him and was stuck from then on. A friend of mine who was an astrologer said, "There's a definite link between the two of you." And we've never been able to get rid of it, no matter what we try and do! [laughter]

■ *BOYD: Didn't Ray live in a car in his early days in Hollywood?*

■ CAROLYN: Yes. His buddy that he bunked with got a girlfriend, and Ray wound up living in a parking lot right around the corner from the studio where we'd first met, on Santa Monica Boulevard. A friend let him take showers at his apartment. My family didn't know about it, but every morning I would get up early and make him an egg, onion and mayonnaise sandwich on French bread and deliver him breakfast before I went to dance class.

Even in the last couple years there've been times when things were really tight: when he'd be down in Hollywood going to the lab and would sleep in the van because cash was short. A night's stay in a motel could mean the difference between an extra roll or two of film. So he'd sleep in the van, even though I'm sure it's not all *that* comfortable. But at least there's more space than in the first car he slept in, which was a little Nash Rambler!

■ *BOYD: Oh, I'd always imagined he slept in that station wagon he drove in* Incredibly Strange Creatures.

■ CAROLYN: No. As a matter of fact, when you look at *Creatures* it's the old yellow Rambler that's in the back when he first walks out of his apartment. It's the one Atlas King was working on when he says, "I can't get this pile of junk to work."

■ RAY: That was a true scene. When we left that place we left the car there.

■ CAROLYN: We couldn't afford to have it towed. If you follow our films you get to know the scenery. (The only other person I've seen do that is Claude Lelouch, who directed *A Man and A Woman*; I've seen him use the same apartment in a couple different films.) Anyway, that flying saucer we used in *Lemon Grove Kids*—we had to get rid of it before we moved. We called this junk dealer and he came and saw the saucer and then saw all these bent-up 35mm film cans we were also getting rid of. He asked if we were in the movie business. It turned out that this junkman just happened to be the first black movie producer; in Hollywood, *everyone's* in the industry! He had gone back into his first business, the junk business.

It was even funnier when we first moved to Lemon Grove Avenue—nice, lovely middle-class couples, and in come the bohemians! The first thing we do is put our flying saucer in the front yard. The next thing we do is start filming. Into this very nice middle-class neighborhood in the mid-sixties we brought a mummy running around, a gorilla running around, the Lemon Grove kids running all around the area, and the first blacks they'd probably ever seen above Franklin Street at that particular time. It was another year before they'd let our kids play with their kids.

■ *BOYD: Were those your kids running around Atlas King's yard in* Thrill Killers?

■ CAROLYN: Our kids and our crew's kids. We couldn't always get babysitters so we just stuck the kids in the film. Incidentally, the cameraman for the *Lemon Grove Kids* filmed the Jonestown massacre.

■ RAY: It's hard to make a movie, Boyd. It's so hard. There are always some people who get a lot of money to make a movie and that's great—but there are a lot of young people out there making a movie on nickels and dimes, and it may be the only movie they ever make. There are a lot of people who put up their homes and things and *bingo*—that's it. You've got to *really want* to do it.

■ CAROLYN: I guess that's one way you might explain some of Ray's films. They really are *organic*. Because what the

original script is, is very rarely anything close to the final product. That's because he's always gone with the flow. Things happen—you adjust.

■ *BOYD: I can't imagine too many other directors in the early sixties having an attitude that would allow them to improvise and make radical deviations from the script, just following their instincts.*

■ RAY: Well, I don't know *any* other filmmakers in Hollywood who have enough guts to go out and make a feature movie without a script, and pull it off and get it out, doing everything from start to end. You have to have a love of what you're doing to make these kind of movies, because you'll never get rich. Even when you make a movie that makes a lot of money, everybody else gets the money! I'm a perfect example [laughs]; all the money I've made in the business is through pure persistence and hounding people, just hounding them. The nicer you are, the more they'll eat you alive!

It seems like the movie industry likes to destroy bridges rather than build them, until eventually there's nothing left.

■ *BOYD: I noticed something odd in* Thrill Killers: *there's a party scene where George J. Morgan appears as George J. Morgan, and Arch Hall appears as Arch Hall, but the credits only list George J. Morgan. I thought maybe it was because Arch was such an obnoxious drunk in that scene that he didn't want to be credited.*

■ RAY: He was playing *himself!* I always do these little things. Of course George had a larger role in that, throughout the picture.

■ *BOYD: I thought that maybe after Arch saw it, he said, "Hey, I don't want to be credited as playing myself, because I look like a drunkard."*

■ RAY: No, not really. In fact he had a great time that night. Arch Hall was a strange guy. I met him right after I did *Drivers in Hell.* Actually, he had a bit part in *Secret File: Hollywood,* which is where I first met him. Then he asked me to do the second unit photography for *Eegah!,* and that's how I came to work for him. After that he asked me to direct a film for him with his son, *Wild Guitar.* And he said, "Now, you mustn't do anything to distract from the script. You must do exactly what the script says." But since I'd never directed a movie, I figured I'd better do the best I could. When I added in the early Lemon Grove kids to the movie, Arch didn't like them at all; he thought they detracted from the story. So he cut out all the scenes with them: the kidnapping, everything, and then the movie only ran for something like 63 minutes.

I tried to give all the touches I could to the kid. Arch Jr is a nice kid, and he was a good singer, but he didn't seem to have his heart in it; never seemed to really care. It was all just handed to him on a silver platter. And I always felt, to be honest, that Arch was just attempting to re-live his youth through his son. It was a big disappointment that his son didn't want to continue in the business. The minute his son stopped making movies, Arch stopped making movies. He didn't have the desire to go out and tackle the industry without his kid in the picture. But I can understand that. You have to have a *love* to make these kind of movies.

■ *BOYD: Wasn't Arch Hall a test pilot?*

■ RAY: Yes, and they made a movie about him: *The Last Time I Saw Archie.* Robert Mitchum played Arch Hall, and it was written by Arch's roommate in the army, Bill Bowers. Bill wrote it, it was a hit novel; the only problem was that he had to have permission to use Arch's name. He told him that he'd take care of him, and Arch signed a paper. Of course, Arch never got a thing for it; the studio never gave him anything.

Mitchum played Arch Hall to a "T". They got together for dinner a few times and Mitchum watched how Arch acted. Arch had that lazy walk, lazy attitude, very lazy. Like he had to make a real *decision* to get up and get a glass of water—really! If you ever see *Eegah!,* watch him running across the desert in his shorts. He used to make sure the lens would only cover a small area so he wouldn't have far to walk. Then he'd sit down.

■ *BOYD: Why don't any Arch Hall movies ever show up? What happened to all of them?*

■ RAY: I don't believe I've seen a group of Arch's films show up on TV since 1964 or '65. His wife sold the rights to all of his films to some guy in New York.

■ *BOYD: So they'll all be re-released?*

■ RAY: I don't know. I don't even know who got them. Did you ever see *The Choppers?* That was his first movie. Then came *Wild Guitar,* then *The Sadist* which was later re-named *The Profile of Terror.* Then he did *Eegah!*

■ CAROLYN: I think that was about the time Junior wanted to get his wings and fly.

■ RAY: Junior got married. Married a nice Vietnamese girl. He's out there somewhere, probably still playing his guitar, sitting on a hill in Boulder City overlooking the Dam. He's probably an old man by now . . . ■

RAY D. STECKLER
BIOGRAPHY
BY JIM MORTON

The films of Ray Dennis Steckler are weird, individualistic, and radical. Sometimes they seem out of control, largely due to his penchant for working without a completed script. The fact that he stars in many of his films (under the pseudonym "Cash Flagg") makes them that much better.

Steckler got his start as a director thanks to Arch Hall, Sr., who was making **Wild Guitar**, the story of a young man named **Bud Eagle** who comes to Hollywood in search of fame and fortune. On his first night in Tinseltown Bud gets—through an incredible set of coincidences—the opportunity to perform. The boy is quickly snapped up by a shifty recording agent (played with frightening conviction by Arch Hall, Sr.), and eventually learns that fame and fortune are not as important as the girl he loves.

While **Wild Guitar** may not win any awards for plot originality, it does give Steckler a chance to display his curious talents. The film also marks the first appearance of Steckler's alter ego, Cash Flagg, who plays "Steak," a sleazy strong-arm man who works for the recording agent. He gives the part a schizoid dimension—shifting in an instant from boredom to maniacal intensity.

Steckler's next effort remains his best known: **The Incredibly Strange Creatures Who Stopped Living and Became Mixed-Up Zombies**. It's the story of Esmerelda, a sideshow gypsy fortune-teller who likes pouring acid on men's faces and locking them up in her secret cages. With help from her sister Carmelita and companion Ortega, she hypnotizes a young freeloader named Jerry (Cash Flagg) and forces him to commit murders. When he no longer proves useful to her, he too is given the acid treatment. No explanation is ever offered as to why the fortune-teller keeps acid-scarred men caged in her tent, but none is needed—from the moment the film begins it's obvious we're no longer in this universe. The world of **The Incredibly Strange Creatures** exists outside the bounds of logic and reality.

Originally **Creatures** was released in "Hallucinogenic Hypnovision." Before the film starts, "The Amazing Armand" warns the audience they will see "actual flesh-and-blood" zombies. This gimmick was achieved by ushers wearing "Cash Flagg" masks who waved rubber daggers at members of the audience. In urban theaters this novelty proved more frightening for the ushers than the audience—several received black eyes and sore jaws while attempting to frighten the wrong people.

Ray Dennis Steckler's next film, **The Thrill Killers** (also known as **The Maniacs are Loose!**) is his most technically proficient. Steckler (under the name Cash Flagg) plays Mort "Mad Dog" Click, homicidal maniac. Three escapees from an insane asylum (one of whom is Click's brother) terrorize people at a roadside diner and elsewhere. In one particularly effective scene Click stabs a prostitute to death in her darkened hotel room, while outside the window a neon light flashes on and off in perfect counterpoint to the plunging knife. Later the escapees terrorize (and eventually kill) a woman while a narrator recites on the radio a grotesque parody of Little Red Riding Hood!

Of all Steckler's movies, none is better cast than **The Thrill Killers**. A lead role featured Liz Renay, a Hollywood glamour girl who gained notoriety for going to prison rather than testifying against her gangster boyfriend. Other outstanding performances were by Herb Robins, Gary Kent and Keith O'Brien, who play the three escaped lunatics.

Steckler's films are schizophrenic. **The Incredibly Strange Creatures** suspends its tension for occasional song-and-dance numbers; **The Thrill Killers** starts with the story of a Hollywood hanger-on and ends with a shoot-out and a chase on **horseback**! But of all his films, none is more schizophrenic than the unbelievable **Rat Pfink a Boo Boo**. At times this film seems to be writing itself—the plot changes suddenly, continuity is non-existent. It's hard to imagine what audiences thought upon viewing this film for the first time back in 1966.

It begins as a straightforward thriller. Three hoods, after attacking a woman in an alley, decide to get their kicks by terrorizing the girlfriend of rock star Lonnie Lord. After a

Carolyn Brandt today. Photo: Boyd Rice

few anonymous phone calls, they kidnap the girl. Up to this point, **Rat Pfink a Boo Boo** is fairly creepy—the hoodlums are genuinely frightening and the situation tense. Suddenly, as if by whim, Lonnie Lord and sidekick Titus Twimbly decide to save the girlfriend by turning into Rat Pfink and Boo Boo, a pair of low-budget superheroes. From this point on **Rat Pfink** drops the melodrama, turning into a slapstick comedy that ends with an interminable chase.

Whatever its faults, **Rat Pfink a Boo Boo** represents filmmaking at its freest. It's hard to imagine what Steckler had in mind when he made this movie; often absurd, occasionally tedious, it is never predictable!

During this period Steckler also made his "Lemon Grove Kids" films: low budget take-offs on the Bowery Boys, short and silly stories about the misadventures of a gang of misfits. Later he compiled them into one incoherent, over-long movie: **The Lemon Grove Kids Meet the Monsters**, featuring the same out-of-control wackiness that characterizes **Rat Pfink a Boo Boo**. Cash Flagg appears again, this time as a perfect imitation of Huntz Hall. In one scene the films actually overlap, with Rat Pfink and BooBoo making an appearance in a retake of a scene in their film!

Although his output slowed, Steckler continued making films during the '70s. He started off the decade with **Super Cool**, a hard-boiled detective story starring (who else?) Cash Flagg. Unlike most of Steckler's films, **Super Cool** (also known as **Body Fever**) seems to have a carefully structured plot.

Steckler's other films during the '70s are less inspired. **Hollywood Strangler Meets the Skid Row Slasher** is an amazing title, but the film—essentially a silent movie with narration—is little more than a curiosity piece. **Blood Shack** (also known as **The Chooper**) has a few Stecklerian

moments, but pales beside his earlier efforts...

Steckler began his film career as a photographer (taking movie stills) for Timothy Carey on **World's Greatest Sinner**; other assignments included being cameraman on **Scream of the Butterfly**, **The Velvet Trap** and **The Erotic Adventures of Pinocchio**. He also worked on music videos for various singers and rock groups, including a rarely seen video of the **Nazz** singing "Open My Eyes."

Currently living in Las Vegas, Ray Dennis Steckler continues to work; he recently began shooting **The Survivalists** (tentative title; after a conflict with producers the film was completed by Ted V. Mikels), and one of his future projects is a sequel to **The Incredibly Strange Creatures**. We hope he never stops making movies **his** way...

FILMOGRAPHY

Drivers In Hell aka Wild Ones on Wheels, 1961
Wild Guitar, 1962
The Incredibly Strange Creatures Who Stopped Living and Became Mixed-Up Zombies, 1963
Sinthia: The Devil's Doll, 1968
Rat Pfink a Boo Boo, 1965
The Lemon Grove Kids Meet The Monsters, 1966
Sinthia, The Devil's Doll, 1968
Bloody Jack the Ripper, 1972 (unreleased)
Super Cool (aka Body Fever aka The Last Original B-Movie), 1969
The Chooper (aka Blood Shack), 1971
The Hollywood Strangler Meets the Skidrow Slasher, 1979

Ray Dennis
Steckler today.
Photo:
Boyd Rice

Ted V. Mikels has one obsession: making movies. He'd like to be remembered as "a hell of a filmmaker who did 28 hours a day, 10 days a week towards the making of films . . . always conceiving, concocting new ideas for stories." And as he put it, "Anywhere somebody will fund my movies, I'll go."

During a recent film shoot near Death Valley (he volunteered to be Director of Photography to help out his old buddy Ray Dennis Steckler), the barrel-chested Mikels worked under a blazing 105° sun from 6 AM straight through to 7 PM without stopping, rarely even pausing for water. And it was **hot** (a stunt motorcyclist fainted from sunstroke). Ted's supportive presence and constant humor—often in different accents—smoothed out a lot of interruptions inevitable during any film shoot.

Born Theodore Vincent Mikacevich to Croatian emigrant parents, in early childhood Mikels began mastering magic and psychology. Originally involved in theater, he's been a movie scriptwriter, cameraman, director and producer for the past three decades, creating classics such as **The Astro Zombies, The Corpse Grinders,** and **The Doll Squad** on budgets below belief. His films explore unconventional territory, from brain transplants to witchcraft to polygamy to a women's hit squad . . .

Although recently relocated to Las Vegas, Ted V. Mikels lived for the past twenty years in a genuine castle just outside Hollywood. Possessed of seemingly endless reserves of energy and enthusiasm, he demonstrates a constantly philosophizing outlook immersed in saturnine humor. Boyd Rice interviewed him in a castle room filled with dueling swords, masks and other colorful memorabilia . . .

■ *BOYD RICE: Ray Dennis Steckler said you have 8 wives—*
■ TED V. MIKELS: "Wife" is a restrictive term; we say "Castle Lady." And the magic number is *seven;* I told Ray that seven was the precise number; otherwise we'd have to find another castle and start seven more there.
■ *BR: Why seven?*
■ TVM: It's very simple: seven is my magic number. When I was in high school I was told that there are seven females on earth for every male, and I want my seven! So, I'm willing to take care of them, and teach them what I know best, which is filmmaking: any area from scriptwriting to still photography.

One of my ladies went on to do her own picture: as writer, producer, director, star *and* editor! I started her out as an assistant script girl. And she made a woman's picture, covering in retrospect a woman's lifetime after having a nervous breakdown at an airport. It reflects on her childhood, living with her father, and how her father made sexual advances toward her. Of course that affected her whole life, in her relationships with men, husbands, and so on. Anyway, that movie was made as the result of the way we choose to live, which is very moral and very decent. It may not be easy for everyone to comprehend, but we don't go around trying to make people understand every single thought, concept and belief we have.
■ *BR: So many people have* one *idea they believe in,* one *thing that's their favorite, and so on carried to every level of their life . . .*
■ TVM: I constantly have this conversation with ladies; they ask, "Why *not* a one-to-one relationship? How can you have *seven* women sharing your life?" I say, "The purpose in life usually is to *fulfill ourselves* and *achieve our goals.* If ladies together can have a place to stay where they can learn and develop an ability in a certain area; where they can achieve their goals in life through this commingling of personalities, talents and abilities; then it's an advantage to them." There are no demands on them; psychologically they're totally free. There are no recriminations.

We *do* have an agreement, and the agreement is that the ladies who live and share their lives with me do not sleep around. They are *not* obligated to sleep with me, but they are obligated to accept this agreement. If they want to be with someone else, then let them be with someone else; let somebody else take care of them if they want. It's a matter of *choice.*

If they no longer want to be here (or if I don't want them here), I don't say, "Leave." But I'll say, "Well, if it's not working, then don't prolong it." *What works works; what doesn't work doesn't work.* If they're here and they're happy, moving toward the direction of fulfillment at a stronger or faster pace than they would elsewhere, then obviously it's to their benefit to be here. And if I can help them learn something, they in turn can help me: answer phones, xerox scripts, work in the editing room with sound effects, etc. I can teach them many things; I probably have started 400-600 people in film, just in various categories. It may be something simple, like showing them how to make apple boxes for the grip department. And then they get enthused, and first thing you know they're learning how to handle lights. I've had people start as grips and end up being First Cameraman . . .

We have enough activity to keep anyone busy, in every realm of the audio-visual entertainment field: from music to motion picture feature films, which is essentially what I do. I write, direct, produce, edit, promote, and distribute (on an international level) feature films. (Then I try to find a way to get the money back.) And my preference in films is for action-drama, adventure-action drama. I've made a number of horror films, and I do that when I have some coiled-up rolls of leftover film and a dozen people who say, "Hey, let's make a movie." Even though there's no movie to make, we create one to do.

Over a period of 30 years doing films, many times I've had a whole house full of people, living with me just to *survive.* And I've found that *men,* once they live with you, don't get out and *do* what they need to do. Whereas *women* can put all

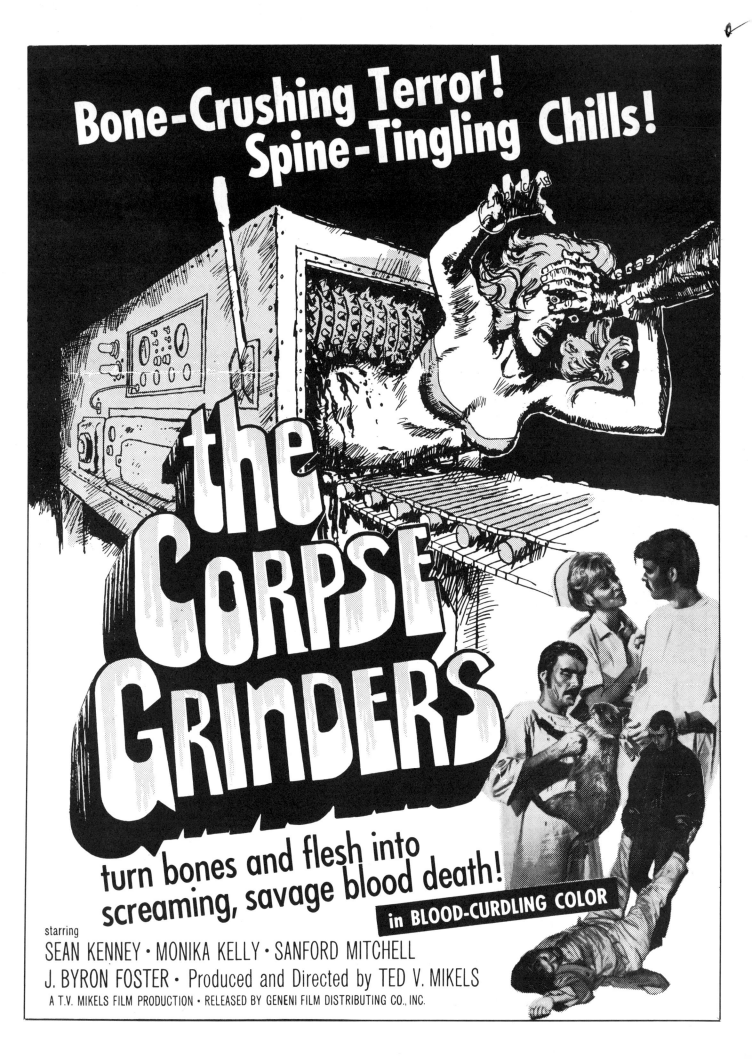

their intensity into a family-type relationship. In my book it doesn't work when it's communal and there are men *and* women—I don't need that! I have to be somehow or other in total leadership of whoever's with me. I don't expect other men who are working toward their *own* family success to work under my wing. But females, on the other hand, can move forward in their lives, achieving what they want to achieve, because polygamy has always worked since the beginning of time.

Every animal you see, no matter what it is, is polygamous. Only the human animal has this concept of monogamy, but then, as often as possible, they break it! A lot of my friends have monogamous relationships, but tomorrow they'll have another monogamous relationship with another lady, and so on, and the female will do the same thing. So they're living a lie! I don't accept that; I don't like it.

> **We built a corpse-grinding machine for maybe $38. If a studio were building something like that, $38 wouldn't even buy the coffee they'd drink while making the machine (which would probably cost $138,000).**

If I have a lady with me, we have a basic understanding: be a responsible person, keep agreements, and don't sleep around. Do what you wish, go anywhere, do anything, but just be responsible. If you say you're going to be back at 10 pm, if you're not here we expect a call, and so on. It's just being responsible. Then they can choose the path of life they want to move forward to, accomplishing things in life (especially with some guidance or teaching). When the dollars are ample, we have a little extra fun—maybe take a little boat trip to Catalina. And when the dollars are tight (which they most often are), it's a real belt squeezer.

■ *BR: What got you interested in film?*

■ TVM: I grew up an entertainer. From the time I was five years old I was doing magic for neighbors—string-and-bean tricks; by the time I was seven I had a 20-minute show, and by the time I was twelve I had a 45-minute show. By the time I was fifteen I was selling a 2½-hour show to all the school systems. I did ventriloquism, accordion solos, and I'd always have some pretty girl as a specialty dancer (maybe a tap-dance routine or Arabic dance) during an intermission to give me a break. I did everything from escaping straitjackets to you-name-it—even fire-eating . . .

At the age of seventeen I started touring the country with the very well-known and famous Mandrake the Magician. When I returned to college after a summer tour with him, my show became larger and more involved, with perfectly coordinated music, etc. But it always seemed pathetic that when the show was over, after you'd worked so hard, there was nothing left but a memory . . .

So I started filming, and discovered that with the camera you could stop motion, snap your fingers and make things disappear *like that!* I had lots of fun! I always wanted to do a feature film called just plain *MAGIC.*

■ *BR: When did you first shoot film?*

■ TVM: When I was ten or twelve I developed film in the bathtub—did all the still stuff. But movies started when I was a late teenager. I started filming shows . . .

I made educational films, sales films, training films, fun films, half-hour melodramas, any which way I could. I bought short ends of outdated film and did anything and everything to be able to put a film together. And I enlisted the help of a lot of people.

I learned that to many people, making a film is *exciting!* I'd have as many as fifty people in a weekend working on a film,

which was an enormous pleasure to me. I've never lost that same feeling: making a film is the greatest pleasure. People ask me why I don't ever take a day off. Well, my greatest day off, so to speak, is making a film. It's a greater pleasure than anticipating a vacation in Tahiti, although I want to do that, too!

■ *BR: I've always felt that* Astro Zombies *or* Corpse Grinders *were different because the people involved really wanted to do them. Most films—it's like a factory put them out. When somebody genuinely wants to do something, they put more of themselves into it, and it shows.*

■ TVM: The camaraderie and the fun we had doing *Corpse Grinders,* for example, was phenomenal. I don't think there were more than one or two people who'd ever been around a film production before. The script girl had never seen a script in her life, and so on.

I was at a studio where a lot of people were coming in from other states trying to get signed up. Now if I were doing a picture where people were getting paid, I would be very selective, in order to get talented, experienced people. But if I was doing a picture with relatively zero dollars, then I would pick people who had a willingness, who had some form of transportation, who had their own place to stay, and who could go a month or two without compensation. And the compensation, when and *if* it came from the theaters, would come later.

That's how *Corpse Grinders* was made. Almost everyone in the whole production had never been around a picture before. The cameraman had done some 16mm, but on the first day of shooting (over at Cecil B. DeMille's residence on DeMille Drive) he yelled out, "Hey, Ted, teach me how to load this camera!" This is opening morning; there's forty people milling around! Everybody was learning their job: the sound man had never run a sound recorder, some people were putting on make-up for the first time, and so on. And it was fun.

We ended up making the biggest grossing picture I ever made [laughs]. And it's still going strong; some people claim it's a little classic in its own right. It happened to be financially successful as well, doing box office #11 of the top 50 grossing pictures that particular week. And it was made with *no money;* baloney sandwiches with no cheese, a little bit of mustard and a lot of heart and soul.

■ *BR: In your life, it seems you've managed to do exactly as you please—*

> **I did ventriloquism, accordion solos . . . I did everything from escaping straitjackets to you-name-it—even fire eating.**

■ TVM: My idea of success, I haven't achieved yet. A lot of people (even fifteen years ago) have said to me, "If in my whole lifetime I make as many movies as you've already made, I'll feel I've really accomplished something." But I don't look at it that way. I've got over 100 picture credits, of which more than 30 are features, but I don't really feel I've *begun.* Number one: I've never looked for, nor found, financing. I just do my pictures any which way I can. (However, I have friends who've been looking for financing 20 years and have never made their first picture!) So, it's just as tough to find financing now as it ever was. Doesn't matter how many pictures you've done, you have to have the right combination of being at the right time and place with the right financial seed to get it going. And there's no easy way—at least *I've* never found one.

By the same token, if I didn't have to spend 90% of my time trying to put bits and pieces together (a little loan here, a little loan there, a few dollars from a bank, laboratory credit,

FILM PRESSBOOK SYNOPSIS

THE CORPSE GRINDERS

Sudden, inexplicable attacks by cats on their human owners resulting in death and mutilation, surge through a metropolis. A young hospital intern, Dr. Howard Glass (Sean Kenney) and his nurse assistant Angie Robinson (Monika Kelly) seek the answer when her own pet feline assaults Glass without provocation. They theorize that an exotic canned cat food could be the cause after learning a fatally bitten woman's pet and Angie's ate the same brand. The food has turned partaking cats into man-eaters!

Sleuthing eventually takes Glass and Angie to a dingy factory where the cat food is manufactured by two diabolical partners, Landau (Sanford Mitchell) and his greedy aide Maltby (J. Byron Foster). The basic ingredient consists of cadavers supplied by an accommodating but disreputable cemetery caretaker Caleb (Warren Ball) and his wife Cleo (Ann Noble). It is in the factory that shirring power saws, red stained chopping blocks, ominous cauldrons and a vociferous grinder transpose human flesh and bone into pussycat puree.

Desperate for fresh supplies of human flesh, Landau and Maltby ply skidrow alleyways to fill the demand. For good measure they include the caretaker when Caleb insists on payment for his raw stock.

Glass and Angie arrive at the factory on a ruse to get food samples for laboratory analysis, but are outsmarted by a suspicious Landau. A determined Angie nevertheless on her own returns late at night, sneaks in, but is trapped by Maltby, who, in the absence of Landau, is about to abscond with his withheld share of profits.

Angie is strapped on the conveyor leading into the grinder. Maltby's lecherous advances halt when Landau unexpectedly appears. A startled Maltby accidentally hits the controls, is dragged onto the running conveyor ahead of helpless Angie toward the flashing tips of the grinder knives. Meanwhile, Glass has alerted authorities. While he and the police, sirens screaming, converge on the factory, a maddened, fiendish Landau proceeds to aid his partner's demise. A freed Angie attempts to evade Landau's clutches as he himself is ironically caught and headed for the grinder, only to be devoured by a band of ravenous cats. Glass releases Angie. ∎

people who are willing to work in exchange for being taught, and so on), I'd be more productive. It's a tough way to go and still compete on the world market with pictures that someone has spent a million or $10 million (let alone $30 million) on, yet we do one with four nickels that's got to compete. And when you get a review in the paper, they don't care whether you've spent 2 nickels on it or $2 million. They rate it and compare it the same as any other picture made at any other price. They say the ingenuity and creativity of the film is what they compare, yet when the creator of one film is working with $20 or $30 million, the comparison is really unfair.

We built a corpse-grinding machine for maybe $38. If a studio were building something like that for a psychological terror picture or whatever, $38 wouldn't even buy the *coffee* they'd drink while making the machine (which would probably cost $138,000). Our corpse-grinding machine consisted of lawn mower blades which had been scrapped, plus odds and ends—some red lightbulbs that were 39¢, a piece of discarded plywood, things like that. [laughs]

However, the total concept of entertainment is (like in magic): if you can make someone believe something, and make them enjoy it, they really don't *care* whether you've spent $38 or $138,000 on a corpse-grinding machine. When they see this silly contraption—a tube, and a body with clothes on (presumably a cadaver) sliding in one end and coming out the other end as hamburger, *they laugh,* and that's what the whole thing's about.

■ *BR: I like the idea of people knowing they can actually go out and do something like that, without a million dollars.*
■ TVM: Anyone can!
■ *BR: People have this mystical reverence for films. Most people's attitude is, "Oh, I could never do something like that."*
■ TVM: But there *is* a method and procedure. That Castle Lady I mentioned could not have made her own picture until she was here and *saw* what it was all about. After we shot the footage, in the editing room she could see, "Oh, *that's* how this comes together. *Now* I know why you did that with the camera." Somehow they've got to have the *opportunity* to learn. And very few of these opportunities are available in the colleges.

When people come from a college to work on a picture, it seems they have only a *theoretical* concept of what it's like to really make a film. Practical, day-to-day filmmaking without total financing is so different, that they're usually at a loss. Therefore, they have to become production assistants, where they're picking up permits, racing around delivering checks, buying Marks-A-Lot pens—that sort of thing. Because even though they might have five years at an accredited motion picture college, they still don't have any *practical* knowledge.

Places like A.F.I. [American Film Institute] offer a bit of an opportunity to jump in, but usually in a situation where there's 500 or 1,000 people who want to get involved, and room for only 5 or 6. Maybe only 5 or 6 people are required—most of these are 16mm or Super-8mm projects. Also, the logistics of their situation (time, locations of their homes and so forth) won't allow it.

All the more this points up how, in a period 25 years ago, I had my house *filled* with sleeping bags and people who were eager and anxious to make a film. I had to take care of them: feed them, fix their flat tires, get them new spark plugs when they needed tune-ups, and so on. I found that by keeping all these people close we could hang together with our energy and our intensities to create a picture. But when they all scatter and go to their own homes, you've got to get on the phone, and if everybody's calling everyone else 20 times a day saying where to meet and how to get there (with people saying, "Gee, I haven't got any gas," etc)—*that's* how the concept of the Castle Ladies originated. *They* can adapt themselves, whereas a man wants to lead his own situation or command his own clan, whether it be his wife or whatever. Actually, I don't believe in *running* anybody, but I also don't believe in letting anyone run me. Running, manipulation,

Scene from Blood Orgy of the She-Devils.

domination, as well as jealousy, possessiveness—all that doesn't work. And when you're making a film you face all the psychological shortcomings and aberrations of every person and personality in the company. But in college "psych" was my major before I left to make my living in the entertainment world. And I feel I have a great deal of practical knowledge from having a large family. You know, 14 grandchildren, six kids . . . [laughs]

■ *BR: You have 14 grandchildren?*

■ TVM: Yes. I don't let them call me "grandpa" until they come over and exercise with me. Because I exercise very hard—as hard as I did when I was 18 years old, or harder. I don't feel any older than when I was about 20. I think there's something about doing what you *love* to do that keeps you out of this *tunnel* that leads toward old age. Every day I think: the drudgery of doing something you don't want to do is *destructive.*

■ *BR: Doing only what you* want *to do keeps you from falling into someone else's context where you just—*

■ TVM: *Drift away!* The only detriment or shortcoming I can see is: when you're not financed, it's tough. And getting money back from a film *after* it's made is just as tough as getting the money to make it with. *Tough!* You get ripped off all over; there's piracy everywhere in the world. Just from knowing what I do about grosses and theaters and box offices and television and videocassettes and so on worldwide, I'll tell you that the handful of pictures that I still own and control have literally grossed far in excess of $100,000,000—

even the ones I made without money. But you can't get your hands on that money.

I'm not a joiner, I don't join *anything.* (I *am* a member of the Motion Picture Pioneers of America, but that's an honorary organization you're asked to join if you've served the motion picture industry 25 years or more.) I'm not in the Directors' Guild, not in *any* guild. I just don't want anyone telling me what to do, or what I cannot do.

But, I know that hundreds of thousands of dollars out there change hands, without any returns to us so we may continue to make films. The biggest rip-off is videocassettes around the world, whether by projections, or stolen tapes that go into a country and are duplicated by the tens of thousands and sold without any copyright participation. I'm a firm believer in free enterprise, but a videotape recorder that allows anyone to copy any picture with the push of a couple buttons, giving them an income . . . !

■ *BR: And you don't have a squad of lawyers to track these down . . .*

> **There's something about doing what you love to do that keeps you out of this tunnel that leads toward old age. Every day I think: the drudgery of doing something you don't want to do is destructive.**

The Doll Squad.

Lil Zaborin plays Mara, evil incarnate, who challenges Lucifer, the devil himself in **Blood Orgy of the She Devils**.

■ TVM: That's right. But I'm not too great a supporter of attorneys—they cause more downfallen projects than they assist. And they take so long to do things; I cannot move in that slow of a time frame. They'll take four-day weekends off to go play, and come back Monday at 11:00, and at 3:30 if somebody wants to have an early dinner or late lunch then *nothing urgent*, so . . .

I'm sure there are some very hard-working attorneys, but I call them the "Monday, Wednesday, Friday, next week boys." It's always "can't get to it 'til Friday"; Friday, it's "sorry, Monday"; Monday, "Wednesday"; Wednesday it's "check me at the end of the week"; and at the end of the week they're gone! And that goes on month after month.
■ *BR: A lot of businesses operate that way—*
■ TVM: Like with a laboratory—you may have to wait 3½ weeks to get your sound transferred. So what do you do for those 3½ weeks? You wait. While your interest goes on and you owe thousands of dollars more on the money you borrowed, but, you know, that's the problem the creator faces.

Almost nobody who finances pictures wants to go into a risk venture. There are people who do, but they want double, triple, quadruple collateral back-ups, interest and payable monthly. These people have no concept of what the creative person goes through in trying to generate money on that money. All they know is that they want it collateralized and covered so there is no risk to lose a *penny*. While the creative person puts his neck on the chopping block every time. That's why I've sometimes made pictures like *Astro Zombies* and *Corpse Grinders* with no money.
■ *BR: I meant to ask you—I went to what was advertised as the world premiere of* Blood Orgy of the She Devils *in San*

Diego, at the Balboa Theater. Was that actually the world premiere?
■ TVM: It *maybe* was. San Diego is a good test city. Did they print the title?
■ *BR: They did.*
■ TVM: We found newspapers everywhere refused to print the title. Silly little title; a little witchcraft picture that's really very innocent. They might have called it *Blood Devils* or *Orgy of the Devils,* but to my knowledge no place, at the time of the release, would print the full title, *Blood Orgy of the She Devils.*

A little horror picture is lots of fun to make; you work hard making it. On the other hand, pictures I enjoy the most are like *Doll Squad,* the forerunner of (and made 4 years before) *Charlie's Angels.* When they made *Charlie's Angels* they used some of the names (like "Sabrina") out of *Doll Squad.* Here we have eight girls who work for the C.I.A., and they're like James Bonds, all working under the guidance of Francine York, who's the top one. Early in the movie a couple get killed (puts the rest on their toes), then they wipe out Michael Ansara's garrison on an island. All of his 300 troops—six girls wipe 'em out! [laughs] It's a fantasy, it's escapist.

In 1972, when we first finished it all the networks wouldn't touch it because they said it was too violent. Yet it was *tongue-in-cheek* violence. The girls give somebody a drink, he stands up and explodes—completely disintegrates! To me that's a *joke,* that's not violence. It's too preposterous, too incredibly unbelievable.
■ *BR: On TV there are programs that use the same formula every week, and it's: one week beautiful show girls are being murdered, next week models are getting murdered, the next week beauty contest entrants—it's always beautiful girls being murdered.*
■ TVM: Like they say, there's only 7 basic story lines, and those 7 mixed and intertwined create 49, and those 49 intermixed make that many more, and so on. But basically my feeling about dramatic action is that there's more opportunity there for sheer artistry.
■ *BR: What was your first picture?*
■ TVM: My first picture was *Strike Me Deadly.* Unfortunately I did it in black-and-white—it never got off the ground. At that point I had no idea of the "Hollywood" point of view as to what should be made and what shouldn't; or what would sell. That film expressed purely the part of me that was directing plays and making short films, putting my feelings and interests into a story. It's a very simple story of a young man and his wife who are college teachers spending the

> **Blood Orgy of the She Devils** was a witchcraft story. And every time we turned around someone was getting burned, or something was catching on fire. It was almost as if there were witchcraft present.

summer working for the U.S. Forestry Service in a lookout tower. On his first day the guy witnesses a murder, and the murderer chases him through the forest, starting a forest fire to destroy the evidence, and so on. There's action: planes dropping borade on the forest fire, flames everywhere; the guy's trying to find his wife and she's out feeding squirrels instead of staying back at the tower. There's a chase through the rocks and the lava beds and the waterfalls . . .

I had thought of redoing it, but now they can change black-and-white (on magnetic tape) to color! So I hope to transfer that film and release it to all the magnetic markets of the world. After we find $95,000 to change that black-and-white negative to a color magnetic master so we can make copies in every format, somebody else can get their hands on it and make copies for free!

We've got a number of other action things like *Operation Overkill* and *I Crossed the Color Line,* the original title of which was *The Black Klansman.* Although the film's promoters advertised it was made in complete secrecy in the deep South and so on, it's still very gutwrenching—quite an in-depth story. [At this point a Castle Lady walks past noisily, bringing the conversation to a halt. When Ted informs her she's interrupting an interview, she assumes the stance of an animal, emitting hisses and growls. Ted smiles, saying, "Thanks a lot, honey," and the interview continues.]

In *Girl in Gold Boots* we tried to do a picture that was non-violent and clean—no nudity, *no anything* that would keep it from afternoon matinees or daytime television. And it was so tame [laughs] that audiences wouldn't support it, even though it had beautiful dancing girls. It was a typical story of a young girl from the Midwest coming to Hollywood, meeting good elements, some bad elements, and being exposed to a choice. After seeing a lot of the undesirable aspects of the "great life" in Hollywood, she chooses to lead the clean, simple life and leaves the area. So it had a moral; something to offer there.

Then I did a story called *Alex and His Wives.* It's a profile of

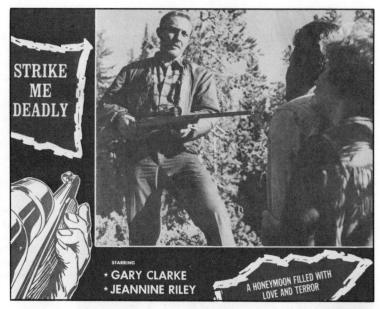

STRIKE ME DEADLY

STARRING
★ GARY CLARKE
★ JEANNINE RILEY

A HONEYMOON FILLED WITH LOVE AND TERROR

a man who actually lives in the Utah desert with 14 wives, and what they do with their life. It's a nicely done, very warm story of a family—a *big* family. For some reason, the people who created the concept for the picture disappeared from the face of the earth.

After that came a couple of martial arts films, the most recent being *Operation Overkill.*

I'm putting my "Doll Squad" into outer space in a picture called *Space Angels.* One of my friends is a *good* animator, Robert Maine, and we've done preliminaries—created spaceships, videotape of our own ships in flight, and so on. The work looks rich and elegant, and it's all done—rear screen, front screen projection, everything—in our own facilities.

Space Angels involves a planet of beautiful females that's invaded by a bad guy. All the females on *his* planet are sterile, so he sends his bad queen to kidnap the good queen and take over her planet. Of course, the female planet is non-violent—they can't fight back in the same manner as the more violent planet that sent its warriors and soldiers to take over. So obviously there's got to be some sort of hero, and the hero's been marooned on another planet after a big war with the bad guy. The girls in search of their kidnapped queen happen to run into him on an island where people get eaten by spiders as big as a house. He gets them out of there, they get their queen back, and there's a happy ending and so on . . .

I've got a big project that's been my pride and joy for about 27 years: *Beowulf.* We've shown the script to major studios and they say, "It's going to cost $60 million dollars." Well, it would cost *them* $60 million, but I could do it for $8 million, and it would be an epic that would bring in money for 40 years. (But where do you go to get $8 million?) It's in the realm of Conan, but Scandinavian in origin, and part fact, part fiction—meaning there's some basis to believe that the hero actually existed, around 600 A.D. It's based on that great piece of English literature, the Beowulf poem, about the tremendous strength and capabilities of a super-human warrior with the strength of 30 men in one arm, who was a champion of the people, a folklore hero.

■ *BR: Do you usually have several projects going at once?*
■ *TVM:* You *have* to! We have a project going on in almost every type of film. I've written one to be done here in the castle, but they don't allow you to film in your *own home*—the number of ways a creative person can be stifled is staggering! You have to go down, file a permit, pay them $200 a day, but we might be starting the whole motion picture with only $200—that's to buy a few rolls of short ends of film, and a few baloney sandwiches. On top of that, we're supposed to hire policemen, firemen, etc. So it's prohibitive.

You have to get away from here to areas where people are still fascinated with the creativity involved in making films, and aren't out to take you ... where people might offer you their homes and vehicles and ranches and so on. Then you get support.

When a dedicated filmmaker finds a way to make a film, he needs all the support he can get (it might take *20 years* to pay for a camera). Imagine you were an artist with your easel set up to paint a picture somewhere, and somebody comes along and says, "What's that thing made out of? Sticks? You can't have that on this beach." Then someone else comes along and says, "That paper you're painting on is flammable; we don't want any fires here," and takes that away. Then someone else comes along and says, "What are you doing on this beach; don't you know it's private property?" [laughs] Anyway, the restrictions are tremendous.

Once we were shooting a picture with people who theoretically had survived a nuclear holocaust—mutants. Well, the actors in make-up and beards looked so bad that neighbors called the police. Now, police keeping an eye out for shady characters is one thing, but when they come and shut you down, that's another.

> **The networks wouldn't touch it because they said it was too violent. Yet it was tongue-in-cheek violence. The girls give somebody a drink, he stands up and explodes—completely disintegrates! To me that's a joke, that's not violence.**

I've always said that making a film is the *easy part.* From writing, producing, directing, lighting, cinematography, editing and so on, making a movie should be simple! The hardest part is: (1) getting the money to make it; (2) getting the money back after it's been made. Last is: making the film. That's the way I look at it.

■ *BR: That film with the mutants; was that* Aftermath?

■ TVM: Yes; we did it here on the castle grounds.

■ *BR: And it was done by Steve Barkett?*

■ TVM: Yes.

■ *BR: Somebody said that he wrote, directed and starred in it, and that it took him five years to finish.*

■ TVM: Yeah, it can take a long time. We started the project as a joint venture, but sometimes having two or three cooks

in the broth ... So I sold out to him. I'd known him for a long time before he came to me with the concept; he wanted to direct and so on, and I wished him well. But that was only *one* picture filmed here. Next week we have a company bringing in a Bengal tiger and everything else! That is, if their plans don't change. As you know, plans for picture production *often* change.

■ *BR: I meant to ask you about Tura Satana—how did you meet her?*

■ TVM: I was flying with some friends from central Oregon down to Mazatlan for about the last vacation I ever took—that was 1959 [laughs]. On the way we stopped in Vegas. When I first saw her she was an exotic dancer; what a gorgeous, lovely lady! I didn't meet her until seven years later. I was about to do *Astro Zombies,* and an agent mentioned Tura Satana. I said, "Wow! I remember her from Vegas." So she came in for a reading, and I revamped the part especially for her, to make her a "Dragon Lady," and promptly fell in love with her (and all that).

She was also in my *Doll Squad* picture. She is a very good lady, and I still consider her a very close friend. And the same with the rest of her family: her daughter Kilani, her daughter's husband and their kids. You become very close when you make films—I don't believe I've ever done a picture where the people involved aren't to this day good friends.

She just moved back to Hollywood after living out in the Valley for years. I don't think she wants to stay out of the public eye; if I had the right picture for her we'd be back in production together again. I was smitten with her the first time I met her, and I've loved her ever since.

■ *BR: Tura Satana should be a household name!*

■ TVM: Yeah! There are those of us who *love* the characters she's very capable of creating. And she's still very beautiful. She did have an accident that caused a lot of grief—she was hit full on in the side of her vehicle, and for the past two years has been out of commission with those injuries. But I understand she's better. Anyway, she's *good,* and I enjoy making that type of film.

Astro Zombies was made with practically no money. When you realize we had people like Wendell Corey and John Carradine in the studio, I'm almost aghast when I think what tiny, tiny pennies we made that picture for. Everything was a creation from nothing. One prop was just a painted plastic thing with little lights flashing underneath ...

One story about the making of *Astro Zombies:* I had some lots I was buying on Mount Washington (later I had to

Tura Satana relaxes and thinks up new evil deeds in **The Astro-Zombies.**

OBADIAH 18

The story you are about to see is true. The names have not been changed to protect the innocent. The film is based upon actual incidents and played by the people they happened to—Alex Joseph and his wives. All 105 minutes of color action were shot entirely on location in southern Utah—where it really happened. Never before has a drama with these ingredients been brought to the screen.

All this was accomplished without the cooperation of any federal bureau. The story was necessarily filmed under armed guard and carried forth despite the attempts of the U.S. Park Service to deny the right of access to public lands during filming.

In all respects "OBADIAH 18" is a unique testimony to American ingenuity.

"The man who has raised the nation's eyebrows with his flaunting of the establishment, the man who claims 10 women—young, attractive, intelligent women—as his wives, the man who dares to do battle with the government ..."

Now comes the true story of Alex Joseph, the one-man revolution whose devil-be-damned courage has arrested the attention of domestic and international press. Set to the long-striding pace of a man who walks through the world as though he owned it, the movie is filled with Joseph's romances and challenges, his friends and enemies. This man lives more in a week than most people do in a lifetime! The movie is laced with the adventures and escapades of the people who look for Joseph. Some of them are comical, some are deadly serious—but they all find out that whoever thinks he has an eye on Alex Joseph should look over his own shoulder to see who's really doing the looking ...

An amazing portrait of an outrageous and beautiful family ... This true story is more incredible than any fiction. In outrage or admiration of this revolutionary polygamist lifestyle, you will be left wondering—what will they do next? ■

> You have to be as obsessed as a religious fanatic! Actually, it's the same with anything you really want to succeed in.

surrender them because I used them as collateral on a picture). I was filming up there on my own property, and *out of nowhere* came the fire department and the police department—they just converged on me. I had about twelve people there. What was funny was: we just turned the cameras on them and used the footage in the film! We edited it in and it looks like part of the movie—*it's great!* For a long time that was our private joke.

■ *BR: Wasn't something burning?*

■ TVM: Well, we had a little bit of a smokepot. I appreciate the fact that someone was concerned enough to immediately come out, but it was just a *tiny* smokepot. There was an old wreck on the property that we'd turned into a car that had just crashed over an embankment, containing a body that was theoretically just killed—the astro zombie—and the demented doctor who was collecting body parts had to get to that body quick so he could take parts out of it. So, it was kind of delightful to see all those police cars pouring out of nowhere onto the property. It made our scene!

■ *BR: Any other fire stories?*

■ TVM: *Blood Orgy of the She Devils* was a witchcraft story. And every time we turned around someone was getting burned, or something was catching on fire. It was almost as if there *were* witchcraft present, in fact ...

There were *no reasons* for fires that started by themselves out of nowhere. Like, somebody in the prop department would get burned, and ... It got to be something that the cast and crew would wonder about: "What *is* this?" [laughs] In the past I'd spent about 2 years researching parapsychology, attending seances, etc, yet I could find *no reason* for the things that took place.

For example, we burned a witch at the stake, and it happened to be a lady very close to me. We had her on top of a wood pile chained to a huge post, and I had instructed the effects people to build the fire on a pallet which could be pulled away with ropes in the event of a problem. (You get the fire started, then pull the pallet away and cut to a close-up, with flames from a different source). Well, all of a sudden the wind changed and we almost *really* burned her at the stake! [laughs] That was hairy!

In almost every picture, things like that have happened. In *Operation Overkill* we had explosions that wouldn't explode, because the weather in Reno was too cold. The basic explosion would go off but everything else would just fall down in white flakes. [laughs]

I was a stunt man in a picture called *Indian Fighter,* with Kirk Douglas and Alan Hale. I played a barebacked Indian shooting flaming arrows. Years before, in central Oregon, I had shot flaming arrows just for the heck of it. I got on the good side of the effects people because I had developed flaming arrows that would *stay lit* in flight. (Whereas the props department just had arrows with a big, dumb-looking glob of orange phosphorus on the end that didn't even look like fire.) I shot 'em into flagpoles; set wagons on fire; and had a lot of fun.

■ *BR: How did you make flaming arrows?*

■ TVM: I used *pitch!* They don't think about pitch in Hollywood, but in central Oregon it's everywhere; you gather it in little cans from trees where it oozes out. That's what you start your fire with at night. With pitch plus turpentine, I was able to create a mixture that would *stay* lit. However, you have to remember that the modern hunting bow shoots so fast that it would put out any fire. So you have to use a true *Indian* long bow that just *lobs* the arrow so it stays lit. They're accurate; you just have to use a different elevation.

Years before, I had won some archery contests. I used to shoot bow and arrow every day; I used to *hunt* with bow and arrow. I still have all my hunting gear.

■ *BR: By the way, do you happen to know Cresse and Frost?*

■ TVM: I knew Bob Cresse reasonably well twenty years ago; I don't know what he's doing now.

■ *BR: I heard he was shot in the stomach and had to leave the country.*

■ TVM: I heard that, too. He was involved in a different type of film than I was! Lee Frost—he's still around; in the past year I've run across his credits in a film somewhere. I'm sure you can find him; check the laboratories.

■ *BR: What do you look for in a film?*

■ TVM: I look for the creativity of the maker. Then, how much I am taken with the story: am I entertained, or am I turned off? I'm often asked in interviews if I have somebody I try to emulate or imitate. And I say, "God, no!" I don't pay any attention to what anybody else does; I do what *I* feel. If someone else wants to copy *me,* fine, but I do not copy. I've never copied.

But I am guilty, a little bit, of using stereotypes. For example, if you need a "doctor" in a bit part who has to rush on, do something and then leave, you're almost obligated to use a stereotype so that people will instantly accept the person as a doctor. But even that stereotype changes from time period to time period. Now, a 28-year-old bearded man wearing faded denims may be a doctor. You'd accept that today, but 15 years ago you *had* to have a man in a 3-piece suit, graying hair and bifocals with a little satchel. So, if I've got to "sell" a part

efficiently and quickly, I use a stereotype. But other than that, I do not copy.

If you want to be a filmmaker, it's like: if you want an automobile and all you've got is a junkyard full of parts and pieces; if you don't have any other way to get it, you build it. If that means you have to learn how to paint the car when it's through, you do that, too. It's the same with making a film: I don't *like* having to write, produce, direct, raise the money, shoot, be director of photography, cameraman, work with the drama teacher, do the make-up and special effects, do all the editing, put on every sound effect, do all the music, handle it through the answer print, then start out with the film under your arm, selling it . . . I don't do that because I *want* to; I do it because sometimes there's no other way. *I do whatever it takes.*

■ *BR: You do the music, too?*

■ TVM: I *taught* music when I was younger. But I do not do the scoring. I may take a library and do the scoring; however, I have a composer friend who's absolutely fantastic and well-talented, Nicholas Garras. He's done most of the music in my films for about 28 years. He composes; then we rent the studio and go in with anywhere from 18 to 30 musicians and record. Later, when he's already scored it, he sits at the movieola and times it along with a click track. If there's something happening that calls for a *sting* at, say, 14.3 seconds, he knows exactly when that sting should hit. Garras is brilliant that way, and that's how pictures are scored.

It would be nice to be able to just hire someone and have all these bits and pieces done. In a way it's an advantage to do it yourself, but it's also a disadvantage because it takes so much time. You start with writing, end up with your first answer print, and it's a year out of your life. How many pictures can you make?

I've seldom ever started two films in a year. I'd love to; I'd love to start one every 90 days. To do that you'd have to hire post-production, hire an editor, hire a sound effects company, have someone writing so that while you're working on one film another one's being written. Actually, I've probably

> **The easiest thing is making the film. The toughest thing is getting the money, the second toughest is getting it back.**

got 6 projects in various stages of preparation at this moment, besides scripts being drafted and so on.

■ *BR: What's your taxidermist script about?*

■ TVM: *Taxidermist* is unusual, to say the least. I can't really give away the plot because I don't own the story; it was created by a relative and close writer/friend of Francine York. It has to do with family wealth in the deep South, the rivalry that takes place, and revenge. Without giving away the plot, I'd say some very startling things take place, because

BLOOD ORGY OF THE SHE-DEVILS

Mara (Lila Zaborin) a "black" witch, practitioner of the occult, black magic, and evil incarnate, is the leader of a coven of voluptuous, scantily clad beautiful young women who vent their sadistic love and passion for pain on helpless victims as they perform the bloody ritual of a hideously macabre dance of death, carrying aloft flaming torches and plunging spears into their human male sacrifices in a gory ceremony to titillate their pulsating pleasures and sanctify the evil desires of this queen of the Witches.

Mara is approached by Rodannus (Ray Myles) enemy agent of a foreign power, accompanied by his henchman, Barth (Paul Wilmoth) with the request that an Ambassador representative to the United Nations from another country be eliminated by means of her magic powers. During this meeting, Rodannus demands proof of her mystical power and she causes a wine glass to shatter in his hands. When the enemy agent leaves, Mara keeps the bloodied handkerchief he had used on his cut hand.

Lorraine (Leslie McRae) a newcomer to Mara's coven, persuades her boyfriend, Mark (Tom Pace) an unbeliever, to attend a seance. Astounded by the results, during which Mara has conjured up two spirit guides and a ghost and worried about Lorraine's involvement, Mark decides to consult Dr. Helsford (Victor Izay) a "white" witch or warlock, and an expert on psychic phenomena.

After Mara has caused the Ambassador's death at a party, Rodannus fears that she may turn her powers against him, and he sends Barth to kill both Mara and her high priest, Toruke (William Bagdad). Barth also kills a young girl, Roberta (Linn Henson), but she manages to scratch his face before she dies.

Meanwhile, Dr. Helsford agrees to help Mark. By means of witchcraft, Mara has caused Barth to kill a cat instead. She now restores Toruke to life and using Rodannus' bloodied handkerchief and Barth's scratched skin from the fingernail parings of the dead girl, Mara eliminates both Barth and Rodannus in a macabre and bloody manner.

Mark and Lorraine are to attend another seance at Mara's residence and they discuss with Dr. Helsford the possibilities of age regression under hypnosis which Mark is to undergo. The doctor warns them of the dangers of dabbling in the black arts. He psychometrizes an amulet Lorraine is wearing which Mara had given her as protection against unfriendly demons.

After the pair leave for the meeting, the disturbed Dr. Helsford, sensing an evil aftermath, enlists the aid of three other scientists interested in psychic phenomena and they decide to visit Mara's home where the meeting is to be held. During regression, Mark is shown to have been killed by Indians in a previous life as a frontiersman and now, drugged by Mara, he is to be offered up as a human sacrifice in an effort to conjure up Lucifer, the Devil himself.

Mara and her coven of witches are soon terrrified as an unseen presence takes over. The building rumbles and trembles as utter chaos reigns. The unseen terror possesses the bodies of the young witches who turn against Toruke and kill him, and they then turn against each other.

Outside, Dr. Helsford fights the evil within by means of exorcism and manages to restore order and sanity, driving the evil unseen presence away. When the quartet of scientists enter the building, all is death and destruction. Mark, Lorraine and all the others are dead. Only a bat clings to the ceiling and dislodging it, Dr. Helsford, knowing its true identity, kills it and throws it on some burning coals. At last, Mara pays for the consequences of evil, as her translucent, vaporous form floats upwards in a raging, screaming death. ■

taxidermy's not limited to animals! [laughter] But that's just *one;* I've got a lot more stories I want to do.

Finding the wrap-up dollars for a picture is sometimes more difficult than finding the initial dollars. All your costs escalate as you go along. You start out making a picture for 28¢, and if your project looks like it's headed for a successful conclusion, you keep requiring more and more money to dress it. Like, it's one cost to use canned music tracks out of a library, and another to have a talented man like Nick Garras write it and score it. It's one thing to do a sound mix at a tiny stage on some back street in Hollywood, as opposed to one of the houses where they've got $20 million invested in sound transfer equipment. So you keep upgrading as you go; as your enthusiasm develops, so does your budget.

Very seldom do pictures bring back the money unless there is the control that only the major studios can exert. *They* can collect the money. An independent like myself cannot enforce collections anywhere. You've got to have legal departments and offices in many cities; you've got to *do things* in order to collect money. Just because your picture grosses a lot at the box office doesn't mean you get any. There are too many places where your money's taken: for promotion, for print costs, for every reason under the sun including a bad date that's rained out that *you've* got to pay for, advertising, etc.

You may get money due you from one theater, whereas a theater in an adjoining town had a storm and all the money for advertising was lost, so the money made from one town pays for the losses in the other. I've had reports from 30 theaters, many of whom did *excellent* business, where instead of getting $500 in film rental for each theater, I get a *bill* for $800. Doesn't always happen, but it happens often.
■ *BR: That's nuts!*
■ TVM: It *is* nuts!
■ *BR: It's hard to imagine that sort of thing happening—*
■ TVM: Remember when I said the easiest thing is *making* the film? The toughest thing is getting the money, the second toughest is getting it back. Of those 3 things, making the film is the easiest, as well as the only thing which goes forward on schedule, providing you've got a dollar allocated for doing a certain job.
■ *BR: Everyone's heard about people who have a Top 10 music hit, yet never see any money from it.*

Dancing beauties in *Girl in Gold Boots.*

■ TVM: I can think of a lot of big pictures that have grossed millions, with the producer *never* having seen a penny. No one I've known has ever found a way to successfully monitor theater receivables. Maybe the big chains can, because they deal with mass volumes and gross revenues. But if you have a play date somewhere in the Midwest, if your picture did $3,200 for one week, theoretically 25% is supposed to come back to the distributor. Of that $800, $200 is kept by the *local* distributor. Then your $600 gets hit with a lot of charges, and you might get your share anywhere from 3 months to 2 years later. And, there is no commitment on anybody's part that they're *really* going to pay you, except that they're in business, and you assume that sooner or later they have to pay to *stay* in business, otherwise no one's going to give them any films.

> It doesn't matter what the ideas are, I get an idea a minute. In five minutes I could write more titles for viable film stories—very realistic film productions—than I could make in the rest of my life. So I don't want to hear that there aren't that many really new ideas.

If we knew a picture played a chain of 100 theaters, for example, and these theaters gave us the box office *gross* receipts, we could figure out a net film rental. But that chain might have 4 theaters in another state which spend more money on advertising than they should, so the money you *might* be getting from the first state will be taken to cover those theaters in the other state. It's funny the way it works; *difficult.* And if the theater or circuit doesn't do it to you the distributor will, or the sub-distributor, or master distributor. We formed our own distribution company, but you *still* can't keep track. It's almost come to the point where you have to deal directly with the theater on a theater-to-theater basis. If you can't, you really don't have any protection against what will happen, from the time people pay their money to get in the theater, to the time you receive it (or don't receive it). I didn't have gray hair when I started; I didn't have *any* gray hair.

■ BR: *You really have to* want *to make films, given all the obstacles—*

■ TVM: You have to be as obsessed as a religious fanatic! Actually, it's the same with *anything* you really want to succeed in. Making films is magic; there's something very fulfilling about it. It's also something that's very easy to become obsessed over. That's why when people ask me why I don't take vacations, I say, "Vacation from what?" Making a film is my recreation, profession, vacation, vocation, *everything!* It's fun! The only time it gets tough is when money is too scarce, and then many times *survival* is at stake. In fact, *very often.* And that's when it's not so much fun. [laughs] You may have pictures all over the world that are feeding thousands of people; you may have 10 different films playing at the same time, yet go a year without seeing a dime. That's the nature of the business.

■ BR: *Again, that's nuts.*

■ TVM: It *is* nuts. And I don't know of anyone who can change it. I tried very diligently, but I wasn't able to. Maybe on this newest picture, *Operation Overkill,* I'll let someone else handle all the legal manuevering, merchandising, promotion, collecting the money and so on—people whose business is just doing that with finished pictures. I'll see if they have better luck than I did.

■ BR: *It's hard to be a creative person* and *hold up the business end.*

■ TVM: A creative person can hold up many ends of business, but they can't hold up *every* end. Anyway, most filmmakers don't deal with all that—collecting money and so on. I'm a firm believer in "all things come to he who waits." One of the outstanding things about our business is that the amount of money you spend making a film has no relation to what you can expect to make in return. On the other hand, the more money you spend telling the world it's a great picture, the better chance you have of getting a bigger return. A film may only cost $1 million to make, but it may cost 5 times that much to tell the world it's a marvelous film, so they'll go see it. And that's not uncommon: to spend far more *promoting* the film than the film actually *cost.*

■ BR: *Your films should have a head start, because the titles are so good.*

■ TVM: I've been told I have a unique ability there; that's part of being a showman. You do your *best* magic trick, you don't use your crummiest one. You use the ones that have the greatest flash, the greatest audience-pleasing ability. You choose music that is most moving, and so on. It's just part and parcel of the game.

You choose titles like *Operation Overkill*—action oriented, CIA, martial arts. *The Doll Squad* dolls are pretty girls; mix that with James Bondish-type artwork and you have an all-female James Bond film. *Blood Orgy of the She Devils* is almost like it sounds. And *Corpse Grinders*—the corpse grinders are hoodlums who grind corpses into cat food for "Cats Who Like People." It has to be very simple; how are you going to reach an audience if you can't say what it is in a few words—you can't give them a dissertation! If you said, "A Story About a Man Who Chased Bears," you've said it all. *I Crossed the Color Line* is a story about a man who passed for white, and of course his blood was not. He went on to take vengeance on the Klan for killing his little 3-year-old daughter in a church bombing. In *The Astro Zombies,* "astro" is futuristic, like astral space, and zombies are dead people that really can't die again, right? So I concocted the title *Astro Zombies* 20 or 25 years ago, long before there was ever any such thing as heart transplants . . .

As with *Astro Zombies,* I'm usually accused of being a few years ahead of whatever's going on. I'm always three or four years ahead, but many times I don't find the money until it's too late. The concepts are there, but concepts get ripped off. Just by presenting screenplays to anyone, they get ripped off. A lot of people are not creative thinkers, they're copiers. And so I'm blessed with being able to *re-create*—if somebody copies something, I can in 2 seconds [snaps his fingers] come up with a different idea. I get calls constantly from people, saying, "I've got a hell of an idea for a movie," and I stop them right there. They say, "Don't you even want to hear it?" I say, "Yes, *in a way* I would, but tell me—most importantly, have you got the money to start it?"

> I'm not in the Directors' Guild, not in any guild. I just don't want anyone telling me what to do, or what I cannot do.

It doesn't matter what the ideas are, I get an idea a minute. In five minutes I could write more titles for viable film stories—very realistic film productions—than I could make in the rest of my life. So I don't want to hear that there aren't that many really new ideas. Anyway, I've got all the ideas *I* need, plus I have an enormous investment in screenplays that are the result of previous ideas. They're ready to go. Why come up with more stories and screenplays when you've got to make films out of the ones you've already created?

■ BR: Corpse Grinders *expressed the idea of cats eating human flesh and then attacking people—I haven't seen* that *particular theme used too often.*

ASTRO ZOMBIES

Multilation murders occur with increasing savagery in a city. The nature of these murders—vital organs ripped from the victims' bodies—leads the C.I.A., headed by Holman (Wendell Corey) to the conclusion that the former chief of the Astro Space Laboratory, Dr. DeMarco (John Carradine) has succeeded in creating an Astro-Man, a zombie with a defective brain!

DeMarco, missing since his dismissal from the Space Center, has secreted himself in an old mansion on the outskirts of the city; there he continues experiments on human bodies with the aid of a deformed assistant. Foreign agents from hostile governments are also trying to locate DeMarco to force him to put his knowledge in their hands. The exotic and voluptuous Satana, working with two vicious killers, reduces the competition by torture and threat, brutally massacring some of Holman's men.

The subsequent multilation of a beautiful technician at the Space Lab leads Holman to set a trap for the zombie, by planting another girl as bait. The suspense tightens when the zombie attacks the girl after Holman's men are gone. After a desperate fight the zombie is tracked down, back to DeMarco's mansion.

Meanwhile the spies are embroiled in ever-deepening intrigue, but manage to find DeMarco's lab with a frequency rectifier. An explosive finale is inevitable. Holman's men surround the mansion, trapping Satana inside with DeMarco and the zombies. A bloody gun battle follows, with the zombies butchering indiscriminately. DeMarco is shot down by Satana, but not before he throws the master switch that deactivates the zombies forever, burying his secret under a mass of electronic rubble. ∎

I sold everything to buy the film to make the film to begin with. I sold my house, car, drums, saxophone, the lots I had, everything.

■ **TVM:** When I say there aren't that many original ideas, what I mean is, every time someone calls on the phone saying, "I've got an idea for you," I say, "But I don't need any more; I've already got so many ideas." But actually, that depends on the mood I'm in. If I'm just finishing a picture and haven't got the pressure of something waiting, then I don't mind listening. But whenever someone calls up with an idea, most of the time all you can tell them is to do a synopsis. *Got an idea? Do a story treatment.* Then let's find out how viable the story treatment is toward making a film out of it.

■ *BR: How can you determine viability of a story treatment?*

■ **TVM:** Well, to me that story about 2 guys who grind human bodies into cat food—that's viable! *The Girl in Gold Boots,* about a girl who comes to Hollywood and is faced with making a choice, to me that's viable. A man with 14 wives and how he makes his life work—to me that's viable. *Operation Overkill,* the CIA using martial artists to overpower terrorists and suppress illegal shipments of weapons, that's viable.

I could sit here and dream up a hundred ideas in five minutes. The mind is a marvelous computer; all you've got to do is tune in and say, "Hey, I want to make a new movie. What do I make it about?" Every few seconds [snaps fingers in quick succession] you'll come up with a thought!

Since I've had very young girls in my life, I can think of a story about that: gray-haired dude, 50 years old, meets a girl

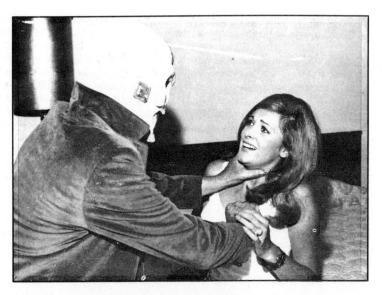

An Astro-Zombie attacks! (The Astro-Zombies)

who's 18 or 19. It turns out she's the daughter of one of his college buddies who gets incensed that the man has a fascination for his daughter. He doesn't realize the little daughter has a fascination for the man. Maybe they both work together—maybe they both do helicopter rescue missions, and one guy has a choice of letting the other fall off a cliff during a rescue operation. I can dream up these things forever, you know . . .

I dreamed up a story based on this old, beat-up castle I live in, called *Castle Ray.* There's a guy living here a bit akin to myself—he's got a beard and moustache; and there's a little mystique about the building—there's lots of secret passages . . .

■ *BR: Are there?*

■ **TVM:** There *are* some places between the wall here, and so on. And the castle is on two acres of trees so it's hidden. I'd put it into a period piece, somewhere around 1890.

■ *BR: How can you do that?*

■ **TVM:** I love special effects lighting; I claim a great capacity there. I don't know many directors who are *really* capable of lighting. I can do things in this place to make it look scary *in ways beyond.* Meaning: taking lights out, putting up gas lamps, using mattes on the windows in order to project an ocean and cliffs out there, instead of trees . . .

I'm going to take advantage of all I've learned in 30 years of filmmaking right here. I've got a screenplay on *Castle Ray,* and I've got screenplays on a number of other things. *Strike Me Deadly* I sat down and wrote in about 3 weeks on a little patio like this, then started filming days later.

■ *BR: Don't you think people could appreciate* Strike Me Deadly *in black-and-white?*

■ **TVM:** Let me tell you what I face. When someone puts the videocassette in and watches it, they love it and nobody wants to turn it off. But when we're talking about buyers from the Middle East, buyers from the United Kingdom, buyers from Scandinavia, buyers for theaters, buyers for cassettes in this country or it doesn't matter where, the minute you say "black-and-white" you're shut off. *Not interested.* Nobody from any country wants to buy a black-and-white film from America; no TV stations, nobody. Pay cable? "Black-and-white—forget it, we're not interested." They don't even want to know what it's *about* . . . or whether it's a good film or a bad film . . . and they don't want to look to find out, either. That's why I'm going to change it to color. We've got bears, birds, geese, ducks, waterfalls, airplanes dropping borade on billowing red flames—all that's spectacular to look at. Redo-

THE WORM EATERS

In the town of Melnick, California an old clubfoot hermit lives near a semi-dried up lake and forest. His name is Hermann Umgar. The corrupt city council leader, Mayor Sunny Melnick, has decided to condemn the old lake and forest where Umgar lives and re-zone to build condominiums.

Inside Umgar's 50-foot-tall wooden water tower are rooms filled with tanks of worms. Umgar talks to them, sleeps with them and grows them bigger and fatter so that they will on command eat all the crops of Melnick and bankrupt the town so he can save the beauty of the trees, lake and forest from the greedy Mayor.

In various scenes Umgar kisses, feeds and sings to his Tenya worms while the secret M Society attempts to burn, hang, and blow him up.

A complication arrives at the lake in a silly rich family and two beautiful teen-age girls who decide to stay at the lake for a vacation. The pretty young daughter, Penelope, who is always sunning herself in a bathing suit, is horrified by Umgar's clubfoot and grotesque looks. The two teen-age girls complain, "The old creep don't even have any hot dogs around here. It's un-American!" The mother Mildred screams at Umgar, "I want eggs with no goo in them and my cream-filled fudgies, you idiot!"

Suddenly one night Umgar is surrounded by the horrifying sight of three worm-like men standing over his bed. They are the Champion Bass Fishing Club men that disappeared in Lake Melnick many months before and were assumed to be dead. The leader Bucky says, "We are not dead. We ate some of your worms that were in the fish we caught and we were transformed into a new glorious breed of half-man and half-worm. We live under the Red Tide in the lake and no longer want to be like the greedy men we were. But you must bring us worm women to mate with so our civilization under the Red Tide will grow." Umgar agrees to feed his worms to women to give to them and they will help him eat the crops.

A dumb waitress named Heidi eats some of the worms in spaghetti at Umgar's tower and becomes the first worm woman. Umgar builds a cage and makes three more worm women with worms in fudgies and hot dogs for the rich mother and teen-age girls.

Back in Melnick the city council votes to re-zone the lake. The young rebel Phil presents a note to the concil from Umgar that the old hermit does have a deed to the lake. A fight breaks out and Phil escapes.

Back at Umgar's tower he hears a radio news announcement that the city council is going to build condominiums and he screams, "I will kill them with the deadly Ana worms! They will not destroy my beautiful trees and mountains." He goes to town and puts the deadly Ana worms in the following foods: triple deck hamburgers, fried chicken, chocolate malts, ice cream, chewing tobacco and Tequila. The city council dies one by one.

Umgar arrives back at his tower to find the Mayor waiting for him with a gun. A fight breaks out and the Mayor gets sucked into the cage filled with worm women and is eaten to death.

The next morning Umgar's neck is pierced by a fishing hook and he is pulled down to the lake by a fishing line held by the leader of the worm men. They feed Umgar his own worms and then go to town to capture tree women in beds, kitchens and showers. In thrilling scenes that follow we see Hermann Umgar the worm man crawl over forests and dried river beds toward the crops to eat all of them by himself. He dies horribly by being splat across a diesel truck windshield in one of the most horrifying messes ever seen on film.

Believe us, folks, a hell of a lot of worms and food are hysterically eaten in the above-mentioned silly, laugh-a-minute motion picture. ■

I've always related making films to magic.

ing all that in color should bring a whole new world of receptivity to that film, because it's very enjoyable, full of outdoor excitement and action. There's no swearing, no nudity; it's just a good all-American film ...

At Goldwyn Studios—I had an office there until about '75—Goldwyn was looking to play host to about 1,700 Boy Scouts and Eagle Scouts. And from all the films *they* had to choose from, they chose *Strike Me Deadly* to entertain them on a Saturday night (theoretically, one of the high spots of the convention). Why, I don't know. Maybe because it's outdoors, action, clean, warm, touching, gripping, and there's enough excitement and enough things happening. So, the film *will* open a new market—but not as black-and-white.

The only reason I made it in black-and-white was because I sold everything to buy the film to make the film to begin with. I sold my house, car, drums, saxophone, the lots I had, everything. But I couldn't put together enough nickels to buy color film; I could only buy black-and-white, which was 2½ times cheaper than color, 2½ times cheaper to process, and 2½ times cheaper to print. The difference in the price would have kept me from shooting. Had I to do it over, *of course* I would have shot color. As that was my first film, what did *I* know?

■ BR: *By having the frame of reference they've been given to judge films by, most people focus their attention in such a way as to miss much of what's going on right in front of them. The films I like have a lot of extra things going on which people miss, because they aren't viewing the films on the films' own terms, if you follow me.*

■ TVM: I've always related making films to magic. Making a film is creating illusion, and magic is the same thing: *causing someone to believe they see something they're not really seeing.* Somebody might be in a little pool by this patio, but if the camera only shows water and a little raft, and you tell the audience they're in the middle of the ocean, then that's where they are. We're doing the same thing: we're doing magic ... *camera magic.*

■ BR: *You mentioned 7, your magic number. Do you have any actual interest in the occult?*

Mara the witch shows a member of her coven what the future holds—death! In Blood Orgy of the She Devils.

■ TVM: I did lots of research into the occult; in fact we called the production company for the witchcraft picture *Occult Productions, Inc.* The occult *is* interesting, but everything has to have its proper place and perspective. I'm interested in everything there is to be interested in, and that means all things! I like to think I don't go overboard in any direction; I believe action-adventure is the top pursuit for me as a filmmaker, because that reaches the greatest market. And in reaching the greatest market, theoretically you have your greatest return.

■ *BR: Back to the number 7—*

■ TVM: It's always sort of been my magic number. I have a *thing* about numbers: 1's, 3's, 5's, 7's. When I do my exercises, which I do every day of my life, everything's got to come out to 7's—I can't tell you *why.* If I do fencing lunges, I'll do 25, 50, 75; after I do 75 I'll do more, because 7 and 5 added together is 12, and 1 and 2 added together is 3, and so I'll do 4 more to make another set of 7. It's kind of a "thing" for me: everything is 7 or 3. Like, with a spoon that's been in soup, I would never tap it just once, I'd tap it 3 times. [laughs] Little idiosyncrasies, you know!

■ *BR: For some reason, everywhere I go, "3" keeps popping up in some important context. It's always been a very important number for me; I have no idea why, or how this started.*

■ TVM: Well, "7" is a very magic number for me. I didn't even think about it, but all of a sudden I realized that for years I had 7 big cables. I could think of 7 in a lot of other ways, like the idea of having 7 Castle Ladies, and so on. I don't know *why* 7 seems to hold such a magic for me, but everything I do (not *everything,* but a *lot*) is related to 7's. And particularly in exercise, where I do 7 sets of dumbbell curls everyday. Don't ask me why, but I have to do 7. It kind of drives me. There's no real reason for it at all. [Talk turns to Ted finding the wrap-up money to finish project *Overkill*].

■ *BR: Didn't you tell me you were making this movie out of used footage?*

T.V. Mikels on location.   **Photo: Vale**

■ TVM: *Used footage?*

■ *BR: Didn't you say that on the phone?*

■ TVM: Oh, no! I said I was going to use *used film.* By saying "used film" I really should have told you I was going to use film that's already been put into the camera. *But,* the *unused* portion of it is re-canned and stuck in a dark bag, and I'm going to use *that* again. But it's not been previously *exposed.*

■ *BR: Oh!* That's *what you meant.*

■ TVM: I said it as a joke.

■ *BR: I thought you were going to get your hands on a lot of footage, and splice it together, composing a story somehow.*

■ TVM: Oh, no; I wouldn't do *that.* I don't redo anyone else's work. I do what I feel is expressing my *own* creativity; I wouldn't for a minute consider using someone else's. Like, I even shoot my own stock footage. If I need Las Vegas, if I need forest fires, I go shoot it myself.

> **If you want to be a filmmaker, it's like: if you want an automobile and all you've got is a junkyard full of parts and pieces; if you don't have any other way to get it, you build it.**

I've got other ones starting, too; I've got *Silent Rage, Sudden Death* that I'm doing. I'm a fine cameraman, too. You know, I'm bragging a little bit, but I've spent my life making films—I've taught a lot of people how to *be* cameramen. A lot of work out there, I've shot; on a lot of pictures playing around the world, I've shot the camera. I don't *just* write, direct, produce and edit and so on. Part and parcel of being a creator is having the total concept of the creativity, meaning: if you're going to expose film, you'd better be able to light it. You'd better be able to put an actor in front of the camera who's going to be able to perform; if he can't, you'd better help him. If he doesn't look right, you'd better be able to do the make-up. If you need a gunshot to go off near his head and make a chip in the wall, you'd better be able to know how to do it, or do without it. That's my whole belief: *you learn to do whatever it takes, to do what you want to do.* You want to climb a mountain?—you put one foot in front of the other and start climbing. Whatever that means.

■ *BR: It means a lot.*

■ TVM: It means to me that I make films.

In Independence CA, Vale conducted a short interview with T.V. Mikels during a break in the shooting of the movie **The Survivalists** that he was directing.

■ *VALE: You recently left your castle?*

■ TED V. MIKELS: We left the castle after living there 15 years; I bought a house in Vegas with a pool and extra houses on about 1¼ acres. It took 14 trips over the mountains to move everything, but now it's all set up, with cutting rooms, etc. The reason I moved was: my money people said they'd finance my films and build studios for me if I'd move to Vegas. So I moved!

■ *V: What do you wear around your neck?*

■ TVM: A boar's tusk. When I direct a picture I've always got my director's finder, a contrast glass, light meter, etc. around my neck, plus the tools on my belt. So when I'm not directing a picture I feel naked—I think that's where this [boar's tusk] came in.

■ **V**: *Could you update us on your last two movies?*

■ **TVM**: *Ten Violent Women*—a fun film—is sold in almost every country in the world; it's on video now from World Video. Fortunately I selected a company that builds beautiful full color jackets, not black-and-white with a little splash on it. So you can get *Corpse Grinders, Doll Squad, Ten Violent Women, Blood Orgy of the She-Devils, Girl in Gold Boots, Astro Zombies* and I don't know what other pictures I've done, on video.

Operation Overkill is in a stalemate. About eighty percent of the filming was finished in Reno. The plot is: disreputable weapons manufacturers are supplying guns to terrorists for use around the world, and the CIA (because they can't use federal government troops) brings in martial artists to try to ferret out the terrorists and blow up their training compounds, etc. There aren't any women in it, it's nothing like

Doll Squad; all my pictures are different. It's what you'd call a pure action picture, like *Force of One* where Tiger Yang decimates 20 guys at once. But not chop-saki; when he hits you, you *go down.* He's two-times world champion; he's got a ball on the back of his hand about as big as this glass.

Earlier we went to do a picture in South Dakota with Tiger. He picked up a *big* river rock in a creek, and I saw him chanting, sitting crossed on his haunches. I thought, "He's not going to hit his hand on that rock, is he?" So I walked over and asked, "Tiger, what are you doing?" He replied, "I break, I break." I said, "Tiger, we've got a picture to do—if you hit your hand on that rock you'll smash your hand and we'll never make a movie." And he said, "No, I break, I break." He sat there for awhile and finally I said, "Tiger, you're going to smash your hand—DON'T DO IT!" He ignored me, hit it once real hard and nothing happened. I thought, "Ohmigod." But he did it again and he cracked that rock in three pieces—a big river rock. I put the pieces in the trunk of my car and took them home. It had to be something *here* (points to forehead), not the force with which he hit that rock. Incredible.

■ **V**: *You told Boyd that you helped one of your Castle Ladies completely make a film—*

■ **TVM**: That picture was entitled *Knee Dancing.* A lovely woman who has four sons who are out of school now and on their own is the writer-producer-director-editor and star. It's a good story about a woman having a nervous breakdown at an airport. Her whole life flashes before her . . . as a child molested by her father, the effect on her relationships with men for her entire life, etc. I did the photography for her. She's gotten several awards—in fact they flew her to Paris not long ago to accept an award for it. Her name is Doreen Ross.

I've spent a great portion of my life making films like that—that I don't consider *my* pictures. I did the photography and worked like a son of a gun on *The Hostage* which was one of the only pictures where I got to shoot and play with light; that picture got critical acclaim for the lighting. Of course my gaffers jumped in and took the credit in the magazine interviews, god bless 'em!

■ **V**: *Any problems on this current film shoot?*

■ **TVMS**: I worry. I worry that my meter might get kicked, because I'm working down at light levels that are unheard of—at very few foot-candles . . . I don't worry providing that all of the mechanical equipment is functioning as I have

created the circumstances for it to function. But if there is any sort of a deficiency in the cycles of the power, or any sort of problem in the soup, or any sort of problem on a meter . . . *although,* if you've put a few million feet of film through a camera you have confidence. So I have confidence in what I'm doing, but *something can always go wrong.*

■ **V**: *Would you ever produce someone else's film again?*

■ **TVM**: After my experience with *Aftermath,* I decided that never again in my lifetime would I allow anybody else to direct a film where my money is involved. It was the end of my producing-only, and the solidification of my intent to always direct-and-produce.

Now theoretically, if I'm paid $10,000 a week as a Director, or $7500 a week as a Director of Photography, and I'm going to go ten weeks on a picture, it seems reasonable that the compensation would be ample. But it seems like every time you get involved in a thing it's a freebie or a near-freebie, and those are the ones that kill you. They destroy your art history, they destroy your soul, because you fight to stay alive while you're trying to be creative.

There *are* circumstances where I would produce for somebody; right now I'm doing this with Ray out of warmth and friendship, but normally you can't—you can't afford to! And Ray will tell you the same thing—I'm sure Ray would never produce a picture for anybody unless they compensated him properly. Because it takes your guts and your entrails and your soul to make a film. It takes everything you possess within you! ■

T.V. Mikels.   **Photo: Vale**

TED V. MIKELS
BIOGRAPHY
BY JIM MORTON

Ted V. Mikels has been a motion picture writer, director, and producer for over 30 years. Until recently he lived in Sparr Castle (boasting a dungeon, secret passageways and 23 rooms) in the Verdugo Mountains near Glendale, Ca. with seven women. With his goatee and Dali-esque moustache, he resembles a sideshow magician—which he once was.

Since childhood Mikels traveled extensively, performing in hundreds of shows as a magician, ventriloquist, solo accordionist and acrobat. At the age of 19 he was presenting a 2½-hour magical extravaganza called "Open Sesame." An expert fencer, weight-lifter, archer and horseman, from 1950-1958 he appeared in numerous films as a stunt man and bit player. In 1952-55 Mikels covered Oregon as a newsreel TV cameraman, and from 1953-1963 he either directed and/or was lead performer in numerous stage plays such as **The Diary of Anne Frank**. Besides working as

cameraman on feature films, he's made dozens of educational and documentary short films, trailers, television spots and commercials including music-rock videos in the late sixties.

As a feature film director-producer, Mikels got his start in 1960 when he sold everything he owned to finance **Strike Me Deadly**. Although no box-office smash, it sparked his career. He worked as cinematographer on **The Hostage** and that same year directed **The Black Klansman**.

The Black Klansman did well at the box office. Released in 1965—a time when public interest in civil rights was at its peak—the film is about a black man who infiltrates the Ku Klux Klan trying to learn who killed his daughter. In true exploitation fashion, the film features plenty of interracial bed-hopping, and was successful enough for Mikels to start his own distribution company: Geneni Film Distributing.

In 1968 he directed and released **Girl in Gold Boots**, about a young couple who, trying to escape the draft, gets caught up in the world of crime. That same year also saw the release of the classic **Astro Zombies**.

If he never made another film, **Astro Zombies** would assure Mikels a niche in film history. Dealing with cryogenics and transplanting frozen human parts, the science fiction-horror plot features a mad scientist and his even madder assistant who create half-human, half-robot creatures out of dead bodies. When one of the Astro Zombies loses its

Doll Squad.

solar-power pack at night, it makes its way home by pressing a flashlight to the solar cell on its forehead! Thrown into this stew is a subplot of enemy agents trying to steal the secrets of the Astro Zombies. The agents are led by dark-haired, fiery-eyed beauty Tura Satana, whose presence contributes immeasurably to the film's appeal.

In 1972—a banner year for bizarre films—Mikels released his magnum opus **The Corpse Grinders** which hit #11 on the weekly Top Fifty box office list. It's the story of a cat food company that uses human corpses in their product. Unfortunately, this secret ingredient causes cats all over town to attack their owners. The premise is weird enough, but the cast is even stranger—what an assortment of misfits!

Wanting to release **The Corpse Grinders** on a double bill, Mikels chose a film he had picked up the rights to called **The Undertaker and His Pals** (1966). It stars a mortician who, enlisting the aid of two brothers—one of whom wants to be a surgeon—drums up business by creating customers. The brothers, when they're not helping the undertaker, run a restaurant. The three have a very equitable arrangement: after dispatching the victims, the would-be surgeon is allowed to practice on the cadaver by removing certain parts. Those parts wind up on the restaurant menu the next day; the rest goes to the undertaker. Not without a sense of humor, the murderers choose their victims carefully. A woman named Ms. Lamb has her legs removed—you can guess the next day's luncheon special . . .

Originally **The Undertaker and His Pals** featured extensive gore, borrowed (as a cost-cutting measure) from old surgery films. Mikels found this solution to be a bit strong, so he removed most of the surgery footage. His final cut of the film runs barely sixty minutes.

The Corpse Grinders/The Undertaker and His Pals double bill proved to be Mikels' most popular release of all. He followed it with **Blood Orgy of the She Devils**, about witchcraft, exorcism and reincarnation among a group of witches in California. Many newspapers refused to advertise the film's full title . . .

1974 saw the release of **The Doll Squad** (aka **Seduce and Destroy**) about an elite group of female CIA undercover agents. Mikels is convinced his film was the source for the popular TV show, **Charlie's Angels**. Partly for her exotic looks and partly for her knowledge of karate, Mikels again cast Tura Satana in a lead role.

Besides writing and directing, Mikels has produced almost all his own films and a few by others. His most notorious production is **The Worm Eaters**, about an old eccentric who turns people into monsters by feeding them worms. They're supposed to be giant worm-creatures, but they look more like people stuck in their sleeping bags. The film stars and was directed by Herb Robins, a talented actor familiar to any fan of Ray Dennis Steckler's films. It's a comedy, but Robins' sense of humor is so askew that the film resembles a horror movie for three-year-olds.

Another film Mikels produced is **The Aftermath**, a low-budget feature shot around Los Angeles. After a disastrous premiere, Steve Barkett, its director/star refused to release it. Briefly, the film is about an astronaut who returns to Earth and finds civilization shot to hell. He adopts a boy and teaches him to be muy macho, and the boy repays the favor by helping the man blow away villains and bad guys.

Other films T.V. Mikels has produced or directed (or both) include **Cruise Missile**, an action-adventure spy thriller shot at German, Italian, Spanish and U.S. locations; **Ten Violent Women**, an action-psychodrama about women taking women's lib to a criminal degree and ending up in jail; **Devil's Gambit**, a martial arts undercover drama involving two large oil and energy conglomerates and featuring **Tiger Yang**; **Kill The Dragon**, a martial arts adventure partially shot in Spain; **Space Angels**, a galactic space fantasy of futuristic intrigue; and **Operation Overkill**, again featuring Tiger Yang in a CIA campaign against terrorists. He recently finished directing a film which Ray Dennis Steckler started, **The Survivalists** (tentative title) and is planning many more movies . . . ■

PARTIAL FILMOGRAPHY

AS DIRECTOR-PRODUCER:
Strike Me Deadly, 1963
The Doctors, 1963
One Shocking Moment (aka **Suburban Affair**), 1964
The Black Klansman, (aka **I Crossed the Color Line**), 1965
The Astro Zombies, 1967
The Girl in Gold Boots, 1968
The Corpse Grinders, 1972
Blood Orgy of the She Devils, 1973
The Doll Squad (aka **Seduce and Destroy**), 1974
Alex Joseph & His Wives (aka **The Rebel Breed**), 1978
Ten Violent Women, 1982
Devil's Gambit, 1982
Space Angels, 1985
Operation Overkill, 1985

AS PRODUCER:
The Undertaker & His Pals, 1965
The Worm Eaters, 1965
Cruise Missile, 1980
Kill the Dragon, 1983

Note: Mikels served as cameraman on **Jungle Hell** (1956), **Day of the Nightmare** (1965), **Night of the Beast** aka **House of the Black Death** (1965), **The Hostage** (1966), **Agent For H.A.R.M.** (1966), **Catalina Caper** (1967), **Snow Monsters** (n.d.), **Ghouls and Dolls** (n.d.), **Children Shouldn't Play with Dead Things** (1972), and other films.

The Astro-Zombies

Probably the best-known filmmaker in this book is Russ Meyer—the Washington Post called him "practically an American institution." Classic films he's made include **Mudhoney, Lorna, Beyond the Valley of the Dolls** and **Faster Pussycat! Kill! Kill!** His 1959 movie **The Immoral Mr. Teas** singlehandedly paved the way for the entire nudie-cutie genre and the later hardcore films that continue to this day. As a force for advancing sexual freedom of expression, Russ Meyer has earned his fame.

Some of the largest-breasted women to walk the earth appear in Meyer's movies, distracting viewers from the fact that his films often present serious socio-critical content and complex moral dilemmas. Characterized by extreme behavior approaching mythic proportions, his films consistently reveal a sense of humor sometimes crass but usually insightful.

Russ Meyer was born March 21, 1922 in San Leandro, California. When he was 14 his mother bought him a movie camera and that immediately launched an obsession that stretched into a life's career. In World War II he worked as a photographer and cameraman, and after the army photographed Hollywood films (e.g., **Giant, Guys and Dolls**) until his "break" in 1959 when he directed **The Immoral Mr. Teas,** immediately reaping a fortune. To date Meyer has made more than twenty features. Recently he remarked, "I have to pay homage to the women in my films and the success they've given me."

Russ Meyer was interviewed at his Hollywood home which was filled with shrines to friends living and dead, and his own movie posters in languages from Tagalog to Danish. Jim Morton asked the questions.

■ *JIM MORTON: I've heard a lot about* The Breast of Russ Meyer. *What's that?*
■ RUSS MEYER: Twelve hours of unfettered beauty, great history and humor! I've been working on it for five years, I've got a million and a half dollars of my own money in it, and it's going to be a sensational film. But I refuse to stop fishing and womanizing and having epicurean meals and generally having a good time, so it'll be ready when it's ready. I estimate in about two to three years—there's a big job ahead of me yet.
■ *JM: Is it going to be released as a movie or a video?*
■ RM: It's too long—it's 12 hours. See—I'm making a film for myself. It's an enjoyable position for a filmmaker to be in; to make a film just for himself. What I mean by that is: I don't have to make any money; it's not necessary. It *will* make a lot of money in video, but that is so far off, just with what it takes to make a video master the way I go through it, with scene-by-

scene color corrections. It will show at festivals like the Cinemathéque Francais or the National Film Theatre in London; already I've been invited to a number of them. So it will be my song. I think the unique thing about the film is that to my knowledge no filmmaker has ever made a film of himself.
■ *JM: Probably not intentionally, anyway.*
■ RM: No, not even intentionally or unintentionally. It will have a ring of truth about it and, I think, also interest and entertainment value. Usually films about a director follow a format; it's generally: get six or seven of John Huston's associates together and we'll shoot 'em and they'll tell little vignettes from his life, and then show the beauty of John Huston's story—some great film clips. The beauty of George Stevens is not his military footage or his friends, it's the great film clips. I have great film clips (which aren't clips, they're condensations of all my films) but I have more—my own particular brand of humor ... World War II footage ... footage of me revisiting the places, photographing friends that I've known through the years. Instead of having them stare at the camera—if the guy's a farmer or if he's a painter or if he sells hamburgers, I photograph him doing that while he's reflecting and talking in voice-over. It's an amazing picture; it's mindboggling to think of the number of scenes I've shot, in addition to compressing 23 films down to 10-15 minutes each.

> I refuse to stop fishing and womanizing and having epicurean meals and generally having a good time, so it'll be ready when it's ready.

■ *JM: So the film will be almost like a book?*
■ RM: Exactly. I'm writing my song. Curiously, a German chap—I've known him for a long time—had obtained an assignment to do a book on me and came over and spent a long time here. I've got ninety volumes of clippings (which we built this cabinet for). But I'm afraid he didn't do a very good job—I'm rewriting it. He was incorrect in the synopses and like most Germans he has no sense of humor. He also did a little bit of the "Philadelphia Enquirer" (which we had an understanding wouldn't be done) in that he assassinated a number of characters in the film—friends of mine—for the sake of trying to get into the Teutonic mind something that's sensational. I think it's really bad, so we have levied upon them: publish it and be forewarned! [laughs knowingly] Anyway, that's the end of the story.

However, the point I'm making is: it's going to be a good book. I have three publishers who want it: one in France, one in England, and one here in the 'States. I'm doing all the synopses and I'm writing them in a very florid style that I didn't think I could pull off—the writing is like the films, with adjective upon adverb, unending punctuation, dots, dashes, etc. What I've been doing is in a sense writing the narration for my big film. So it has value ...

Tura Satana in action in **Faster Pussycat, Kill! Kill!**

■ *JM: Your films usually have fairly heavy narration.*
■ RM: That's because I have a very strong background in documentary films. After the war, I worked for four years doing—we can call them documentary, but they were more employer-relations films for oil companies, paper mills, railroads, things of that nature. I worked for a producer in San Francisco, and it was a great training ground for me. I've always loved the documentary format with the serious, intoning narrator. And generally at the end there'll be a scene where we try to straighten everything out by reviewing the film and pointing out where a character went wrong, or point out the characters' shortcomings and frailties—things of that nature. It adds to the whole tongue-in-cheek aspect of the movies.

■ *JM: Educational and industrial films can be quite wonderful—*
■ RM: They don't seem to make them like they used to. They're too loose now; I think television has had a lot of influence. The older ones were really marvelous; *well* structured, maybe hambone by today's standards. A lot of my stuff seems almost unintentionally funny now.
■ *JM: John Ford directed an old "training" film called* Sexual Hygiene.
■ RM: I'm familiar with it—remember the guy with the soft chancre in his throat! It was always *dreadful* to look at. In the army they would terrorize us with that—remember the short arm and the chancres and the guy in the crib: "Honest, doc, I won't do it again!" I often thought it would make an interest-

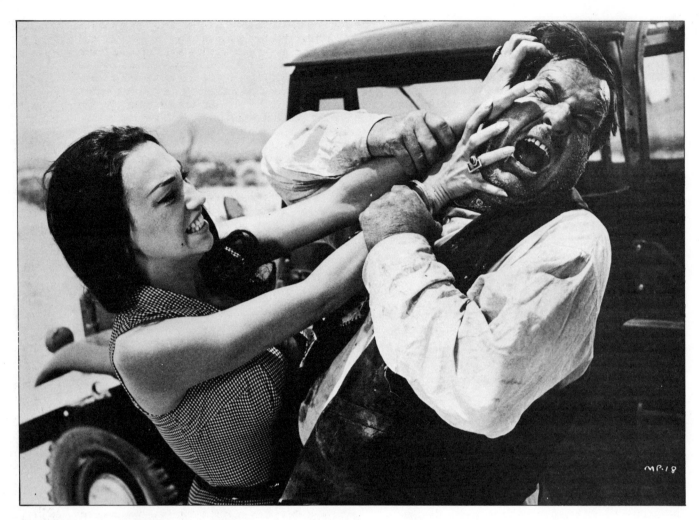

Haji in action in **Motor Psycho.**

ing film: to take that and intercut it with my kind of drama, then cut to these [venereal sores]. I'm afraid, though, the military wouldn't release it to me for that purpose.

■ *JM: You could show lots of terrible slides interspliced with Playboy bunny pictures. Incidentally, where do you find your women? I walk down streets all the time and never see anybody quite like—*

■ RM: There's only a very few, and I've been fortunate to find a few of them. Those that I find and can't use, it's either because of a difficult boyfriend or a husband who doesn't

> I've always loved the documentary format with the serious, intoning narrator. At the end there'll be a scene where we try to straighten everything out by reviewing the film and pointing out where a character went wrong, or point out the characters' shortcomings and frailties.

want the bird to flee the nest, as it were. That's the most-asked question in interviews. That, or, "Does your mother have big breasts?" They kind of go even-Steven.

By and large the girls are from the show business world—premiere strippers that make four or five thousand a week, or

others that someone will recommend to me. They're not easy to find; in fact, I'm arduously searching for two more. I've got five superwomen in the new film intercut throughout the opening which is seventy-eighty minutes long, and I need to find two or three more. Hard to find, very difficult.

■ *JM: They also have a certain larger-than-life quality to them. I remember watching* Faster Pussycat *and you had Susan Bernard, the Playmate, in it and she looked like a tiny dinky thing compared to Haji and Tura.*

■ RM: She was a little squirt, very definitely. In *Playboy,* when you get that foldout, it's pretty hard to tell how tall anybody is unless you look at the spec's. By and large women are not that tall, you know. If you get a woman that's five foot seven, that's pretty tall for a lady. In the instance of Tura, she was wearing boots and she was so voluptuous—big hat, big pair of hips, big boobs—a great Juno-esque looking lady . . .

■ *JM: She takes on a kind of mythical quality in that film.*

■ RM: A lot of people draw all sorts of conclusions about it . . . "Gotterdammerung" . . . "Flight of the Valkyries." She's part Cherokee and part Japanese; her father was a well-known chef in a restaurant in Chicago. That was one of the few times I've really lucked out in casting a role—I couldn't have found another girl that had the configuration, and really knew judo and karate and was as strong as a fucking ox, and had never acted before. She'd been a stripper. Another time was when we found Z-man who played SuperWoman in *Beyond the Valley of the Dolls.* We could never have found another man who would have done that whole Shakespearean shit and the whole works. He still to this day believes that I ruined his career—he didn't have much of a career to begin with, but—he's another one. I don't mean him any disrespect, 'cause he made that part.

And again with Charles Napier, the guy with all the teeth who was in *Supervixens*—without him, the film wouldn't have had anywhere near the kind of success it had—I'm certain—in spite of the big boobs and seven girls. Napier, I think, has a quality that few actors possess: Wallace Beery, Borgnine, Alan Hale. There can be just a thin edge separating evil and humor, and they can work both sides of that line. Napier's got that quality: smiling on one side of the mouth and sneering on the other. He's had his good shot now with a picture called *Rambo*, and I think he may be off and running. He wants very much to be Clint Eastwood but I think he's just a great character-type. Who knows? Who would have known that Bronson would have such great success?

> Z-man played SuperWoman in **Beyond the Valley of the Dolls**. We could never have found another man who would have done that whole Shakespearean shit and the whole works. He still to this day believes that I ruined his career.

■ *JM: It was a rather long time before he made it, too. People always talk about your women, but I notice that certain male characters show up in your films, like Napier and—*
■ RM: Stuart Lancaster. I have a band of players. Lancaster was in *Mudhoney*: Uncle Luke with the bad heart, kindly and totally good, always rising to the defense of his niece. He played the narrator on *Ultravixens* which was a take-off on *Our Town*—remember the man who would sit at the corner of the stage and say, "Well, I don't know what's going to happen. We'll see what's going to happen tomorrow when the sun comes up." I didn't use him exactly that way, but that was what it was patterned after. Super guy, but never having done anything, largely because he inherited a fortune from his mother. But she was wise enough to set it up in a trust so he gets, I think, $8,000 a month. He spends it every month. If he had gotten all the money, he would have made/produced 200 bad plays—he's *really* into theater. Dave Friedman said that the first sum of money he got was $400,000, and it all went in like two months, producing plays.
■ *JM: Another male character that comes to mind is Hal Hopper—what a sleazy guy!*
■ RM: Poor Hal, he's passed on. Hal wrote an all-time great song, "There is No You." He was one of the Modernaires. It's hard to imagine him sitting there by the microphone singing . . . He was brought to my attention by an actor named James Griffin. Hal made a great nasty son-of-a-bitch . . . but he was also the guardian of little Jay North of *Dennis the Menace*. So here's this whole other side of him. He's gone now, regrettably. In *Mudhoney* he had *no* redeeming qualities; at least in *Lorna* he did an about-face—he realized that he had met more than his match. I wanted to use him again in *Beyond the Valley of the Dolls* but he was very ill. I've always felt comfortable using certain people, like Haji—she's been in a lot of my films; she's just a great standard-bearer. Even today she really looks great.
■ *JM: She's one of the few women characters that crop up again and again in your films.*
■ RM: She's been in *Beyond the Valley of the Dolls; Motor Psycho!; Faster Pussycat, Kill! Kill!; Good Morning and Goodbye*—very substantial part in that. She was in *Supervixens* and *Up!* With some of these people I feel *comfortable*.

Trouble is, with girls—generally I use them once and not again. It's almost like having a wondrous affair, even though I might not have one—I have an affair with the camera with them. I think I've extracted all the vital juices that are available for a given film, and I think there's a great shot in the ass if you have someone new to work with for the next picture. But in a supporting role it isn't quite the same thing. I've only used Haji as the main lady in one film—*Motor Psycho*. The others she was always in a secondary position.

The girls often don't have the same kind of freshness and newness; often they don't have the same kind of dedication. There's a tendency to not take it as seriously the second time. Maybe they're thinking a little too much; maybe they're listening to too much pillow talk—I don't know what it is. That's a tough one for a director that's dealing with matters sexual—to fight off that pillow talk when they go home at night. The "ace" I call it—the husband or boyfriend who is terribly insecure himself and has got to give them a lot of advice. In the morning when you start up again you can sense that someone's been feeding that chick's computer, and you've got to try and work around it—listen and discard things.

Anyway, to put it very simply: it's a miracle that these films are ever completed. Just a miracle. I mean the emotional problems, the insecurity, the loss of interest after three or four days, and all the cajoling and bullshitting and ass-kissing and ass-licking—it's a miracle the films are finished—certainly mine.
■ *JM: Is that your first camera there?*
■ RM: No; I have a couple of shrines in this house. This house was bought to film *Beneath the Valley of the Ultravixens*—you can see some scars on the ceiling. I bought it because of this room—we built all the sets in this room. It did not have that big bookcase, it was just a completely big room and then I converted it into an office and a work area and now it's my second home. I stay here occasionally and edit films.

That shrine there is for a Chinese chap (an American); he and I shot movies together when I was 14 or 15 years of age; he recently passed away. He was instrumental in my getting my first job before World War II. His wife gave me this camera and that's my little shrine for Henry . . .

Over there I have another camera that belonged to an old

Beyond the Valley of the Dolls.

army buddy who just passed away, who was more brother-like than just about anybody I've every known. The one lower with an exposure meter in it is for the camerman who was in the service with me, who shot a lot of series like "Twilight Zone" and "Hatari," and he also shot my *Seven Minutes*. He was a combat cameraman in the Spanish Civil War.

They're my little shrines—at their husbands' behest their wives have given me these things because we were so terribly close. It's nice to walk by them and stop for a moment and reflect on the individual. Displayed is the one object—or objects—that really represents the basis of our friendship—the one indentifying thing that can bring it to a point immediately. I think of Henry—I think about that camera.

> **In the instance of Tura, she was wearing boots and she was so voluptuous—big hat, big pair of hips, big boobs—a great Juno-esque looking lady.**

■ *JM: When did you get your first camera?*
■ RM: I think I was 14. My mother got me a Univex—it's the camera that probably did more for home movies than anything Eastman Kodak ever came up with. It sold for $9.95 and the film was 60¢ a roll—orthochromatic Single-8 (meaning sprocket holes down one side). The projector was $14.95. By today's standards that might be fifty dollars, but it was the thing that got me by the short hairs. I tell you, when I got that camera, from then on every nickel I could get my hands on went to upgrading and so on. It got me into the services as a G.I cameraman, simply because of my very strong amateur background.
■ *JM: Getting back to the leading ladies, Edy Williams—*

■ RM: Edy Williams plays Edy Williams better than anybody else in the world! She did a pretty good job with *Seven Minutes*. The film wasn't so successful because I was told I had to have an R rating (and when I say X, I mean an MPAA X: not hardcore but softcore). It just doesn't have the content, and people do react to it in a poor way, but Edy did a pretty good job on that.

We were married for four years or so. I think the best thing she ever did (and not just because I was involved) was *Beyond the Valley of the Dolls*. She gets a great reaction in the theater every time it's shown. She's been in a lot of other, much lesser films, but I have to admire her—she's in there trying all the time and does her publicity and—here's a recent picture—she still manages to look very good. But I couldn't have used her as leading lady because you've got to have a little more control over a person than your wife. There's a tendency for things to not go as smoothly as when you're working with a stranger.

I have to take one exception: that's my wife Eve—wonderful lady whom I lived with for 12 years. She was killed in Tenerife in a terrible airplane crash. We did *Eve and The Handyman* together. There were just four of us: the guy who played the handyman, my assistant, and Eve, and she cooked for us and we really had a tight thing. She said "Okay, half of this is my money, I like the idea of doing it, and let's do it," and she broke her ass—there was never any static from her. She just said, "Look, whatever you want to do, let's do it, okay? I'm here, I'll get up early in the morning and I'll look right" and so on. She was special in that area and in many other areas as well, but with her I could do it, you know.

But I would never have given Edy a shot at being a lead—there would have been head problems, definitely. There's a tendency to have a wife take advantage of her position, and I'm not just talking about her, but I'm sure any filmmaker—there have been occasions where they've used their wives

Tura Satana again.

Scene from Common Law Cabin.

and it's not been a good idea. I guess that's one of the reasons why I've tried to be at arm's length with the leading lady and not have any hanky-panky; a couple of times I did—three times, four times—and it really wasn't best for the picture.

> **The last lady was Kitten Natividad—we were very close, we lived together for four years and she was fine, because she was a total sex object and a sex machine and she knew that what we were doing was going to be beneficial to her.**

The last lady was Kitten Natividad—we were very close, we lived together for four years and she was fine, because she was a total sex object and a sex machine and she knew that what we were doing was going to be beneficial to her, and it's proven to be because she was able to get more money. But

she liked it, she liked that whole thing of turning on people; it was a big game and it was fun, you know. She never had any real big aspirations of becoming some kind of "actress" or anything like that, but she did fine, she did very well. She came equipped with what I need for a leading lady more than anything else. She had a great body and she had done a lot of fucking in her time, so she knew all the positions and everything in the way of turning on a guy—two necessary prerequisites for the success of any leading lady's performance in one of my films. But, when you get that passionate intimacy, there's a tendency (*I* think) that either person will take advantage of the other. Best to be at arm's length, I've found.

A great lady I really cared for—we'd been together quite a while—played the deaf-mute in *Mudhoney*. Very pretty lady. We had become intimate years before when I was in Germany shooting *Fanny Hill*—that's where I met her, and then I brought her over. One night she decided she didn't want to appear naked in front of the whole crew, and no matter what I said, like: "You did it in Berlin and there were fifty Germans hanging around," she would reply, "Well, it's different now." I ended up very angry. There's an example of being placed

Publicity shot from **Finders Keepers, Lovers Weepers**.

in a position where you're getting your nuts wrung out. Sure, you could do several things—you could punch her out and then you fuck up your picture, and I'm not prone to punching women out anyway. Or, you can have a giant fight, somehow managing to force her to do what you wanted and not getting the results—the only best way then is to break your ass and do the best you can ... Anyway, it worked out, but it affected my feelings toward the lady for as long as we were together from there on out, because it represented a down deep solid lack of trust ...

There can be just a thin edge separating evil and humor.

■ *JM: When you work with a person all day long, and then come home at night and see them there as well, sometimes—*
■ RM: No, no, the women I've known have been turn-ons. I'm lusting all day for them. Even if I'm not having them I'm lusting for them—it's very healthy to feel that lust. They're great enough—we can bear witness that it's difficult to tire them early in the game. Unless you're a fuckin' wooden Indian ...
■ *JM: When you started making films did you come up with a story and say, "Hey, this would make a great sexploi-tation movie?"*
■ RM: I didn't know what sexploitation *was*. *The Immoral Mr. Teas* was the first breakthrough film in the sense that it popularized and established the "nudie." It was Number

One; as *Time* said, "it opened up the floodgates of permissive-ness as we know it in these United States." *Teas* simply was an idea which I scripted out in a document and we shot it in four days. I knew exactly how it was going to begin, I knew how it would be in the middle, and I knew how it would be in the end. It was based on my experiences doing stills for *Playboy*. There's a lot of stuff on the girl-next-door, the common man, the voyeur—little nude photo essays. So *Teas* was a film that was imitated by so many people—I imitated it, in a sense. I did *Eve and the Handyman* and I made other nudie films, but *Teas* was a huge, huge success and it's still a collector's piece. *Teas* came out in '59 and it's still kicking.

[pointing to photo of man] He's up in Frisco. I've done some filming with him; we were a tight group. He was in the army with me; he was an army photographer, so we see each other as often as we can—a friendship extending past 40 years. In fact next week I go to Philadelphia, and we'll have a reunion in Bloomington, Delaware, then have one down south. I'm kind of a ringleader-historian. All those guys played a pretty heavy role in my life and in my films, too.
■ *JM: There's a certain almost "G.I." quality to your humor—*
■ RM: Best time of my life, I'll tell you that. Never had a better time—I was sorry to see the war end. People say, "What?" but I was sorry to see it end; I was ready to go to Japan, the whole shot, you know—the damn bomb interfered with all that. 'Cause I had a feeling like, "Son-of-a-bitch, I'm having such a good time, I'm doing just what I want to do, it's exciting; what kind of a job can I get when I get out? How can I get some kind of a job?" And it worried me: "God, what if I have to go back to that same job I had before?" I liked very

82

much that whole living by your wits, with each day being a new piece of excitement. I had mixed emotions about coming home; I probably was the only one in my group who felt that way. Everyone else wanted to go back to Alabama and start a family and all that. Not me, I just: "Gung ho, let's do it again!" Just like I feel about my art now: I'd like to start it all over.

■ *JM: When you got out of the army you went to Hollywood?*
■ RM: I just got off the train here. With the other guy that was with me—just fishing—we went over to the studios. We went to the union to see about getting a job and they said, "Forget it, we got guys that are gonna get their jobs back." So I went home to San Francisco/Oakland—I even went back to my old job for about a month. Then I managed to find this industrial job which was great for me. However, I have the feeling that I would not have given in—that I certainly would have been persistent.

> I would never have given Edy a shot at being a lead—there would have been head problems, definitely. There's a tendency to have a wife take advantage of her position.

■ *JM: Well, your memorabilia here is a testament to that.*
■ RM: You haven't even seen the other room yet, with props from each picture. As fast as I find something that I want to put on a plaque, I will. I'm starting to put them on the ceiling now—great ceiling for that purpose, slanted like that. My films are having a great rebirth in Germany, France and England now.
■ *JM: There's a French book on your films.*
■ RM: It's a book by my distributors; Jean-Pierre Jackson wrote it. The captions are all wrong, but otherwise it's great! There was one photo of that great big black woman, June Mack, titled "Erica Gavin."

That's why I'm so concerned about this movie [*The Breast of Russ Meyer*]; it's damn well going to be right. I like the video aspect of it, too—projectionists can no longer cut scenes out of it. Projectionists are great slide collectors—they cut out two or three frames and then crudely splice it so the action goes WHAAAP! and the soundtrack ends up harsh. But in video you can't do that. You buy it, and you can go over the juicy roles over and over again.
■ *JM: Video seems to be opening up a whole new market for sexploitation films from the '60s.*
■ RM: For me there aren't many that hang in there. Fortunately I have a big, strong following and it grows. Not many softcore—not many hardcore films, for that matter, have become real classics. You can count six or seven hardcore films that are steady sellers—Radley Metzger's stuff (he goes under the name of Henry Paris or something like that), and *Deep Throat*, of course, which is like *Mr. Teas;* it started the whole shooting match.
■ *JM: The hardcore pretty much drove out the softcore.*
■ RM: I never suffered, but of course there wasn't really much good softcore except mine. There were some things like Jonathan Demme's *Caged Heat* and so on—films that prefer not to be called softcore, but there's nudity, a plot and whatever.

When hardcore came in I was over at Fox making $150,000 for five months' work and doing a couple of films. All those other guys were jumping in there making these hardcore movies and I was making a film that was so-called big time, you know. When hardcore was at its strongest I made a picture called *Blacksnake!* which was the only unsuccessful film I ever made. I thought it was a great idea,

but it was about two or three years too late with its slavery aspect. It played mainstream houses.

Hardcore has always been at some shadowy little place where you skulked in and out, with the exception of *Deep Throat*—women went to that because it became so popularized. The others were all guys in raincoats. That's one good thing about hardcore now—people can take it home. You don't have to parade into a theater.
■ *JM: I've been to a few adult theaters; they're kind of depressing.*
■ RM: Now they're really falling by the wayside—folding very fast. Video, of course, is killing them off. People can rent it rather than go to the theater. But still there's nothing like looking at something—I don't care what it is—on a big screen in a dark auditorium—it's great! And until they get video in some *size* you're going to always have that comparison. People like to sit at home and be lazy and look at video, but it doesn't have the *quality*. My stuff I dub from the negative, with scene-by-scene color corrections, but even so there's nothing to replace something being projected on the screen. This *Breast* will be a monster, just considering the scenes there are in it.
■ *JM: Are you going to have somebody else playing yourself?*
■ RM: Oh no, it's me. Throughout I introduce the films in a kind of P.T. Barnum way, and it's not bad. If it's me and I'm doing it, it works, you know—I'm a type, I'm a character, I'm not acting—I'm just introducing. In the beginning I'm driving a car and I go to Europe and retrace my steps from Ireland to England to Normandy, Omaha Beach and so on. I'm driving a Mercedes, then I cut to my black-and-white GI footage. And there's always a girl like Kitten in the back seat playing with herself naked, but I'm not aware of it. And I have a narration (which I haven't written yet) which has got to be unpretentious, just matter-of-fact—not trying to be funny or anything—just reflections. I've got some pretty good photography of me driving the car, stopping and looking, and then I move down to the city ... go down the road and there's Tammie Roshea—now *there's* some cups! Great lady—she's intrigued watching the Mercedes go by. She represents the guardian angel. Then you cut to a room/window and there's Candy Samples doing something to herself. It's for the audience to realize that they are in the right theater. There's this referral, this new stuff all the time.

> The Immoral Mr. Teas was the first breakthrough film in the sense that it popularized and established the "nudie."

■ *JM: Tammie Roshea—did you use her in any films?*
■ RM: No. She's a great stripper; I met her through Kitten. She's got a great body; she'll be awesome in the picture.
■ *JM: I just got a magazine from France called* Nostalgia. *It seems like the French picked up on what you were doing quicker than the Americans.*
■ RM: Yeah, but they had a lot of time to get ready. If it wasn't for my distributor—a real film buff—I don't think we'd be playing as well as we play. He was a schoolteacher; he got out of schoolteaching and decided he wanted to distribute these films because he believed in them so strongly. Now we get calls from people wondering if there's any others where the rights have not been given to Mr. Jackson ... so I owe him a great deal.
■ *JM: ... Tura Satana is a woman that everybody likes—*
■ RM: She appeals to gays, lesbians, the whole bag, everybody. She has a very strong following now with young people. Musicians look upon *Pussycat* as a remarkable film; Warner Bros wanted to use an excerpt for some new female group on

MTV but I turned it down, period. It's gratifying to have young people today see and hear it—I get phone calls, "Where can I get the soundtrack?" or "I heard there were T-shirts," and so on. Tura's developed into a real heroine, or anti-heroine; whatever.

■ *JM: A group called* The Cramps *does a cover version of* Faster Pussycat.... *There's something about Shari Eubanks that really appeals to me.*

> Strangely enough, what I've achieved on film with her and her brother really represents the kind of way I like to screw—I mean like a football scrimmage. That's the way I like it—I don't want any funny stuff or all this cocksucking and everything else—I just want to get in there and whale away at it.

■ RM: She wasn't so outrageous in her body (although she had a great body and a real presence), but ... She got in with some guy that kind of screwed her around, but she did end up pretty well—she inherited an awful lot of money from her family. I admired her; I liked her very much. She had balls, she had real guts.

We were traveling, promoting the film in the Midwest—her home was Farmer City, Ill. I had to go to Milwaukee and I remarked, "Well, they got an opening in Champaign" and she said, "I'll go." I said, "That's awfully near to your home, isn't it?" She replied, "I might as well" and went down there and it turned out a huge share of the audience knew her.

She sat next to her father (who is an ex-G.I.) and I said, "God, you got guts." (*I* didn't want to sit next to him, he'd probably punch me out.) She did something where she's sitting up on this peak, nude, and her father shouted, "MAH GOD, SHARI!"—you could hear it all over the auditorium. She retorted, "I told you you weren't supposed to come see the film!" She could handle it, you know. I never met the family, but they probably would have stoned me or something.

Shari was gung-ho; there was never an ounce of trouble with her—she just loved doing what she was doing. We always had a lot of privation, difficult conditions—no showers, sometimes—and she was there—she carried water, carried the battery up the road. I'll take my hat off to her.

Ushi Digart's another great trouper. She was in a number of films—very special lady. I've really been privileged to know some great people.

Most filmmakers are generally not one-to-one on a project; they have a lot of people who are sharing responsibilities. Whereas I've always done a kind of one-man band, where there's something like an umbilical cord tying me to one or two of the people, where you have that tight feeling and that dependency on one another to make the whole damn thing work—and I think how fortunate I've been to have had people like Shari Eubanks or Ushi Digart or Kitten Natividad. All these ladies and I had a communion, a marvelous communion, and a meeting of the minds. It went beyond just being an actress in some kind of little television show, because we were doing so many little things together. It was like qualifying for the Olympics every day—it was the 440 and the high hurdles and everything all rolled into one. And they performed, they did it with a minimum of complaints, and rebounded at night when we had dinner and enjoyed the evening, then got a good night's sleep and got out of bed at five o'clock in the morning and they're putting on body makeup, you know ...

Brother and sister conserve water and have fun doing it in Vixen.

Once we were up in this cabin where I had shot *Vixen;* we went back to do *Up!* Makeup always has kind of a heady odor, and I walked in and both Ushi and Kitten were naked (Ushi just sleeps in the raw; she had a great body), and I said, "God, it smells like breasts in here!" It broke them up; they never forgot that line. There was something about this musk odor that was permeating the entire room, and here were these two women with giant tits making them up and so on and I was smelling breasts—sounds like a W.C. Fields line.

> **Never had a better time—I was sorry to see the war end. People say, "What?" but I was sorry to see it end; I was ready to go to Japan, the whole shot, you know—the damn bomb interfered with all that.**

This umbilical cord thing—I don't know if I explained it quite the way I feel it. I've always been my own man, but when I worked at Fox I was dealing with an awful lot of people, trying to outwit an awful lot of boyfriends and outside influences, and I was in town—which made it very difficult to isolate these people from bad influences, because they go home at night. You can't sequester them there on the lot. When I'm in Miranda, Ca, we have an arrangement: no boyfriends come up, no husbands come up. We're up here, we're going to do it in three weeks; hang in there until we get the film done, okay? And that's what I meant by becoming close (and I don't mean it in a purely physical sense): working together, arguing, fighting, cooking, eating good food, having a drink, swearing, whatever—"God, my feet hurt," and all that . . . nobody to really cater to them and kiss their ass as they do in these major productions. It brought out the best and the worst in all of us.

■ *JM: Sounds like good times.*

■ RM: You just felt it down there in your own scrotum when you're shooting a scene. I know when I was shooting *Vixen,* the scene with Erica Gavin and her brother was the best of them all. She really displayed an animal quality that I've never been able to achieve ever before—the way she grunted and hung in there and did her lines. It was a really remarkable job; I have to point to her always. I've done a lot of jokey screwing, but there's something about Erica and her brother there that was just remarkable. Nothing made the adrenalin flow like that—that was a great experience.

■ *JM: That whole movie seemed more intentionally erotic; your other films are more like ribald humor.*

■ RM: I wonder about the word "erotic"; a German I know uses the word all the time. I said, "Do you mean filming through a bunch of dirty wine bottles . . . people caressing each other?" Europeans have a kind of feeling for this kind of eroticism; it's totally unlike what I feel, I know.

When I was rewriting the synopsis on *Vixen* I'd just finished that particular part about her brother and I said, "Strangely enough, what I've achieved on film with her and her brother really represents the kind of way I like to screw—I mean like a football scrimmage. That's the way I like it—I don't want any funny stuff or all this cocksucking and everything else—I just want to get in there and whale away at it." And this is what her brother was doing. If you're going to thrust at the woman [knocks rapidly on the table], I want her to meet me halfway! You know—just strong physical fucking. And here it is, and that's the thing that I like—it's part of me.

When you see her in that scene when she's hanging onto the iron bedstead (I love the iron bedstead because that *really* represents the basic workbench in life, with the rungs you can hang onto), and she was just grunting almost animalistic, like the mating of the wildebeest and the water

buffalo—wonderful, wonderful stuff.

■ *JM: I think "erotic" means it gives you a hard-on.*

■ RM: Exactly. The Germans and the French—it's not the same feeling. I get tired of them when they talk about, "Well this isn't really erotic." Maybe "erotic" is *sick* or something! Give me the good ol' American way, with lots of grunts and cum in cunts—you know, get in there and whale away at it.

I have a girlfriend now that's that way—no foreplay, nothing, just climb on and do it. That's wonderful. You feel great about it . . . I say you need a girl who just yells.

I told this one lady, "I read where women need something like four minutes to get ready for sex," and she says, "Well, I'm more like 22." And even now she'll do it; she'll call, "22! 16! 12!" You're walking upstairs with a hard-on, and she's like a viscous sponge. She's so in tune with her whole mind—remarkable lady to get laid. And that's transferred to me as a person. So I'm living a film fantasy right then and there. It's marvelous to have that kind of union with somebody, where you just *have* each other and then you (exhales deeply) say, "Okay, let's do something else here, take a swim, whatever . . ."

■ *JM: Were any of the women in these films difficult to make movies with?*

■ RM: Every one of them had a moment of some difficulty, just as I'm sure I came off as being one son-of-a-bitch at times. When I said earlier that it's been a miracle that every one of these films was finished, well, every damn film I ever made had monstrous problems, there's no question about it. For example, after three days of filming I was looking at one girl through the reflex and she stuck her tongue out at me—not in a jokey way, but really pissed off. And I remembered what Preminger told me one time: "You treat these actors like cattle—don't treat them like human beings." And from then on I was really a very difficult guy: never said anything rewarding about the performance, never complimented her, I barely spoke to her. I would use my assistant to say, "This is what we're going to do." And that girl did such a better job; she became so apprehensive about me, and whether or not she was *pleasing* me from the standpoint of doing a good job on the film. See—it worked. It wasn't a master stroke but I *had* to do something; I knew I was losing grip there.

Sometimes people get a little too merry or too funny, laughing it up, so I'll have to say, "C'mon, we've got to be serious about it. I want you to break your ass; now stop it—enough of this lunch break!" So each woman presents a problem—no question about it, and they wouldn't be special ladies if they didn't have some sort of problem to present. If they were some kind of mush-bag that you could . . .

One time I had a girl quit in the middle of a film. She quit because she couldn't handle the privations—she was used to Miami Beach.

Ushi Digart—we threw her into *Cherry, Harry and Raquel,* and we used her as a wraith-like character who ran through the scenes and did strange things. A guy named Cohen, who is a critic for *Women's Wear Daily,* wrote, "I can't explain the presence of Ushi Digart cast in the role of 'Soul' . . . but thank God she's there!" [laughs] That was exactly right. I mean, he said what I felt so much better than I could have ever said it.

So they all present a little bit of a problem, there's no question about it. Actually, Shari Eubanks is one person that never presented a problem—I have to say that in her behalf, rather than to say, "Well, such-and-such was a real bitch at times." In the final analysis we were always able to look at it square in the face and kind of joke about it and laugh and say, "Well, we did it, it's okay, everybody's friends." But Shari never let me down, she was a super lady, and Ushi was the same . . . Ushi never presented a problem, she would extend herself beyond the limit. So I have to say those two ladies are above and beyond any woman I've ever worked with who are 100 percent.

Anyway, I have to go. ■

Russ Meyer is probably the only sexploitation director to garner acclaim from mainstream critics without abandoning the fans or the field of sex films. His movies return us to the days when men were men and women were wet dreams. Meyer likes to describe the women in his films as "pneumatic." An odd word to use for human flesh, perhaps, but Meyer doesn't deal in flesh—he deals in fantasies. The narrator in **Mondo Topless** says it best: "Until now you've only dreamed there were women like these. But they're real! Unbelievably real!"

Meyer got his first camera at the age of fourteen and promptly began filming everything. At the outbreak of World War Two he used the military to pursue his love of film. Assigned to the 166th Signal Photographic Corps, he ended up in Europe filming General Patton's advance toward Germany. Thirty years later, footage by Meyer ended up in the film **Patton**.

After the war Meyer tried getting a job in Hollywood but, finding the way barred by tight union control, he moved to San Francisco and worked as an industrial filmmaker. At the suggestion of army buddy Don Ornitz, Meyer began shooting photos for pin-ups and girlie calendars, and his early work remains some of the best in the field. Several of his photos appeared in early issues of **Playboy** and graced the walls of gas stations and garages all over America.

While working as a photographer Meyer met Pete DeCenzie, an Oakland burlesque owner who convinced him to return to filmmaking. Meyer started by shooting a burlesque film starring stripper extraordinaire, Tempest Storm. By this time, however, the burlesque films of the early fifties were already giving way to nudist movies. DeCenzie wanted Meyer to shoot a nudie, but Meyer was reluctant, for nudies lacked two elements important to him: outstanding bodies, and eroticism.

In 1959 Meyer began filming **The Immoral Mr. Teas,** casting as lead an army pal, Bill Teas. Meyer introduced the perfectionist trademarks his training had engendered: razor-sharp cinematography, parallel montage, excellent sound, and percussive editing. **The Immoral Mr. Teas** broke box office records everywhere; the Wall Street Journal estimated it had inspired 150 imitations within a year. For most people this was the first time they had seen a naked woman on the screen. The plot concerns itself with the misadventures of a dirty old man whose peculiar biological gift is the ability to see every woman in the world naked, whether she is or not. The women in it are gorgeous; the narration bawdy yet straightforward . . . and the "nudie-cuties" were born.

Meyer continued in the same vein with light-hearted, innocuous films like **Eve and the Handyman** (starring his then-wife, who became his associate producer), **The Immoral West** aka **Wild Gals of the Naked West, Erotica, Europe in the Raw** and **Heavenly Bodies.** All were characterized by another Meyer trademark: the deep-voiced, authoritative (and ironic) narration. **Immoral West** was an oddly stark abstraction—almost like a Beckett play—of the cliched elements associated with the "Wild West"—the quick-draw gunfight, fist fight, etc, all tied together by a liquor-drinking narrator. When the box office for nudie-cutie films began to wane, Meyer took a big step: if sex alone wouldn't sell a film, how about a dash of violence to spice things up?

Lorna (1964) was the first in a series of outstanding films in which the bright colors and ultra-pink flesh of earlier efforts is replaced by the starkness of black-and-white. Likewise, the story abandons the earlier happy-go-lucky optimism in favor of a more realistic and downbeat mood.

Lorna is an Erskine Caldwell-like story of a rural couple. The husband, handsome but dumb, loves his wife but doesn't appreciate her need for sex; for him, their monthly two-minute tumbles

are enough. The wife needs more but cannot tell her husband. One day, after hubby has gone to work, Lorna encounters an escaped convict in the woods. The man rapes her, but Lorna doesn't mind—at least it takes him more than two minutes to come. The fugitive returns with Lorna to her house and they engage in more sex play. When the husband comes home the battle is joined, and in the confusion Lorna is killed. Throughout the film a preacher pops up, spouting the Gospel and warning people of their impending doom.

Lorna was a hit and, like **The Immoral Mr. Teas,** opened the floodgates for a host of imitators. It marked the beginning of sexploitation's **noir** period, with the "gosh-I'm-being-naughty" ambience of the nudie-cuties replaced by a meaner, more sadistic attitude. Although Meyer's primary reason for shooting in black-and-white was monetary, it matched the subject matter perfectly—had **Lorna** been shot in color, its impact might well have been diminished.

Meyer's next film was **Fanny Hill,** a color 18th-century period piece shot in Berlin and starring Miriam Hopkins. The elegant costumes and sets seemed out of place in a Meyer film—in fact, two days before the end the producer, Albert Zugsmith, took over the film and did the final edit. Meyer doesn't consider this movie his own.

Back in America, Meyer next filmed **Mudhoney** (1965), another black-and-white profile of rural low-life: Missouri in the '30s. This time the sexual interloper is not an escaped convict, but one who has served his time and seeks to rebuild his life. The husband is not a well-meaning dolt but a vicious miscreant—outstandingly portrayed by Hal Hooper. The wife is (as usual) a gorgeous blonde with excess cleavage. **Mudhoney** is even bleaker than **Lorna.** Resembling a cross between **Tobacco Road** and **The Ox-Bow Incident,** it rails against American morality and religious hypocrisy.

Meyer next explored the genre of the motorcycle film with **Motorpsycho** (1965), about three "bikers" (riding on mopeds!) who go around raping and murdering in a small town in the California desert. After they kill one man's wife, the husband seeks—and gets—revenge. Especially notable for the time is the characterization of the lead heavy as a psychotic Vietnam vet who, in the final conflict, suffers flashbacks that he's killing Vietcong.

The most talked about—and best—movie from Meyer's sex and violence period is easily **Faster Pussycat, Kill! Kill!** (1966) The film stars Tura Satana, a woman whose extreme sexuality and menacing screen presence are unrivaled. The story concerns three go-go dancers who release their tensions after work by driving fast sportscars out to the desert and laughing a lot. A squeaky clean square challenges Varla (Tura Satana), the leader of the pack, to a race. After beating him, she—much to the horror of his young girlfriend—ends up killing him by breaking his back. The trio then abducts the girl and retreats to a secluded ranch owned by a crippled old lecher with two sons: one a mental midget with the body of a Hercules, the other a scholarly milquetoast. With the arrival of the women the fireworks begin.

Faster Pussycat, Kill! Kill! has a rhythm and feel to it that defies description. The dialogue rings in the ear like beat poetry, and some scenes, such as the shoving match between Varla's Porsche and the brawny simpleton, are unforgettable.

At first Varla appears to be nothing more than a sadistic bitch, but by the end of the film she seems almost supernatural. The plot mechanics of the film are similar to those of a monster movie, with Varla the monster. We know she is evil and will die, but we can't help rooting for her; next to her, the "heroes" are a washed-out and bloodless lot.

After **Faster Pussycat,** Meyer shifted back to color with a documentary on large-breasted women entitled **Mondo Topless,** his only non-fiction film. In it, his camera takes a look at the "topless" craze that was sweeping the nation in the mid-sixties, while a narrator offers hilarious insights into what this "new movement" is all about.

By now Meyer had established a standard for quick-witted, sardonic screenplays. **Good Morning . . . and Goodbye** (1967)—Meyer's study of impotence in marriage—is outstanding for Alaina Capri's merciless upbraiding of her husband, and Haji's role as a **femme fantastique** existing in the sex-fevered imagination of the husband. **Common Law Cabin** (1967), set at a rundown, isolated tourist resort, also starred Alaina Capri as a voracious sex huntress with deadly wit, but Babette Bardot (Cf. her primitive fire-dance and dive from a spectacular rock) is equally memorable. **Finders Keepers, Lovers Weepers** (1968), inspired by Don Siegel gangster movies, is about a robbery attempt in a go-go dancing bar that gets out of hand. Memorable parallel montage sequences include a couple making love underwater (in the bar's pool) cut with a demolition derby, and other erotic scenes cut with footage of a little girl and boy in 18th century costume playing and the colored fountains of Century City! In this story, the eruption of violence is the logical result of promiscuity in an insular group.

Vixen (1968), Meyer's next film, was a straightforward narrative of a bush pilot and his oversexed wife who live in the Canadian wilderness. Into their lives are thrust several people, including a black conscientious objector, a militant Irishman and a Royal Canadian Mountie. By the end of the film, **Vixen** (played spectacularly by Erica Gavin) has made love to almost everyone, including a man and his wife, the Mountie, and even her own brother.

In many ways **Vixen** is the progenitor of modern porn. The storyline—something about racism and Vixen's sociopolitical awareness—exists to give the film the "socially redeeming" value necessary (at that time) to stave off prosecution on pornographic grounds. But Meyer, saving the political chatter for the end, first lets the raincoat crowd see what it came for.

Vixen was a hit, shifting the focus away from '60s violence back to more straightforward sex. It cost $76,000 and returned more than $7.5 million at the box office. Upon noticing these figures, a major studio, Twentieth-Century Fox, hired him to do a sequel to **Valley of the Dolls**, a moderately successful film based on Jacqueline Susann's roman á clef about the Hollywood underbelly. Roger Ebert, a young film critic, was hired to write the screenplay, called **Beyond the Valley of the Dolls**. Ebert showed a strong affinity for Meyer's rampaging sexual excesses, and together they came up with the most "Meyeresque" film ever made. When Susann threatened a lawsuit the characters and action were changed, but the name remained the same; a disclaimer denied any similarity to the previous movie.

If there is such a thing as a perfect motion picture, **Beyond the Valley of the Dolls** is it. In a world of Hollywood glitz it combines elements of sexploitation with experimental camerawork; and narration worthy of the best educational film with the bouncy good nature of a Beach Party movie. It has sex and violence, rock 'n' roll, drugs, Nazis, hermaphrodites, lesbians, cripples, blacks, pathos, bathos, and a woman giving head to a .45 automatic . . .

Meyer's next two features were in striking contrast to his previous work. The first was **The Seven Minutes** (1971), based on Irving Wallace's indictment of the censorship process. The title referred to the average amount of time it takes a woman to achieve orgasm. The film implied that all the people in favor of censorship are old, ugly and corrupt, while the people against censorship are young, beautiful and relaxed. While centered on the trial of a man incited to commit rape after reading a "pornographic" novel, most of the movie concerns the search for the author (who of course had written the book under a pseudonym). Lacking Meyer's exuberant sense of humor, the film's commercial failure coincided with the end of his relationship with Fox.

Marking a return to independent productions, **Blacksnake!** (1972, aka **Sweet Suzy**), tried to mix two genres: sexploitation and blaxploitation. Set on an imaginary 19th century Caribbean island and featuring a white lady plantation owner who rules by sex and by the whip, the film begins with the arrival of a British agent who has been sent to find the lady's husband who mysteriously disappeared. After numerous episodes of torture and whipping of slaves interspersed with interracial affairs, he discovers the husband was turned into a zombie. Finally, the slaves revolt and burn down the plantation, killing the tyrannical slaveowners. Despite beautiful color cinematography and some memorable scenes (including a snake in a bathtub, and the white villainess's comeuppance at the end), the film didn't please blacks because of its sexploitation, and didn't please whites because of its blaxploitation.

After two years of false starts in other new directions, Meyer decided to return to his familiar—and successful—comic-strip elements: the isolated community, top-heavy women, promiscuity, etc. **Supervixens** (1974) detailed the picaresque adventures of a young man who, wrongfully accused of having killed a woman, is running from the crooked policeman (who actually commited the murder), incidentally falling prey to several super-females along the way. Scenes such as the placing of a stick of dynamite between a bound Supervixen's spread legs marked Meyer's return to his tried and true mixture of sex and violence.

Up! (1977) was a direct descendant of another Meyer film, **Cherry, Harry and Raquel** (1969), Meyer's last film before venturing onto the Fox lots. Set in a dusty Arizona border town, **CH&R** depicts double-crossing drug smugglers involved in power struggles, interspersed with various sexual encounters both hetero- and lesbian. The film is wildly edited—in one instance switching from a lovemaking scene in the desert to a hospital gynecological exam.

Up! tries for the same accumulation of delirious scenes. At the beginning, Adolph Schwartz, a homosexual Nazi, pays a young man to sodomize him aided by three large-breasted women. Afterwards, he takes a bath . . . and a gloved hand releases a carnivorous fish into the bath which attacks his vital organ and then eats him. Abruptly the next scene depicts a young woman running down the street who is picked up and raped by a man who drags her into a river . . . etc.

In 1972, **Deep Throat** had initiated the collapse of film censorship, yet Meyer steadfastly (to this day) refused to depict hardcore sex, arguing that it negated sustained interest in the plot and mise-en-scène while deactivating the imaginations of viewers. Meyer's healthy cult following kept him afloat during the seventies, but his movies of this decade are problematic: the elements are all there—outrageous bodies, bizarre dialogue and extreme plots, spectacular camerawork, perfect editing—but the films seem more like parodies of earlier works.

Meyer's last theatrical release, **Beneath the Valley of the Ultravixens** (1979), starred Kitten Natividad, his most overdeveloped discovery of all. The story chronicles the problems of a man who, much to his wife's horror and disgust, finds sexual satisfaction only in anal intercourse. His "sickness" is eventually "healed" by a local radio evangelist whose bustline is hardly less impressive than Kitten's. Although occasionally too reminiscent of previous plots, **BVU** represents the extreme limit of Russ Meyer's sexual parody.

Currently 13 of Meyer's films are available on videotape (write PO Box 3748, Hollywood, CA 90028). For Winter '86 Meyer is preparing the video release of a "Grand Luxe Preview" of his autobiography, **The Breast of Russ Meyer**, as well as **Mondo Topless 2**. In retrospect, Meyer's 23 films to date stand as a formidable achievement of true originality. ∎

During the late fifties, dozens of films concerning the perils of juvenile delinquency were released. Anyone who has seen some of these has almost certainly seen Dick Bakalyan. Almost forgotten today, Bakalyan holds the record for punk portrayals in J.D. films.

Bakalyan got his start in 1957 with **The Delinquents**, a good, low-budget film made in Kansas City by aspiring filmmaker Robert Altman. Bakalyan's portrayal of a hoodlum in this film set the tone and style for most of his later efforts. That same year he again played the heavy in Jerry Lewis' first solo film, **The Delicate Delinquent,** and in the Sal Mineo film, **Dino.**

Bakalyan's beady eyes and smart-ass smirk helped make him the quintessential delinquent. In 1958 he hit his J.D. peak with **Juvenile Jungle, Hot Car Girl** and the anti-marijuana classic, **The Cool and the Crazy.** In the latter film, Bakalyan is teamed up with the only person rivaling his record for hoodlum performances, Scott Marlowe.

The sixties saw the end of the J.D. films along with the birth of the Beach Party movies. Bakalyan's screen appearances were considerably diminished. During this period most of his work was in television, where he often reprised the thug roles he had previously created. He did get one more chance to play a teenage heavy on the silver screen in **Panic in the Year Zero,** an "after the bomb" film starring Ray Milland as a man determined to save his family, no matter what the cost.

In Los Angeles, Dick Bakalyan was interviewed by Boyd Rice.

■ *BOYD RICE: Tell us about the early days of Juvenile Delinquency films.*

■ DICK BAKALYAN: *The Delinquents* was my first experience in films. Two weeks after that I was signed to do *The Delicate Delinquent* with Jerry Lewis—the first film he made without Dean Martin. Then I believe I did *Dino.* Sal Mineo was good in that; I could relate to a lot of the people in that film.

Those kind of pictures were a lot of fun! The writers thought they were making some kind of *statement,* but they really weren't—they were just doing them hoping the kids would run to the drive-in's to see them! Although, a picture like *Dino* SAID something, you know. It was about a troubled kid and his problems; I played a gang leader but I wasn't a *bad* gang leader. This was not a gang that went out and raped women or killed or stole; in those days there were gangs because it was part of "the thing." When I was a kid *everybody* was a member of a gang.

■ *BOYD: You were in a gang?*

■ BAKALYAN: We *all* were—you did it to survive. Your

clique, the guys you hung out with, was called a "gang." You had to have an identification with a group, otherwise you were all alone. Unfortunately the media glamorized the gangs in such a way as to imply you had to be a real *bad dude* to be in one. And that's why you've got so much trouble on the streets today: most of these kids are just trying to emulate what they've seen in films!

I'm trying to remember how many of those we did ... *Juvenile Jungle, Hot Car Girl* ... I remember shooting those films in 10 or 12 days; *The Delinquents* took maybe 5 weeks. In those days the word got a lot of press: "delinquency." In the beginning my mom would always say, "Why can't you play nice guys?" especially after she saw *Delicate Delinquent.* I said, "Ma, there's no money in it. It's crime; *crime pays."* She said, "What will the neighbors say?" "Hey, ma, what do I care?"

■ *BOYD: How'd you decide to go into acting?*

■ BAKALYAN: I'd been a boxer; was in the service, got out. Me and my wife came to California. I got a job parking cars in Beverly Hills, went to U.S.C., just grabbing a job here and there wherever I could. I couldn't figure out *what* I was going to do—I didn't know how to do anything except box, but I couldn't do that anymore.

Laura Brooks, an acting coach, asked me to study with her. For about 3 months I became involved in her workshop. There was this little theater-in-the-round called Players Rink and if you did anything in that theater, *everyone* saw you—all the people from Central Casting, producers. I was lucky enough to catch a part as a J.D. (juvenile delinquent) in a thing called "Mrs. Goodwin's Boys," and from that time on work came.

■ *BOYD: Does your acting career affect how people react to you?*

■ BAKALYAN: People think I am who I play. Sometimes it works to an advantage; sometimes it's a disadvantage. The disadvantage is when they *underestimate* you; they think you're what I call a "dis-dat-dem-and-dos-er." But those guys are *fun* to play! Most of the leading men I know—most of my friends—would love to play gangsters and/or the bad guy, 'cause that's the *meat.*

In the service I was involved in psychological warfare; it taught me how to get the message across in more subtle ways, and that has helped me as an actor. The great thing about being an actor is that things are constantly changing and there's a constant flow. I mean, in this business I have friends that range in age from 18 to 70. So my life is a lot of different things. Most people my age (51) are stuck somewhere, in with their own little clique and that's *their world,* you know! My world is still out there; every day I'm waiting for the next chance to do what I do. It's always, "Quick! What's next? Let's go! Action!"

■ *BOYD: What would you like to do next?*

■ BAKALYAN: I'd like to do things for kids that deal with integrity and self-respect. We don't have that in our country today. Kids try to be like television heroes, but that's not what it's about. There was a time when if you gave someone your word and didn't keep it, you were a *villain,* no matter what

88

Bakalyan in The Cool and the Crazy

side of right or wrong you were on. Today, that means *nothing* to people. I talk to a lot of young people and they just don't care.

When I did *Delicate Delinquent,* nobody was wearing long hair. But I let my hair grow long (by today's standards it wasn't long, but by 1956 standards it was *long*). The attitude was, "Hey, what the hell do I want to get a haircut for? I'm gonna be drafted. I'm gonna be killed in some war. So let 'em cut it when I go in the service." And that was the attitude of this character—that was the *key* to this character. It's not in the script, but it's what you *bring* to the character. Now the audience doesn't grasp all of that, but they notice a roundness or fullness in the character.

You can never divorce "you" from you. You've got to bring *you* to the role. *Always.* First, there's physical presence: you're going to be cast according to how you look. Then it's what you do to try and make it for real.

■ *BOYD: Did you actually get arrested on location for* The Cool & The Crazy *because of your wild haircut?*

■ BAKALYAN: It was *The Delinquents.* Peter Miller said to me one day, "Come on, we're gonna go get a lemon ice cream soda." I'd never heard of a lemon ice cream soda. I thought "All right," and we went into this soda fountain in the basement of his apartment building in Kansas City. I wasn't there a minute when this cop came in and spun me around and threw me up against the counter. I thought, "What is this shit?" and started to laugh 'cause I thought Peter had put him up to it—I thought it was a *joke.* But the cop went bananas because he thought I was laughing at him.

People were staring. Evidently some guy had escaped from somewhere and was wearing the same color shirt or was about the same size, and the cop thought it was me. When I found out it wasn't a joke I got nervous and said, "Pete, tell him who I am." And Pete said, "I don't know this guy; he followed me in here. I've never seen him before in my life!" I said, "Huh? Tell him I'm an actor; we're here making a movie." The cop said, "Nobody makes movies in Kansas City!" We laughed about that, *later.*

I've been stopped lots of times in different cities. You see, cops look at pictures of "wanted" people before they go on duty. They see a face that's recognizable—Boom! They make a move on you.

It's been fun being a character actor. People will recognize your face and stop you and say hello. It's nice because [at this exact moment a man passing by recognizes Dick and greets him excitedly as though seeing a long-lost friend]. See! People you've never seen will stop you just to say, "Hi." It makes it nice. Some people think I work with them: "Don't I know you from work?"

■ *BOYD: What kind of neighborhood did you grow up in?*

■ BAKALYAN: A tough neighborhood in Boston. I was little; that's why I became a fighter. I never really liked to fight but I was good at it—you had to be if you were small. That's the only way the big guys would leave you alone: if you could scuffle, they respected you. I never went out *lookin'* for beefs. Today, if someone did the wrong thing, I'd go over the table after them. My brother's always sayin', "Dick, you're going to get sued." It's just my nature (thank god for it), that *attack* thing. I'm not afraid to do anything, I'll do whatever. If it's absurd, we'll talk about it first. Then, if it's justified, we'll do it. Some guys get cute and I have to set 'em straight.

■ *BOYD: Well, you have to deal with nuts any time you step out the door! But all in all, it sounds like you've had a good 27 years in the business.*

■ BAKALYAN: I feel really lucky to have been in this business. I feel like a youngster, always looking forward to what's happening next. It's exciting. Of course there are slow times, when you wait to be called and you go bananas because there just isn't anything to do. But what else *could* I do? Be a crook? ■

During the past three decades Joe Sarno has made approximately 200 feature films—so many that he's lost count. Although generally classified as "sexploitation," these films often reveal archetypal and moral dimensions not usually found in the genre. A former psychology major at New York University, Sarno has never ceased exploring the behavioral conflicts engendered by individual desire vs. social reality.

Additionally, during his long career Joe Sarno has made educational and industrial short subjects, documentaries, commercials, music videos, children's films, news programs (from a helicopter he filmed the aftermath of Mt. St. Helens), etc. He currently works as a "film doctor," revising and repairing other people's imperfectly realized projects.

Dividing his time between Sweden and Manhattan, Joe lives with his wife Peggy (actress and multi-talented assistant on many of his films) and son Matthew in a comfortable, book-lined apartment near the Museum of Modern Art. The following conversation took place over a gourmet pasta dinner which Joe himself prepared. Vale and photographer Ana Barrado asked the questions . . .

■ VALE: *How would you describe yourself as a filmmaker?*
■ JOE SARNO: Categories are set up by people who are basically part of the "in crowd," with all the attendant thinking and definitions, so it is difficult for me to answer that question outright. I was born a *rebel*. In film, I got outside of the acceptable framework as often as possible. I think that is what a filmmaker's goal should be—to get outside of what, at the time, is the established framework. I think the established (the word "establishment" is overworked) thinking is always to be *gone beyond*. I went beyond the framework; I said things that were not always acceptable, and that's one of the reasons I did feature films: I wanted to say things that were not, at the time, acceptable.

I have a great affection for the Navy in which I served, but I almost became an expatriate because of the war in Vietnam. That war was wrong from the outset. My Navy and the Marine Corps, the US Army—all the might of America—was thrown into crushing a people who had struggled for freedom for over 200 years against the Chinese, Japanese, and French. I thought Korea was wrong, but not like I *knew* Vietnam was wrong.

In Sweden, people interviewed me and asked me about being in World War II and I said I fought against fascism. But young people sometimes don't understand; some of the people in Sweden said, "You're against this war now, but you weren't against Hiroshima." But I was long out of the war by

that time; *I* couldn't have dropped that bomb. I never dropped one bomb on civilians; the war I fought was against guys with guns who wanted to kill me.
■ VALE: *Self-defense!*
■ SARNO: In a left-handed way. And when I went to war I knew nothing about who the Japanese were. We were the last "innocent Americans." I went into the war a teenager and became an old man overnight!

> I was born a **rebel**. In film, I got outside of the acceptable framework as often as possible. I think that is what a filmmaker's goal should be—to get outside of what, at the time, is the established framework.

The last person I voted for was Lyndon Johnson because he promised he wasn't going to get involved in Vietnam—and he got involved. When Nixon came in, I lived for 2½ years in Sweden! Now, any country that can elect somebody like Reagan—I listen to some of his statements, and I'm *floored*. I look at some of his old movies and think, "This guy can *not* be President—God! He had both legs cut off in *King's Row!*"
■ VALE: *Reagan's a blinding example of media control—*
■ SARNO: But it can work the other way, too. By his death *one guy* was responsible for Nicaragua going to the Sandanistas. An American journalist went up to show his press papers and some government guardsmen blew his brains out—but that was all *on camera*. Practically as soon as people saw it on TV, Somoza was out—he had to get out. The U.S. had to get rid of him. Now, I'm not a big leftie, but I think that just like we did in Vietnam, we've backed the wrong people in Latin and Central America.
■ VALE: *. . . How long have you been making films?*
■ SARNO: Since the '40s.
■ VALE: *Do you own copies of everything you've done?*
■ SARNO: No, I wish I did. Once I stop a film, I start another—I never have time to tarry, I'm so overloaded with work. And to begin with, I've done so many films—
■ VALE: *200 or more, right?*
■ SARNO: Yes.
■ VALE: *How did you get started? You flew with the Navy during World War II; did you see combat?*
■ SARNO: Oh yes. In the Pacific, the Marshalls, the Gilberts, the Marianas, the Solomon Islands. That was a thousand years ago.
■ VALE: *I'm glad you survived to make films.*
■ SARNO: I survived, that's all. Back to film: in the Navy I knew very little about it but I was brought in to assist in a training film based on a low altitude bomb sight invented by Warrant Officer Johnson and used by me in combat. I fell in love with the realm of film forever.
■ VALE: *So that's how you broke into film?*

the
sensation
clubs!

partners
in
pleasure!

wild
bottle
parties!

SIN IN THE SUBURBS

the whole scandalous story...
shock by shock !

FOR ADULTS ONLY!

Starring ALICE LINVILLE • W. B. PARKER • AUDREY CAMPBELL • LAHNA MONROE   Produced by Burton BRADLEY • Written and Directed by Joe SARNO • A Jovin Films Release

Britt in a photo from **Young Playthings.**

■ SARNO: Yes, quite by accident.
■ *VALE: Do you have a filmography or biography available?*
■ SARNO: No. I've never done a biography on myself even looking for work, because I've been a freelance film director all these years and I've never been out of work. But I went from one area of film to another, sometimes burning the ships behind me. For instance, I went from commercials, training films and industrial films that got me a reputation early on to those features with sexual themes. And I *always* succeeded in burning my ships behind me.
■ SARNO: In 1959, I had just come back from Europe. A friend of mine asked, "Look, you want to make an exploitation film?" I said, "What's an exploitation film?" He said, "Well, it's got sex in it." I said, "Will I get arrested?" (I didn't even know what it was, then.) He said, "I want you to do something based on a magazine article you did."
■ *VALE: You were writing as well?*
■ SARNO: I had begun writing when I went to college—I started college before the war, then came back after the war a little worse for wear, got my degree and began writing mostly on psychological and historical subjects, along with some short stories. In those days there were a lot of magazines—if you were *different* you could sell your stuff. Today it's not so easy.
  Anyway, this man brought me to someone, and I did a film

called *Sin in the Suburbs*. An extraordinary film. Again, it was based on fact. It was very carefully researched, and had great people in it. There were a couple of quick flashes—scenes in which you saw Audrey Campbell's body. She was a very beautiful model at the time—in her forties, but *beautiful*. She was a nude model, had acted a little and she wanted to be in a film. Woody Parker, a very good actor, was also in it, along with Alice Linville.
  Flash forward: several years ago, a secretary called me up and said, "Listen, if you can get me a copy of *Sin in the Suburbs* I'd be eternally grateful." I said, "Well, I'm not sure; I don't know where any copies are." She said, "Please try, because my boss was in the picture and we want to surprise him!" It turned out her boss was Neil Bogart who lived in San Francisco and started Casablanca Records. Neil was in the picture and he was a good young actor in those days; he also had a music group and he was the vocalist. Anyway, Andrew Sarris loved the picture. It was counter-establishment and all the other critics hated it, but Sarris saw what was good in it.
■ *VALE: Which friend suggested you make it?*
■ SARNO: George Carmen, a film editor who was much older than I—he died a few years ago. I already had a background of documentaries and commercials, so . . . He read the story in the old *Coronet* magazine (a small format magazine in '46 or '47) and I wrote the script. I've got a copy somewhere—actually, I'm not sure I do.

Over the years you lose everything; I don't keep very good files. Just now Steve Bono was on the phone; he wants me to do a script for a feature called *The Witch of Hominy Hill,* a country-and-western film. He and I were going to do this several years ago—he's a union production supervisor on big films. Well, I *had* a script but *I can't find it,* so I'm rewriting it—which is sort of difficult because I've really forgotten it.

I made little money out of *Sin in the Suburbs* for a very curious reason. George Carmen's friend who produced the film was a vice-president of the 9th Federal Savings & Loan, a big bank here in NYC. I did a second film for him, a comedy called *Pandora's Box* which was not very good. I was cutting

> My point of view is more or less always from the woman's point of view; the fairy tales that my films are based on are from the woman's point of view. I stress the efficacy of women for themselves. In general, I focus on the female orgasm as much as I can ... women have much more imagination than men! I think sex is supposed to be a lot of fun.

the second film at 1600 Broadway when all of a sudden two tall guys come in with Texas accents, wearing the hats and the whole thing. "You Joe Sarno?" "Yeah." It was the FBI! "Where's Earl Bradley?" "Jeez, I don't know." (I didn't know, but he was in Tangier.) They said, "Do you realize that Earl has been *peculating*" (I had to look the word up, because I thought it was a dirty word) "money from the 9th Federal Savings & Loan?" I was stunned—I didn't know anything about this.

It ended up that any money that I might have been entitled to was eaten up by the government, the insurance company and so forth, because he had been peculating almost $400,000 plus interest over a matter of five years. And that's why he went into the film business, because he figured it would bail him out—and it almost did. The film was very successful. If he had been able to curb his appetite for young women long enough he would have had enough money, but he met a Miss Denmark in New York, ran off with her, and wasn't covering himself at the bank. That's why he was caught. Consequently, I didn't do well on that film.

■ *VALE: So* Sin in the Suburbs *was based on an article you wrote?*

■ SARNO: My article was on drinking among women in the suburbs; in those days "alcoholism" wasn't ever brought up. One of the young women whom I was interviewing said, "Listen, you think *that's* a story—I've got a *story."* As a side-light I wrote this little bit (which was part of a series) about how people get involved in fantasies ... how they *allow themselves* to become involved in fantasies.

The story happened in upstate New York—I'm not going to give you the name of the town. These men and women— all comparatively wealthy people—wore black hoods and cloaks (but were naked underneath) and would have group sex without knowing who their partners were. For light all they had were these huge candles—very occult! Curious thing: there was a guy like a ringmaster—he had on a ring-master's suit with top hat, whip, the whole thing (although there was no full-fledged flagellation—at least none that I know of).

These people were all married couples; it was a throwing the key into the ring type of thing. Nearby was a motel that got big business because some people (who nobody knew) were from out of town. I was allowed to witness one of these

events as long as I preserved the anonymity. And it worked marvelously as a film—it was black-and-white but very cinematic because it was all a matter of *shadows* ...

■ *VALE: So you filmed the actual people?*

■ SARNO: No! I filmed actors. I had robes tailored for them and we went through the entire thing. It was a big turn-on for the actors, too, because of the kind of contact itself. Even though the cameras were moving—we did a lot of free, hand-held shooting—it turned out to be a very good film.

The whole thing had been the idea of the ringmaster and his wife. They were "swingers" and they got others involved. The ringmaster's wife was the one who started the idea—*she* was the one with the imagination. By putting her husband in a position of power it gave her power over these people. At the beginning she went around to the women, mainly, and got them to participate. I must say there were homosexual contacts also, especially among the women.

■ *VALE: The thrill of making sexual contact without the disadvantage of identity—*

■ SARNO: Exactly. They wore masks and all kinds of weird things. There was no problem of dialogue—everybody was groping around. And the crux of the story (and it was actually true) was that one woman discovered that her 17-year-old teenage daughter had been in the thing from the very beginning—unbeknownst to her. That was really the denouement of the story as it was told to me. When the film came out it was a sensation—Catholic bishops denounced it from the pulpit.

The main problem the film dealt with (just like in *Moonlighting Wives*) was: *how* did she get these women to come into this life?

Moonlighting Wives elucidates and explains how one woman persuaded these other women. Actually it was very simple. To begin with, she found that a lot of the women were gambling (playing the horses), so she went to these women gamblers first. She thought, "These people really have a drive; I'm going to explore it." Money only means one thing to a gambler: they can gamble it. So the young women who were gamblers were her first and most willing recruits. After she had her business going, she had bankers who were coming in and using her girls, so she'd find out who in the area was behind on their mortgage—who was having trouble.

> Often in movies the hangover from the Victorian age or the '30s is: if you enjoy sex you get killed, especially if you're a woman.

The curious thing was: for most of the women it became not the money but the adventure of the whole thing. Even after it was clear that their debts were settled, they were not dropping out, because it was *exciting.* They'd meet other guys; they'd meet other women; they had lesbian situations and everything else that they could never have thought of in their housewife lives. And they didn't have to commit their identities to it. It was a living fantasy, after which they went back to their kids and husband ... The film had a lot to say; I feel the same way about *Young Playthings.*

Moonlighting Wives made a lot of money. *I* didn't, because I didn't have a percentage of it, but I got a good fee plus bonuses.

■ *VALE: How did you come to do* Moonlighting Wives?

■ JOE SARNO: That was based on an actual incident. A man who had been a vice-president of United Artists came to me and said, "Joe, listen—would you do a script for us?"

I did the research and groundwork and came up with a story based on a young woman living in the suburbs who with her girlfriend were freelance stenographers—they went out and did typing and so forth. The girlfriend was very sexual, and it seemed like every time they went out they had sex! Not for money either, just for . . . ! So the first woman said, "Wait a minute—we're *giving* it away. But we could probably turn this into something." So she went out and recruited a number of housewives—attractive young women. (Not all of them were attractive, so she sent them to Slenderella so they'd be more attractive and appealing.) In the afternoons while their husbands were away, they went out "on call" as stenographers.

Finally a policeman got really bugged that all this "filth"

> Sweden is more or less the mother of women's independence—they're far ahead of us psychologically. The Viking philosophy was matriarchal to a great degree, and perhaps that's partly why Sweden is the way it is.

could go on under his nose. He was an Irish Catholic—really against all this kind of activity, and he busted the young woman. But the interesting part was: she had in her possession a little black book. This book had names and phone numbers of politicians, prominent attorneys, local public relations people and executives from the defense industry based nearby.

Finally this young woman got off without any fines or anything; she got off completely. She had been sending the girls out as stenographers, and had paid withholding taxes and social security on them, so when the income tax people came in *they* couldn't get anything on her. But this didn't appear in the picture—the producers thought otherwise. In the movie she loses everything, but that's not the way the real, true story ended.

■ *VALE: How did the policeman find out?*
■ SARNO: He was a vice cop. The way it was really broken was: a young woman got involved with a guy who beat her; the neighbors called the police, and that's how they tracked things down and discovered she was working for this woman, etc.
■ *VALE: So you interviewed the actual people involved?*
■ SARNO: Yes, I interviewed many people including the judge who finally sentenced her—I didn't include *that* material in the film. Then I wrote the script based on all that.
■ *VALE: It's too bad you couldn't have gotten away with the real ending for* Moonlighting Wives.
■ SARNO: I couldn't have at the time. The people who financed the film knew where they wanted to play it—it was a very big film at the drive-ins which were a large market at that time. The young British actress who played the lead really was a dancer—she was working as a dancer in Las Vegas then. *Moonlighting Wives* was produced and financed right here in New York.

Then there was *Young Playthings* which was based on a Swedish story, sort of a fairy tale; it was in the public domain. I listened to people talk about it—everybody told the story differently. It was about a young woman toymaker who could entrance people. The Swedish woman who played the toymaker—a *marvelous*, intelligent young woman—never did a film after that. She became a missionary; she went with a Swedish mercy mission to Biafra and worked there (actually, I don't think she truly became a *missionary*). The other long-legged young woman, Christina Lindberg, is now a journalist working for major magazines; some of what she writes is sexually-related. As you probably know, Sweden is more or less the mother of women's independence—they're far ahead of us *psychologically*. The Viking philosophy was matriarchal to a great degree, and perhaps that's partly why

Sweden is the way it is . . .
■ *VALE: So you fashioned the concept and the script?*
■ SARNO: The concept I did, but I had a lot of help. Many people from different parts of Sweden told me their version of the story as they knew it: "Oh no, *that's* not how it goes—it really goes *this* way . . ." I tried to make a version *in between,* and naturally I updated it—it supposedly happened in 1848, a time of unrest in all of Europe.
■ *VALE: Again, you did a lot of interviews before writing the script?*
■ SARNO: I always do! Whenever I do a film, I always find a *basis*—a psychological basis or a basis in an old story. And my point of view is more or less always from the woman's point of view; the fairy tales that my films are based on are from the woman's point of view. I stress the efficacy of women for themselves. In general, I focus on the female orgasm as much as I can . . . women have much more imagination than men! I think sex is supposed to be a lot of fun, and—
■ *ANA: Well, women like it too—*
■ SARNO: Exactly—that's the point. And that's what my films usually are about. The toymaker is a woman and at the same time she also appeals to the women in the relationship,

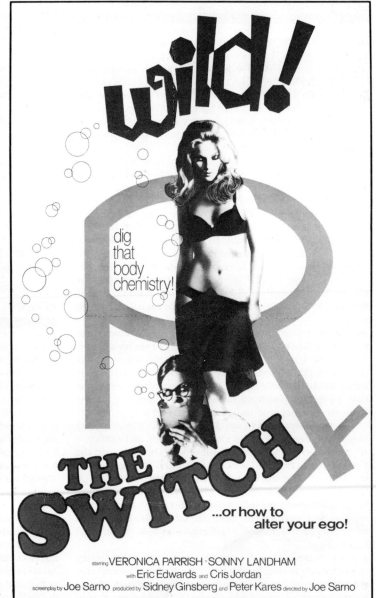

Scene from The Love Merchant.

knowing that the men are more difficult to deal with, to bring them into her fantasy. That's what the whole film's about: the toymaker brings them into *her* world.

■ PEGGY: Joe said: "This is their fantasy, this is what they want to be." We discussed the make-up. You don't think about it, but most people don't realize how much eyebrows make the person. When you put whiteface on someone and take away their eyebrows, they have nothing—they're just eyes staring at you—*nothing.* (We never think about it because we *have* eyebrows and they are automatically used as expressions of whatever we feel.) But you can make the actors angry, happy, risible—anything you want—with eyebrows. From studying Italian Renaissance paintings I had already decided what I wanted, so then it was even harder—

■ *VALE: Because of preconceived notions?*

■ PEGGY: Because when I wanted a certain expression or feeling to go with a costume, I had to *draw it* on the face. It was a small crew, so the same people turned into many different costumes/characters. And when the people turned into those characters that were painted—there were many different layers . . .

I remember doing the make-up in the day and making the costumes all night. I never slept—it was the long Swedish night which never got dark; at 12 o'clock it would get a little dark but by 1 o'clock it was bright again. I was so far behind because I'd set myself such big tasks. I was script and make-up as well, so I was really exhausted.

■ SARNO: She did everything—she *designed* the production.

■ PEGGY: We went to Leningrad right after that and I think I slept through every play we went to.

■ SARNO: That's right—*Young Playthings* almost got Peggy arrested in Russia!

■ *VALE: How?*

■ SARNO: We flew directly from Sweden to meet Peggy's parents in the Soviet Union. Peggy took along these little photos of the make-up she'd done, to show her mother (but the girls had their breasts showing). The state police grabbed Peggy and said, "This is pornography!" They were so upset you wouldn't believe it. She demanded, "Give me back my things!" but they wanted to keep them. I thought for sure we were headed for Siberia.

■ PEGGY: That film really was a group effort. The people were inspired by the concept of this toymaker getting people into make-up and working out different things, so they were quite excited about their costumes and make-up and they really enjoyed it. And you could really *feel* it—when that happens on a film and you film it, it's there forever. Because the people really liked each other and they wanted to work *for* the film.

When I was putting on make-up I was so tired, because I'd stayed up all night. But everyone put up with me with great senses of humor—like every time I put the wrong eyebrow on someone . . . But it was a group effort. We had no pressure from a producer—we had a marvelous producer from the West Coast, Seymour Borde, who would just send Joe money. People would say to him, "You're crazy, just sending him money. You don't know what he's going to do with it." Because most people would take the money, eat out, take girlfriends around the world, and with the rest of it make the film. But Joe isn't that way—never was that way, and Seymour felt this, somehow.

■ *VALE: So the films are done with a small, almost telepathic staff?*

All the Sins of Sodom

■ PEGGY: Very small. We made *Young Playthings* in early June, '72, in ten days or less. Sven Grankvist was the on-set producer, Gunnar Westfelt was the cameraman, his son Lasse Westfelt was the assistant director, and the man he lived with, Jimmy McGann, helped me with make-up and costumes. There was also a sound man, Rolf Kings; an editor, Lasse Grankvist; and that was the crew. All the people really wanted it to go, and worked very hard—and it wasn't easy for them in English.

Lasse Westfelt's father had a summer house on an island outside of Stockholm, and we went there to film. Since Joe's the editor and the director and the writer, he knows just what he's going to do, what he's going to shoot and who he needs. And if he has a good producer who gives him free rein (so that he doesn't have to hire the producer's girlfriend, or whatever), he can hire a person whom he feels something *with*.

If it's a young girl, usually she *trusts* him, and that's very important: they don't feel they're working with someone

who's going to take advantage of them. So they have long discussions about the character before, and they see that Joe's really a legitimate person who's interested in filmmaking, and that's why he's gotten such good performances out of young amateurs.

If you could see this movie *Inga,* Maria Liljedahl was extraordinary—she's since given it up. She was an extraordinary find—a young ballet dancer; I think she was fifteen when we used her first. Such a sexual person you have never seen! But also potentially a *very good* actress, and the combination was unbelievable.

Anyway, I'm glad that for a long time we worked in Europe rather than here, because by the time we came back, here it was pornography in a really different way. In those early days it wasn't pornography—all the people who worked really wanted to make their character so real, and the sex was part of it and came out of it. But once you start working with porno people it's different—they're very involved with their *bodies,* and it's not the same.

We did so many European films between 1967 and 1971—we did one called *Daddy, Darling* made in Denmark—again a very psychological story. The Swedish actress in that had a great tragedy—her husband had died earlier of a heart attack, and her two children later burned up in a fire.

Those days, when we made *Young Playthings*—those days are gone. The man who was the assistant cameraman is now a postman. We still give him great hugs when he delivers the mail . . .

> The curious thing was: for most of the women it became not the money but the adventure of the whole thing. They'd meet other guys; they'd meet other women; they had lesbian situations and everything else that they could never have thought of in their housewife lives. And they didn't have to commit their identities to it. It was a living fantasy, after which they went back to their kids and husband.

■ *VALE: Do you do any improvising during the making of the films?*

■ PEGGY: The films are totally scripted. But when things go well and get carried away, Joe will write more scenes.

■ SARNO: If I see that the chemistry's good, I'll say, "Oh jesus, let's add something here," knowing that you have somebody good who will produce for you. If you've got people who don't go along with the flow, then . . . They *must* go with the flow, or it's no dice.

■ *VALE: Which films did you improvise on?*

■ SARNO: Not *Young Playthings*. The people were so involved in it that you didn't need any improvisation, because they became the *characters* rather than *themselves*. You see, improvisation sometimes permits people to be themselves too much. What people should be is the character, but filtered through their own personality.

■ *VALE: Who casts the people?*

■ SARNO: I do. I find out where they live, as it were, and determine how to put them with other people.

■ PEGGY: Wherever he was, even when people couldn't speak English, Joe always found good people. Nadja in *Veil of Blood*—she's marvelous. One German actress had a fire in her home—her father was burned and died—but she came to work despite that, and finished the film.

Veil of Blood was a Dracula kind of film shot in an old castle; one of three "flesh" films which we did in Germany outside of Munich; the others were *Wall of Flesh* (not a bad film) and one called *Butterflies* (not sure what the English title is) with Harry Reems who was the doctor in probably the most infamous of all hardcore films—*Deep Throat*. He administered the "deep"!

Veil of Blood was retitled in Germany *The Revenge of the Black Sisters*. It was about four people who become stranded during a storm—naturally—at a castle. The housekeeper believes she is waiting for the return of a young woman who is a vampire that has died (but being undead they don't really die).

One of the young women who comes in becomes involved psychologically in *being* this vampire—almost through self-hypnosis she believes she is this vampire, and everyone else believes it . . . So she goes through the entire "thing" and finally in the end she has to be killed because now she *is* the vampire. In the denouement when she's about to inflict herself on the other young woman who is her friend and partner, she is killed by a wooden stake that goes through her heart quite by accident. This film more or less is about *persuasion*, just like *Young Playthings* was. There are a lot of Freudian symbols in both films.

■ SARNO: Another film made in Sweden was called *Laura's Toys*. I think Playboy bought it for cable television. It deals with an American archaeologist looking for runes, runic stones. He's got his wife with him and an assistant (a young Swedish woman who was a music conductor. This was the first film she'd ever done, and she was fantastic). The story is about this triangle. The wife is jealous of the young woman because she demands so much of his time—they have no affair, but the wife's jealousy pushes them into one . . . as well as pushing *her* into an affair with the young woman, to the point where she actually falls in love with the young woman because—you know, if you say to a kid, "Don't touch that!" the kid touches it! Same thing. The exteriors filmed in the Swedish islands were so lovely, adding to the eroticism; the acting was superb. The jealous wife has this background: when she was at Swiss boarding school, she was sort of controlled by this other woman who now appears on the scene—the fourth person, Karen.

■ *VALE: What* were *Laura's toys?*

■ SARNO: The people. The two young women who were at the Swiss Boarding School were the only two kids who were left alone. The other kids' parents would take them away on vacation, but *they* were left there because their mothers had too many things going for themselves to care about the kids. So the kids grow up and get to be so close that one couldn't go to the toilet without the other going, too.

The story follows in a line from these two women; this closeness permeates all the relationships that Laura enjoys. It starts with her reciting all the sexual things they used to do when they were young. This recitation, periodically, pushes forward the story, because things happen parallel with that. In the end Laura breaks the relationship with Karen completely, even though Karen *seemed* to be the one who had the upper hand.

Power is a theme in many of my films: people have power over others just by force of will and their overwhelming personalities. I'm a great believer in the force of will. And I believe in "the force." Combat pilots try to develop this force. You know: "flying by the seat of your pants"—when the pilot must react so quickly that the reaction in a split second means the difference between life and death . . . when a microcosm of seconds, an almost infinite time that's nothing, means survival. When I saw *Star Wars* my hair stood on end because Lucas defined what I recognized as the force that vibrates within all of us to be developed or repressed by each of us. In my films I often tell about people who have this tremendous power and who use it to dominate others, who use their personal magnetism and drive to achieve whatever good or evil they will.

■ *VALE: Also, your films often portray people discovering their own* true *unconscious desires.*

■ SARNO: Yes, this is the big thing in living—*most people don't recognize their own truest feelings.* That's why when they see them on film they don't say, "Jeez, I'd like to do that," even though they *would* like to do that. But they do get caught up and empathize with the people on the screen.

■ *VALE: There's a realm of freedom these people discover when they surrender their identities and will for awhile to somebody else.*

■ SARNO: Absolutely true. I found that in *Sin in the Suburbs.* I used to sit in the theater and then listen to people after the film; I was curious as to what people thought. And I would talk to them—I wouldn't let them know it was my film. And women especially would identify with the people, and some would say, "This is the kind of thing that if I had the guts, I would do it."

■ *VALE: All guts is, is will.*

■ SARNO: Most people don't permit themselves to exercise

97

their fantasies ... or even their imagination. Consequently they will identify with a picture like *Sin in the Suburbs* but they'll say, "Oh, but nobody ever *does* that."

In movies often the hangover from the Victorian age or the '30s is: *if you enjoy sex you get killed,* especially if you're a woman. That was such a hare-brained concept to begin with. In Spain there's a famous true story about a Swedish doctor and his wife who were in an automobile accident and were thrown from the car. The wife was lying in the street bleeding and the doctor ran over to her and said, "My god, I hope she isn't dead!" And one of the bystanders said, "Don't worry, señor, at least her dress didn't go over her head!"

The world has such a distorted view of sex—and a distorted priority regarding sex—and political awareness is often correlated to people's ideas about sex. My films present

sex without violent endings, and I think that's one reason my films have had a market—they're satisfying, without murder endings. I never go for violence in my films; the most violent film I've ever thought up has been a script for urban guerrillas—it ends in a shoot-out.

I've written a script about urban guerrillas—terrorists—that is based on the Weathermen who in the '60s used to make bombs and plant them in places. Finally they killed themselves in an explosion right down on 10th Street. The Weathermen were largely led by women—Kathy Boudin, Kathy Wilkerson and 8 or 9 other young women who had all gone to upper middle class schools and who finally were on the wanted lists. The FBI thought they were just nuts.

What happened was: there were 16 bank robberies netting about 8 or 9 million dollars, and the FBI had no idea who had pulled them off. (They said they did, but they had no idea.) The robbers had done things that the mob would never have thought of. Now, over the years the ['60s] "revolution" had gone away, disappeared. And these girls were so upset that the revolution had just frittered away that they decided the thing that would help the Black Liberation Army or the Sandanistas most was *money.* So they robbed these banks.

Now whenever there's a robbery, why are the people always caught? Because they spend the money. But not Kathy Boudin, Kathy Wilkerson and those people—they shipped the money away. *They* lived like cockroaches, believe me! They slept on pallets in lofts, they took jobs as dishwashers, and nobody could ever point to them. They had a way of getting the money away—I won't go into exactly how, it's too long-winded—but there was a Swedish national doctor, a young woman, who helped them get the money away to the third party, Cubans or whoever handled it.

To make a long story short, the young woman who led this became so frustrated that there was no focus on the revolution, that she decided there had to be some blood. And there was. They killed 3 cops and now they're all under arrest. That's the story, but nobody will do it because they feel it's too close to the real story; the people are on trial, and the trial's gonna last a hundred years.

■ *VALE: You did interviews for that project, too?*
■ SARNO: Yes. I think they held a view of an Amazon society. Interesting story; I've got the script and am hoping somebody would like to do it ...
■ *VALE: In* Young Playthings *you had people who had relinquished their former "respectable" occupations who were now pickpocketing and stealing for a living—but not violently.*

■ SARNO: Their morality became the morality of the young toymaker, which was not to be violent, but to flaunt in the face of the establishment the law that was for the "haves" not the "have-nots." They would use any means to get money, short of robbery with a weapon.
■ *VALE: After your Swedish period what films did you make in New York?*
■ SARNO: I made a black-and-white film on Fire Island called *The Beach House,* about people using sexuality to hide their own fear of sexuality ... One called *Abagail Leslie Is Back in Town* was based on something that had actually happened. A young woman returns to her home town after having left in disgrace because she had an affair with another woman's husband. She tries very hard to show the people that they're no better than she is, and she succeeds to some degree ...

I'd love to get a copy of *The Switch,* which was a comedy

All the Sins of Sodom

with very good people in it like Ray Serra and Kathy Christopher. It's a very funny film about a spinsterish chemistry professor who makes a potion that she believes is going to change her, like Dr. Jekyll & Mr. Hyde. She takes it and she does change, but she changes sexually—when she's under the influence of the potion she goes after sex, and she *really* goes after it! Ray Serra who always plays Italian gangsters—

■ *VALE: He was great in* The Honeymoon Killers—

■ SARNO: In *The Switch* he plays the part of a stevedore whose wife is always hounding him for sex, but he's too busy watching "Duke" Wayne films. He talks with such a heavy Brooklyn accent that you can hardly understand him.

■ *VALE: You don't have a complete listing of these New York films?*

■ PEGGY: I started compiling a filmography, but I never finished it. He did *so many* films a year, low budget black-and-whites as well as color. I don't like the comedies like *The Switch* as much as I like the "exploitation" films, because the latter were like "Eugene O'Neill exploitation"—there were all these psychological "things" that made the characters act the way they did. In films like *Young Playthings* you also had the right chemistry, like between the toymaker Margareta and Christina Lindberg—and that's luck. Because if there's one person very uptight about sex, then . . .

All those years, Joe wanted the real feeling and spirit. And some of these sex people were used to just faking it—and they overdo the faking. They would just give the "uh, uh" sounds and think that was it. And he would say, "You call it in on the telephone to me, because I'm not interested."

■ SARNO: Another good film was called *What They Say About Young Stuff*. That's not *my* title, but it's a good film with some very good acting in it. A film I did for Les Baker.

■ PEGGY: We used to do a film in a week, two weeks.

■ *VALE: Can you always get funding?*

■ SARNO: I can get funding ordinarily if I want to make a film in this milieu: a little on the sex side—not *heavy* on the sex side, but a little. But I haven't done anything in years because I've been so busy on documentaries and so forth—I make a great deal of money being a "film doctor." Right now I'm working on something for cable television. There was a hardcore film made a couple of years ago called *Inside Seka* and now we've made a soft version. I'm cutting it a little more to make it even *more* palatable for cable.

Several years ago I did a film called *Confessions of a Young American Housewife*, which included somebody who—in her 40s—later became a hardcore porno superstar: Jennifer Welles. (I knew her when she was a chorus dancer on

> **The Russian state police grabbed Peggy and said, "This is pornography!" They were so upset you wouldn't believe it. She demanded, "Give me back my things!" but they wanted to keep them. I thought for sure we were headed for Siberia.**

Broadway. I also knew Georgina Spelvin who went by the name of Chelly Graham when she was also a chorus dancer—she became a superstar for being in *The Devil in Miss Jones*.) These films were all written from the woman's point of view.

I did another "inside" picture called *Inside Jennifer Welles* which we just cut for cable. I've gone from commercials to big documentaries which I still do, to architectural films, to children's films. I used to work with Chuck McCann who's now an actor in Hollywood—he used to have a children's show and that was great fun. But basically I haven't really focused on any one spot in this business. I've done rock 'n' roll films—I did a thing called *Step Out Of Your Mind*.

■ *VALE: Great title—was that during the psychedelic sixties?*

■ SARNO: *Early* sixties. A young woman who was married to Richard Burton had one of the first discotheques in New York, it was an "in" place. The film featured The Four Kings, Ronnie Dante who now produces for MTV; it was a fun thing. We just did a documentary on the Nolan Sisters—they're Irish, had number one hits in England and Japan but they're unknown here. I do work for Video Shack—they're one of the biggest video retail outfits in the world—and they had this in-store promotion by Duran Duran for their new videocassette. That was a mistake! They figured they'd have a few hundred kids, but 4000 kids showed up trying to get into the store all at once—it was a riot! They had the riot police out; it was on television.

■ *VALE: What happened to* Step Out of Your Mind?

■ SARNO: I don't even know.

■ *VALE: What's another film you did in New York?*

■ SARNO: In 1963 I did a black-and-white film called *Flesh and Lace* which was also interesting, with a young woman who'd worked in Hollywood and came to New York and wanted to do a film with me. But I wouldn't know where you could get a copy of it. It was about a toy store, but the toy store owner was really a collector for the mob. He used it as a front for gambling and so forth; he was the "banker." This strange young woman wanders in who's homeless; she has no place to go. So she stays in the store and she becomes involved with the toys, because she's simple (not simple-minded but *simple*) and this is her refuge—she almost doesn't want to go out again because she's afraid, so many things have happened to her. Another guy who befriends her *uses* her—he finds out that this is where the money goes, and he uses her to rob the store in the middle of the night. And he's killed by the rather good guy—the guy who's a collector for the mob is rather a good guy! (With my partial Italian background, I believe that not all the mob guys are bad guys.)

> **Power is a theme in many of my films: people have power over others just by force of will and their overwhelming personalities. I'm a great believer in the force of will.**

■ *VALE: These were films that you had artistic control over?*
■ SARNO: Oh yes; I don't want someone sitting over me. What happened with *Pandora's Box* was—the same guy who went to jail said, "Now you'll make *this* film for *me.*" He wrote the script and everything—terrible! Good people in it—but a terrible film.

I did a fun film called *Warm Nights and Hot Pleasures,* but it wasn't that unusual. It was the story of three girls who come to New York on different careers—they had gone to college together and the whole thing—and it ends up that they are really in competition; the intensity of their competition almost destroys them. I *knew* three people who went into a commune in the '60s; they wasted a great part of their young lives trying to live an inadequate ideal.
■ *VALE: Have producers ever changed your films?*
■ JOE: I made one film, *Every Afternoon,* with a British actress, Diana Dors. It had good people in it, but the producer screwed it up. I didn't have the editing rights on it and he actually added in scenes and wrote new material for it. The basic story was about two people meeting in the park—a young guy and a young woman—back to fantasies! The young woman is in a ballet outfit—practice clothes—and the guy is wearing "pilot's wings," and he tells her he's a pilot. Well, neither one of them is—he works at an airline loading cargo and she is a prostitute who reads a lot, etc. Each day they meet and they have this tremendous fantasy.

Finally he finds out who she is. He's given a birthday party and a girl is brought there, and she's the girl. Then they avoid each other for a long time, but finally they meet again in the park and they carry on the conversation. She now knows that all he is is a freight handler, but they talk as if he's still an airlines pilot and she's a ballet dancer. It's one of those weird little stories that could have been beautiful, but the producer totally wrecked it. It should have been a small film but he tried to make it a big one. The little sensitive story was lost . . .

Producers are always a problem—usually I *don't* have problems with producers, but on this one I did.
■ *VALE: Peggy, when did you meet Joe?*
■ PEGGY: There was a Joe Sarno repertory company in New York, and I joined around '65. I worked with him first as an actress in 3 or 4 films. "Repertory" means that the same group of people would play different roles in different films. If he knew that you were going to be in his film, he would write a part for you and change the script according to what your potential was, what your limitations were. These were not pornography; we did *exploitation*—as much as I saw Elizabeth Taylor do in *Cat on a Hot Tin Roof.*

From '65 to '67 we worked with the same people—not only the same actors, but the same crew. Bruce Parks always shot the films, Bobby Balin was always the assistant camera-man, Jimmy Lynch was always the sound man, Kemper Peacock was the editor, and we all worked together for I don't know how many films. When someone hired Joe they knew that he had the freedom to choose *his* crew, write *his* story, and choose *his* actors. So he had great freedom at that time.

It was that same kind of joint effort that people talk about in the young days of film: when money didn't matter, when you worked because you really believed in it—you believed in the story, you believed in the film, and it wasn't just a job or just the money. That camaraderie and that feeling really does show up on a screen. Whether it's a multi-million-dollar film or a $250,000 film—the money doesn't matter.

By 1967 I had moved in with Joe. Then this producer said, "We'll go to Sweden." I wasn't working as an actress on the film and they didn't want me coming. So I worked unpaid because I was his *girlfriend,* making sets and costumes. The second film I got paid for, and then I worked with him—never as an actress again. On small films you have to do *everything.* I had to be yelling at the people—Joe's too soft-hearted—and I'm like a German general, I am.
■ SARNO: Peggy's been in a number of films. She was a star in Adolph Mekas's *Hallelujah the Hills.*
■ *VALE: So it's not just luck that your filmmaking team functioned so efficiently—*
■ SARNO: No! It's not an accident. You *choose* it. I think by force of will (back to the "force") you avoid things and people that don't fit in.

For example, there are many people who shouldn't be doing pornographic films, or who are doing them for the wrong reasons. The right reason is one that is not commercial: because they *like* to perform in front of people (in a sexual way or otherwise); because they're *turned on* by doing it. Otherwise they shouldn't be doing it. I *tell* people they shouldn't be doing it, or that they *should* be. For example, Annie Sprinkle should be doing it, because she loves to and is so involved in this whole feeling of sex. She is so crazy and sweet and nice it kills you . . .

The big thing with films—*a film is the result of a human relationship,* and when you write it to begin with, it's got to be about a real human relationship. Each actor or actress must filter the character through their own personality. And that's the whole secret of the thing. Without that, you have *nothing.*

> **I'm glad that for a long time we worked in Europe rather than here, because by the time we came back, here it was pornography in a really different way. In those early days it wasn't pornography—all the people who worked really wanted to make their character so real, and the sex was part of it and came out of it. But once you start working with porno people it's different.**

■ *VALE: What most interested you when you studied psychology?*
■ SARNO: General motivations and behavioral patterns. I wrote a lot on behavior patterns.
■ *VALE: I'm always amazed at the process of belief—how people will select (or not select) what they believe in, and how people will live out their lives based on belief in something totally unsubstantiated or arbitrary.*
■ SARNO: They select to believe in what's *safest* or *easiest* for them to believe in. The Catholics say, "Give me a child until he is six and I'll give you a Catholic on his deathbed." That's probably true of any religious belief, pretty much.

Each society encourages the beliefs that will make the society function to the benefit of the few who *want* it to function that way! ■

100

Joe Sarno on the set.

Joe Sarno today. Photo: Ana Barrado

PARTIAL FILMOGRAPHY

DAVE FRIEDMAN

David Friedman is a sexploitation movie pioneer and the producer of Herschell Gordon Lewis's first three gore films. Here he chronicles, among other topics, the development of sexually liberated cinema in this country. In Hollywood, Jim Morton asked the questions . . .

■ *JIM MORTON: How did you get started in sexploitation films?*

■ DAVID FRIEDMAN: I was too young to work and too nervous to steal! This was the only other thing I could do . . .

I've been in the motion picture business all my life. God knows X-rated or adult/exploitation films have been around as long as there have been movies. After getting out of the army I was with Paramount, then I decided I'd better get into something for *myself*. So I went into independent film distribution which soon came to mean *skin*-dependent film distribution, because the only pictures which were available to independents were foreign films and cheap little pictures that flashed a tit—something you couldn't even *do* in those days.

A lot of the theaters that became nudie or porno theaters originally were art theaters. We used to call them "coffee" houses because all the intellectuals and pseudo-intellectuals would go in to see foreign films with subtitles and would sip coffee and talk about how Buñuel is doing this and that, and now he's in *Cahiers du Cinema*—all of that bullshit. Around 1955 *And God Created Woman* came along, starring Brigitte Bardot. Suddenly these nice little coffeehouses that showed these pictures with the subtitles had lines around the corner. The theater manager said, "My god, what happened? Where did all these people come from?" Well, they'd all come in to see Miss Bardot's bare ass!

Then there was another French film called *The Lovers*. And a few distributors found out that the French weren't the only ones; the Swedes were making films with a little skin, too. That's where *One Summer of Happiness* and *Naked Night* came in. Nobody was buying Ingmar Bergman for his creativity or because he was a great film director; they were buying it because he showed some ass and some tits!

■ *JM: So these foreign films influenced American filmmakers toward showing more skin?*

■ DF: I've always said that Russ Meyer's *Immoral Mr. Teas* was nothing more than a cheap American version of *Mr. Hulot's Holiday*. He said that *well, it influenced him a little*, but . . .

■ *JM: Back then an exploitation film would play an "art" theater one week, the next week it would play a grind house. I remember going to see* Ulysses *and seeing a trailer for* Love Camp Seven *playing next week—*

■ DF: That's why so many adult theaters have the word "art"

on them—they were art theaters. They became sex houses because the art films later moved more and more into the mainstream. Now you've got pictures like *The Gods Must Be Crazy* that play for years in one theater. Today, if you've got a picture like *Das Boot*, a company like Columbia picks it up and the minute they put *their* label on a film, it suddenly attains a new respectability it doesn't have if an independent handles it.

I became partners with a really fascinating fellow, Kroger Babb, who had been involved with everything from the famous "birth of a baby" films to a spook show, *Dr. Chasm's Chasm of Spasms*. Kroger just passed away a few years ago. He was one of the great geniuses in motion picture exploitation; one day I'm going to do a book about him—in fact I've got the title: *Country Boy with a Shoeshine*. He was from an era of Americana that should be chronicled: a combination flim-flam man, P.T. Barnum, and W.C. Fields . . .

Babb was a big imposing guy who used to drink like a fish (he could drink a bottle of whisky at one sitting); came from a miserable little town in the middle of Ohio: Wilmington. His real name was Howard W. Babb. Back east there was a chain of grocery stores called Kroger stores; he worked in one so all the other kids called him "Kroger" Babb. He kinda liked the name and kept it.

> **Nobody was buying Ingmar Bergman for his creativity or because he was a great film director; they were buying it because he showed some ass and some tits!**

His story started when he was managing the Checkers circuit of theaters in Ohio. He was traveling through a little town and saw two carny types, Cox and Underwood, with a show called "Dust to Dust." "Dust to Dust" was a copy of Brynie Foys' old picture *High School Girl* with a "birth" reel and a "clap" reel added. He went in and watched this production and (they've got 'em lined up all around the block) he said, "You guys got something great here. All you need is one thing." They asked, "What's that?" He said, "Me." They asked, "Why do we need you?" He said, "Because I'll show you how to sell it."

So the three of them started a partnership going from town to town (down south) showing the birth reel, the venereal disease reel and selling the books—Babb always figured one thing: no matter what the subject was, have money coming in from a book sale. Of course this was a book on sex.

They got into Indianapolis. Kroger went out to lunch after the first show and came back and the theater manager was about to have a duck: "Ohmigod, Mr. Babb, Marilyn Horn was just here and she was just infuriated. She thinks it's the worst thing she's ever seen and she's going to have us closed

down." And Kroger said, "Who the hell is Marilyn Horn?" "Oh, Mr. Babb, for god's sake she's the reviewer for the Indianapolis newspaper. You don't understand, Mr. Babb, her uncle is the Catholic bishop of Indianapolis; her father is the Chief of Police; her brother is the captain of the Vice Squad; and her aunt is the Mother Superior of the nunnery here. She's a very devout Catholic girl; she's the reviewer for the *Indianapolis News* which is the biggest afternoon paper in town, and *she is mad!*" To make a long story short, at the end of the week when Babb was leaving town, Marilyn left

> [How did I start in exploitation films?] I was too young to work and too nervous to steal! This was the only other thing I could do.

town with him! And she lived with him for 30 years until he finally did marry her. And she's now his widow. Talk about a salesman! This guy could charm the birds out of the trees.

They all got to Cleveland about the beginning of the War. And Babb came up with an idea: he is going to make one great "birth of a baby" picture and he's got the title: *Mom and Dad*. And Marilyn has written it; she's even named the lecturer: "Eliot Forbes, America's foremost hygiene commentator." Cox and Underwood wanted to take their money and they did; Underwood went back to Kentucky, became a big horse-breeder and never surfaced until years later with a pirated copy of *Uncle Tom's Cabin* which he made a fortune with. *Uncle Tom's Cabin* was made by Universal just before sound, with Raymond Massey playing Lincoln. Underwood put a soundtrack on it and traveled through the South, making a lot of money.

Kroger came out here, made *Mom and Dad*, and from then on school was out! The film got a lot of heat from the Catholic church; it was on the condemned list. Kroger was the only man to fight back: he'd run ads in the trade papers: "Kroger

Babb, America's fearless young showman, announces that his next film will be *Father Bingo*, an exposé of gambling in the parishes!" I learned a lot from Kroger—he had a superb command of the language and could write an ad that you couldn't believe. He would plant these little stories in the paper, claiming that he had played a town a few weeks before and the mayor had written him:
"Dear Mr. Babb,

"Before your show came into town I opposed it, and I did not want to give you a license to play the picture. But the common council outvoted me. But, I was delighted to see that the film was everything you said it was: a fine, educational attraction. As a matter of fact, it probably saved the life of one of our fine young high school students, a young girl who found she was in trouble.

"She did not know where to turn; she could not tell her teachers and she didn't dare tell her parents. Her friends suggested she go see your movie, which she did. From that came the courage to tell her parents. The parents understood. The girl had the baby which has been placed for adoption, and I want to thank you . . .

"P.S. The girl was my daughter."
That's the kind of thing that Babb could do!
■ *JM: What did he do after* Mom and Dad?
■ DF: He tried everything. After *Mom and Dad* came *Prince of Peace,* with which he was selling a beautiful, four-color litho of "Jesus Christ Our Savior" and a miniature Bible. There was a Passion Play down in Lawton, Oklahoma, and he went and filmed it. He had discovered a little girl in Atlanta named Virginia Prince and he was going to make her into another Shirley Temple. Well, that never came about.

I ran into Kroger one night at a variety club in Atlanta where he'd opened *Prince of Peace* and the audience had simply walked out. I asked him, "What the hell happened, Krog?" He said, "I don't know. Will you go out and take a look at it?" I said, "Yeah, I will."

Well, the Passion Play normally is done in pantomime; you don't need the words because we all know them from the Four Gospels. But these guys were mouthing the words. So when it came to the scene of the Last Supper, Jesus said in his Oklahoma voice, "Wel-ll, one o' y'all's gonna betray me to-naight," and Judas Iscariot yelled when the Romans came in,

Friedman satirizes the Hollywood image in the softcore film, Starlet. Friedman makes an appearance in this movie, playing himself.

"Dat's him! Dat's him ovah 'deh!" I said, "You better redo the soundtrack." So we dubbed English into English; I got some radio voices from Atlanta and we laid down a track where the people at least were speaking without any trace of an Okie accent. Babb stayed up about 3 nights drinking martinis and came up with this beautiful campaign of Christ on the Cross: "Kroger Babb presents The Prince of Peace," and school was out on that one!

Then he had one on alcoholism, *One Too Many*, starring Ruth Warrick. *One Too Many* is a lost picture. It was about the evils of alcohol and women getting drunk—a real preacher movie—it wasn't that great and the book didn't sell well. In the middle of that Babb got involved with a picture called *The Secrets of Beauty*, where for $10 he was selling women a make-up kit and a book on how to be beautiful. *Secrets of Beauty* also didn't work because in those days nobody had $10 to spend; most of the girls who saw the movie went to Woolworths for their cosmetics. That was before Revlon and all the fancy cosmetics lines.

She Shoulda Said No (about marijuana) was originally called *The Devil's Weed*. Kroger made this picture right after Lila Leeds was arrested in a bust with Robert Mitchum—they were both smoking some joints. He did about six months at the county farm; the judge let her go because she was a good-lookin' blonde. We had Lila out on the road telling about the evils of dope, but unfortunately she was blowing the operators and blowing the stagehands and messing around with the ushers, and we were getting closed up on morals charges because of her ...

Kroger never stopped. He was something unique; a combination medicine show man, carny, flim-flam man, what have you. I've always said there are four generations of exploitation films, and I am a senior citizen of the third generation. Babb would have been in the second generation; Babb was 20 years older than me. Dan Sonney's father, Louis Sonney, would have been in the first generation—they're all forgotten; those are the guys who came right after Edison. The second generation was with the Forty Thieves, the Sonneys,

Ecstasy on Lover's Island; one of the many films released by Louis Sonney and son.

Pappy Golden, Dwain Esper, Steve Foys, Kroger. Russ Meyer, Herschell Lewis and I are in the 3rd generation. And all these kids today who are grinding out porno—that's the fourth and last generation. In my generation I would have to put Roger Corman, Sean Cunningham, a guy in England named Peter Walker—I don't know if you've ever seen any of his stuff. I had the rights to one film called *Flesh and Blood Show*.

■ *JM: Did you work for Babb?*

■ DF: Babb and I were partners in a Chicago company called Modern Film Distributors with a fellow named Irving Joseph. How this came about was: there were four "birth of a baby" pictures. Irv wrote one called *Because of Eve*. A fellow named Floyd Lewis owned one called *Street Corner*. A character named Talley down in Texas owned one called *Bob and Sally* that was made by Universal; that was really the best. Then, of course, there was *Mom and Dad*.

These guys used to fight each other tooth and nail. One day I was sitting playing cards with Joseph and I said, "You guys are crazy. The four of you should get together." So Joseph and I brought the other three into Chicago and it was agreed that we would operate out of Chicago, it being more centrally located. And where a guy played *Mom and Dad* this year, next year he would play *Because of Eve*, the next year *Bob and Sally*, the next year *Street Corner*. We kept the West Coast kind of an open city, because you didn't have to play that many dates out here; there were beautiful drive-ins all

over where all you had to do was play two or three and you made enough money to last you for a year.

The only thing Babb did after that—after Babb had shot his wad with *Karimoja,* he and I brought to the U.S. an early Ingmar Bergman film starring Harriet Anderson. We played around and came up with a campaign: "Monica: The Story of a Bad Girl." Babb got his share of the profits for years and years; finally, that too came to an end. But I'd see Babb quite a bit; we remained very good friends until he passed away ....

■ *JM: Tell us about your involvement with Herschell Gordon Lewis.*

■ DF: Herschell and I made *Blood Feast, 2000 Maniacs,* and *Color Me Blood Red.* Then he and I split up and he went on. But before that, we had made *Daughter of the Sun, Lucky Pierre, BOIN-N-G!, Scum of the Earth,* and about 6 or 7 nudist colony films filmed in Miami.

■ *JM: What inspired you to make your first films together?*

■ DF: I owned a drive-in theatre in Joliet, Illinois that was playing a lot of junk on the weekend. One day I said, "Christ, I can make a better picture than that!"

So, Herschell and I made a couple of pictures in Chicago. One was called *The Prime Time* and the other was called *Living Venus*. Neither was too successful. I was on a road trip in Toledo, Ohio and Rosa Rose, a famous old stripper who had a burlesque house, said to me, "I could sure use some shorts with some pretty girls showing their tits!" So I went back to Herschell and said, "Let's you and I make some shorts for the burlesque houses." We kicked it around and ended up writing 4 or 5 little sequences. I said, "Why don't we just put 'em all together?" and that became *Lucky Pierre,* which was released in 1959, the same year that Russ (Meyer) made *The Immoral Mr. Teas.* The whole nudie-cutie craze was then on. That's how I got lucky and drifted in, like everybody else.

At the time we made *Lucky Pierre,* New York State had a censor board. And a man had come up there with a picture he'd made down in Tampa, Florida called *Garden of Eden.* New York State's Supreme Court told the censor board that nudity was an accepted form of life and was not obscene, and

they had to okay the picture. So everybody ran into New York City with a nudist colony picture. Dan Sonney had a couple of old ones; he had one made in 1933 called *Elysia* that was made by Bryan Foy who was one of the "Seven Little Foys."

So Herschell and I immediately went down to Florida and started grinding out nudist colony films. The first one we made for ourselves was *Daughter of the Sun*. That girl was so gorgeous it wasn't even funny. Then Tom Dowd, who was an exhibitor in Chicago, wanted to make some. So we made *Goldilocks and the Three Bares*, *Nature's Playmates*—we ground those things out like sausages! Then we made one for

> We got the bright idea to shoot **Blood Feast**. We made it in 4 days; it cost $26,000. That was the first of the blood-and-guts films, all the slice 'em and dice 'em, smash 'em and mash 'em films that ever came down the pike.

Leroy Griffith called *Bell, Bare and Beautiful* starring Virginia Bell. Virginia was married to Eli Jackson who was a partner of Griffiths, an old friend of mine—they were burlesque and carnival people.

While we were down there shooting that, we got the

bright idea to shoot *Blood Feast*. We made it in 4 days; it cost $26,000. That was the first of the blood-and-guts films; the forerunner of *Friday the 13th*, *The Texas Chainsaw Massacre*—all the slice 'em and dice 'em, smash 'em and mash 'em films that ever came down the pike. Herschell and I followed that with *2000 Maniacs*. During the last one we did, *Color Me Blood Red*, Herschell and I got into an argument and I finished it. Then he went his own way and I went mine. In the last year we kinda got back together and we might make *Blood Feast Two* together.

■ *JM: A lot of people have this concept of the director as "auteur"—that the director does everything and the producer is just the shmuck that hands out the money. But whenever Herschell Gordon Lewis talks about the movies you did with him, he always uses "we."*

■ DF: Herschell and I have had many ups and downs. Herschell is probably the single smartest individual I ever knew in my life. First of all, he has a Ph.D in English Literature; he was a professor of English. He could write faster, quicker and better than anyone I've ever known. If he sees somebody doing something, whether it's making an automobile or performing brain surgery, he can do it; he's unbelievable. On *Lucky Pierre* he was doing the camera and I was doing sound; there was just one kid to help us pick up. That was the whole crew; we did everything together. We did the campaigns together; we distributed together; it was the greatest team since Barnum & Bailey. I learned an awful lot about production from Herschell ... I already knew something about sound, and I knew how to handle a movie camera—I've had cameras all my life.

Herschell and I did everything together; we could anticipate each other. *Lucky Pierre, Daughter of the Sun, Nature's Playmates*—we would write 'em together. I would dictate and he would type for a couple of pages; then he would dictate and I would type, etc. We knew who all the characters were and everything else. That's how we wrote the scripts.

■ *JM: You knew Bob Cresse and Lee Frost, who made many sexploitation films together—*

■ DF: Well, Cresse was a weird, weird kid. I first met him when his father was on a carnival with me in Allentown, Pennsylvania one week, and his father brought the little monster out to visit the show . . .

■ *JM: I noticed that Frost filmed* Love Camp Seven.

■ DF: Frost was the director; Cresse was the producer. Cresse was very domineering. That whole thing was Cresse's idea; Cresse really wants to be a Nazi more than anything else in the world, that's his whole thing. He *really* believed he was

> After working with Herschell, I came out here and started grinding crotch-hoppers. I resisted explicit sex almost to the end; I didn't get into that until '73 or '74. I had a lot of fun with the soft things: **Trader Hornee, Zorro.**

a Nazi. But Cresse handled Frost like a fine violinist would handle a Stradivarius. Cresse would say to the industry as a whole, "Lee Frost is the best; there is no one who can approach him. He is the finest." And that's all Frost wanted. Cresse didn't need to *pay* Frost; he just told him how *good* he was . . . That's sad but true!

■ *JM: I remember seeing* Love Camp Seven *and thinking, "Gosh, there's wall-to-wall flesh, yet no pubic hair!"*

■ DF: I know the scene you're talking about. Remember the scene when they put the girls on that bloody sawhorse? That was Cresse's bright idea!

Cresse and I would always talk: "What are you gonna do, Cresse?" "I'm gonna do a war picture!" "Well, then I'm gonna do a sea picture." "Well, I'm gonna do . . ." So, at the same time we both get the idea we're going to do a western. His was called *Hot Spur,* mine was called *Brand of Shame.* We don't say anything, and then we both announce it at the same time. We both said to Vince Randolph (who owned the Pussycat Theaters—he just passed away), "I want to be first." Randolph, being smart, said, "Look. You two guys are my most important suppliers of pictures. Without you two guys I couldn't run this chain. I'm not going to get in a fight with either one of you, because you're both insane. You both work it out and you both come to me together and tell me who's going to play first. Otherwise, I'm not going to play either one of them! Here's the two dates: I got a date in July and a date in August. You either both come to see me together, or send me a letter that both of you sign."

So, Cresse and I went at it: "I was first!" "Bullshit, I was ten minutes ahead of you!" "You stole my idea!" "I didn't even know you were making it—how could I steal your idea?" "Well, my picture's better than yours!" "Who says?" I said, "I got beautiful blonde girls in mine; you don't . . ." So it went.

Lee Frost was one who believes that auteur theory. Although Lee and I worked very well together on *Defilers,* I still felt he considered the director superior. But I'll tell you who I consider the superior person in all filmmaking: *the writer.* That's where it starts from! Although . . . the writer Byron Mabe was impossible to work with . . . but maybe Byron Mabe isn't that talented. *Normally the less talented you are, the bigger ego problem you have!* Take the most talented

cameraman in the world, Ferd Sebastian—he's the easiest man in the world to work with. And there's the cameraman who started with me, Laszlo Kovacs, who was the cameraman for *Daughter of Fanny Hill* and *Smell of Honey.*

■ *JM: I heard that Cresse got shot in the stomach—*

■ DF: Yeah, he got shot. I was in Australia at the time. Cresse always liked to carry a gun. One night he was in a bookstore at Hollywood and Western. He looks up and there's 3 guys beating the hell out of this broad. They got her down on the ground and they're kicking her. Cresse runs over and goes to his car and takes his gun out and holds the gun up, saying, "Stop! I'm calling the police! Stop or I'll shoot!" And this guy whirls on him and says, "We *are* the police, motherfucker!" and shot him twice right in the stomach. And then the guy shot his *dog.* He almost died . . . and he never really recovered from that, mentally. LAPD—they're "Dirty Harry's" down here!

After working with Herschell, I came out here and started grinding crotch-hoppers. I resisted explicit sex almost to the end; I didn't get into that until '73 or '74. I had a lot of fun with the soft things: *Trader Hornee, Zorro . . .*

■ *JM: I'd really love to see* The Defilers, *but there's no theater where you can see films like that.*

■ DF: They have no value today; the video people don't even want them. *The Defilers* was not a bad little picture; I made that in '64 with Lee Frost, who had been working with Bob Cresse most of the time. One I made after that, that I like even better, was called *A Smell of Honey, A Swallow of Brine!* I wrote the story for Stacey Walker, whom I met when we were shooting *Fanny Hill.* It was a pretty fair little film. Those pictures were kinda like the Roger Corman films of their day.

■ *JM: Maybe the Playboy channel will show them.*

■ DF: What Playboy's doing is almost unbelievable; they're buying X-rated films and then cutting all the sex out of them and just playing the story part, which in a lot of these pictures you can get rid of in 15 minutes! [laughs]

■ *JM: It seems like a bad idea. I wrote them begging them not to do that and to just show the old sexploitation films instead.*

■ DF: They would be better. But, at least they've been showing *The Erotic Adventures of Zorro.* There is a very good *cool* version of both *Chorus Call* and *Seven into Snowie,* and they were showing both of those. But most of the stuff that Playboy has programmed themselves has been pretty sorry.

■ *JM: Do you know anything about a film entitled* How to Undress in Front of Your Husband?

■ DF: Chris Warfield made that. Did you see that compilation film I did with Arthur Knight on the Playboy channel—it had footage from *How to Undress in Front of Your Husband* in it—no, I used *Virgin Bride.* It also had a lot of old footage in it like *The Girls from Loma Loma.* The compilation film we're doing now, *Sex and Comedy,* is even better.

■ *JM: How did you get involved in the project for cable?*

■ DF: The project that Arthur Knight and I have been working on was called to have been a feature documentary film called *That's Sexploitation!* We've been working on this at least 7 years. We accumulated films for years doing this, but we never could get a major company to listen to us; we never could get *Playboy* to listen to us. And Arthur even writes that continuing series in *Playboy.*

■ *JM: I've got* Playboy *magazines from the '60s with his film articles in them.*

■ DF: Do you remember Connie Mason? She was playmate of the year in June of 1962. Then she made *Blood Feast* and *2000 Maniacs,* the Alpha and Omega of her screen career. Herschell and I used to argue over her; she couldn't act at all. I said, "Herschell, she looks great, and she's got a bit of a following; a bit of a name." She was a great-lookin' gal.

■ *JM: Whatever happened to her?*

■ DF: I saw her about 15 years ago at the Beverly Hills Hotel. She was lying around the pool. She still looked great! ■

Few men have done more for sexual freedom in this country than David Friedman. From the earliest days of nudist films he has been an integral part of the adult film industry, not only as one of the better producers, but also as a collector and historian of early exploitation films.

Friedman's history is a colorful, hyperactive one. As a young man he worked at various jobs in carnivals and even owned one. He graduated from Cornell with a degree in electrical engineering, wrote speeches for a former governor of Alabama and worked as a craps dealer in Phenix City—a town so sleazy they made a movie (**The Phenix City Story**) about it. After World War II, he worked as a press agent for Paramount Pictures before striking out on his own in the world of independent film distribution.

He worked with Kroger Babb—one of the most outrageous and ingenious men in the history of exploitation films—traveling around the country with "birth-of-a-baby" films like **Mom and Dad**; pretending to be "Eliot Forbes, famous hygiene commentator"; and selling pamphlets like "Secrets of Sensible Sex."

In the late fifties, Friedman teamed up with Herschell Gordon Lewis to make nudist films, including **Daughter of the Sun,** about a school teacher forced to defend her nudist practices against bluenoses; and **Bell, Bare and Beautiful,** a vehicle for former strip-tease queen Virginia Bell. **The Adventures of Lucky Pierre** was one of the first "nudie-cutie" films to appear after Russ Meyer's **The Immoral Mr. Teas.** Other early Friedman-Lewis efforts include **BOIN-N-G!, Scum of the Earth** and **Goldilocks and the Three Bares.**

But the films Lewis and Friedman are best remembered for are the world's first gore films: **Blood Feast, Two Thousand Maniacs!** and **Color Me Blood Red.**

While filming the latter, Friedman and Lewis had a falling out. (Whatever the reasons, they have since buried the hatchet.) Lewis continued to explore the world of gore, while Friedman went back to sex, distributing titles like **Trader Hornee; A Smell of Honey, A Swallow of Brine!** and **Thar She Blows!**

About this time Friedman teamed up with the sons of one of the earliest exploitation pioneers, Louis Sonney. An Italian immigrant, he gained fame in 1919 for capturing a notorious railroad bandit, Roy Gardner. Sonney took the reward money and started Sonney Amusement Enterprises, in 1921 releasing the film **The Smiling Mail Bandit** based on the story of—Roy Gardner. Sonney went on the road, appearing in person to talk about his capture of the bandit, and warning against a life of crime. When "The Dangers of Crime" theme began to wear thin, Sonney switched to "The Dangers of Sex." Altogether he produced nearly 400 movies—all dealing with the dangers of various exploitable evils.

Friedman is full of stories about Louis Sonney. When Sonney was touring the country with his "Dangers of Crime"

show, he brought with him a collection of wax figures of desperados from the Old West, including the outlaw Elmer McCurdy. After dismantling the Crime show, he sold McCurdy to a wax museum at The Pike, an amusement park in Long Beach. When the wax museum folded, the figure ended up at the Laughter in the Dark Funhouse in L.A. There it mouldered until one day, during the filming of an episode of **The Six Million Dollar Man,** a technician found that the body was real. It was discovered that years ago Sonney had bought the body from a traveling carnival show and coated it with a layer of wax. Eventually it was shipped to Guthrie, Oklahoma (McCurdy's home state) for a proper burial.

The late sixties were "Golden Years" for sexploitation. Sex films symbolized the new sexual freedom sweeping the country. As the Supreme Court swept away more and more restrictions, the industry flourished. During this time, Friedman worked with many top talents such as director Lee Frost. They made **The Defilers,** a dark and moody B&W film loosely based on John Fowles' novel **The Collector.** It featured a man so obsessed with a woman that he kidnaps her.

A somewhat more humorous Friedman movie was **Starlet,** the story of an actress's climb to the top. The film trashes every Hollywood myth, from **All About Eve** to **Valley of the Dolls.** The studio portrayed in the movie, Entertainment Ventures, is the real name of Friedman's company, and

> Cresse always liked to carry a gun. One night he was in a bookstore at Hollywood and Western. He looks up and there's 3 guys beating the hell out of this broad. Cresse runs over and goes to his car and takes his gun out and holds the gun up, saying, "Stop! I'm calling the police! Stop or I'll shoot!" And this guy whirls on him and says, "We are the police, motherfucker!" and shot him twice right in the stomach. LAPD—they're "Dirty Harry's" down here!

Friedman appeared in it playing himself!

Most of Friedman's movies feature screenplays either written or co-written by him, which may explain why most of his films "are as rigid as a medieval morality play: a heterosexual scene, an S-M scene and a lesbian scene . . . something for everyone." Well, not really everyone—mostly lonely men. Friedman continues, "I must admit the carny in me plays on that most basic emotion that conmen use—loneliness."

Besides producing and screenwriting, Friedman occasionally acts. Easily his most outrageous appearance is that of the Nazi commandant in **Love Camp Seven.** The irony of such a portrayal is not lost on him, but Friedman is a man who realizes a little outrageousness is good for the soul. Interestingly, the film was made by Olympic International, a rival company to Friedman's Entertainment Ventures. (However, the rivalry was always friendly.)

The advent of hardcore sex films in the seventies killed the market for softcore. At first Friedman rejected the anatomical explicitness of this new breed of film, as he preferred the plot-oriented sexuality of sixties sexploitation movies. But the "raincoat crowd" was taking its business to the porno theater across the street. Reluctantly Friedman followed the

A scene from **Love Camp Seven.**

PARTIAL FILMOGRAPHY

AS PRODUCER:
The Adventures of Lucky Pierre, 1961
Nature's Playmate, 1962
Daughters of the Sun, 1962
BOIN-N-G!, 1962
Bell, Bare and Beautiful, 1963
Blood Feast, 1963
Goldilocks and the Three Bares, 1963
Scum of the Earth!, 1963
Two Thousand Maniacs!, 1964
Color Me Blood Red, 1965
The Defilers, 1965
The Notorious Daughter of Fanny Hill, 1966
A Smell of Honey, a Swallow of Brine!, 1966
She Freak, 1967
Brand of Shame, 1968
The Lustful Turk, 1968
Starlet, 1969
Thar She Blows, 1969
Trader Hornee, 1970
The Erotic Adventures of Zorro, 1971
Seven into Snowie, 1977
Chorus Call, 1978
Matinee Idol, 1984

AS ACTOR:
Bell, Bare and Beautiful, 1963

Love Camp 7, 1968
The Pick-up, 1968
House of a Thousand Dreams, 1969
Starlet, 1969
Matinee Idol, 1984

market and began producing hardcore films, among them: **Chorus Call** (an erotic rip-off of **Chorus Line**), **Seven Into Snowie** (an erotic rip-off of **Snow White and the Seven Dwarfs**) and most recently, **Matinee Idol.**

Friedman has no illusions that his films are great art, but he does think they're entertaining. "Most people are making pretentious garbage," he says. "I make funny garbage." Indeed, Friedman's films are notable for their hokey, rib-poking humor. In **Trader Hornee** he parodies virtually every jungle movie cliche—the lost treasure, the white woman raised in the jungle, the girlnapping gorilla. In **The Erotic Adventures of Zorro** the hero is a flaming gay by day and a womanizer by night—a concept George Hamilton borrowed for his film **Zorro, The Gay Blade.**

With the rise of the videocassette market stimulating demand for almost anything obscure, perhaps films like **The Defilers, The Acid Eaters** and **Daughter of the Sun** will be re-released. And, whatever comes from Entertainment Ventures in the future will surely be worth watching. ∎

INTERVIEW:
DORIS WISHMAN

For the past thirty years Doris Wishman has kept a low profile, making her nudist and exploitation low-budget films with almost no critical attention, much less acclaim. Yet her films—difficult to obtain and view—are indicative of a spontaneous playfulness and uninhibited imagination all too rare. When Andrea Juno interviewed her she seemed genuinely surprised, even skeptical, that anyone could find her work worthy of study, probably because at first glance her films often reveal such trademark low-budget production values as dodgy lighting and interiors resembling rundown motel rooms. Yet behind her economically deprived visuals lie a wealth of the imagination: wildly improbable plots, bizarre "method" acting and scripts yielding freely to fantasy.

Even though she says she's no feminist, Doris Wishman is definitely a positive woman's role model, persisting as she has in a field saturated with men. Somehow she simultaneously uses the exploitation genre and transcends it, as when she came up with the bizarre idea of implanting a spy camera in Chesty Morgan's 73" mammaries in the film **Double Agent 73.**

Despite never having gotten rich, Doris Wishman continues to work in her field of choice: independent filmmaking. The following interview took place in her film editing studio in New York City's warehouse district.

■ **DW:** As I said, my life really isn't that interesting—
■ **AJ:** *The fact that you've been making these films is interesting enough. When did you start?*
■ **DW:** About 20 years ago. My first films were nudist camp pictures. Then I went on to do other things like dramas and comedies. Now I'm making my first horror film. I can't say I was very successful with comedy—on the contrary I wasn't, so of course I won't attempt *that* again!
■ **AJ:** *How did you get into nudist films?*
■ **DW:** Well, I was in distribution. Then, when my husband died, I decided I wanted to do something that would be so different that it would keep me occupied *every second.* I didn't know what I was doing when I started production. Of course when I was finished with the first film, then I knew where to go, but making it was very difficult. I really didn't know what I was doing!
■ **AJ:** *That's the opposite of a lot of filmmakers—they know how to make a film but they don't know how to distribute it.*
■ **DW:** The thing is, I felt that since I knew distribution, production should be simple, but it doesn't work that way. They're completely different; there's no connection until

you finish the film. Then of course you have the edge because you know where to go.
■ **AJ:** *Did you have film crews?*
■ **DW:** Yes, but I did pretty much everything myself. Except for camerawork and editing, because I'm very clumsy with my hands . . . !
■ **AJ:** *How did you know the nudists? Did you search them out? Were you a nudist back then?*
■ **DW:** No, I wasn't. In fact I was rather astonished when I first went to the nudist camp, although the people were wonderful. The woman who ran the camp said that everybody in the crew had to be nude, and I said *under no*

> Sometimes you just get a title, then you work around the title, which I've done many times. It's ridiculous, of course, but that's how I work. [Take, for example] **A Night to Dismember:** I got the title first; [also] **The Amazing Transplant.**

circumstances! So *we* weren't nude. But of course the nudists were. It was an interesting experience; everybody was very nice and very cooperative.
■ **AJ:** *How did people think about you, a woman, working in a very male domain?*
■ **DW:** At first everybody was rather surprised, and it was a novelty. Of course, now women are in it as much as the men. I found it very exciting, very challenging. And I am a frustrated actress, so that helps. But really, there's nothing more to say except that I've been working very hard. I don't consider myself successful because I haven't made very much money, and that's how I judge success at this point.
■ **AJ:** Bad Girls Go to Hell—*when was that done?*
■ **DW:** It's an oldie . . . about 7 years ago.
■ **AJ:** *Do you know where a lot of your films are?*
■ **DW:** No, I really don't because I've sold most of them, and once I do that I have no more interest in them.
■ **AJ:** *Who do you usually sell them to?*
■ **DW:** Distributors
■ **AJ:** *You haven't made much money on these films?*
■ **DW:** I did until I made a comedy; then that was the kiss of death! I won't make any more comedies, that's for sure!
■ **AJ:** *What's most profitable for you?*
■ **DW:** Exploitation films.
■ **AJ:** *Do you invent the scripts yourself?*
■ **DW:** Yes, I write them myself. Then I direct them, choose the casting, crew, location—almost everything, although I don't edit. I know what I want. And I can't use a camera; I wish I could.
■ **AJ:** Double Agent 73 . . . *there was something so wonderful about the concept!*
■ **DW:** Chesty Morgan was very difficult to work with. She's made a lot of money because of this picture—she appears in

nightclubs and earns a great deal of money.

■ *AJ: How did that film help her? Just by giving her exposure?*

■ DW: Sure! That film made money. And actually, if not for the comedy, I'd be all right now.

■ *AJ: What year was this comedy?*

■ DW: About five years ago. We thought it was funny but nobody else did. The people working on it—we all thought it was hilarious, but obviously we were wrong! That's part of the game. I wish I could tell you something more interesting.

■ *AJ: Believe it or not, this is interesting: the fact that you're doing these films, you've done them by yourself, and have the motivation and drive to do them. . . . How many films did you make with Chesty Morgan?*

■ DW: Two; one called *Deadly Weapons.* That wasn't as good as *Double Agent.*

■ *AJ: What was the plot?*

■ DW: Chesty Morgan's lover is killed by some gangsters, and she seeks them out and kills them by smothering them with her breasts. It's a gimmick. Because there's no sex in either picture, you have to have *something.*

■ *AJ: Yes . . . so she can constantly show her breasts. Now you're doing* A Night to Dismember?

■ DW: Yes, I'm just finishing it, but I'm changing the title. How did *you* hear about it? I'm not through with the film; I've changed it about 4 different times.

■ *AJ: When did you start it?*

■ DW: About two years ago. But I'm surprised that you knew the title!

■ *AJ: By the way, did you ever use any pseudonyms? Did you write screenplays under the name Dawn Whitman?*

■ DW: What picture was that? I can't remember.

■ *AJ:* The Amazing Transplant. *Did you write that screenplay?*

■ DW: Yes, that was mine.

■ *AJ: That was great! Did you direct it as well?*

■ DW: Yes, I do the same with each film: I write, direct, and so on. But I used another name because it looks bad; it's not wise.

■ *AJ: That's what Herschell Gordon Lewis does.*

■ DW: Sure, everybody does that. What other films do you have written down?

■ *AJ:* Another Day, Another Man—*did you do that?*

■ DW: That's not on video. Where did you get that?

■ *AJ: Michael Weldon, who is writing a huge filmography*

Bad Girls Go To Hell

> There's a lot of blood in this, but that's what the public wants, and if you're in the business you have to give them what they want, if you have the courage.

for Ballantine Books, catalogued this. You know, certain obsessive people go around and do research.

■ DW: But I can't imagine where he got that, because I didn't sell it to video, and it's an oldie.

■ *AJ: I don't know. But* The Amazing Transplant—

■ DW: That was sold to video. Do you have any other films listed there?

■ *AJ: No. Your film company is J.E.R.?*

■ DW: J.E.R. is a distribution company that isn't mine. My company is J.U.R.I. Productions.

■ *AJ: But Jerry Balsam distributes some of your films?*

■ DW: Most of the time.

■ *AJ: What do think of the role of women in films these days?*

■ DW: Of course it's very exciting, but in many areas I don't

feel that women are as capable as men.

■ *AJ: Which areas?*

■ DW: It depends. I don't think I should speak this way, because I'll have the women down on me! I think men are more enterprising; I think women are much more cautious, because they have to be, I suppose. I don't believe in Women's Lib, I really don't.

■ *AJ: What does Women's Lib mean to you?*

■ DW: Women are coming into their own—if they can do a man's job, I feel they should be paid for what they can do. But I don't always think they can *do* a man's job. But then, by the same token, a man can't always do a women's job, so it sort of equalizes.

■ *AJ: Then how do you feel about what you're doing? Because traditionally, a lot of men would say that women should not direct sexploitation films.*

■ DW: You say "sexploitation," but that's not quite true because these days those films are not considered sexploitation. *Double Agent* and *Deadly Weapons* haven't any sex. *The Amazing Transplant* has very little sex. So they're not *sexploitation.* Anyway, as far as sex is concerned, men and women are on the same level, so that has no bearing! What I'm doing and what other women are doing—anybody can do if they have that talent, it has nothing to do with sex. But I don't feel that women can do everything that men can do in the business world. Especially where *prowess* is concerned. But anyhow, I have other problems; I'm not interested in women's lib. I'm really not.

■ *AJ: Are you married?*

■ DW: Not right now.

■ *AJ: You're pretty much on your own?*

■ DW: Oh yes, very much so. I like it.

■ *AJ: What were your budgets like? When you did* The Amazing Transplant *how much did that cost?*

■ DW: That was only about $250,000, I think. Which is considered very low, but that's because I do everything myself, and I don't take an actual salary, I just take what I need.

■ *AJ: How about* A Night to Dismember?

■ DW: That will be more costly; at this point I'm not sure, because I'm not finished.

■ *AJ: Do you have special effects in it?*

■ DW: Oh yes; these days you *have* to, unless you're making a terror film. There's a difference. There's a lot of blood in this, but that's what the public wants, and if you're in the business you have to give them what they want, if you have the courage.

■ *AJ: You think of the plots yourself?*

■ DW: Oh yes, you know—it's *just* imagination. And then you develop it. Sometimes you just get a *title,* then you work

---

I was rather astonished when I first went to the nudist camp. The woman who ran the camp said that everybody in the crew had to be nude, and I said under no circumstances! So we weren't nude. But of course the nudists were.

---

around the title, which I've done many times. It's ridiculous, of course, but that's how I work.

■ *AJ: Can you name a title?*

■ DW: *A Night to Dismember:* I got the title first. *The Amazing Transplant . . .* well, *most* of my films.

■ *AJ: Do you think people could tell if a woman had done your films?*

■ DW: Oh no. They know whether they like it or don't, or whether they think it's good or bad, but how can they tell?

■ *AJ: How is softcore sexploitation currently marketable, now that there's a whole market for hardcore?*

■ DW: I don't think there *is* any market for softcore, frankly, and I *don't* know what I'll make after this. I haven't the vaguest idea. I'm not thinking about the future; I just want to get finished with this film. But I really don't think there's a market for this sort of film anymore.

■ *AJ: Would you do hardcore?*

■ DW: No. Not that I disapprove, but I don't think I'd be capable. Well, I *could.* At first I thought it was horrible, but it's not. If you don't want to go see the movie, don't—they're not twisting your arm. If you want to see a hardcore film, fine. But I couldn't make those films.

■ *AJ: So if this is successful, you'll stick with horror?*

■ DW: I don't know. I haven't the vaguest idea at this point. Normally I'd be thinking of about ten other films, but this is one time where I'm not going to until I'm finished and know which way to go. Because the market changes constantly, and truly I don't know what's going to happen. Speaking of horror films, there are millions of them out, and I don't know how long *they'll* last.

■ *AJ: Do you still take a hand in the distribution?*

■ DW: Not if I can help it. I do because I have to sometimes, but I don't like to. I don't like distribution.

■ *AJ: That's where you started, though.*

■ DW: And that's where the money is, too. The distributors generally don't invest anything, so they have nothing to lose. Let's assume your picture cost $500,000. By the time you've gotten your money back, *if* you've gotten it, they might have made $150,000. Whereas you might not have gotten your money back. So actually, the money is in distribution. But I don't like it. This is more of a challenge, more exciting.

■ *AJ: Do you have any interests besides films?*

■ DW: Well, I'm writing a novel, and right now that's my hobby. Every time I have a spare minute, I write. It's a

wonderful story, I think, called *In a Dark Corner.*

■ *AJ: Is it romance-gothic, or horror?*

■ DW: It's not horror. It touches the lives of many people, has a most unusual ending—a fantastic ending, very different, and it's just—I can't really describe it, it's not horror. You cry a little bit, and yet it's not drama. There's some love story, naturally, some sex (which I find very difficult to write, I don't know why), and it's just good, *I* think—*naturally,* or I wouldn't write it.

■ *AJ: How long have you been working on it?*

■ DW: Oh god, a long time. About two years. But I don't work on it all the time. And sometimes when I *do* have the time I just can't think, so whenever I get in the mood. I don't know if it'll ever get published, but I'm going to try anyhow. It would make a great film, but it would have to have a very costly budget, a very high budget. And I find it difficult to find investors; I don't like to ask for money even though it's an investment.

■ *AJ: How do you get money?*

■ DW: I've used my family's money, my friends', and some of my own. And then I get a lot of credit because I have a good reputation, thank goodness. And that's about it . . . you're waiting for me to talk but I really have nothing to say!

■ *AJ: You've said quite a bit. Do you have any other hobbies?*

■ DW: Right now, I'm just working, thinking. And I've written some scripts.

■ *AJ: Do you ever send them out?*

■ DW: No, I'm keeping the scripts, because when I finish this I want to work on the others—I have two other scripts that are great. I'm really busy writing when I have any free time.

■ *AJ: Do you ever watch any films?*

■ DW: Strangely enough, no. I don't go to movies if I can help it, and I should.

■ *AJ: Why not?*

What I'm doing and what other women are doing—anybody can do if they have that talent; it has nothing to do with sex. But I don't feel that women can do everything that men can do in the business world.

■ DW: Because I become too critical. And if I'm with anyone I think I become annoying, because I see things that they don't see, and it bothers me. For example, in the Lindbergh kidnapping case which they had on last week, it was a three-hour TV movie . . . [disruption]

■ *AJ: How did you know Herschell Gordon Lewis?*

■ DW: He's in the industry; I met him someplace, I can't remember where. Do you know Dave Friedman? I think I met him through Dave Friedman.

■ *AJ: Do you know how to get in contact with Dave Friedman?*

■ DW: No, it's been years since I saw him. He's in Los Angeles as far as I know.

■ *AJ: Have you ever seen the Herschell Gordon Lewis films?*

■ DW: No, have you?

■ *AJ: Yes, they're great and quite witty.*

■ DW: Which?

■ *AJ: The Wizard of Gore, Blood Feast . . .*

■ DW: What is *Blood Feast* about?

■ *AJ: It's about an Egyptian man who worships the goddess Ishtar (a dummy they dressed up and painted gold). In order to worship her he has to provide a feast of body parts. So basically there's a series of killings in preparation for this "Egyptian feast," and—it's great.*

■ DW: I never saw it; I *should* see those films.

■ *AJ: There's probably a market in cable for your films—*

■ DW: I don't think in cable; maybe in video. I don't think so; I may be wrong.

■ *AJ: There's a lot of film festivals now devoted to more obscure films.*

■ DW: I haven't heard of any. You mean devoted to horror films?

■ *AJ: The older exploitation and horror films ... By the way, are there any other pseudonyms you've used, other than Dawn Whitman?*

■ DW: Maybe, but I don't remember—I didn't even remember Dawn Whitman until you mentioned it. I doubt it, but I don't remember.

■ *AJ: How do you feel about your work?*

■ DW: Well, I think I'm good!

■ *AJ: And do you like your films?*

■ DW: Yes, otherwise I don't make them. I have to think they're marvelous, great, and wonderful, otherwise I don't get involved. Of course they may not always turn out that way, but I have to feel that. It's a challenge, it's exciting, and I enjoy what I'm doing, and that's very important.

■ *AJ: Your films are good, and tastes are changing—*

■ DW: [softly] Well, I don't know how good they are, but—

■ *AJ: They are, because they reflect a creativity that's spontaneous and naive and uniquely affecting—qualities you usually can't find in the midst of a $20 million budget. I think people are really craving that now.*

■ DW: You really think so?

■ *AJ: There's a small but growing community of people around the world who realize that almost all big budget films like* Star Wars *are sterile. It's obvious that a corporation made this film, and—*

■ DW: Doesn't have that personal touch.

■ *AJ: You're also interesting in another dimension—it took a lot of courage to do this on your own.*

■ DW: It's not easy, but I guess most things that are worthwhile aren't that easy. ■

DORIS WISHMAN
BIOGRAPHY
BY JIM MORTON

During the early '60s hundreds of entrepreneurs and filmmakers jumped on the sexploitation bandwagon and began to crank out nudist films. Some, like Russ Meyer and Herschell Gordon Lewis, became famous. Others were regularly ignored, one of whom is Doris Wishman.

When nudist films first surfaced, Ms. Wishman was there with **Nature Camp Confidential** and **Blaze Starr Goes Nudist.** And under the pseudonym "Doris Wisher" she appeared in a Herschell Gordon Lewis film. Later, when the thrill of watching naked people play volleyball wore off, Wishman added the novelty of plotlines. She continued making nudist films until the mid-'60s when, like virtually every other sexploitation director, she switched to themes of violence, vice and death. It was during this period that Ms. Wishman directed the superbly titled **Bad Girls Go To Hell.** Whether the film is as good as its name is difficult to say—like many sexploitation films, prints of it are difficult to find.

In the early '70s Wishman teamed up with sex star Chesty Morgan and directed two films that assure her a place in the history of strange films: **Deadly Weapons** and **Double Agent 73.** Chesty Morgan is best known for her upper torso appointments: a full 73 inches of mammary excess. In **Deadly Weapons** (a title whose meaning the attentive reader may well discern), Chesty turns in an exquisitely bad performance—so crippled that in her next film, **Double Agent 73,** her voice is dubbed.

Supremely tacky, **Double Agent 73** makes **Pink Flamingoes** look almost genteel. And the film does not merely strain credulity—it tears it asunder. Chesty plays an agent assigned to ferret out and eradicate members of a dope-smuggling ring. To learn the identities of her victims after dispatching them—no need, apparently, to know before-hand whom she's killing—Chesty snaps their photos. The camera is implanted—really quite routine, medically—in her left breast. Naturally, every time she wants a photo she must first remove her clothes. Moreover, agent Chesty is working under a lethal deadline—she must complete her assignment by a certain time or the camera will explode!

Ms. Wishman, in addition to directing films, also wrote several movies under the pseudonym "Dawn Whitman." Her best effort is **The Amazing Transplant,** the story of a sexually frustrated young man named Arthur who wishes he could be more like his satyric friend, Felix. When Felix dies, Arthur—hoping for a virility boost—forces a doctor to transplant his friend's penis onto him. The operation is a "success." Arthur turns into a sex fiend, traveling around the city raping women. When his girlfriend Mary calls him "sick," Arthur strangles her and goes on the lam; finally he's tracked down by his uncle, a New York police detective who assures him that his problems are psychosomatic. Arthur reluctantly agrees to turn himself over to the authorities, and the movie ends in **Lady Or The Tiger** fashion—the outcome is left to the viewer.

Doris Wishman's style is all her own. Only Jean-Luc Godard can match her indifference to composition and framing; if two people are talking and one is partially obscured by a post, so be it—the camera will not change its angle. Sometimes we are treated to static shots of feet—or torsos, or hands—while voices talk off-screen. At other times Ms. Wishman will trade off shots in such a way that we never see the person who's talking—instead we watch the listener, his head nodding thoughtfully to words from a speaker we can't see. Often her camera imitates a human eye roving restlessly around the room, occasionally allowing insignificant objects to hold its attention. For example, the camera might follow a person to a dresser, then stop to dwell on the various items (objects completely irrelevant to the plot) it finds there.

Unlike the performances in the films of Herschell Gordon Lewis and Russ Meyer, the acting in Doris Wishman's films is usually underplayed; half-baked, even. This, coupled with her singular camera technique, gives Wishman's work an unmistakable look and feel. Some filmmakers work on the periphery of accepted styles, but Wishman is well beyond the fringe. No hints here of Hawks, Welles, or Eisenstein—in fact, no hints of **anything** seen before; and because of this, critics and viewers have hastily—and unfortunately—shunted aside the work of this uniquely inspired filmmaker.

The sexual freedom of the '70s—unkind to many other sexploitation directors as well—hurt Ms. Wishman's career; as hardcore films took over the market for softcore dried up. In 1983 she began work on a slasher film entitled **A Night To Dismember.** While not rejecting the possibility of making more movies, Wishman is pessimistic about her filmic future. We wish her luck. ■

INTERVIEW:

LARRY COHEN

One of the most politically aware, sardonic, and resourceful directors in this publication is former New Yorker Larry Cohen, whose films over the past 15 years all bear anti-authoritarian, anti-religious or other socio-critical themes. His films **God Told Me To, Q** and **It's Alive!** question commonly held assumptions about God, aliens, religion and family ties, while other efforts such as his screenplay for **I, The Jury** (which links the C.I.A. to sex-crime assassinations of political radicals), and **The Stuff** (critiquing the F.D.A. and corporate/governmental collusion) round out a career devoted to destabilizing the status quo . . .

On a warm fall afternoon Andrea Juno and Vale interviewed Larry Cohen at his old Spanish ranch-style mansion off Coldwater Canyon Drive in Beverly Hills, once the home of his friend, director Samuel Fuller. Posters in many different languages from his movies, flyers for his theatrical productions, photos of friends and his five children, as well as a **Variety** sheet listing **It's Alive!** as top-grossing movie of the week, lined the walls of his office. At the end he brought out wonderful memorabilia, including props such as the **It's Alive!** babies and bird models from **Q**.

Soft-spoken, hospitable, and very funny, Cohen freely offered his philosophy, political and religious views, career history, industry overview, and many anecdotes in a four-hour conversation over a kitchen table, interrupted only by apple pancakes supplied by his daughter Melissa.

■ *ANDREA JUNO: Why do you prefer filming in New York?*
■ LARRY COHEN: I *like* filming there—I like the streets, the activity, the texture of the city. There's always something happening—there's always *life* going on. Here in Los Angeles the streets are devoid of people—there are cars going back and forth, but you don't see *people.* And you don't see the contrast in architecture that New York has, where there's brick, glass, an old building next to a brand new one . . . Here it's like looking at a blank, clean sidewalk, as opposed to one that has all kinds of cracks in it and levels of steps, where everything looks like some kind of multi-layered piece of art. It's more fun to shoot *that.*
■ *VALE: Your films are multi-layered, yet accessible—the audience can get simple messages right away, but other, more complex implications are there.*
■ *AJ: Do people get mad at you because they can't put a simple label on your films?*
■ LC: They don't get mad at you, they just ignore you—if they can't get a "fix" on you they ignore you. But cable video and the videocassette stores are a wonderful thing, because people see your pictures years later under different circum-stances, or maybe they're just able to concentrate better in their homes.

It's like having your books in the public library; people'll read the book, but you're not going to make any money. But you can't worry about it, you just go on and make your next picture. Revival houses are the same thing; the pictures play, but they change the picture every day, so . . . You get your chance to make money when the picture comes out theatrically *the first time,* and after that it's *art for art's sake.* I like the fact that my films keep surfacing. They're like people; they have a life of their own. They go out into the world and make friends on their own.
■ *AJ: Have you experienced any resurgence of critical acclaim?*
■ LC: As time goes on, more and more people—whether in France or England or wherever—discover the whole succession of pictures. I knew that if I made enough films that would happen; sooner or later somebody's going to see them, someday.

Although . . . my films were all made in the commercial marketplace of Hollywood. They were financed by commercial companies that expected to make money on the pictures, and in most cases they did. The only one that didn't was *The Private Files of J. Edgar Hoover,* and you never can tell—something might happen with *that,* someday.

The reason I got to make so many pictures, one after another, was because they made money for people. They were low-budget and able to make back their investment with substantial profits for everybody, even though they weren't what you'd call blockbuster hits. (Except for *It's Alive!* and *Black Caesar,* which were top of the list for awhile.)
■ *AJ: Was* Hoover *a personal indulgence?*
■ LC: It was not in my usual cycle of horror or sci-fi. I just wanted to do it because Hoover was a flamboyant and unusual character, and because no one else would make it and thus risk incurring the wrath of the FBI and causing a lot of trouble for themselves.
■ *AJ: Did you get in any trouble?*
■ LC: No! They knew I was oblivious to any pressures they could apply. Being an outsider, I wasn't subject to the same pressures or fears that somebody else in "the system" might have been afraid of. And the picture didn't turn out to be *too* derogatory to him, anyway. It was a picture where everybody was bad, everybody was a little bit crooked. He was just one more phenomenon of the system which encourages a lot of hypocrisy. Roosevelt didn't come off well, and neither did the Kennedys or Johnson; everybody came off as kind of unscrupulous.

Hoover didn't come off any worse then anybody else in the picture, which was the truth of the matter. Those who liked Hoover were fairly satisfied with the film. I had more trouble with people like Arthur Schlesinger who felt that we slandered Franklin D. Roosevelt. He wrote in the *Saturday Review* some nice things about the picture, but withheld his approval because of the shabby way we treated President Roosevelt.

We took a big chance on that; people felt there was no market for a picture like that, and when they think this they can make it come true. If the distribution department of a movie decides beforehand that a picture is not going to be successful, they will put it in the wrong theatres, give it bad play dates, won't spend any money for advertising or TV advertising, so inevitably the picture will fail. Then their pre-judgment is verified and they go on thinking, "See, we really *know* if a picture's going to make it or not!" On *J. Edgar Hoover* they didn't think it would have any market, and they made sure it didn't. But it still has slipped onto TV and into repertory theaters, and I get inquiries about it all the time. You never know *where* these films can turn up.

■ *AJ: Your movies don't seem to have pat, dogmatic politics. They have complexity, they can't be pinned down to simplistic "Left" or "Right" messages. And yet they all have underlying anti-authoritarian themes.*

■ *V: Yes, they seem to be anti-"Control Process"...*

■ LC: That's true. *The Stuff* is an indictment of the food industry, mass market advertising and the cynical way it's all handled by the U.S. Government Food and Drug Administration. In the end of the picture, they uncover that "the stuff" is a poisonous food that takes over people's minds and kills them, so they finally get it off the market, destroy the factory and blow up the franchises. But then the people who are merchandising it just re-emerge under another name. They dilute it, saying their new product contains only 12½% of the stuff—the rest is "natural dairy products"—and put it out under a new name with a new advertising campaign.

That's what they always do, right? Like with saccharin—now it's *Nutrasweet*. If you examine the label you'll probably find the product has just as much saccharin as before, but they just put in a little drop of Nutrasweet so they can feature that on the label, giving the impression there's no more saccharin in it. But all they did was *add* the Nutrasweet without *taking out* the saccharin. Now you really don't know what you're getting!

They'll sell you anything. Ford Motor Company'll sell you a car that goes out of control and runs you over. They *know* about the defect, but it's easier for them not to do anything about it and pay off the lawsuits than to recall all the cars. Even though a few people get killed—*so what?* When they find it's a defective part that makes the cars go out of control and kill a few old ladies, they say, "*Oh well,* if you bring the car back we'll fix it for you."

> I don't relate to anyone who is a professional religionist . . . who has the ego to tell us that they know God's will, and can tell us what God thinks and what God likes and what God is, and how God feels about integration, and South Africa, and AIDS.

What *should* happen is—they should be forced to refund the entire original purchase price of the car. I don't care if I've driven my car 20,000 miles—if it was defective to start with, they should give me back the whole $10,000 I originally paid. *Then* they wouldn't put defective cars on the market! But try and get that passed. It would be "bad" for American industry; we'd have to start loaning money to Chrysler to keep them from going out of business . . . [laughs] There is nothing as bizarre in my movies as what happens in real life. I think all my pictures are *understatements.*

The whole system is amazing. Recently Sparkletts Water Co. here, who put out "natural, pure, clean bottled water," were given the biggest fine in history, $500,000, because they were caught pouring the paints they use to paint their tanks

Larry Cohen with his two monster babies from It's Alive Part I & II and newly hatched killer Mayan bird-god from Q.

with into the city water system, a violation of the law. But it was cheaper for them to do it and pay the fine than to dispose of it properly.

■ *AJ: That's just one or two executive salaries a year for them. A drop in the bucket, so to speak.*

■ LC: See, they don't put anybody in jail. If they started putting people in jail there would be a change! But they don't want to put a few "nice persons" in jail when all they did was poison a few hundred thousand people . . .

There was a recent story about someone putting plutonium in the New York City water supply. But after a couple of days you didn't hear about it; imagine the panic if they went on the air and told 8 million people they're going to die! They just dropped it: "Keep on drinkin' it, folks!" So, my movies are definitely an understatement. They're not exaggerations; they're *conservative!* They don't go as far as they *should.* And probably no one would believe it if you told the *real* truth.

■ *V: Why was the title of* God Told Me To *changed to* Demon?

■ LC: Well, nobody could remember the title; they kept saying, "God Made Me Do It" or "God Told Me To Do It." Finally Roger Corman said, "We'd better change the title to something people can remember." *The Omen* had been out, and I thought that Omen spelled sideways is *Demon,* so . . . !

■ *AJ: Did it work?*

■ LC: Oh, I don't know. It didn't turn it into a blockbuster,

Photo: Vale

Larry Cohen with Broderick Crawford on the set of **The Private Files of J. Edgar Hoover.**

but the picture played and was distributed by Roger Corman.

■ *AJ: Did it make money?*

■ LC: Yeah, it made money—for *us,* anyway, who made the picture. Money still comes in on a regular basis from foreign sales and things like that. All these pictures bring in money every quarter or every year, just like a songwriter getting royalties on some hit song he wrote twenty years ago.

■ *AJ:* God Told Me To *was such a bleak statement about religion. What do you feel about religion, God, etc?*

■ LC: I don't relate to anyone who is a professional religionist ... who has the ego to tell us that they know God's will, and can tell us what God thinks and what God likes and what God *is,* and how God feels about integration, South Africa, and AIDS. Everybody's got a different idea what God thinks; the crazy guy on the street corner knows about as much as the guy in St. Patrick's Cathedral—none of them know *anything.*

People say, "Reverend Moon—what a crook!" and I say, "But what about the *Pope?*" It's all the same; anybody who starts telling you what God thinks should be locked up *immediately!* Get them off the streets because they'll cause a lot of trouble for everybody. I don't want anybody telling me that so-and-so's going to heaven but not this guy. I'd hate to get there and find a line of people with reservations; they give you a number like in a bakery and you're standing there, then they call your number and some guy comes over and says, "But you're not wearing a necktie!"

I think heaven, the way it's depicted, would be too horrendous to imagine, with everybody up there telling you who's good enough to get in and who's *not* good enough to get in, like some kind of a club. I think it's really sad when I see all these guys on television "healing" people and asking people to send their money in. I find it hard to accept that anybody falls for this. But then, I guess if you're desperate

enough, and you've had enough tragedy in your life, for some people the only alternative to giving up completely is finding something to put their faith in.

But it would be better to put your faith in nature, and go out and pray to a big tree, or the clouds which are beautiful, or go out into the woods somewhere where God really had something to do with it. Forget about all those stained-glass windows which are pretty, but ...

I guess I got the idea for *God Told Me To* from going to the National Gallery in London. I was walking through it, looking around and thinking, "Jesus, they talk about *movies* being violent—look at all these paintings. This saint has 77 arrows in his back, this guy's got his head over here and his hand there, and here are all these women being raped and ravaged. Look at this scene and think what it would cost to reproduce it: a big canvas with bodies strewn from one end to the other; here are babies with spears through them. And it's a religious painting."

Jesus, there's nothing as violent as the Bible. God kills everybody—drowns the entire world, destroys the cities of Sodom and Gomorrah, burning people to a crisp. "This is a *tough* guy," I said. "Boy, if he ever came back, look out! Talk about Godzilla—what if *God* ever walked in here and took a look around? He's one tough cookie. This man is *strict.*"

So that gave me the basic idea for this movie: what if a messiah came back, bringing with him the kind of ethic that really *is* the basis of our religion, which is: *kill and destroy anybody who doesn't do EXACTLY what you tell him to do.* Why should the Angel of Death fly over and strike down every firstborn male child of the Egyptians who didn't do anything except be born; why should those little babies have to die? This is an *unreasonable, mean person.* Right? This is *not* a nice guy.

Back in the '20s when Cecil B. DeMille was making sexy

comedies and sexy movies about philandering wives with big orgy scenes, the Motion Picture Board of Review came down and said, "You cannot make these kind of pictures anymore." So DeMille decided he would make Biblical movies, because in that context he could have orgies, he could have all these women taking baths, he could have all this infidelity; *everything* he was no longer allowed to do he could get away with, because he was invoking the name of the Lord. If you have the Bible you can get away with *anything*. The Bible is a book that's full of sound and fury, sex and violence, and the best-selling book of all time, you know.

■ *V: However, the author never got any royalties.*

■ LC: That's what you think; we don't know who wrote it! Believe me, religion is a big business—bigger than the movie business, that's for sure. Before movies came along, people had to go *somewhere* on the weekend so they went to the church. And if they had a good minister who ranted and raved and created a lot of excitement—

■ *V: And painted illusions—*

■ LC: —With hell and damnation, where you could see all those people consumed by fire—boy, that was hot stuff!

> **Jesus, there's nothing as violent as the Bible. God kills everybody—drowns the entire world, destroys the cities of Sodom and Gomorrah, burning people to a crisp.**

■ *V: They prey on all those fear emotions.*

■ LC: Sure. Now you've got different people doing it, like that guy in Oregon—Rajneesh. On a recent news program you could see these people going crazy when he arrived, chanting, screaming, hollering, having virtual orgasms of delight. Now, because of AIDS, when they have sex they have to wear plastic gloves, and they're not allowed to kiss, and they have to wear prophylactics during intercourse. He's got them convinced (like others have done before) that everybody's going to die in a nuclear holocaust if they don't go to some out-of-the-way place. Also, he's got his sect believing they will be the only survivors when the plague of AIDS sweeps America and the world, and everybody else dies but them. You can get people to believe anything!

■ *V: A doomsday scenario has been an essential part of so many of these religious movements through the ages.*

■ LC: Well, everybody's expecting the "last judgment"—the whole church is based on the belief that some day Jesus will return and the "last judgment" will come. If you look at the painting "The Last Judgment" by Michelangelo—talk about horror movies, there's a guy holding somebody's *skin* in his hands! I got a print of that when I was at the Vatican. Michelangelo painted himself actually as the skin; this man's holding his outer skin all hanging down, but it's Michelangelo's face. For all-time gruesomeness you don't need Rick Baker or "The Thing"—just go look at some religious paintings! Originally I wanted all the main titles of *God Told Me To* to be religious paintings of exquisite violence.

■ *V: Why didn't you do that?*

■ LC: Well, I'd gotten all these slides from different museums, but we didn't have the rights to reproduce these paintings, and I was afraid, after we shot it, that we'd be involved with all kinds of litigation with museums across the country.

■ *V: Those paintings from the 16th or 17th centuries aren't public domain?*

■ LC: I don't know. I think you could argue you have the right to use a painting like the *Mona Lisa* that's been around so long it's just become part of our society, there's no ownership to it. Just like the Sphinx and the Pyramids have become part of our culture.

Merely showing the actual painting should be okay. But if we were to actually paint in a naked woman performing a sex act on a religious figure in a painting—that might be considered "obscene"; we wouldn't necessarily have any right to deface a painting or change it in any way. But just to *show* the painting seems to me like showing Mt. Rushmore. I didn't have the time or legal fees to get into it.

Anyway, I thought all those violent religious paintings would tie the whole thing together and solve the problem of: how can I bring "aliens" into the plot? Aliens are like an alternative religion—the belief that aliens are going to show up. There's probably a better chance that aliens will show up than Jesus will appear! "Make your bets now on who's coming first—*ET* or Jesus!"

■ *V: The* National Enquirer *periodically runs stories about tiny men in crashed space capsules being found. Maybe this actually happened.*

■ LC: Probably just as many people say the Virgin Mary appears and tells them to go do something. All these fantasies! There are so many interlocking things people believe in—stories in the Bible, ancient drawings and carvings supposedly depicting "spacemen" with antennae coming out of the helmet—you've seen *Chariot of the Gods*.

There's some of that in *God Told Me To*—the idea that ancient aliens may have founded our religion. In the movie this guy's an alien and he's here on earth. If Superman were real—if there really were a Clark Kent, and Mr & Mrs Kent found the baby in the space capsule and brought him up, when he reaches five or six years old he doesn't know who he is, right?

He starts to go to church, they tell him about Jesus Christ and he thinks, "I can see through walls and I can fly; I have superior powers. I look like a man, but I'm not one of them—I'm sure of that. *I* must be Jesus Christ."

He's not going to think he's Superman; he's going to think he's Jesus because we have a religious belief that says God comes down to Earth looking like a man but with superior powers. So he doesn't go to Metropolis and become a reporter; he starts a religion. The alien in this movie could easily be deluded into thinking he's God, just by the fact he's not a human being. If you're not a human being, who are you?

My movies aren't so different from what was done all through ancient societies. So many of the ancient books and plays are based on gods appearing in human form; the Minotaur is half-human, half-beast. God's always coming down and having sex with a woman, and she gives birth to a child who's half-human and half-monster. That was the principal Class A entertainment in those days; today that's an exploitation film!

Some people ask, "How can you make a picture where people give birth to a monster baby?" [as in *It's Alive!*] Well, it's not the first time this story's been told. Mythology has loads of monster babies; I mean, in those ancient days it was unusual if your kid was born without a tail. Often you see the combination of man-beast people—the head of a man with the body of a beast and vice-versa.

For example, in Egypt there's Anubis with the head of a dog and the body of a man. These kind of monsters are not new, but they always have some religious connection to them. And in ancient times people thought that malformed children had some kind of religious significance. In some societies they worshipped them, and in others they sacrificed them. But they always thought they were in some way God-like or a manifestation of God.

■ *AJ: Were you thinking about this when you did* It's Alive!?

■ LC: To some degree. I didn't think *It's Alive!* was all that different from a picture that came out years later called *The Elephant Man*. It wasn't the same story progression, but I was trying to create the same feeling of a compassion for someone who is *different*.

It's funny, because today *The Elephant Man* is sold just like the Elephant Man was sold when he really existed. You show him in the ad with a caftan on so you can't see his face, and you tell everybody to go to the movie and pay five dollars to get in—to see what he looks like when they take it off, right? Just as in an old-time freak show. And *It's Alive!* is the same thing. The audience *almost* gets a look—we hardly show it, but they get a little glimpse. But on the same token, both *It's Alive!* and *The Elephant Man* are trying to tell a compassionate story about feelings.

It's Alive! tries to tell about parents' feelings for a child that's different. In today's world it could be *anything* wrong with the kid—psychologically or physiologically—and yet parents have to come to terms with their feelings for the child. At the time I made the picture, people were afraid of their children because their kids were wearing their hair long, smoking grass, and fucking. All of a sudden they were taking acid, fathers were shooting their teenage sons in the house because they couldn't control them anymore, and there was a general fear of the younger generation by the older generation—they were suddenly *afraid.* This was a big, prevalent feeling at the time, and I felt that the story fitted in. This was a picture of that time: the early seventies.

> I never got into anything, so I never changed. I never got into any of the fads in terms of clothing, drugs, or anything. I just did my work, lived my life and kept out of all those things. I believed in certain things politically but I wasn't out on the street throwing bags of shit at the police. I didn't believe in that.

It's funny how things even out as time goes by. These movies become a part of the culture or the subculture and they're there, but everything else changes. The hairstyles change, the compulsions change, the political things change. The people stop marching in the streets, and they get jobs, and get on the pension plan, and they get conservative ... people go through the big drug thing ... then they get off the drug thing, and then join the gym and the healthclub and they jog and eat wheat germ and take colonic enemas—these are the same people that were wasting their bodies years before.

The world changes but the movie stays the same; it's just there. It's made in one culture and emerges ten years later in another. And sometimes it's understood better by people who are no longer in the culture that the picture was about. Ten years later they've changed into different people; they see the picture on cable and say, "Hey, this is very good! Why didn't we like this when we first saw it?"

You can see how the world is changing constantly. I know all these people who once were wild, crazy kids, and you meet them now and they're older than I am. What happened to them? [laughs] How'd they get so old? And now, you've got kids running around with the spiked hair—orange, pink, and blue. It's great, but wait and see these same people ten years from now—you won't recognize them. They've got to get it all out of their system *now.*

All that rebellion they'll get out of their system by dying their hair green or red or purple, without ever dealing with anything *mentally.* So that when they're all through with it, they can become the same boring people that their parents are. Meanwhile we go on making the movies. It's like painting on the walls of the cave—years later another society discovers those paintings and says, "That's what things were like in those days." Those movies really have something to do with the time in which they're made.

Full Moon High [points to poster] was made about seven or eight years ago. Two weeks ago a picture came out called *Teen Wolf* which is basically the same film but not nearly as funny. *Full Moon High* was really *about* something—about a

kid who's a werewolf. (Ever read *Interview with the Vampire?* In it there's a little girl who's a vampire—she never gets any older. Werewolves and vampires never age; they stay the same age forever.) The kid's a teenager in high school who becomes a werewolf; then he goes away—he doesn't want to bite anyone in his hometown. Twenty years later he comes back and of course all the kids he went to high school with are middle-aged, but he's still seventeen.

So he goes back to the high school posing as his own son. His ex-girlfriend is now a forty-year-old woman, his best friend is now the forty-year-old Chief of Police ... They always say *werewolves* change—the full moon comes out and they change into a wolf—but he's changed less than anyone. In the past twenty years all these nice, idealistic sweet kids have become these hideous people; he's less of a monster than they are.

So it really was a picture that was *about* something; also, kind of a fun picture. Again, this is what I was talking about: how people change so much. In a ten or twenty year period they change totally into different people. That's why people get divorced, I guess; they marry one person and find out ten years later they're living with somebody else. But the pictures, like my werewolf, stay the same!

■ *AJ: How about* you? *What were you like ten years ago?*
■ LC: The same. I never got into anything, so I never changed. I never got into any of the fads in terms of clothing, drugs, or anything. I just did my work, lived my life and kept out of all those things. I believed in certain things politically but I wasn't out on the street throwing bags of shit at the police. I didn't believe in that.
■ *V: Too ineffectual for you?*
■ LC: Yeah. When I lived in New York we went for training in Civil Disobedience to close down nuclear power plants, etc. We went to a course in that, but I didn't like being manipulated; I felt that the ones running the whole thing were manipulating and brainwashing people just like these religious people do: giving them dogma. You weren't allowed to think for yourself; you had to do it the way they wanted you to, there were no questions asked. You were supposed to lie on the street and let yourself be dragged down the block.

I didn't want to become a drone, no matter what the cause was. I've never been able to get into any of those things. You do what you can, but without becoming part of a mob or group or movement.

Strangely enough, if you stand back it all kind of goes away. The people all change; usually they become totally hypocritical, like all those guys who were the "great leaders" in the anti-war movement—Jerry Rubin ... Woodward and Bernstein, who were such great media heroes—such "wonderful guys" turned out to be a couple of assholes!

You've just got to stand back, look at it all and say: *this too will pass away.* Because that's the truest statement I've ever heard, truer than any Biblical statement. I don't know if it's from the Bible, but it sounds like it is: *This too will pass away.* Whether it's success or failure, or misery or whatever, if you stand back it will pass away, it will change. If you're a big success—don't worry, you won't be for long! If you're Number One—don't worry, somebody else will take it away from you. If you're madly in love—don't worry, it will pass away. If you can't stand someone—that's all right, it will go away too—hate also goes away. Everything will eventually pass. Your great success or great depression will go away, eventually. That's what I think when I see all these people coming up who know all the answers and—
■ *V: Have all the 'hip' attitudes, like* hate Reagan—
■ *AJ: Or love him.*
■ LC: Yeah, they know it all. Reagan's a phenomenon like everything else. I think that at the end of his speeches they ought to come on and say, "The part of the President was played by Ronald Reagan." I mean, he's good casting for this

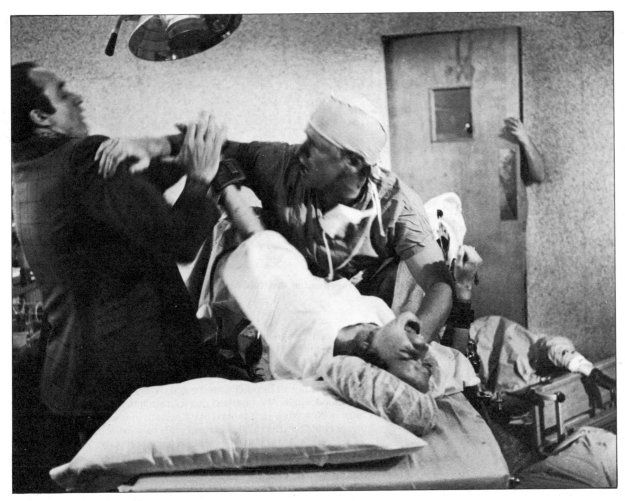

It's Alive!

part. All the Presidents have been terrible disappointments . . . including Kennedy.

■ *V: He fooled a lot of people.*

■ LC: Well, he fooled them because he was attractive and had the media on his side—they'd finally found the first real Television President. Eisenhower before him was an old man. He was a World War II hero, but in terms of speeches he wasn't very good on television. But Kennedy was *made* for the TV tube. He looked so extemporaneous and so relaxed and so casual, and could answer any question, and charm and make jokes, and act sexy to the women. He loved his kids, and

> **Now, you've got kids running around with the spiked hair . . . All that rebellion they'll get out of their system by dying their hair green or red or purple, without ever dealing with anything mentally. So that when they're all through with it, they can become the same boring people that their parents are.**

loved to walk on the beach; always had a kid or a little boy under his desk (making all the decisions; people didn't realize that). He was a wonderful guy—beautiful wife and everything. They didn't mention that every day at 3:00 PM there was a hooker coming into the White House . . .

If you read the speeches Kennedy made they're really amazing in the context of what really was going on. He said that he and Winston Churchill had something in common:

Churchill was able to function so well because every day at 3:00 he took a nap, and Kennedy did the same. And it wasn't just lying down on the couch, he put his pajamas on and got into bed for one hour. What he didn't tell everybody was: the reason Winston Churchill went to sleep at 3:00 was because he was *drunk*—every afternoon he got drunk on brandy and passed out, and they had to put him to bed. And the reason *Kennedy* went to bed was because there was always a broad being brought in at 3:00 PM. These are the *true facts!* You get the famous statement, then twenty years later you get the true facts. You can imagine what absurdities are going on today—we'll only know in about twenty years. So what's next?

■ *AJ: God Told Me To was very filmic, with your use of camera angles and particularly your use of sound.*

■ *V: Yes; why did you dedicate the film to Bernard Herrmann?*

■ LC: He was supposed to do the music for the film, but he died before he could. He was a good friend of mine. Actually, we had been together the night before he passed away; we had run the film for him over at Golden Studios. Then he and his wife and my wife and I went out to dinner. The next morning we got a call from his hotel saying he had died in his sleep. We had been with him till about 12 midnight, and then he died a few hours later. So of course he couldn't do the music. Frank Cordell, a good British composer who had known Herrmann, wrote the music.

■ *V: The sound editing was incredible, with layers upon layers of sound.*

■ *AJ: The film has almost a timeless quality, like a morality play or an opera that makes it much more than just a story set in New York.*

■ LC: There were a lot of things going on at once in the story, with the religious choir and the parade music *and* the score.

■ *AJ: A lot of times at the end of certain scenes you had the music swell, and somehow that lent the quality of a Noh play or something very stylized.*

■ LC: We mixed it at Golden Studios which is the best mixing place in Hollywood. We had a guy who worked for Robert Altman who often is complimented for good sound and good sound mixing. The mixer was Dick Portman, who has won an Academy Award for some of the work he's done.

■ *V: But didn't you tell him what you wanted?*

■ LC: You always tell them what effects you want, for sure, and for the most part you get what you ask for. Sometimes you don't; then you have to stop in the mix (which is very expensive) and find an effect that the studio has available on cassettes. Sometimes you have to create them right there at the soundstage.

God Told Me To was a New York picture and it had a lot of real street sounds and street noise, recorded live. Some of it you can't keep out of a picture because it's on the dialogue tracks. If they don't want that extraneous noise in, some studios will then "loop" the scene. But New York street noise is like the New York "look"—it has a *texture* to it. I usually feel that reality is the best thing you can give people in a movie.

■ *AJ: A lot of times a director works on an intuitive level that is not logically thought out at the time . . . How did you do that parade scene?*

> Now I have to figure out how to get the Masons' parade into a picture. . . . ! Parades are fun—you get a million free extras, and it looks very rich and opulent because you have all these people marching along.

■ LC: Well, we actually shot part of it at the real St. Patrick's Day Parade in New York.

■ *V: You had your actors there in the parade?*

■ LC: Yeah; that scene was one of the first things we shot. I thought, "Wouldn't it be great if we could have a shootout in the middle of the St. Patrick's Day parade which is next week? But it's not in the script, so I don't *have* to deliver the scene. If it doesn't work out, I won't be penalized by people saying, 'Hey, you didn't get that big parade, so we don't want to give you the money for the picture because you didn't give us the picture you promised.'" I thought, "But if I can bring this off, it will add a big, spectacular scene to the movie."

What could be more fun than to have the police looking for one particular cop in the middle of a big parade where there's 5000 policemen? So we went down there wearing badges like we were covering the parade for a newsreel company. We had three cameras and three crews, and we put Andy Kaufman in the parade (who played the guy with the gun). It was the first thing he ever did in a film, by the way. We told him, "Get in there with the police officers!" So he got into the formation, and the cops who were there played along with it. They probably thought we were allowed to do it, anyway.

■ *AJ: Were you?*

■ LC: No. We had no permits to shoot an actual movie, we only had permits to shoot a normal newsreel of a parade. They didn't know we were going to have people falling down, running around, pulling guns and stuff like that! But we didn't actually fire off any guns there.

Later, we came back to Los Angeles and contacted all the

Parade scene in **God Told Me To.**

Irish-American groups there. I told them we were going to re-stage the St. Patrick's Day Parade downtown. We got a permit, and all these groups came and brought their bands. They came in costumes and marching clothes, and *that's* where we shot all the stuff with the guns *really* going off and the blood squibs. We matched that footage into the footage shot in New York so it looked like it was all-in-one. But we *never* could have had all that carnage and chaos in the middle of the real St. Patrick's Day parade in New York City!

■ *V: I wondered; I thought the parade scene alone must have cost a million.*

■ LC: It would have, because you would have *had* to have thousands of extras, and you really would have had to shut down the entire Fifth Avenue, and they never would have gone along with *that*. As it was, I'm sure to this day they're trying to figure out how we managed to do that in the middle of their parade and get away with it! Anyway, we got the sequence. But if it hadn't worked out, I just would have done something else, that's all.

Now I have to figure out how to get the Masons' parade into a picture. I'd love to see a gun fight in their parade, because if a few bullets go into some of those balloons and they start popping or dragging all the people up on those strings, then . . . ! Parades are fun—you get a million free extras, and it looks very rich and opulent because you have all these people marching along. They're all there, anyway!

■ *AJ: What was your budget?*

■ LC: Oh God, I don't even remember. They're all low budget films—a million this or a million that. In those days a million dollars was more than it is today. You'll notice prices never go *down!*

■ *AJ: Remember the silver scandal?*

■ LC: That's right. The price of silver went up so they raised the price of film. Then the silver market collapsed, but they didn't lower the price of film; they kept it high and that was that.

Everything costs more money; wages are more and benefits are more. So even if your budgets go up, a good portion of that raise is eaten up by inflationary costs, and you still don't have any more real money to make your picture with than before. You're still working on basically a limited budget, no matter what.

But sometimes, *imagination* is required to come up with something when you can't squander money aimlessly. You may end up doing something cleverer than you would if you had all the money in the world. If we had staged the St. Patrick's Day Parade like a normal movie studio, it might not have been as good, because it never could have been the *real* parade. But we had the real parade—*nothing* could be better than that.

If you set out to do something like that, you have to enter into it with a great deal of trepidation: "Am I really going to be able to bring this off? Is something going to go wrong?" Because remember, they only hold the parade once. They start off walking from 42nd Street up to 86th Street, and when they get there that's the end of the parade. If you don't get the scene by the time it's finished, then . . .

We were running our asses off! We had to keep getting ahead of the march each time. We'd shoot them going by and then we'd have to run our asses off and get up ahead of them in enough time to set up the shots, set up the camera, get the readings and focus and be ready when they came by again. And you'd be carrying all that equipment—batteries, extra loads of film, running like crazy. It was like covering a real news event.

■ *AJ: But it had that "special feeling": a kind of gritty feeling of reality.*

■ *V: In both Q and* God Told Me To *you have similar scenes showing death coming from above. Did you use some of the identical footage in both movies (of people falling down after they'd been killed)?*

■ LC: Yes. I didn't have much footage of people falling—you know, the shots from overhead. We didn't have many shots of a massive number of people running around and falling down. I got thrown out of New York and I couldn't get any more footage. That was after we fired the machine guns from the top of the Chrysler Building!

■ *AJ: How did you get the Chrysler Building as a location for Q?*

■ LC: We were able to rent it from the management because they didn't know what we were going to do. They didn't know we would bring actors, cameras and crew all the way up those ladders into that skinny little needle at the top of the building, and that we'd have helicopters flying around, and guys firing machine-gun blanks off the building.

When we got up there they were doing repairs, so there were these little metal baskets hanging off the building that steeplejacks work in. We got the idea of putting the police with machine guns in those baskets. We hired the steeple-jacks, dressed them up in police uniforms and taught them how to fire the guns, because no *normal* people will go into those baskets and hang off the side of the Chrysler Building. Even stunt people don't want to do that—it's really scary.

> Reagan's a phenomenon like everything else. I think that at the end of his speeches they ought to come on and say, "The part of the President was played by Ronald Reagan."

They fired the machine guns, and of course the shots carried—unfortunately—down into the streets. The *Daily News* Building is down the block, so the *Daily News* sent over a camera crew and photographers and put a big headline in their paper that said, "Hollywood movie crew terrorizes New York!" Then they wrote an editorial saying, "It's time we stop allowing movie companies to come in from Hollywood and frighten our citizens"—they said people were running for cover and that old ladies were terrified. Of course it was a total lie. I *had* a camera crew down on the street to try and get footage of people's reactions in case there really *was* a panic, but no one ran away! That's why I had to use footage from *God Told Me To*; I couldn't get footage of anybody running because they all just stood there and looked, that's all. Nobody thought there was anything dangerous about it.

All these guys were up there pumping machine gun blanks. We had mostly off-duty policemen; we had a police sergeant and we had all the permits, but when the *Daily News* decided to lead this crusade, then Mayor Koch called up the lady who's in charge of the Motion Picture Division and bawled her out. Then she called me in and said, "You're not going to be allowed to shoot any more scenes on the streets. You can finish your picture here but you can't shoot any more chase scenes or scenes that will disrupt the streets. And no guns are to be fired in any scenes, period. No gunfire." But, at least we got the key scene with the people in baskets hanging from the Chrysler Building.

> Sometimes, imagination is required to come up with something when you can't squander money aimlessly. You may end up doing something cleverer than you would if you had all the money in the world. If we had staged the St. Patrick's Day Parade like a normal movie studio, it might not have been as good, because it never could have been the real parade. But we had the real parade—nothing could be better than that.

■ *AJ: How can you hire cops as* actors?

■ LC: We hired off-duty cops. They show up in their own uniform, whereas if you hire an actor you have to pay them for the day, and send them to Western Costuming (and that's another $75 for the costume), and you have to rent them a gun and a badge, so by the time you're through you've spent over $100 just on *wardrobe*. But if you hire a regular cop, they come in their costume. Everybody does it!

Every time you see a movie made in New York the cops are the same cops who are members of the Screen Actors Guild. They work in movies on their days off—they make a lot of money that way! Plus, they know the procedures of handcuffing or searching somebody, so they do that in a realistic manner.

■ *V: In Q it looked like you used a genuine police headquarters.*

■ LC: We rented a police station. You can rent police stations in New York just like you can out here; if you go to any city they cooperate with you because it's good for the economy of the city. Usually they'll give you police cars and policemen for very little dough.

When we made the second *It's Alive!* picture in Tucson, they gave us the whole police department. Actually, there I overdid it—I used *too many* policemen. When the protagonists came out of the back of the hospital the entire Tucson police department was waiting for them—it was immense! They give you everything in these cities; everybody wants to get in the movie.

■ *AJ: What's your situation now with New York? Can you go back there and shoot?*

■ LC: Oh yes, I've been back since. The business has changed. The lady who was there is not there anymore. I told you everything changes, everything passes away. She's now a production manager herself and she came to me for a job! The guy who used to be chief of the Police Liaison Squad left the police department and became an Assistant Director! The guys who once gave you a hard time being hard-nosed cops—a year or two later they've retired from the force and they're working for you as production guys. As I say, you shouldn't really worry about things for too long, because it all changes. And you meet the same people over and over again in different contexts.

■ AJ: *How did you get the idea for Q?*

■ LC: I don't know ... I got the idea from looking at the Chrysler building with all those bird motifs on it, thinking it would make a great nest for a giant bird to go up into. I always look at that building—it's gorgeous, particularly when the sun hits it in a certain way—it's the most beautiful building in New York. I thought, "Jeez, the Empire State Building gets all the attention, what with King Kong and all. But this is a much better-looking building." Then I had to figure out some way to get a story out of this—a story with a character. Then I got the idea about this little punk who learns the secret of the bird's hideout; for ten minutes he becomes somebody important. Then he's gone again. But for ten minutes he has his glory.

■ AJ: *But you ended the film with a title card: that he sued and won the million dollars—tax free—he'd been promised for revealing the giant bird's location.*

■ LC: That ending title wasn't on the original prints, but after the picture opened in New York and I went to the theater, I thought, "You know, the audience would like it better if he got that money at the end."

■ AJ: *Yes, it makes everybody feel triumphant!*

■ LC: He's such a punk, but so *likable* that you feel it would be great if he got the money at the end. So I said, "Let's make up a title card and stick it on, and we'll cut my credit down by a few frames." But that was all an afterthought.

■ V: *What research did you do to write the screenplay,* Quetzalcoatl—

■ LC: I got a couple books on Aztec history, etc, but there was a lot we didn't put in. Like, when the Spanish came to the Aztec temple in Mexico, they found about 18,000 skulls there—18,000 human beings had been executed and their hearts cut out in that temple of *Quetzalcoatl*. Think about all the people who were victims of that human sacrifice! But I didn't want to get too gruesome and inaccessible; a little suggestion of it was enough.

Plotwise, there had to be *some* reason why that bird showed up there; there had to be *something* that brought it

> We hired the steeplejacks, dressed them up in police uniforms and taught them how to fire the guns, because no normal people will go into those baskets and hang off the side of the Chrysler Building. Even stunt people don't want to do that—it's really scary.

there. I had to find a way to tie all the pieces together—the human sacrifices, the bird, the Moriarty character—and bring everything together at the conclusion. The last scene, when the "priest" tries to get Moriarty to say the prayer before sacrificing him, brought the whole thing back full circle.

■ V: *That was brilliant when Moriarty refuses to pray!*

■ LC: Near the end of the picture I made up that scene and we more or less improvised on it—it wasn't in the script. I said, "Tell him to say a prayer" and he said, "Fuck you! I ain't sayin' any of your fuckin' prayers!" Michael Moriarty's good about those things—if you give him an idea on the spur of the moment and he's in character, he'll put the idea right into the character.

■ V: *That's one of the closest marriages I've seen between a written character and an acted character.*

■ LC: And he's not that way at all, in reality or in person. In his other movies, like *Pale Rider, Bang the Drum Slowly, Holocaust, The Glass Menagerie* with Katherine Hepburn—he's *nothing* like that. It was a total acting job.

■ V: *But he's got it in him, because when he scat-sang with the piano—*

■ LC: Well, he wrote that song. That's another thing; we were on the set and in between takes he was sitting around listening to a Walkman. I said, "What are you listening to?" and he replied, "I'm listening to these songs I wrote." I said, "Let me hear them." I put it on and I said, "That's good, and I like the one about an 'Evil Dream.' I'll tell you what we should do: this guy shouldn't just be a little street punk, he wants to be better than that. He wants to be a singer, he writes songs, and he wants to get a job playing the piano in a club. We'll make up a scene where he goes to a club and tries to get a job, and they reject him. *Then* he'll go along with the robbery."

So we can see that if *only* they had given him the job, he would not have gone on the robbery! He would not have been up in the Chrysler Building, he would not have found the nest—none of this would have happened if they'd just given him that job! But they don't. And he gets rejected in a very insulting way when the guy turns the jukebox on.

So we went down, rented a club in the East Village and did that scene. All that wasn't in the script, but that's how things happen in the making of a picture. You discover something about the actor or the character that leads you off in a direction different from what you'd originally anticipated. I thought the nightclub audition gave him a lot more character and made him a lot more interesting person than if we had just had him be a little crook. And he loved the fact that he got to sing one of his own songs!

■ AJ: *Q again had the same kind of theme as* Demon *and* It's Alive! *with the gods coming back—*

■ LC: That's true, *rough cookies* ... picking people up off rooftops for no reason! Like I say, God just knocks people in airplanes right out of the sky for no reason! They're just flying along, all these men, women and children, on their way to Kansas City or somewhere, and he knocks that plane into a mountain. And you say, "Why does he do such things? Does he have a reason for this?" But he's just like that bird—he's flying around and notices you down there: "Oh! There's Larry Cohen!"

■ V: *Splatt.*

■ LC: Don't be up on the roof when *Quetzalcoatl's* flying by!—that's the whole thing. People go to church and they're making a mistake. They say, "Hey God! Look at me! Hey, it's *me* here, *Sam,* I'm praying!" And God says, "Oh ... *Sam,* I'd forgotten about him ... no plague on him lately? Well, let's do something about it! Give me a report on him. Children: how many? *Too many* children! *Burn his house down!*"

Don't call attention to yourself. It's like being in the army: you never look at anybody, you never look the sergeant in the eye, you just never make eye contact with *anybody*. Pretty girls who walk down the street and don't want to be talked to don't make eye contact. *Look away!* Wear sunglasses, wear a Sony Walkman, don't look at anybody! Don't call attention to yourself when you're dealing with God, just keep a low profile and maybe he'll go away. I just think: It's not so much "God help me," but "God leave me alone!" *Q* was just like all the other gods—indiscriminate and brutal!

■ AJ: *That was David Carradine in it?*

■ LC: Of *Kung Fu*. It was nice of him to do that part for me. He was in Cannes with a picture he had directed himself. I got him on the phone and said, "Listen, I'm going to start making this picture in a couple of days, and I've got Michael Moriarty and Candy Clark, and I've got a part for you." He says, "What do I play in it?" I said, "Do me a favor, just come on back here and do the part. I promise I'll write you some good stuff; I'll write you some funny scenes. Just come back and do it."

So he arrived the same day we're shooting the scene with Michael Moriarty playing the piano in that bar. He called up from the hotel and I said, "Put a suit on and come down here." When he got there we were already shooting; I said to him, "Here's what you do: you come in and sit at the bar. The guy's going to say to you, 'What's new? Did you find that guy's head yet?' And you say, 'Oh, it'll turn up!'" So he says, "What's this about? What does this mean?" I said, "Well, it's too long a story to explain, but you're looking for a guy's head that was chopped off or something." So he does the line.

Later on (after the picture was finished), he told me, "I had never worked in a situation where I didn't know what I was doing beforehand. I didn't know what my character was or what I was supposed to be doing in the picture, I didn't know what the story was, I had never read the script, I had just gotten off an airplane from Europe, I had no idea what was happening. I go down there and you tell me to say these lines. As soon as I did the scene I was so upset I went out into the street and threw up!" I said, "Well, you never would have known it—you did fine." He said, "Well, I liked Moriarty playing the piano—that relaxed me. But I still didn't know what was going on." It was wonderful that he was a good enough friend to come all the way over and do that for me on faith. Of course, that night he got to read the script and it was

> **Don't call attention to yourself when you're dealing with God, just keep a low profile and maybe he'll go away. I just think: It's not so much "God help me," but "God leave me alone!" Q was just like all the other gods— indiscriminate and brutal!**

all right after that.
■ *AJ: He had one of the best roles.*
■ LC: He got a chance to be funny. Usually he's so stoic, having played "Grasshopper" for so long, where everything has to be cloaked with an inner meaning and a higher implication—you know what I mean, *too serious*. That picture was unpretentious and he was unpretentious in it. He ended up having a great time.

When you work with somebody like Moriarty who gives so much, who takes chances and is willing to really mug and do stuff, and who acts with his whole body, then you see that and think, "Gee, I can do that, too. I can use my whole body, I can use my head, I don't have to look so good, I don't have to play the handsome leading man." Carradine said that he learned something from doing the picture, because it *loosened him up* as an actor.
■ *AJ: How do you elicit* more *from your actors?*
■ LC: I give them things to do all the time; I give them new lines, new pieces of business. So when they come to the set they already know from previous days that they're not going to do just the things they studied last night. They're not going to just go through the motions like they do on a television-type of show, where they have a script, they go to the set, they know the lines, they stand here, then they go there, and . . .

Whereas I'll come in and say, "Wait a minute, I got another idea. Let's make up a thing: you're talking to him, and then just as the waitress comes over you'll say something vulgar like 'Fuck!' and she'll look at you and you'll be embarrassed." We'll make up something like that right in the middle of a scene, and that breaks it up with the actors because something new is going on.
■ *V: In that one scene the waitress was great, because when the character swore she kind of smiled tolerantly, but as soon as she left her expression changed to disgust.*
■ LC: You see, you make up things that make the day an enjoyable experience for the actor, because *something's happening*. Rather than just *coming to work* and going through the ritual of it.

■ *AJ: Is that why most actors seem so sterile?*
■ LC: Well, actors are like everybody else—they go to work every day! Except you get up earlier, because you've got to be there at 8:00 AM in make-up and costume, so you get up around 5:30, and the actresses get up even earlier because they've got to do their hair and make-up. They get there and work all day, 10 or 12 hours, and then go home and learn the lines for the next day. It's a job—a *hard* job.

Most of the time they had a good career on Broadway and then came out to Hollywood and got into TV or movies and made good money, bought a house, and now they can't afford to go back to Broadway anymore because they have a "life-style." So they have to take almost every job they're offered because, in order to live in the style they've become accustomed to, they have to work.

So every day just becomes the routine, going-to-work situation. Once in a while they get a part that has some life to it, or they meet somebody who tries to make the filmmaking experience *fun* for them. *Then* they're able to do something other than give you the routine performance they can give you in their sleep.

Most actors can give you their routine performance in their sleep, because it's the same performance they give in every picture. The director will say, "Okay, we need a guy to play a general. Let's get so-and-so—he always plays a general." So you see the same guy come in and play a general. Another guy always plays a District Attorney, another guy always plays the Chief of Police . . . So if you don't want a guy to play the part the same way, you've got to make up something so that he'll play it *differently*.
■ *AJ: There's complicity all around in a system that keeps perpetuating the stereotyping—*
■ LC: Well, it's *simpler* to hire somebody you've seen playing that part in a previous episode of a TV show, than to hire someone new. Movies are usually better than TV, if only because you find new faces and people you haven't seen before. Like in *The Year of the Dragon*, you get to see a lot of interesting new faces—all these Oriental gangsters.

But when you get someone like David Carradine who is an established actor, who is known for a certain kind of performance, you try to give him something different he can have some fun with. You try and loosen him up and let him do things that are a bit more *fresh*.

The main thing is—you always hire competent actors who could give a performance even if you weren't *there*. And for some things a director isn't necessary. Everybody knows that you're going to shoot a close-up of this guy, and then a close-up of the other guy, then an over-the-shoulder-shot, then an over-the-shoulder shot of the other person, then an entrance to the room, exit from the room—I mean, a computer could direct the picture! There's no need to have a human being there to do this. And you're hiring actors who have all played the same parts before, so they don't need to be told what's required of them.

Most directors are just traffic cops: "You stand *here* . . . you stand *there* . . . on to the next scene!" The difference is: if you can give people something different, and call on different muscles to be used so they can't do their same old act, then they can't revert to giving you the same old performance. Actors can't help it; they'll give you the easiest performance they can give you. You want to make things more difficult so they'll have to call on something *special*. And in doing so it will kind of *wake them up* and make them *interested* in the picture.

When we're making pictures, often the other actors want to watch what's going on. Whereas on most sets the actors are all in the corner, reading the sports page. They're there for the job, but often they don't read any scenes they're not in. When they get the script they look for their part, circle their lines, and never read the rest of the script—it's just a *job*. But I like to turn it into something that they're involved in—with an element of the unexpected. Also, it makes it more pleasurable for me, otherwise—if it were just a matter of doing it by rote, it would be better to let someone else direct the picture, and I'll stay home!

■ V: *Do you use friends as actors in minor roles?*

■ LC: Some people have been in so many of my pictures that they've *become* friends. But they're all actors.

■ V: *How about the guy with the heavy Italian accent working in the produce market in* God Told Me To?

■ LC: Yeah, he was working as stage doorman of the Golden Theater in Manhattan when I went to meet my friend Ben Gazzara. He said, "You're making a picture? I'm an actor—how about giving me something to do?" He wasn't just your usual person, he was a *type,* so I thought, "Let's give him a line."

I pick up actors, but usually they're professional actors. Like Andy Kaufman—I'd seen him at the Improvisation Club. I asked him if he'd ever done a movie and he said, "No," so I said, "I think you're going to be a star. I tell you what: I'll give you a part just so I can say I gave you your first part in movies." And it was true! But usually it doesn't work out to use people who are friends or just off the street. I prefer actors who have been in picture after picture, whom I can rely on, so that if I get into a problem I can say, "I need some help; can you try and get us a hotel where we can shoot in the lobby this afternoon?"

If you work with people over the years, they become kind of like Assistant Producers. Again, it's because they want to hang around even when they're not working. As long as they're there, you may as well give them something to do that makes them part of the production. So I ask them to help me out with this, that, and the other thing.

Usually I send the actors off to buy their own wardrobe: "*You* know what this character would wear; go out and buy a suit he would wear, and here's some money." They go out, and now they're not just *acting,* they're *involved.* Instead of handing them something, saying, "Here—wear *this!*" and they say, "Gee, the character wouldn't wear that; he wouldn't feel comfortable wearing that." If it's something they pick out themselves, it helps them to get into character while they're doing it. You use any device you can to bring people into the production as *participants,* rather than making them feel like they're outsiders.

■ V: *I was impressed by the performances of the blacks in* God Told Me To—

■ LC: We shot those scenes in a real pool hall up in Harlem. Those were all actors. You tell 'em you want black actors, they send you black actors. Believe me, the door opens and they parade in—there's a lot of 'em out there. The guy who was the ringleader was a model, but he looked right for the part so we used him. I don't think he wanted to be an actor and I don't think he's ever done anything since, which is amazing.

■ AJ: *How did you happen to do the two blaxploitation films?*

■ LC: The first picture I did, *Bone,* had Yaphet Kotto, a very fine actor. I showed that picture around and then American International called me up and said, "Listen, we want to make some pictures with black casts, and you know how to direct those black actors." (One black actor in the whole film and "you know how to direct those black actors"!)

I'd been approached by Sammy Davis, Jr.'s manager, who said they would pay $10,000 if I wrote up a movie treatment. I had suggested making an old-fashioned gangster picture like Warner Bros used to make with James Cagney and Edward G. Robinson, but do it with a black cast, because the black underworld was pretty active in New York. The idea was the rise and fall of a black gangster called *Black Caesar* (instead of *Little Caesar.*) He said, "That's a great idea." I wrote the outline and gave it to the guy, but no $10,000. I kept chasing him for the money but couldn't collect.

In the meantime I got a call from American International who said they wanted me to do a black project. Thanks to Sammy Davis, Jr., I happened to have the outline! So I gave it to them, we made the deal right away and I went off and made the picture. It was easy as pie—we just happened to have the right thing at the right time.

But it wasn't a typical black exploitation picture. Usually the black guy beats up all the white people, gets the white girl, becomes successful, and it's kind of a victory of the black over the white society. But *Black Caesar* is a picture about a guy who tries to live this dream but is destroyed by it. He doesn't win, he loses—he loses his own girlfriend who's a black girl, things don't work out with the beautiful white woman, and he tries to buy the white people's apartment and live like they do—in short, he tries to be a white man and fails. He tries to take his mother who's a maid and turn her into a lady, but just makes her very unhappy. He fails in trying to resolve his relationship with his father; he fails on every count.

> Most directors are just traffic cops: "You stand here . . . you stand there . . . on to the next scene!" The difference is: if you can give people something different, and call on different muscles to be used so they can't do their same old act, then they can't revert to giving you the same old performance.

The film's more like *Public Enemy* or *Little Caesar,* where you see the guy rise and fall. The flaw in his dream is that when he reaches a certain point there's no place to go but down, because he has never resolved his personal problems. He has never resolved *himself,* he's just killed a lot of people and gotten into a position of power, and now everything's going to be taken away from him.

At the end of the picture he ends up betrayed by his girlfriend—double-crossed, shot by a policeman and staggering through the slums in Harlem to the building where he grew up, now a big empty wreck with broken windows. He comes back to where he began, as James Brown sings, "Down and Out in New York City."

It's a good picture, but it's not a black *exploitation* picture. The title *Black Caesar* was almost enough to make the picture a big hit. At the beginning he starts off as a shoeshine boy and works his way up to the top, and in the end the crooked police captain finally gets the gun on him, saying, "Before you die I want you to do one last thing for me. I want you to shine my shoes." And he makes him get down on his knees and do it. But then Black Caesar gets the gun away from him and, taking the black shoe polish, tells him, "Before I kill you I'm gonna make you a nigger first." Then he blackens him up and kills him. This is a really good scene—*operatic.* It all happens under an American flag; I really made the whole picture just to do that one scene.

I wish I could remember the name of the guy who played the villain. He was a great big powerful guy who used to be a singer back in the forties—he was a band singer who had a couple of hit records and everything. In the film we had him sing "Mammy," and the totally black audience went wild! It was a total catharsis; black people were getting all that anger out of their system while enjoying the film at the same time. I went to the theater in New York where it was playing—

■ V: *42nd Street?*

■ LC: No, no, it played the Cinerama on Broadway. The film started at 9:00 in the morning and ran all night long—it was a big hit. People would say to me, "How can you go in there;

Black Caesar.

you're the only white people in the whole theater!" I'd say, "It doesn't matter; the audience has such a good time that when they leave they're the most peaceful, friendly people—if anybody bumps into you, they say, 'Excuse me.'"

I went there almost every day for awhile and never saw any hostility whatsoever. But that's exactly what people have always done with movies: get out all their suppressed anger, suppressed sexuality, and live out fantasies up on the movie screen—so you don't have to do it in real life, you know. That picture more or less gave everybody what they needed—nobody left wanting to kill or hurt people, and still at the end it wasn't a cop-out. It didn't have one of those fake happy endings where he ends up with everything—he ended up losing everything. The moral of the picture was: he tried to play the white man's game, and he lost. *He should have been true to himself.*

But then we made a mistake: we made a second *Black Caesar* picture. The first was such a hit that the producers called me up: "We have to have another picture right away; we have to have a sequel!" I said, "Well, the actor's going off for a year to make another picture; we can only get him if we shoot right away. I could start shooting next week, but we don't have a script, so we'll just have to make the whole picture up as we go along." Which is what we did—and it looked it.

The picture was a conglomeration of scenes that you probably would like individually, including some of the best action scenes I've ever done. There are good chase scenes, good action scenes, but it's a mishmash of exposition—like an hour-and-a-half montage. Instead of having a gradual development of character, things kind of just jump from one action scene to the next; there weren't the necessary scenes in between which develop a picture. We shouldn't have

made the film, but that's what happens when greed gets in the way!

■ *V: Your greed?*

■ LC: Yes, *mine*. If I didn't want to do it, I didn't have to. But greed sometimes takes control, and . . .

■ *V: Tell us a little more about the good scenes—*

■ LC: Anything we could think of, we did. We had an underwater sequence with frogmen; a chase through Times Square and up through the theater district where the guy strangles the girl in the alley behind the stage door of the Majestic Theater. We had a long chase that was a good idea. The bad black guy is trying to get away, and the hero, Black Caesar, chases him to the airport but arrives too late—his prey is already on a plane to Los Angeles. So he runs across the airport to TWA and gets the next plane to L.A. The bad guy's on American Airlines, and in the middle they both sit there for five hours, drinking, smoking and watching the movie. When the planes land, the chase starts all over again in the L.A. Airport. The bad guy gets off his plane and is waiting for his luggage while Black Caesar runs across the airport and catches him in the luggage area—he's chased him 3000 miles! I thought this was unusual, and fun.

■ *AJ: I wanted to touch on the whole subject of violence—*

■ LC: Well, in England they give X-ratings for violence. But here there's no such censorship; you see terribly violent, gruesome things in movies here.

■ *AJ: There's no overt censorship, but if you don't get an R rating it's difficult to distribute your movie.*

■ LC: But look what you can do with an R-rating—look at those *Friday the Thirteenth* pictures. They stick knives in people's eyes. They invent new prosthetic devices to do Grand Guignol gruesome tricks—right on camera they can cut somebody's nose off. The more they're capable of, the more

125

they do; then you get really unpleasant horror where people are totally dismembering other people—chopping them up. I don't like that kind of stuff myself!

■ *AJ: I read that you and the main actor in* I, The Jury *complained to Warner Bros—*

■ LC: We complained to Twentieth Century-Fox (who distributed the picture domestically) about the scene where the twins were stabbed to death—it seemed very unpleasant and unnecessary. I felt it ruined the picture—took all the fun out and made it too gruesome. And that scene where the guy gets fried on a hibachi grill—it's no good if you just throw a guy down and burn him, unless there's been a big fight first and *he's* got a few licks in, too. Nobody minds when Indiana Jones shoots down the guy with the sword—it's fun because there's been some build-up to it. But if it's done abruptly, it becomes just an act of violence that is unredeeming—also it takes the fun out of it. So if you can't do the *whole* scene, doing only the end of it becomes just mere brutality.

■ *AJ: In your films violence is usually implied rather than overt. Like in* God Told Me To *when the Judas character sticks his head in an elevator shaft—*

■ LC: We didn't show his head coming off. Some people would do that—if they could afford to build a false body and crush it, they will.

■ *AJ: If you could afford to, would you?*

■ LC: I'd probably do it the same way I did. But after *The Omen*, which was the first time somebody got decapitated (the scene where the sheet of glass cut off the guy's head), then everybody wanted to do a scene like that. So in horror pictures there was a whole syndrome of heads flying off, because they had found ways to make these prosthetic heads more realistic.

We had a little gore in *Q* when the guy cut the other guy's chest open, but I didn't have him stick his hand in and pull the heart out so you can see it pulsating—which other people have been doing lately. I don't do that—it's too unpleasant for me. The picture should be fun.

■ *V: But in* Q *you also had a flayed human body lying in a bed—*

■ LC: It was gruesome, but it wasn't *that* awful.

■ *V: And you did show a guy's skin being peeled off—*

> **That's exactly what people have always done with movies: get out all their suppressed anger, suppressed sexuality, and live out fantasies up on the movie screen—so you don't have to do it in real life.**

■ LC: [laughs] You've seen people on TV or in movies like *The List of Adrian Messenger* pull latex masks off their face—that's nothing. But in context the audience thinks, "Oh, he's skinning him alive. That's really horrible." But it really wasn't anything! It wasn't like bringing out a gory heart with veins hanging out and having it pulsate in somebody's hand.

I like to show 'em very little, but make 'em think they're seeing a lot. That's more fun. But of course, with the preponderance of huge budgets as in John Carpenter's version of *The Thing*, people want to show every possible piece of gore . . . which isn't nearly as satisfying as the original version, which shows you nothing.

■ *AJ: The same with* Invasion of The Body Snatchers—

■ LC: The first one was *so* good. The second one wasn't *bad*, but for that story the small town atmosphere seems to be better. It's easier to believe these aliens could take over a small Northern California town than the whole city of San Francisco!

■ *AJ: You're a genre director and perhaps that's part of why you haven't gotten more widespread recognition. But in the sixties it seemed there were more "mainstream" directors who were genre directors, like Howard Hawks and Sam Fuller—*

■ LC: Sam used to live here—this used to be his house. He's a good friend of mine; a few months ago in Paris we saw each other almost every night. He and his wife live in Paris.

■ *AJ: Really? Because it was the French who first pointed out that what Howard Hawks and Sam Fuller were doing was "art." Only afterwards did Manny Farber and Andrew Sarris echo that in the U.S.*

■ LC: Nobody paid any attention to Sam Fuller for years. It's still tough; he's still trying to find people to let him make movies. It hasn't changed; every picture's a struggle. This was his house in the late fifties, but he'd sold it long before I moved in here. But that's how I met him.

I found some empty cases in the basement that said "Samuel Fuller" on them. Then John Ireland, the actor, was here one day and he said, "I was here before; this used to be Sam Fuller's house." Then I met Sam Fuller at a party at the Beverly Hills Hotel and said to him, "I think I own the house you used to live in on Coldwater Canyon Drive." Then he got to be friendly; he and his wife came up a couple times and spent the evening. Recently I was in Paris and found out where he was, called him up and they were delighted to see me. So I spent almost every night with them. He's a wonderful guy—a great man to talk to; he's got so many good stories and great anecdotes to tell.

But, you know, the genre I'm working in is the most popular genre of this time: science-fiction and fantasy. All the big success pictures now are science-fiction/fantasy, and usually they're big budget, $25 million dollar films. My pictures play, and all I can do is hope people will go to see 'em and like 'em. And if they don't see 'em in the theater, then they see 'em on cable where they watch films they ordinarily wouldn't. And hopefully they'll say, "Hey! This is good; I like this better than a lot of big budget pictures." So, then your picture's being seen, and that's all you can ask . . .

Cable is "The Great Equalizer," and so is the videocassette—people can go to a store and choose whatever movie they want to see tonight. They don't have to worry about whether or not it's playing . . . So it's becoming a democratic process, and that's why pictures like mine will get a chance to be better seen.

Cable's different—you already paid for it, and if you don't want to look at it that's your hard luck, so finally you end up even looking at pictures you didn't expect to, 'cause the damn picture's on so many times. And if it turns out to be good, you're surprised. Then word gets around, and people want to rent it on cassette because they missed it on cable, and you've created a life for the film other than the theatrical life.

If I were a writer I wouldn't care whether people read my book in hardcover or in paperback, just as long as they *read* it. To me, cable and cassettes are like paperback, and theatrical release is like the hardcover. So if I'm a paperback novelist—so what?!

■ *AJ: What kind of films influence you?*

■ LC: Oh, I see almost everything.

■ *V: You've even seen* Dynasty—

■ LC: Once or twice. If you go over to somebody's house, it's inevitable—like my mother *has* to watch it . . . But I can't sit through it or any other episodic series week after week. I do like to watch old Warner Bros or Fox movies with the big bombastic musical scores.

■ *AJ: Were any filmmakers a big influence on you? Or genres, like film noir?*

■ LC: *Black Caesar* was film noir. I used to like crime movies, police movies, but I never was a big reader of science fiction—I don't like to read books that are 800 or 900 pages long and where the characters have long names. And I don't like to read books that have a chronology of characters with arrows showing whose son is who . . . where I have to go through six generations to find out what happened to someone.

As far as movies go, I like them all. When I grew up, the big event was going to the movies twice a week—every week the Loews and the RKO theaters would have new double-features.

■ *AJ: Where was this?*

■ LC: New York. Usually the second feature was bad, but sometimes it would be a little gem. In my neighborhood we only had one theater that would run foreign movies, and they ran the original French *Diabolique* and *Wages of Fear*—great stuff—and *Rififi,* a robbery picture which was one of the first foreign movies to make any impact here, before *A Man And A Woman* or the Truffaut pictures came along in the sixties. I like to go to the movies, but I don't want to make homages to people or remake their pictures . . .

People say, "Reverend Moon—what a crook!" and I say, "But what about the Pope?"

■ *AJ: How about books?*

■ LC: I always read four or five books at the same time—I've got them all over the house, a different book for each room!

■ *AJ: Has any book changed your life?*

■ LC: No one book has changed my life. Take a best-seller like *The French Lieutenant's Woman*—I didn't think it worked as a movie, but Fowles wrote it in such a way that you can see the writer at work while you're reading—for that reason it's an interesting book.

At one point he thinks he should give these characters a break—give them a chance to have a happier life, so he changes the story right before your eyes. You're put into the author's mind. I can identify with that because it happens to me when I'm writing a script. I'm thinking, "Maybe we should give this a happy ending. I like this character; maybe he shouldn't die."

Like with *Q,* in the original script the Moriarty character gets killed by that zealot at the end. But that would have been a disaster, particularly as he turned out to be so lovable. So I had to improvise that scene with the prayer in it. But when I first wrote the story, I had no idea this guy would turn out to be such a lovable character.

A film can come to life when an actor like Michael Moriarty appears; when he does it, you realize how funny some of the material is. I knew we'd get laughs, but I didn't know Moriarty would end up being as innocent as he did. He came out as kind of a soiled innocent—he had a childish sort of bliss about him, so we couldn't kill him.

After I read books, it takes time to decide which one was good, in retrospect. If you ask me *next year* what my favorite book was *this* year, then I'll be able to tell you. When I'm finished with some books I can't remember *anything,* I know I went through 400 pages, but . . . Like John Le Carre—when *Smiley's People* was over, I didn't have any idea what the plot was, or what happened to anybody, or why. And I can't read any of Robert Ludlum's books.

■ *AJ: Ever read Timothy Harris? He's like a modern-day Raymond Chandler; he wrote a good book called* Goodnight and Goodbye *that was somewhat similar to your* I, The Jury *script. A couple years ago we discovered the mystery writer Jim Thompson—he's incredible.*

■ LC: I used to read the Lew Archer books by Ross McDonald. Recently I picked up an old Dashiell Hammett, but I don't like to get too involved with things like that—suddenly you end up writing scripts with names of obscure characters from old Dashiell Hammett books, or you put in hot little *homages* or somehow connect yourself to some person you idolize.

I would like to have made the movie *Hammett* because I could have made a much better movie—that picture was dismally dull. And Frederic Forrest, who's a very good actor, had no charisma at all in that part, the lethargic way he was directed. I've heard of "sleepers," but this is one you can *really* sleep through! But if I go to the movies and don't like the picture, I fall asleep immediately!

■ *V: The sleep cure for boredom.*

■ LC: Usually I say to the girl I'm with, "Listen, I can dream a better picture than this one, so I'll go to sleep." I can let myself go to sleep almost instantly—I'm gone, and that's it until it's over and I can leave.

The same thing with stage plays: if the play is no good, I fall asleep. But then I'll feel guilty because it cost so much money to get in—thirty or forty dollars a ticket! Sometimes I prefer to buy standing room, because then if I fall asleep, I'm standing in the back of the theater and I fall down and it wakes me up—"Wha? Huh? Oh yeah, here I am—oh shit!"

I go to everything . . . I go to most movies. Actually, no, I'm lying—I stopped going to most movies. I *used* to go to everything, but now I don't go to movies about teenagers! There are too many of them, and they all seem the same. They're always telling you about how somebody finally gets laid. And now they got 'em about kids making inventions. These are all Spielberg-clone movies—they take a formula that works for *him* and *they* try to do it. That doesn't interest me.

■ *V: You don't have any formulas, do you?*

■ LC: Me? I just have to be outlandish enough so that people will know it's *my* picture.

■ *V: Your films always criticize some aspect of the "status quo."*

■ LC: Well, that's true.

■ *AJ: The art of screenwriting a really good story, with subplots, subtexts and characters that are complex and alive—that seems to be a lost art these days.*

■ LC: Well, when you try and put a scene in that doesn't have anything to do with the central story, you have a hard time keeping people from cutting it out. Particularly if the releasing company has any power over re-cutting the picture. If they see something that isn't integral, they think it should be cut.

■ *V: But that's never happened to you, has it?*

■ LC: On *The Stuff* they cut out ten minutes—a couple of funny scenes that were not essential to the plotline of the picture. But they were funny, though—*I* enjoyed them.

■ *V: Was that the first time your creative independence was impinged upon?*

■ LC: Yeah. I wouldn't say they *damaged* the picture, because they made a few cuts I thought were improvements. So you have to take the good with the bad. But they left a few sloppy holes in the picture that would have been worth the extra ten minutes. In the long run it would have been a better film if they had just left it alone.

■ *AJ: Is that the first time that happened to you?*

■ LC: Yeah. I've had people before who wanted to cut scenes out and I could talk them out of it. Or, I've had suggestions and agreed with them: "It's a good idea to make that cut; I think you're right." Or, "That scene would work better if it were placed later in the picture . . . or, "this scene would work better earlier in the picture."

Sometimes they're right, but in this particular case they wanted to take out a few "romantic" or "relationship" scenes that "slowed the picture down," because "the kids" would rather get on with the action.

■ *V: Did previews prompt these cuts?*

■ LC: You preview a picture, and if you don't get a good reaction, the producers fall apart. Generally I feel that you *can* preview horror pictures, but you shouldn't give out response cards. Because if a picture's outlandish like *It's Alive!,* no matter how much they like the picture they're going to write wise-guy remarks on the card, like "This picture needs diapers!"

Years ago when we previewed *It's Alive!,* the audience seemed to really enjoy the picture and screamed or laughed in all the right places. But when it came time to write the cards they wrote these terrible responses. And the Warner Bros people were so disheartened they almost killed the picture. Fortunately they released it and it turned out to be a big hit, but if they had just followed the cards they would have given up and thrown it into a hole somewhere.

People who want to be clowns or comedians are going to write something funny on the cards, or something wise-guyish. Basically the same thing happened with *The Stuff*. The audience laughed and seemed to enjoy the picture, but wrote negative things making fun of the picture because it's about a food product that kills people; they wrote wise-guy cards. I say we should never have given them out in the first place.

> If I were a writer I wouldn't care whether people read my book in hardcover or in paperback, just as long as they read it. To me, cable and cassettes are like paperback, and theatrical release is like the hardcover. So if I'm a paperback novelist—so what?!

■ *V: What did the producers cut out?*
■ LC: With producers, it's very hard to get good, rational judgment when there's *fear* involved. So, the scenes they cut out are not even really noticeable, but there *was* one very funny scene where the character was reciting part of "The Tell-Tale Heart" by Edgar Allan Poe. Maybe I could persuade them to let me restore it for the video.

Sometimes the scenes that really make a movie work are the little scenes that have nothing to do with advancing the action, but just add a little *something*. The scene where Michael Moriarty auditions for a job as a singer has nothing to do with the monster on top of the Chrysler Building, but . . . That's exactly what they did with *The Stuff*—they cut out scenes that would have enriched the endeavor.

■ *AJ: Do you have more control over your pictures than most directors?*
■ LC: Sure. They leave me alone when I'm making the picture, and they leave me alone when I'm cutting it. On low-budget pictures they don't bother people too much because they're usually too busy with problems and responsibilities relating to their high-budget pictures, which take up most of their time. They figure, "Oh well, we're going to make our money back anyway just from certain ancillary sales."

At the same time they don't consider the pictures important enough to spend advertising on them. And again, if you don't get the advertising, you don't get the box office. So it has its pluses: freedom of direction, but it has minuses in that they don't want to allocate any time or personnel to work on your picture. So in terms of getting any attention, you get a *very* short shrift.

■ *AJ: But don't you prefer low budgets? In one article you said you probably wouldn't spend that much anyway.*
■ LC: Believe me, if you had the money you could spend it! I'd like to have had more special effects in *Q*—to have had more sequences with the bird. The effects we had were good, but they could have been better. I had many more inventive ideas but we just didn't have the money to do them. But the things we *did* do looked good, so . . .

■ *AJ: What are you doing next?*
■ LC: I'm writing some scripts. In about two or three weeks when the scripts go in, they'll decide which one we're going to make. I always make something every year, anyhow!

I'm really enjoying this particular time now—just being home, working for a few hours every day writing, and not having to have a whole bunch of employees working for me. Because that's a lot of hassle—just dealing with all those people, and everybody has to be paid, and you gotta send in tax forms, and send in this and that, and then people file for unemployment insurance, and you have to send in forms for them, and your whole life is—

■ *AJ: Do you have to do all that?*
■ LC: Well, after you finish up a picture and let everybody go, all sorts of paperwork starts popping up that you hadn't anticipated. If you don't have anybody to do it for you, you have to do it yourself.

After everybody goes away, you get bills that people have forgotten . . . then you get some more bills. The whole picture's closed down, but then the letters for workman's compensation arrive. Finally that goes away. Then finally no more bills, no more employees, no more hassle, no more mail and it's so peaceful right now—nobody to be responsible for but yourself.

As soon as you start another picture, you've got to do the whole rigamarole again—having to deal with all these people, and schedules, and people not delivering things on time, and not doing things on time; having to be the boss and the disciplinarian and the sergeant and the captain and the general. By comparison, writing the script is so peaceful—you go into a room and do it all by yourself, and you don't have to have anybody else around you.

■ *AJ: You once said you firmly believe that people dream cinematically.*
■ LC: I think that people do dream like a movie; they see shots and angles—I dream like that. I'm not sure if I dream in color or black-and-white, though. But as I say, I can dream better movies than some of the pictures I see. I mean I close my eyes and go off, and I don't always remember what I dream but I know it was more satisfying than the picture that was playing there.

Actually, there should be a theater where you go and there's no movie playing; everybody goes into the theater, sits there and goes to sleep, and everybody dreams their own movie. Then everybody gets up and goes home and tells each other what they saw: "Oh, I saw a great movie!"

Or maybe they could just play the movie music on the screen while you sit there in the dark and dream your own movie. Then you come out and go to coffee and discuss the movie: "I dreamed a great comedy" or "I dreamed this Western." "Hey, nobody's dreamed a Western in years!" "You know what I dreamed? I hate to tell you—I dreamed a low-budget picture!" "No! You could've dreamed anything—you could've dreamed a $30 million picture, a $40 million picture. What did you dream?" "I dreamed this low budget picture where these people were trapped in a dark house. What did *you* dream?" "I dreamed this great big galactic fantasy with spaceships coming down from an enormous space station; explosions were going off—it was wonderful. And *you* dreamed a low budget picture?" "I don't know what's the matter with me!"

■ *V: Actually, how do you write? You don't just get an idea out of thin air, do you?*
■ LC: Yeah! Sometimes I just write and don't know what I'm writing, then it starts to come to me . . . I just jump in and start writing a scene, and as you're writing the characters start to talk, start to take over, start to play their part. Sometimes you want it to go *this* way but the characters want to go another way, so you let them go, let them keep talking and see where they're taking you.

Writing is a process of discovery; *it comes to life*. Once it starts coming to life, it becomes *very interesting*. Like I said, if you read that book by Fowles, you'll get that feeling he captured—that feeling of the characters starting to take life into their *own* hands. The characters start to take over and speak in their own style and rhythms; each character starts to have his own way of talking.

Like with painting, there are two ways of working: you can make a pencil or charcoal outline that you can see, then fill it in with paint. Or, you can go in with paint and a blank canvas and start making this shadow and that shading, and rubbing this and that. And you think, "This looks like a terrible mess." Then all of a sudden it starts to come together; you step back and see something you didn't see before: people and background and trees and—where's it all coming from? It's coming out of that brush.

And then other people buy a kit that says "green there, red here, blue over there" and it looks like a horse when you get finished! And you go, "Shit, that *does* look like a horse, doesn't it?"

■ *V: The last way is how most Hollywood movies are made—*

■ LC: No!—the way a Hollywood movie is made is this way: you paint a picture that's supposed to be a pasture. Now there's one guy who paints good horses, so he's brought in to paint the horse. Another guy does grass; another guy does good trees; and then you bring in Sam who does beautiful clouds. Now, because this guy's the best painter of horses, this guy does the best clouds, and this guy does the best trees, you should have the best picture, right? Certainly better than the slob who's running around slopping paint on the canvas! Well, I must admit my pictures can be a little sloppy at times, but I think there's something on the canvas at the end that's—

■ *V: —unique . . . One of your best scenes is the detective's interview with the father who has just killed his children in* God Told Me To. *That summed up perfectly what's repulsive about religious fanaticism.*

■ LC: Robert Drivas played that. Again, I thought it was much better to do it this way than to show the overt violence. Tobe Hooper (*Texas Chainsaw Massacre*) would have shown the husband shooting the kid in the back, killing the wife, and then getting the little kid to open the bathroom door so he can blow the kid's head off, complete with head and skull fragments flying! I chose to do it by the less cinematic method of having the husband recount the story, because people killing their children was just too horrible to show on the screen.

■ *AJ: But that scene is so chilling; it's better—*

■ *V: He's so psychotic—the way he smiles; his expressions—*

■ *AJ: —That peaceful bliss, like religious people telling about their faith and conversion.*

■ LC: Well, it's in the Bible! I got the idea from Abraham and Isaac when God said, "Go out and sacrifice your son!" Then He said, "All right, you don't *have* to do it! I just wanted to see if you'd do it or not!" "God, you mean you just teased me?!"

The moral of Black Caesar was: he tried to play the white man's game, and he lost. He should have been true to himself.

■ *V: You know the Bible pretty well.*

■ LC: I always have to explain religion to people who have had a religious upbringing but don't know anything. Somebody was describing to me the film *Agnes of God:* "There's this nun who has a baby, and they think it's an Immaculate Conception," etc. So I said, "No, you're talking about a Virgin Birth. Immaculate Conception and the Virgin Birth are two different things." They said, "No, no, what are you talking about?" I said, "Jesus being born is not an Immaculate Conception, it's a Virgin Birth. Don't you know the difference?" Nobody knows the difference!

The difference is that the birth of Jesus without his mother ever having had intercourse with anybody is the Virgin Birth.

The Immaculate Conception, which is entirely different, rests on the premise that since the Garden of Eden, everyone on earth is born with Original Sin. Only one person was ever born *without* Original Sin, and that was Mary who was absolved in advance so she could be born pure and be the mother of Jesus. So *Mary's birth* is the Immaculate Conception.

Nobody knows this, including all these people who *think* they know about religion. They always *talk* about it, but they don't know anything. We all talk about everything that we have no information about!

■ *AJ: Were you raised in a religion?*

■ LC: Part of my family's Jewish and part of my family's Irish Catholic, but nobody *practiced* anything. It was kind of a Mexican standoff—nobody did anything, then nobody's feelings got hurt. So basically I became a *filmmaker* as a religion! How about "Filmmaking as a Religion" as a lead for your story?

You have to have your own faith, your own belief. Just because you don't go to a recognized church doesn't mean you don't have any faith in God, or a belief in some higher power, or something that you just worship in your own way or that you just let be.

I think it would be very selfish of me, in my state of affluence, good health and good fortune, to be trying to attract God's attention when there are so many people who are in need of a good meal, or crutches, or anything else. What right do *I* have to pray to God that when my movie opens next Friday, it's going to be a hit? I mean, there are *people* out there, you know!

How about when people win the Academy Award and they say, "I want to thank God for my winning this award." I guess the other 400 people who were up for it just weren't good enough—God smiled on *her* and those other people are shit! Ever think about that? "God said Sally Field should win!" "Oh, thank you, Lord." "Yeah, she did the Flying Nun years ago— let's give *her* the award." Two Academy Awards—God must really be crazy about this girl; everybody else is a piece of shit. Paul Newman never won—even after all his nominations. God just must not like Paul Newman! The *nonsense* of an actor getting up and thanking God . . .

■ *V: I still can't believe that* prayer *precedes the President's speeches—*

■ LC: I think that if people want to, they should be able to say a prayer (or not say one)—if thousands of people want to drop down to the sidewalk and pray, let them do it! What kind of a thing is this: if they catch you praying, you get expelled? Like, "I got caught praying in school today."

If these parents want their kids to pray, they should tell them to go to school and "Just go in there and pray, and pray loud. Let 'em try and stop you!" They break into the bathroom and find all these kids praying: "All right you kids, OUT! I GOTCHA!" If you want to pray, you pray. The way you get things done in this country is: do 'em, that's all. That's how you effect change; all the talk in the world means nothing.

They talked about Civil Rights for years, but until they started boycotting the buses and sitting-in in restaurants, they got nowhere. When they did something about it, change occurred. So if you want prayer in school, everybody should send their kids in and tell 'em to pray their fuckin' heads off!

■ *V: There was a line in* Q *that the creature was* prayed *back into existence.*

■ LC: Well, I guess that high priest thought *he* did it. I'll tell you the truth—*I* don't know how that bird got there, unless maybe it flew all the way in from Mexico.

Originally, we were going to have a whole scene about bringing an egg up in a truck from Mexico and putting it up there, but I dropped it. I said, "Listen, if anybody wants to know how this fuckin' egg got in the top of the Chrysler Building, they can figure it out for themselves, 'cause *I* don't know the answers to these things. I don't know why the *It's Alive!* baby was born; I don't know all the answers to every one of these questions."

People are always saying to me, "How come there are so many holes in your stories?" Well, I don't think it's necessary to know all the reasons behind a legend or fantasy; how can we know everything about it, anyway? The mystery is what makes it interesting.

Again, religion is full of mystery. Priests or ministers say, "Well, if all the facts were there for you, you wouldn't *have* to believe, would you? The Lord doesn't tell us everything because He wants to leave that room for doubt so that you *can* have a belief." That's what they always tell you, right? Well, that's what I say to the audience: "Don't ask me questions, just *believe*. If you can believe what they're telling you in church, you can believe my movies."

■ *V: I like the idea of "sleepers" in your script of* I, The Jury—*people who have been in mental hospitals where they were programmed to—*

■ LC: —commit political crimes and stuff like that—

■ *V: —disguised as outrageous sex crimes.*

■ LC: Well, people always think that all these assassins came about that way. It's a good idea, isn't it?

■ *AJ: How come you didn't direct it?*

■ LC: I couldn't get along with the company that was making the picture. They bought the script and then it was chaos; they were going bankrupt, which they did after the picture was finished (Fox bought the picture in a bankruptcy sale). The picture ended up costing $11 million and it didn't look any better than any of my movies! I think some of that $11 million very well may have gone to places it shouldn't have; I don't know. But it seemed to me that the thing was being operated in a very strange way, and I was better off not being involved.

■ *V: You really changed the plot from the original novel.*

■ LC: Nothing was the same except the opening scene with the shooting of the guy with the missing arm, and the last scene with the woman psychiatrist.

■ *V: Did you film any scenes?*

■ LC: Not a one.

■ *V: You weren't fired two weeks after shooting began?*

■ LC: No, I was only there six days. I shot in wide screen Panavision and the picture was reshot in 185, so they didn't use any of my footage.

■ *V: I was shocked when it turned out to be a real guy without an arm!*

■ LC: Well, I cast the guy. I cast all the actors with the exception of Alan King and the actress who played his friend's widow—I don't know *where* they got her! An awful, terrible actress—she was so *homely,* too. I had shot that scene with somebody else who was very good, and when they went to shoot that scene again they used this person.

Anyway, I cast all the parts including the guy without the arm, and I picked most of the locations and stuff. But I just didn't think the picture ended up very good.

■ *V: But the plot was good.*

■ LC: Well, the idea of the government using psychopaths to commit murders, and using a sex clinic to *find* the psychopaths so they could program them—that was all good.

David Carradine with adversary in Q.

■ V: *I thought that was very strong stuff!*

■ LC: And having Mike Hammer being manipulated also—he's kind of a psychopath himself, a little crazy . . . a nut! They're sending him around killing people also, so he's just one of the psychopaths, though he never realizes it.

■ AJ: *In your movies the heroes are also* anti-heroes—*they're never quite real heroes.*

■ LC: This was a *subversion* of the Mike Hammer character. Like when Barbara Carrera gives him a psychiatric report, he reads it, but in the movie they don't specify what was in it. But the report was supposed to state clearly that this guy had a hang-up on him. So then you've got a very good dramatic scene where Hammer finds out that his best friend all his life has had some kind of sexual ideas about him, and what a repugnant thing that is for someone like Mike Hammer who is Mister Macho, fucking all these women and everything! It was great stuff, but they destroyed it.

> **Sometimes the scenes that really make a movie work are the little scenes that have nothing to do with advancing the action, but just add a little something.**

■ V: *What else did they change?*

■ LC: In their version of the ending Hammer brings his friend's prosthetic arm to the girl in a bouquet of flowers—I didn't write that. In our version he takes it with him to the climax with the leading bad guy and beats him to death with it! That was like my shoeshine scene in the other picture—a very bizarre touch where a dead man's arm is used to kill his killer.

Anyway, once I was off the picture the new people came in and just mangled it up; they did what they wanted with it. What could I do? I went off and made *Q*, so I think I ended up better off.

■ V: *So* I, The Jury *gave you the money to make* Q?

■ LC: No, I got the money from backers. I had been very depressed when *I, The Jury* fell apart, and I felt, "Oh my God! Now I'm off this picture and everybody's going to think I got fired!" The only way to keep going is to make another picture right away, otherwise you're going to be sitting around for six or eight months with everybody saying, "Oh, that Larry Cohen got fired and now he can't get a job!"

I was still in the same hotel in New York where everybody from *I, The Jury* was still living, making the movie. And every morning they'd all get up and go off to work while I'd be in my room looking out the window, thinking, "Gee, this is weird!" Because last week I was directing this picture, and this week all the actors I hired are all working, but I'm sitting here doing nothing.

Then, as fate would have it, I ran into Michael Moriarty in a restaurant on the corner. We chatted and then I said, "You know, I've got something you might like to do." I showed him the script for *Q* and he said, "I like this part!" Then I said, "Wait a minute! Maybe I can make this picture!" I called up David Carradine (who I told you was in Cannes) and said, "Listen, if you'd come back and be in this picture, and Candy Clark will do it, maybe I can get money put up and I can make it right away." Carradine said, "Sure! I'll come back and help you out."

I went out and got the money, which took about two weeks. So about three weeks after I was off *I, The Jury* I was shooting *Q*. Then *I, The Jury* ran into all their problems; I caught up with them and passed them and we ended up finishing the picture almost the same day.

Then, as fate would have it, six or eight months later both pictures opened in New York on the same day on opposite sides of the street! Fortunately for me, *Q* did three times as much business as *I, The Jury*, so I was vindicated. My picture

outgrossed their picture; their picture cost $11 million and ours cost about $2 million. So it all worked out okay in the long run.

But I don't like to ever have problems or conflicts like that—it's unpleasant. It's a *weird* experience to be captain of a ship one day and not have anything to do the next . . . and to see everybody going to work on what had been *your* film. Also, I had a girlfriend who was in the picture and naturally she had to go to work every day and be in it, and I had to hear about it every night!

I'd see the blue pages and the pink pages coming in on her script, and I'd think, "Oh God! Now they're changing the whole script! Don't show it to me—I don't want to read it or know what's going on, because it'll just depress me." And they'd say to her, "Don't let Larry Cohen see any of these new pages. In fact, we'd appreciate it if you wouldn't even *see* Larry Cohen while you're working on this picture!"—thus terrifying the poor girl who just wanted to act . . .

■ AJ: *Which role did she play?*

■ LC: She played the secretary, Velda.

■ V: *What inspired your version of* I, The Jury?

■ LC: I read the book and then I had to figure out how to keep certain elements, which were the beginning, the ending, and the sex clinic which I felt was an important element (in the novel she was a woman psychiatrist); I changed it to a sex clinic.

■ AJ: *Actually, Velda was a great character—she was* gutsy. *She was the one with the guns, who shaped him and took care of him. Also, she was very strong.*

■ LC: Yes, it was a very nice part. But for me it was a weird experience to have gone through. But it all worked out for the best; *Q* might not have been made otherwise, and certainly not with Michael Moriarty at that particular time. So it all happens the way it happens . . .

■ V: *Where did that CIA plot development come from? Do you have any particular point of view on CIA operations?*

■ LC: Well, I think they're into a lot of things, for sure. We know the FBI in the past has operated brothels and things like that to get information on people. The Russians do it in Russia—they have houses of prostitution to get information. I would imagine that psychiatrists could be used to get information.

Psychotics are often used, like the guy who shot the Pope (the so-called Bulgarian Connection) where the guy talks like a complete looney—so he probably *is* a psychotic. The question is, were the Russians and the Bulgarians involved in getting him to shoot the Pope? If so, they probably did exactly what we talked about in the movie: they had a secret intelligence agency making use of mentally ill people to carry out killings they're inclined to do anyway.

Take somebody who has an inclination to kill an authority figure—that's their psychological make-up. Then you program them to kill the particular person you want them to kill, and in *I, The Jury* it's supposed to look like hideous sex crimes.

I think that most of the elements of that picture were overlooked. I don't think people could focus in on the plot, because most of the time they were just trying to understand what the leading actor was saying—his diction was so unintelligible. But in the original script, what was going on was very clear.

The people who took over the film were more interested in action scenes: blowing up limousines, staging an elaborate chase sequence with shooting and fighting in trucks—stuff like that. That to me is not important. The important thing is to have an *unusual angle* about everything and an unusual look at the psychosis of the detective.

A picture like *The Maltese Falcon*, which people can see over and over again, doesn't have a single car chase or gun fight; there are no chases over rooftops, no fist fights. Bogart gets knocked out one time. It all happens in a couple of rooms; there's a lot of talk, interesting characters, but no so-called production values in the picture.

Now if somebody were to remake *The Maltese Falcon* today, they'd say, "Okay, we've got to have Sam Spade in a car chase—it's *San Francisco;* how can you *not* have a car chase? Sydney Greenstreet'll be driving one car, and—!" That's what they'd do. Again, *I, The Jury* would have been a better picture if there had been less money spent on it and it had been left alone.

> **Being murdered is a very private thing, and it seems an invasion of privacy to me to have a movie company come in and exploit that for profit. I mean—you died, and you're dead. If anything belongs to you, it's your death.**

■ *AJ: Do you have a favorite movie of* yours?
■ LC: I guess I like *The Private Files of J. Edgar Hoover*—not necessarily the picture, but the experience of having done it. That was fun because we went to Washington, D.C. and shot it at the F.B.I. headquarters, and the F.B.I. training school at Quantico, and we had all these old actors like Broderick Crawford—
■ *V: How did you get him?*
■ LC: Broderick Crawford wasn't hard to get, because after all, he's an older actor and they don't get many offers for leading parts—today there are very few parts written for older actors, especially good parts. So he was very happy to do it—there was no problem there.

We also had Dan Dailey in the film. Most of the people who were cast were happy to be in the picture, because it was an important subject and there were good acting roles for them. But the main problem was if we could get permission to shoot or not.

At first I thought it would be best to keep everything real quiet so we wouldn't create too much attention. But sure enough, the first day we shot in the restaurant in the Mayflower Hotel, the hotel called their publicist and their publicist called the newspapers and the newspapers came down and took all kinds of pictures, so it was spread all over town that we were making the film. The cat was out of the bag.

Then we got lucky. Ford was President at the time and his wife Betty Ford was a former chorus girl. And she loved Dan Dailey, who used to be a tap dancer and a hoofer in movies with Betty Grable, etc. So we got a call at the hotel that President and Mrs. Ford would like to invite Dan Dailey and Broderick Crawford to lunch at the White House the day after tomorrow.

I thought, "Oh my goodness, I've got to close down a *whole day?* The crew and everybody's on *per diem* and salaries, and there's nothing to shoot if they're not around. But if I *don't* let them go to the White House, I'll have two actors who are so pissed off I'll never be able to live with them. So I've *got* to let them go."

Then I got an idea: "Wait a minute; this is a good time to call up and try and get locations." So I called up the F.B.I. and said, "I'd like to shoot at your offices, but I can't tomorrow, because the stars are going to be having lunch with President Ford. But I'd like to shoot the day after tomorrow." I got, "Please hold the line" . . . then they came back on and it's, "What time would you like to be here?"

So that was *it.* I called up all the locations and always managed to mention that the actors were going to be at the White House, and they'd always check to see if I were telling the truth, and then come back and give permission. So that ended up being the best thing that happened to me!

Again, it was one of those things that *looked* like a detriment, but ended up making things much better for us in the long run. That opened up all the doors; in fact Crawford met

Nelson Rockefeller who loaned us his limousine for a scene in the picture. So we got Rockefeller's limousine, and we got permission to shoot here, and there, and we got in every place.
■ *V: Do you think the film's an indictment of Hoover?*
■ LC: It's not; the film shows good parts of him and bad parts of him—it's a fun picture. I tried to make it look like an old Warner Bros picture from the '30s and '40s, with Miklos Rozsa's music and the color and everything. It looked like a pulp movie. Whereas *The Stuff*—the reviewers call it "junk food." One *Playboy* guy said, "It's as enjoyable and nutty as a Snickers." How about that—other people are making movies; I'm making candy bars.
■ *V: Wasn't the ad campaign changed for* It's Alive!? *Didn't the* second *campaign feature a little claw coming out of a baby carriage?*
■ LC: The first campaign ads featured the dead body of a woman on the ground with blood all around it, saying, "Whatever it is—it's alive!" I said, "This is a terrible campaign, because it doesn't tell you what the picture's about. Where does it say it's about a monster baby?" They said, "Our research shows that women will not go to a movie about a monster baby. It turns the women off."

I said, "I'm sorry, but you people bought a picture about a monster baby and that's what it's about. If you don't advertise it for what it is, we're not going to sell *any* tickets." So they went out with their campaign and didn't do any business. Then they tried my campaign, and they did a lot of business. It turned out that most of the audience were women; the picture did very well with the female audience. So what can I tell you? They were wrong.
■ *V: Back to how you write a script—*
■ LC: Sometimes I'll get an idea and just jump in and start writing a scene that happens in the middle. Then I'll go back and write something toward the beginning. I don't write in chronological order because it's too orderly—there's not enough surprises, you know. If I get bored with the direction of the script, or get a block and can't figure out where it's going next, then I'll jump off into a scene somewhere else in the story.

Sometimes I'll make up a scene that isn't even going to be in the script, just to keep going. Because in the course of working on something I'll think of what I need; I'll discover what I need to get out of the corner I've painted myself into. Then, if the script runs 130 or 140 pages, I'll cut it down to the 103 or 104 pages it must be. But the best thing is to just keep going.

Occasionally I'll write two or three scripts at the same time, so that if I get tired of writing on one—after a couple of hours I get *tired* of that—I'll just jump off into the other one and it gives me kind of a renewed energy.
■ *AJ: Do you force yourself to write every single day?*
■ LC: I try to write every day because I feel better if I do something every day. But today is the interview—when you people get through with me I'm not writing anything! This is straight work—enough for one day!
■ *AJ: I read that at age 11 or 12 you were writing scripts—*
■ LC: I just saw movies and then I wanted to put on shows, but I didn't have any cameras or anything. Somebody had bought me an overhead projector; you put on a comic book and it projects a huge picture of Flash Gordon or Batman; the whole wall will be Batman. I would find a postcard or picture and project it on the wall, put on a costume, stand in front of it like it was a set, and act out a scene. To get kids in school to be in it with you, you'd have to bribe other kids to come see it (because they didn't want to). You'd do something like announce that everybody who comes gets a free comic book, just to get 'em in there, to have an audience. I'd make up my stories and give the kids their lines and put on these little productions.

When I was old enough to get my father to loan me his 8mm movie camera, I started running around the park (or wherever) shooting movies. I had to bribe kids to be in them.

Generally you had to cut these movies in the camera; there was no facility for cutting. So you'd do a close-up of this one, then run around and do a close-up of that one, return to where you were, then do an over-the-shoulder shot—everything had to be planned that way. As soon as it came back from the lab it was all finished and ready to show—all made inside the camera.

■ AJ: Didn't Hitchcock do that?

■ LC: Oh, they all say that, but it's not true. He said that so many times in interviews that he came to believe it himself. But he covered everything just the way everyone else does. If you interview any of the actors who were in his pictures, I'll bet they'd say that he covered all the angles and everything. He did a take of Ingrid Bergman, then he did a take of Gregory Peck, then he'd do the dolly shot in—the elaborate shot and maybe that would be the one he'd end up using. But I'm sure he did the other coverage, too.

It's just too dangerous not to do the coverage on the people, particularly with good actors like Gregory Peck and Ingrid Bergman who give it so much. I would assume he shot like everybody else when he shot *Rebecca* and all those pictures. There may have been certain key sequences that he had all worked out a certain way. But the dramatic scenes and the romantic scenes he probably shot just like everybody else. He used to tell stories so many times he'd get to believe them himself. That's what happens if you get interviewed too much—if you get interviewed to death!

> Sometimes I just write and don't know what I'm writing... and as you're writing, the characters start to talk, start to take over, start to play their part.

■ AJ: You do get heavily involved in your editing?

■ LC: Oh yes, I'm to blame for that. I usually stand over the poor editor and never give him a moment's peace. They always tell me, "The scene won't cut. There's no way we can make it work," and I have to figure out some way to make it work. It's like a puzzle; there's always *one way* that it'll work. Then I say, "I tell you what: suppose we take the line at the end and put it at the beginning. *Then* it'll work." He'll say, "Yeah, but then you're rewriting the scene!" I say, "Well, what's the difference as long as we make it work?" He says, "Well, *I* can't do that—you have to do it. I'm only the editor, I'm not the writer."

Basically you have to stay there and do it, because nobody else is going to do it but you. Sometimes you have to reorganize the scene to make the cutting all work, if for one reason or another it doesn't work the way you planned. If you want to take out the whole middle of a scene because it goes on too long, you might find the people are in the wrong place. Then you've got to figure out some way to get them back in the right place. Sometimes you can do it by running the scene backwards—playing the first part of the scene backwards so that the people say the things out of order and then they're back in the right positions by the time the second half of the scene has to come on. Or sometimes the second half of the scene plays first and the first half of the scene plays second.

Editing is fun, because it's like writing, in a way. But instead of moving words around you're moving images around. At least you're not surrounded by 30 or 40 technicians and all that time that is so expensive—camera equipment, lights, location rentals, everything. At least editing is done in a little room somewhere, quietly, at leisure. You take your time—it's like writing in your room. It's not as pressurized a situation as the actual shooting of a picture which is expensive—you have to keep something going because the clock is ticking.

■ V: When you're writing a script, do you start working at a regular time every day?

■ LC: No, no, it depends on what my day's going to be like. I try to get in a block of time, and if I don't do it during the day then I'll have to do it at night. Just like at school when a kid says, "I've gotta do my homework, but I'm going to go play ball, and then I've got a date and a movie, but I've gotta do my homework even if I have to stay up all night, because it has to be done." So I know that if I don't do it now, I'll have to stay up all night and do it—*I've got to get it done.* I use a typewriter, I use a tape recorder.

■ AJ: Do you use a word processor?

■ LC: No, no. *That* I would never do. I think that writing is a wonderful art form and all it requires is a pencil and a piece of paper.

Now they're trying to change it into a system where you have to have a $2500 piece of equipment in order to write. All these young people are going to grow up thinking, "I can't write—I'm helpless—unless I have my $2500 word processor." I wouldn't want to be dependent on that. I think it's wonderful that you can write on on the back of an envelope or a yellow pad or *anything*—it's wonderful freedom! You can take that with you wherever you go.

■ V: But you do dictate words into a tape recorder.

■ LC: Sure; then I have a typist type it up. If they come up with a word processor you can talk into and it types out the script, then I might get one. *That* might be nice to have; I'm sure that'll happen—that's another step forward. But I still like to know that I can go out and do it the old way.

People say, "Yeah, but if you had the word processor you could take that paragraph at the bottom and move it right up to the top if you wanted to." I go, "Well look—I can take this arrow and go like *that* (moves paragraph up). And if I want to get rid of the words on this line I go like *that* (crosses them out).

You see these manuscripts of great books and plays that have been preserved in museums, and you see the way people write—it's in the margins, up on the corners of the page with arrows going down here, and the whole page is crossed off—it's delightfully sloppy. Just like if you go into a painter's studio, it's a *mess*—there's paint all over the place. The same with a sculptor's studio. *Art is messy!* You want to get in there and get it all over you. I don't like the idea of sitting in front of one of those sterile things pushing those buttons and watching the words come out on television. I don't think that's great—maybe I'm in the wrong century!

■ V: When you were making God Told Me To were there any major problems to solve on-set?

■ LC: The big problem was that Tony Lo Bianco, the star, was in a play and had to be off at 6 o'clock every night. Also, he couldn't work on Saturday—there was a matinee—and he couldn't work on Wednesday which was a matinee. We only had the guy three or four days a week. So he's not in half of the scenes; it's a double. But you'd never know it—and to this day he'll swear he was there, in scenes that he wasn't in! He's seen the picture a few times so now he's *sure* he was there, but he wasn't there. Sometimes even I, when I look at it, have trouble remembering that wasn't him, that was the double. There were certain locations he was never even *at*. So, that was the major problem in that picture.

But I enjoyed it—I enjoyed the *power*, that I was taking the leading actor and putting him into scenes he wasn't even in! Talk about *manipulation*—the plasticity of film is such that you can make a picture with an actor who isn't even there! And have *him* convinced that he was really in the movie.

■ AJ: What a special effect. Actually, can you tell us about your movie of that title?

■ LC: *Special Effects* is an old script I wrote a long time ago. It was the first thing I wanted to do, before *Bone*, even. It was one of the only scripts sitting in the closet that I hadn't sold to anybody over the years, about a movie director who has a crack-up and accidentally kills somebody and then decides to make a movie about the murder, and have the real people play

The reincarnation of a Mayan bird-god takes on the Chrysler building in **Q.**

themselves in the picture.

I got the idea from a movie called *In Cold Blood* where the production company went and rented the actual house where the family was murdered, and shot the scenes in the actual rooms where the murders took place. I thought, "That is really gruesome!"—to have those people killed all over again in the rooms where they were actually murdered.

■ *V: Why is that gruesome?*

■ LC: It's just something weird. Being murdered is a very private thing, and it seems an invasion of privacy to me to have a movie company come in and exploit that for profit. I mean—you died, and you're dead. If anything *belongs* to you, it's your death. They're taking something from you.

Just like sex is a very private thing—if you were having sex, you wouldn't want somebody to run in and take pictures of you and then project them on a screen, claiming they have the right to do it. Well, dying is also very private. I just think it's a tremendous invasion of decency and privacy for the purpose of making a profit-making venture.

Anyway, I wrote this script and nothing happened. After the Polanski murders occurred people said, "Oh, you based your script on that!" I said, "No, no," but people didn't believe it. So the script sat in the closet for years . . . fidgeting around,

waiting to be let out.

Then this company asked me, "We have some money to make a picture; have you got anything?" So we made it. But I updated it a bit; I made the director like a Michael Cimino or somebody who's just made a $25 million picture that's a total disaster; he can't get a job in the industry anymore because he's made these high-budget pictures that have been flops. He's trying desperately to find some subject he can make a movie about . . .

His whole bedroom has been rigged up with cameras, and one of them happens to have been rolling when a murder takes place. He decides to make a picture about this and involve some of the real people. He'll have somebody play the part of the girl victim, but when the time comes he'll actually mix in real footage of the murder with the fictitious footage.

Bit by bit he creates such a reality that the people involved start to believe what's happening themselves; they start to change and get into his mind and act out his fantasy. Then the footage gets destroyed, and he has to recreate the murder again.

■ *V: Interesting idea involving illusion vs. reality—*

■ LC: Right. The main character keeps running these shots of Oswald killing Ruby back and forth . . . run it one way, you kill him; run it the other way and you bring him back to life.

The picture's got a lot of interesting ideas about current celebrityhood in America, where you go out and make a $10 or 12 million dollar movie about Dorothy Stratton, who never did *anything*. The only thing she ever *did* was to get herself murdered. That makes her an instant celebrity?

On the other hand, you've got Jessica Lange as *Frances Farmer* who was not an actress of any real note or repute; hardly anyone knows who she was. Her only claim to fame is: she went insane and was put in a mental institution. So that's what stardom is today: insanity, suicide and murder! That's the essence of stardom—it's bizarre, but that's why these people are "interesting."

Nobody's interested in somebody unless they get decapitated in some horrible accident or took poison or committed suicide like Marilyn Monroe. If you *live*, you just get forgotten completely. Your movies get forgotten, and nobody knows who the hell you are! You have to really die in a bizarre fashion or go mad or something to maintain your celebrityhood forever. *Then* you're really a star! So . . . that's what this picture says.

■ *AJ: I read you were watching Vietnam atrocity footage, flipping back and forth to* The Big Valley *when you were making* Special Effects.

■ LC: There was something about that in the picture—about make-believe violence and real violence. When you're watching the 6:00 PM news on TV and there's bodies lying there, and the next show comes on and there's bodies lying there, that juxtaposition negates the difference. *Bodies are bodies!*

People never used to see so much death before. Now it's "Run out there and get a shot of that corpse; we want it for the six o'clock news." Everyone wants to be as graphic as possible—show 'em everything! We were talking about that in movies: if you can figure out how to knock somebody's head off or chop their arm off and make it look real—that's great movie magic, because people want to see all that graphic stuff. They've seen everything, and now they want to see *more*.

> I got the idea from a movie called **In Cold Blood** where the production company went and rented the actual house where the family was murdered, and shot the scenes in the actual rooms where the murders took place. I thought, "That is really gruesome!"

■ *V: I like that scene in* Q *where the window-washer gets decapitated peering into that shoestore with all those racks of shoes.*

■ *AJ: You have all sorts of jokes in your movies. In one scene in* It's Alive, *there's a sign near the killer babies that reads: "Children At Play."*

■ LC: When making a movie, you can never tell *what* you'll find. You see a vehicle go by that says, "Danger! Children," and you say, "Quick! Run up the block and give that guy $25; we want to use his truck for a minute." And you bring it back and use it, but a minute before you hadn't thought of it. You just see these things as you're going along and you say, "Wow! That would be good—let's grab that and put it in the movie."

■ *V: You've found some great symbolic locations for your films, like the warehouse with the miniature Statue of Liberty on the roof—*

■ LC: That's real. I thought, "If we've got to go to a warehouse, let's go to one with the Statue of Liberty on the roof." It's an icon, like the Chrysler Building with the gargoyles, or the top of the temple the creature in *Q* finally lands on which is shaped like a pyramid. If our society was unearthed 2000 years from now, what would people find? They'd find the Statue of Liberty, and they'd say, "Oh, this must have been the god that they prayed to." Just like some statue discovered in ancient Greece: "That must be their god, Aphrodite."

■ *V: You also take advantage of transient events to provide interesting locations, like parades or fairs—*

■ LC: In *God Told Me To* we went down to shoot at the St. Genaro's Fair where they have processions, floats with religious figures and crosses on them, etc. It was a street fair so they had ferris wheels, rides and merry-go-rounds. It provided an interesting free location and it all fit together. The film also contained the St. Patrick's Day Parade which is at a totally different time of the year, but who's going to know?

■ *AJ: Films create their own sense of time and space, anyway.*

■ *V: Can you tell us a bit more about how you came to make films?*

■ LC: Nowadays everybody takes film classes in school; then they do MTV, documentaries, commercials, news and special events—there are all kinds of jobs for people in the visual media other than just making entertainment movies. Probably the majority of people who go to film schools end up working in the business in one way or another.

■ *V: Did you go the film school route?*

■ LC: I went to New York City College; there was a film school there. While there I began writing scripts and submitting them to television shows in New York. I started selling right away, because if you can write *you can write!*

The easiest way to break in is through writing, because it doesn't cost anybody anything to read it. I mean, if you want to direct even a little movie, somebody's got to give you about $50,000. But if you want to write something, your investment is 30 pages of paper and their investment is the half-hour it takes them to read it. And if they don't like it, they're going to tell you right away, and it doesn't cost anybody anything.

But I would suggest that if anybody writes a script, they try and put some good scenes at the beginning. Don't expect everybody to read 30 or 40 pages to get to the good stuff. Put something at the beginning to make 'em want to stay. The same with a movie—you have to give them something interesting to start with.

It was a waste of time to go to college, but who knew? It was the thing to do—to go to college.

■ *AJ: Why was it a waste of time?*

■ LC: Well, I think I could have gone out into the world and started selling material when I was sixteen, rather than having to spend four years in college. If I'd done that, I would have been selling stuff sooner and I would have been making movies earlier.

The first TV series I wrote for was *The Defenders*, a very popular courtroom series about lawyers, etc that won the Emmy award; E. G. Marshall was in it. The show already was a big hit when I submitted an episode, "Kill or Be Killed." I went down and they were nice; they gave me a chance to write for the show. They liked the first scripts, gave me another assignment, and before I knew it I'd worked on it for three years. I was about 22 years old at the time.

Then I came out to California and I was "hot" because *The Defenders* was a top New York show, equivalent to *Hill Street Blues* today. I started getting work immediately, and then someone asked, "Do you have any ideas for a TV series?" I said, "Yeah," and one of the ideas was *Branded*, about a guy who was court-martialed in the U.S. cavalry for cowardice. It was a humiliation series; every week at the beginning of the show they court-martial him—tear off his epaulets and break his sword. Then he has to ride around trying to redeem himself—prove he's a hero to dispel the fact that everybody thinks he's a coward. That was on for a couple of years.

Then there was *The Invaders*, another series like *The Invasion of the Body Snatchers*. Aliens who look like human beings infiltrate our society and this guy knows about it and tries to convince people, etc.

135

■ *V: They can't bend their little finger—*

■ LC: That's right. They could do everything else—they could fly hundreds of thousands of light-years through the air in their spaceships, but they couldn't bend their little fingers, which was really illogical.

■ *V: You created the concept for both of these series?*

■ LC: Right.

■ *AJ: Branded was really about black-listing, right? They didn't really know that, did they?*

■ LC: No. And *The Invaders* was like a witch-hunt; a paranoia series. Kind of like everybody running around accusing other people of being a communist. I didn't have much to do with the show once it got going; gradually they turned it into a rather simple-minded program.

For instance, it would have been more interesting if the invaders weren't all bad. But, at least we did have Michael Rennie as the leader, who you remember from *The Day the Earth Stood Still*. We had some fun with it, but it was more or less running around doing stuff that had been in other science-fiction movies, but doing it for television. This was when *The Outer Limits* was on; '67-'68.

Then I wrote three screenplays, *Daddy's Gone a-Hunting* which was directed by Mark Robson, a Western called *El Condor*, and another one, *The Return of the Magnificent Seven* with Yul Brynner, which is not really the script I wrote (but I got credit for it, anyway). They screwed that one up; they cut out the whole middle of the picture, saying there was no development in it.

After that I thought, "This is a waste of time. If you want 'em to turn out like you want, you gotta make 'em yourself. It means getting up and leaving the swimming pool." I had already become successful in television and was writing screenplays; I had already bought this house.

■ *AJ: In your twenties?*

■ LC: Yeah. It was easy. Then I said, "Oh god, now I gotta get up at six o'clock in the morning and go running around."

I used to write scripts in such detail (with all the camera angles and everything) that the directors would get angry and deliberately change everything, just because they felt they had no position unless they changed everything. It was like following a very detailed blueprint; the picture was already almost pre-cut, pre-directed and everything in the script. So they'd change things arbitrarily for no reason, and then find out that it didn't make any sense. I had to stop writing the scripts in such detail.

So directing the scripts became the only way to do it, I'm afraid. Unless you have a partner who directs—you write, he directs and you have an understanding or something.

■ *V: How did you get money?*

■ LC: I knew people who hired me and were accustomed to paying me a lot of money for scripts. So I went around asking them for money for a whole picture, that's all.

■ *V: Didn't they say, "Well, you've never made a movie before, so ..."*

■ LC: No, there's always people starting out, particularly in the low-budget area. They're not going to get Robert Wise directing their low-budget pictures; Robert Wise directed low-budget pictures at RKO for Val Lewton, but then he began directing big-budget pictures like *Sound of Music*. There always has to be *somebody* coming along to make the

Michael Moriarty receives a lecture from Candy Clark in Q.

low-budget pictures. People get started going to places like American International or Roger Corman. *Believe me, anybody who wants to get started will get started.* It may not be now or next year, but sooner or later, if they're going to stick with it they're going to get it done. It's just the way it happens.

The people who give up weren't meant to do it in the first place. Because it's a hard business—even after you write the picture and finish it, then you have to run it for these people—people who don't like it because they don't understand it, or who advertise it wrong, or who open it on a weekend when the World Series is on—there's a million heartbreaking things that happen.

If you don't have the resiliency to stay with it and keep going—a lot of people just withdraw; they can't stand the pressure and the sense of defeat. So the best thing to do is: just keep going on to the next picture. When you finish one, be ready to do the next one, or be working on scripts for the next one—have something on your mind so you're not going to be plunged into hopelessness.

■ *V: Do you think you're always two or three movies ahead?*
■ LC: Yeah. It's a wonderful business, though. People do let you go off and play-act your dreams . . .
■ *V: So basically, it was disgust at the abuse of your screenplays that brought you to directing?*
■ LC: I was being paid well for the abuse, though, so I didn't get *that* uppity about it. But I wanted to find out if I could make a good picture. I had written that script for *Special Effects,* but I couldn't find anybody to fund that. Then I wrote another one, *Bone* (the title was later changed to *Housewife*), and I got the money from somebody to make my first film. They always change the titles; If I made 13 pictures I have 26 pictures to my name. That gives me more posters to hang on the wall.

Bone is about an affluent family who live in Beverly Hills. He's a super TV car salesman and she's his bored wife; they hate each other. They have a son they claim is a prisoner-of-war in Vietnam, but really he's in a jail in Spain for smuggling drugs. But they tell everybody he's a Vietnam War POW so they can look better.

Into their midst comes a black thief who breaks into their house to rob them, only to find out they don't have any money. They have this big house, swimming pool, Rolls-Royce and everything, but they owe money to everybody; they're absolutely bust. In searching the house the thief finds a bank book listing a $5000 savings account that the wife doesn't know about—the husband's holding out on her. So she's furious, screaming at him. The thief says, "I'll tell you what. You go into town to the bank, get the money, and be back here in one hour. I'll stay here with your wife. If you're not back in one hour, I'm going to rape her, kill her and everything else."

He goes into town to the bank, and then says to himself, "Why should I go back? I hate that bitch." So he takes off. He meets a hippie girl—this picture was made a long time ago when people used to get Blue Chip stamps at gas stations—he meets this girl who makes her living by finding unlocked cars and stealing the Blue Chip stamps in their glove compartments. They take off for the afternoon to have a little sex.

Meanwhile the burglar is waiting for the husband to return, but he never shows up. The wife gets drunk, and before you know it a relationship evolves between them and they realize how much they have in common, etc. It's a comedy. And they fall in love, and then join forces to go find the husband and kill him for his insurance. So it's a wacky, satirical movie about affluent people in Beverly Hills.

We made the picture and I thought it could be controllable because it had a small cast.
■ *V: Did you film it in this house?*
■ LC: Yeah, we did. It was my first picture; I decided to use my own house—the pool was in it, too. This made it easy;

there was no need to go to work every day! I was making movies but I didn't have to leave the house; it was a nice compromise.

That picture got a minor release from a small distributing company, Jack H. Harris Enterprises, whose prime claim to fame was: they had made and distributed a small picture called *The Blob.* The owner was known as Jack "The Blob" Harris.

> **About make-believe violence and real violence. When you're watching the 6:00 PM news on TV and there's bodies lying there, and the next show comes on and there's bodies lying there, that juxtaposition negates the difference. Bodies are bodies!**

It was my first experience with someone who liked the picture for the wrong reasons. He thought, "Oh boy, this is going to be another *Superfly!* or *Shaft!* I said, "Jack, this picture's not a drama, it's a comedy." He said to me, "Listen, am I going to stand in the aisle and tell them not to laugh?" I said, "If you advertise this picture as a drama, they're not going to know what to make of it. If you pay to see a drama and it's really a comedy, you're not going to be happy." He said, "Well, you know, *leave it to me*—I've been in this business since 1900."

Anyway, it was released as a drama and got reviews like, "The most unintentionally funny movie of the year." Horrendous. Then he said, "*I* know what to do." Next thing I knew, he's changed the title to *Housewife* and now it looks like a porno—what the idle housewife is doing in the afternoons. Beautiful, great.

However, that led to me being called in to do that black exploitation picture, *Black Caesar,* which was a big hit. And shortly after that I made *It's Alive!*
■ *V: Where'd you get the concept for* It's Alive!
■ LC: I think I had the idea of a super-monster baby when I was a kid. I thought it was an interesting idea, and that we could could get all the suspense through the implied presence of something you didn't see.
■ *V: It's ambiguous; you feel sympathetic toward the baby, but you also fear the baby.*
■ LC: That's right. And that was a big hit, so I had two big hits. After that people are always looking to see if you'll have another big hit, so you get financing.

The second *It's Alive!* picture did okay, but not as good as the first. Then the business changed a little when American International went out of business. It was a good company for me because they kinda let me make anything I wanted to. But they sold the company, the new company went out of business, and that was the end of that. Then I had to make my pictures wherever I could find a company that was interested.

Ocasionally I still write a script for somebody if I like the idea or the people I get to work with. Like, I wrote *Dr. Strange* in conjunction with Stan Lee, who's the Marvel Comics guy. We enjoyed working together, and now he wants me to do something else with him, so I will. He's a very nice guy and one of the really greater people; he created a whole new look in comic books which revolutionized the comic book industry. Now Marvel's way ahead of *Superman* and *DC* in terms of sales.
■ *V: Back to your filmography. You did* It's Alive *in 1973 and* God Told Me To *in 1977, but what did you do during the four years in between?*
■ LC: I know I did *something* during that time! I lived in England for a year—I guess that was 1975—and wrote a stage

play called *Motive*. There were two productions of it, one with Honor Blackman, the other with Carroll Baker. Then I came back and made *Hoover*, which I think was made in '76 but released in '77.

■ *V: You wrote a screenplay,* Success.

■ LC: That was in '80 or '81, before *Q*. It was a cute script that had been laying around for years; I didn't have anything to do with making the picture. Then I did a play in New York called *Trick*.

■ *V: How come you never turned that into a film?*

■ LC: Oh, I don't know . . . it was too deep! It was so serious; at the time it was too heavy for a movie, maybe not now. I always think about rewriting it, but I never get around to it. I think maybe the experience of having done it on Broadway was enough; I suffered enough with that one, so maybe I better not suffer again!

■ *V: That takes us up to* Perfect Strangers.

> If our society was unearthed 2000 years from now, what would people find? They'd find the Statue of Liberty, and they'd say, "Oh, this must have been the god that they prayed to."

■ LC: *Perfect Strangers* is a little movie we made in conjunction with *Special Effects*. The deal was to make two pictures back-to-back. *Perfect Strangers* stars a two-year-old child; it was kind of an experiment in manipulating the audience into believing that a two-year-old child could act. Since he can't talk, it has to be a non-speaking child.

Anne Carlisle (who was in *Liquid Sky*) is in it. And *Special Effects* has Zoe Tamerlis who was in *Ms. 45*. I made these pictures with these underground movie queens in the Soho section of New York. It was fun! I had nothing else to do at the time, and it gave me something to do for six months while we were raising money for *The Stuff*.

Perfect Strangers is about a little boy and his mother, Anne Carlisle, who's separated or divorced from her husband, raising a kid. The kid witnesses a murder in an alley behind the house. The killer, an attractive young guy, is haunted by the fact that the child may be able to identify him. But then, the child's only two and can't talk.

He starts following the mother and child around the neighborhood to see if the child reacts to seeing him, because he isn't sure if the child can actually recount what he saw. The mother sees him following them around, and thinks that he's interested in her as a girlfriend. They meet and strike up a relationship, and he's convinced that the kid doesn't remember him.

He starts hanging around the house, taking the kid out, and they become like a family. Gradually he becomes aware that the child *does* remember him and knows exactly what he did. There's a policeman hovering about; the people who hired him to commit the murder are pressuring him to kill the child, and Anne Carlisle's like a feminist who runs afoul of her feminist friends because she's taken up with this boyfriend. Meantime the husband wants his kid back and tries to kidnap it. Naturally she gets the kid back, but we know that the only hope it has of surviving is if the father comes around and abducts the boy. Everything's working at cross-purposes.

Anyway, there's a surprise ending which I'm not going to ruin the picture by telling you. Basically it's a kind of love story with a convoluted suspense plot, but a little different from the usual run-of-the-mill "child witnesses murder" stories. It was made before *Witness*, which has some of the same exact shots we have, with the little child looking through a

crack in the door seeing the murder take place. It was a three week shoot—an economical little picture, and I had a good time doing it, working with a lot of these new East Village people who have a whole kind of subculture society. And they're good actors.

■ *AJ: When were you born?*

■ LC: July 15, in Manhattan. I don't like to tell budgets of films or birthdays.

■ *AJ: What's your favorite part of the picture?*

■ LC: Well, my favorite part of every picture is probably just going to the theater and watching it after it's been released, because then I'm safe—*it's over!* ■

Larry Cohen holding promotion container of **The Stuff** for his latest movie.

Photo: Vale

GENRES

Throughout 1965, Hell's Angels had been the targets of countless news reports, magazine articles and pieces of fiction. Most of the press was negative, overblown, and substantially inaccurate. By the end of the year an Angel couldn't even go to the local tavern for a beer without a journalist or TV crew noticing.

■ In January of '66, "Mother" Miles—leader of the Angels' Sacramento branch—died, and when his comrades geared up to attend the funeral, the press was ready. Every Angel in the state of California turned out for the event, as did nearly every other motorcycle gang, rival or not. The procession was spectacular: wall-to-wall Harley-Davidsons rumbling down the highway as far as the eye could see. Strangely, the death of "Mother" Miles sparked the beginning of a new kind of cinema: The Biker Film.

■ While thumbing through an issue of *Life* magazine, producer-director Roger Corman came across a picture of the Miles funeral. Struck by the graphic power of the photo, it occurred to Corman that the Hell's Angels would provide good subject matter for an interesting *and* profitable motion picture. He and scriptwriter Charles Griffith paid a visit to a gang of Angels, and after an evening of drinking and exchanging stories, Corman and Griffith walked away with the material they needed for a screenplay.

■ The movie was to be called *All the Fallen Angels*. The script was written by Griffith, author of some of Corman's best films, including *Bucket of Blood* and *The Little Shop of Horrors*. Corman wasn't completely satisfied with the script, however, and turned it over to his young production assistant for extensive rewriting. For an added touch of realism, Corman employed the Venice chapter of the Hell's Angels as extras. Corman required that all the actors who played bikers in the film know how to ride a Harley, and when lead actor George Chakiris asked for a stunt double to do his riding for him, Corman booted him from the film, replacing him with the man who was to play the second lead: Peter Fonda. By the time it hit the theaters, the title of the movie had been changed from *All the Fallen Angels* to *The Wild Angels*.

■ *The Wild Angels* is less a story than a series of misadventures. Peter Fonda plays "Heavenly Blues," a brooding young misfit and leader of the motorcycle gang. Bruce Dern plays "Loser"—so named because of his uncanny knack for getting the short end of the stick. When Loser is shot by the police while trying to steal a motorcycle, his friends decide to bust him out of the hospital (figuring it would be easier to get him out of the hospital than out of prison). Naturally, without proper medical attention, Loser dies shortly after he is abducted. A funeral is held, and Blues attempts to express his "frustration with society" to the minister. Failing, he and the Angels disrupt the funeral, raping Loser's wife and turning the service into a free-for-all. At the end of the film Blues is left alone, feeling his role as a biker is played out, and won-

Jack Nicholson, Harry Dean Stanton (background) and friends go for a spin in Rebel Rousers (1967).

dering what lies ahead.

■ The Corman film did little to enhance the image of motorcycle gangs, portraying the Angels as being only slightly brighter than your average circus bear on a bike. Upon seeing the film the Angels felt they'd been betrayed, and sued Corman for defamation of character. The original claim was for $1 million dollars, but after years of dickering they settled for $300.

■ *The Wild Angels* was a hit, especially in the South and Southwest—traditionally the market for exploitation and action films. Much to the chagrin of some American officials, the film was chosen to play at the Cannes Film Festival.

Russ Tamblyn laughs maniacally and displays the dead bodies of three of his victims in Al Adamson's classic, Satan's Sadists.

America was ready for bikers; the slapstick Erich Von Zipper image of the motorcycle menace in *Beach Party* was being replaced by a more malevolent image. Outlaw gangs were no longer something to laugh at—they were a real and present danger, and the public flocked to see them.

■ As is always the case in Hollywood, a successful film is seen as a successful formula, and the race was on to produce biker films. First out of the starting gate was *Devil's Angels*. Like *The Wild Angels,* it was produced by AIP and had a screenplay by Charles Griffith. AIP had wanted Roger Corman to direct it, but he was busy working on *The Trip. Devil's Angels* starred John Cassavetes as an aging biker who leads a pack much younger than himself. Cassavetes as a gang leader was an odd and clever piece of casting. At the time he was busy directing independent features, and took the part in *Devil's Angels* to raise money for his own projects. During the '50s Cassavetes had made his mark as a gang leader in a television drama called *Crime in the Streets* (later made into a movie by Allied Artists), and playing a gang leader again twelve years later added a touch of pathos to both parts: the grown-up delinquent with nowhere left to turn.

■ *Devil's Angels* is a better-than-average biker film, but its box office draw was nowhere near that of Corman's films. The big hit of 1967 was *Hell's Angels on Wheels,* produced by Joe Solomon.

■ Biker movies were good to a lot of producers, distributors and actors. They were quick to make, required minimal scripting, and made few demands on anyone's talent. And of the people who profited from biker films, none profited more than Joe Solomon.

■ By the time the biker craze had rolled around, Joe Solomon was a seasoned expert in the field of exploitation. As a child he had made theater signs working in his father's print shop, and later he became the advance publicist for the infamous *Mom and Dad.* After several ups and downs in the movie world (including a failed venture making black light movie displays), Solomon invested everything he had in *Hell's Angels on Wheels.* The film cost $200,000 to make and pulled in several million at the box office. Joe took the money and invested it in another biker film, *Angels From Hell,* and yet another, *Run, Angel, Run* . . . until he had enough money to start his own company: Fanfare Productions.

■ *Hell's Angels on Wheels* is one of the best of the biker films. It starred Jack Nicholson as a loner who meets up with, joins, and then splits from a group of Hell's Angels. Like *The Wild Angels,* this film has very little plot and features real Hell's Angels, including Sonny Barger, their current leader. Unlike the Corman film, the Angels liked and endorsed this film—a gesture few critics could figure out. The director of *Hell's Angels on Wheels* was the talented (if self-indulgent) Richard Rush, but the real star of the film was cinematographer Laszlo Kovacs. Kovacs (who has since gone on to become one of Hollywood's most sought-after cameramen) pulled out all the stops for this film. Sometimes fluidly, sometimes jerkily lopsided, his camera zooms ahead of the Angels.

■ Another film that fared well that summer was *Born Losers.* It told the story of a half-breed Vietnam veteran who comes to the aid of a young woman being raped by a gang of bikers and gets thrown in jail for his troubles. The film was directed by "T. C. Frank," a pseudonym for the film's star, Tom McLaughlin. The character McLaughlin played was called "Billy Jack." Later he would resurrect the character for the execrable *Billy Jack* and its sequel, *The Trial of Billy Jack.*

■ The biker films released in 1967 did well at the box office. Over the next two years no less than fifteen more biker movies were released, and many talented actors used the genre to keep bread on the table. A few actors played in so many of these that it's hard to find a biker movie without at least one of them: William Smith, Robert Dix, Jeremy Slate, Bruce Dern, Scott Brady and Jack Nicholson.

■ The market for these films was teenagers, so combining the motorcycle gangs with another favorite teen genre—the horror film—seemed a natural. The resulting films are hardly scary, but certainly worth watching. The first attempt was *Werewolves on Wheels,* a film about a gang that crosses paths with a witch and ends up as werewolves. Barf bags were handed out at the door when the film first opened. A more intriguing blend of monsters and motorcycles was *Psychomania,* also known as *The Death Wheelers.* It tells the story of a British motorcycle gang led by an occult fanatic who promises the gang members immortality if they kill themselves. They do, and get their wish, but are eventually undone. The name of the gang is (logically) "The Living Dead," and the creature they worship is a *bullfrog. Psychomania* is one of the few biker films to come out of Britain, and definitely one of the weirdest.

■ A belated attempt to combine Harleys and horror was *Northville Cemetery Massacre,* made in 1977 and set in a small redneck town that decides to solve its biker problem once and for all. The gang fights back and the two warring parties meet in the local boneyard. The townspeople make mincemeat of the bikers, but by the end of the film, they learn the futility of their hatred . . .

■ Herschell Gordon Lewis, who carved a career from the depiction of extreme violence, added his own twisted brand of filmmaking to the genre in the form of *She Devils on Wheels:* the story of an all-female motorcycle gang that takes on—and demolishes—a rival male gang. As with all Lewis films, the stage blood is not spared. Another film, *Sisters in Leather,* explores the concept of an all-female gang in a similar and even more exploitative manner.

■ 1970 marked the beginning of the end for the biker genre. America was growing tired of the shenanigans of these motorcycle maniacs and, as if to drive the final nail into the coffin, Avco-Embassy released *C.C. and Company,* a worthless film starring Joe Namath as a lone biker who defends Ann-Margret against William Smith's gang. 1970 was also the year *Black Angels* was released; the first (and last) blaxploitation biker flick. Producers sought new ways to pump life into the dying genre, and one of the goofiest attempts was *The Losers,* the story of Hell's Angels who are recruited by the President to rescue soldiers in Cambodia. In addition to an idiotic premise, the story saddled the bikers with *dirt* bikes, and *The Losers* met with scant approval from press and public.

■ By 1973 the biker film had virtually disappeared, but New World Pictures tried one more time to revive the moribund genre with *Bury Me an Angel,* which tells the story of a young woman setting out to avenge her brother's death. The film stars Dixie Peabody—a woman who can ride a Harley better than she can act. It's also the only biker film written and directed by a woman, Barbara Peeters. Probably the best thing about this film is its advertising, which, in a shameless burst of alliteration, proclaimed: "A Howling Hellcat, Humping a Hot Hog, on a Roaring Rampage of Revenge."

■ Several factors led to the demise of the biker genre. Altamont, billed as the "Woodstock of the West," turned into a series of bloody confrontations between former allies the hippies and Hell's Angels. The federal helmet law (since repealed) took much of the joy out of motorcycle riding for many bikers, although most gang members tried to compensate by wearing helmets shaped like those used in Nazi Germany. Gas prices drove the highway speed limits down to 55, making a true rip-roaring highway run a thing of the past. Several states passed laws aimed against choppers. Size limitations on forks, handlebars, and wheels—plus countless other nit-picking details—kept some beautiful machines off the road for good. Finally, the genre simply did not offer enough variety to sustain the public's interest, and the biker film, like the motorcycle gangs they helped promote, quietly dropped from view. ■

After World War Two was finally over with, everyone thought they were ready to face the future. They thought the future meant vacations on Mars, 200 mph highways, and nuclear-powered cars. No one foresaw the development of the electric guitar and rock 'n roll and the birth of a new kind of movie for a new kind of teenager: The J.D. Film.

■ Films dealing with the problem of juvenile delinquency had been around long before the fifties. In 1921 *As the World Rolls On* chronicled the exploits of a gang of young hoods. A year later *The Angel of the Crooked Street* became the first film to tell the story of a reform school girl. In 1937 Leo Gorcey, Huntz Hall and several other young actors made their debut as a gang of street-smart kids in *Dead End,* a stagebound but entertaining film about a big-time hood coming home to visit his mom. The "Dead End Kids" were so popular they soon appeared in another film, and another— each succeeding film a little less carefully crafted than the last, until by 1957 the boys were cranking out some of the most consistently goofy movies this side of The Three Stooges. Along the way they changed their name to "The Bowery Boys."

■ Early efforts to portray juvenile delinquency were markedly different from the J.D. films that came later. Usually the delinquency was based on the dehumanizing effects of urban life, or on some wrong turn made by the protagonist as a child. From this point of view it's not inconceivable for one boy to grow up to be an upright citizen while his brother turns to a life of crime, as in *Public Enemy Number One. City Across the River* (based on Irving Shulman's gritty novel *The Amboy Dukes*) was one of the first films to blame delinquency on the parents, even though the parental neglect was caused by the high cost of living in the city—forcing the parents to work all the time. It's *the city* that's seen as the villain, and for most of America juvenile delinquency was strictly an urban problem.

■ All that changed in 1954 when Marlon Brando and his gang roared across the screen in *The Wild One,* a film based on an actual event in a small California town.

■ The bikers in *The Wild One* were a bit too old to be considered *juvenile* delinquents, but their antics, attitudes and slang portrayed a colorful archetype for would-be rebels across the country to emulate. Unlike the young thugs in urban dramas, the rebels in *The Wild One* weren't out to became big shots or millionaires—they broke the rules just for the fun of it . . . because they were there. When *The Wild One* demonstrated that even the smallest town could be overrun by toughs, delinquency became *everybody's* problem.

■ 1955 was a banner year for teenagers. Until then, popular music meant Perry Como and Patti Page. *Your Hit Parade* and *The Dotty Mack Show* offered television viewers a chance to see current hit songs acted out in pantomime by Giselle MacKenzie and Snooky Lanson. Songs like "How Much is That Doggie in the Window" ruled the airwaves. But a new kind of music began to force its way into the national consciousness—a raucous fusion of black rhythm and blues and white country and western that some people thought was the Devil's Music; most just called it rock 'n roll. Because this

IF YOU'RE 16 you're old enough to see it!

MY MOTHER–
"I call her Mother only because I don't know what else to call her."

MY FATHER–
"Now there's always some woman at the house–he says they 'just drop in'!"

MYSELF–
"All I know is–no matter what I do it's wrong!"

A grown-up motion picture for grown-up emotions!

20th Century-Fox presents

TEENAGE REBEL

STARRING
GINGER ROGERS · MICHAEL RENNIE

with Mildred Natwick · and three stars of the future
BETTY LOU KEIM · WARREN BERLINGER · DIANE JERGENS

Produced by CHARLES BRACKETT · Directed by EDMUND GOULDING · Screenplay by WALTER REISCH and CHARLES BRACKETT

new musical spirit and juvenile delinquency arose at approximately the same time, many parents and teachers blamed wailing electric guitars and pumping pianos for the rising crime rate among teenagers.

■ When director Richard Brooks decided to make a movie based on an Evan Hunter book about the problems of juvenile delinquency, he included "Rock Around the Clock" as part of the soundtrack—a song that teens loved and parents loathed. The film was *Blackboard Jungle,* and not since *Birth of a Nation* had a film raised such controversy. After an advance screening of the film, U.S. Ambassador Clare Booth Luce declared that if *Blackboard Jungle* went to the Venice Film Festival, she would not. Ms. Luce, an influential and headstrong woman, won the battle but lost the war; her outrage at the supposed degenerate nature of the film only served to spark people's curiosity—*Blackboard Jungle* was a hit.

■ *The Wild One* started the ball rolling, *Blackboard Jungle* gave it momentum; then came *Rebel Without a Cause*. Originally *Rebel Without a Cause* was intended as drive-in fare, to be filmed in black-and-white on a limited budget. The director, Nicholas Ray, had managed to sign an up-and-coming young actor named James Dean to play the lead role. Warner Bros, sure of the film's success after seeing MGM's profits climb with *Blackboard Jungle,* had Ray scrap his footage and start over in Cinemascope and color—thus destroying much of the film's potential impact. *Rebel Without a Cause* is a borderline J.D. film—Dean hardly seems like much of a rebel, appearing more befuddled than delinquent. A better title for the film might be *Cause Without a Rebel.* The film did, however, establish certain J.D. conventions that would be

used in films to come: it was the first movie to portray teenage hoodlums in a suburban setting. James Dean's character—the misunderstood "good" kid—would crop up again in many motion pictures, including *Invasion of the Saucer-Men* and *The Blob,* and it was also the first movie to feature the game of "Chicken." The number of subsequent films featuring variations on Chicken is staggering. Usually it was used as a device to get rid of the "bad" kid—teens lost their lives driving over cliffs, running into trains, smacking into walls and colliding with each other. The creative abilities of Hollywood scriptwriters were sorely taxed as they struggled to think of new ways to destroy the youth of the nation.

■ As always, producers—hot on the scent of profits in the new teen market—scrambled to cash in. None scrambled faster than Sam Katzman, nicknamed "Jungle Sam" because of his work on Columbia's *Jungle Jim* serials. His specialty was producing movies quickly on very low budgets. Just weeks after *Rebel Without a Cause* was released, he hired his favorite director, Fred J. Sears, started filming, and hit the theatres with *Teenage Crime Wave.* Over the years Katzman added many more teen-oriented films to his filmography, including such favorites as *Rock Around the Clock, Don't Knock the Rock* and *Calypso Heat Wave.*

■ Nobody took better advantage of the burgeoning youth market than American-International Pictures (AIP). Started by a lawyer (Samuel Z. Arkoff) and an ex-theatre manager (James H. Nicholson), AIP aimed at the teen market exclusively. Many critics at the time decried AIP's movies, accusing them of pandering to society's basest elements in shameless

Dick Bakalyan, caught in the act in Juvenile Jungle.

bogo-(88)-9

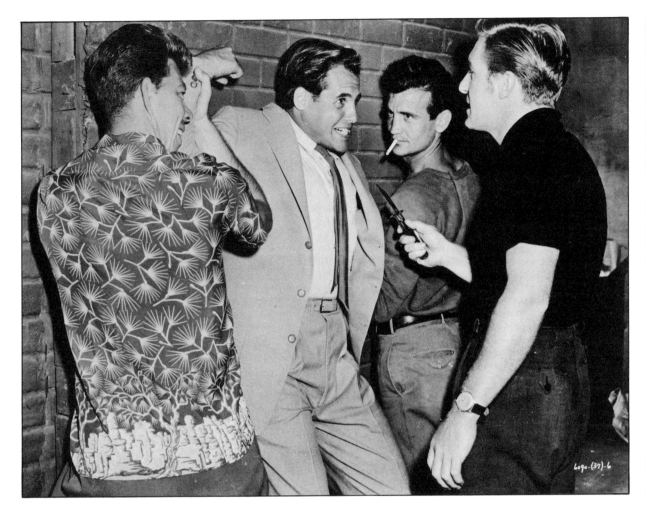

Bakalyan (with cigarette) and friends pour on the friendly persuasion in *Juvenile Jungle.*

pursuit of the fast buck. Arkoff and Nicholson were undaunted, and soon AIP was one of the most successful film companies in Hollywood. In retrospect, AIP gave us some of the very best J.D. films of all, including *The Cool and the Crazy, Reform School Girl* and *Hot Rod Girl*.

■ But Sam Katzman and AIP were by no means the only ones taking advantage of the teenage film market; two other film companies, Allied Artists and Howco-International, also released many films similar in content and style to those of AIP. Allied Artists (formerly Monogram, a long-time institution in Hollywood) kept itself afloat during the fifties with films like *Joy Ride* and Roger Corman's classic *Teenage Doll*.

■ Much smaller than either Allied Artists or AIP, Howco-International joined the teenpix race with *Teenage Thunder* and *Carnival Rock*. They also released, among other of his films, Ed Wood, Jr.'s *Jail Bait*.

■ By showing a side of life most Americans preferred to ignore, the J.D. films annoyed and angered many people. See this review from *Films in Review:*

HIGH SCHOOL CONFIDENTIAL

Were this anti-social film merely a poverty-row amorality made by fast-buckers for the titillation of morons and would-be criminals, FILMS IN REVIEW would take no notice of it. Instead, it was made for, and distributed by, a reputable company (MGM); it utilizes well-known actors and actresses; and its producer, Albert Zugsmith, protests it is an exposé of a social evil.

This film is itself a social evil.

It begins with Jerry Lee Lewis* banging out the rock-n-roll beat on a piano as he "sings" a monosyllabic "lyric" suitable for the intelligence of a baboon. Gathered about him are seemingly wholesome high school boys and girls. Their juxtaposition to Lewis is deliberate, and plants the suggestion, later explicitly reiterated, that the primiti-

vism of urban polyglots has become the American norm. Later, the ghastly nihilism that life affords nothing of value greater than a "kick" is asserted, explicitly and defiantly, in an existentialist "poem" recited for no story-line reason. Its purpose seems to be to provide a "philosophical" rationalization for bop-jabber, juvenile delinquency and dope addiction.

*Lewis, who seems to be in his early twenties, recently married the 13-year-old daughter of a cousin, five months before his divorce from his *second* wife became final.

■ The J.D. films are, in some ways, the direct descendants of the *film noir* of the forties. The heroes are usually outcasts or misfits, and the stories do not always have happy endings; indeed, even the happy endings are tinged with feelings of doom and despair. Only rarely, though, does a J.D. film exhibit the moody photography and sophisticated dialogue of the *film noir*. Miniscule budgets and two-week shooting schedules prevented much in the way of artistic indulgence. Besides, sophisticated dialogue had no place in the world of "cool, man," "Crazy, Pops!" and "Hey, Daddy-O." Most were filmed by directors like Ed Cahn, who worked at breakneck speed shooting fifty set-ups a day. Night shots were filmed "day for night," and chiaroscuro was replaced with a flat grey tone. Most of the movies of the fifties were filmed this way; you could call them *film gris*.

■ By the end of the fifties, America's teenagers were suffering from J.D. burnout. They had had enough switchblades, chicken runs and reform school girls. Chuck Berry was in jail, Elvis was drafted and Buddy Holly was dead in the ground. Also dead was the feeling of the fifties; it was time for something new—something as different from the fifties as they had been from the previous decade. It was time for *Beach Party*. ■

BEACH PARTY FILMS

BY JIM MORTON

In the early sixties teen-agers were bored with the grease-and-leather look spawned by Marlon Brando in *The Wild One*. The new look was clean, scrub-faced and wholesome, with bikinis, bright colors, hula shirts and bleeding madras pants. Amid a prospering economy these kids weren't the social misfits of the previous generation; they all planned to go to college and settle down into well-paying jobs someday. But before they did they wanted to have One Last Fling.

■ The hedonistic happiness and antics of this new breed of teenager did not go unnoticed by Hollywood. Teens composed a sizable portion of the movie-going public, so Hollywood scrambled to find the type of film these new kids would flock to. They came up with "Beach Party" movies. But why? Let us backtrack to August 21, 1959, when Hawaii became a state. The entire country went Hawaiian; women took hula lessons in dance schools across the nation. Albums of Hawaiian music sold out in record stores and supermarkets. People held "luaus," and suburban backyards filled up with tiki gods, tonga torches, hula hoops and women in muu-muus and leis.

■ Along with this came a sport that had long been popular on the islands: surfing. There had always been a few eccentric devotees on the California coast, but now surfing was *hot*. Kids took to it with a fervor formerly reserved for cars, sex, and rock 'n' roll . . .

■ A new culture headquartered on the beaches of America sprang up. Spurred by songs of the Beach Boys and other California bands, the kids of America went surf-mad, and Southern California became the place to be. Strange new words like "gremmy," "ho-daddy," "hang ten" and "cowabunga!" crept into the language.

■ An early film examining this phenomenon was *Gidget*, starring Sandra Dee as a young beach bunny caught between childhood and maturity. In the airheaded plot, Gidget becomes a kind of mascot to a group of beach bums whose strange ideas and lingo she finds intriguing. *Gidget* was so popular it spawned several sequels (each with a different

Beach Bunnies display their charms in Wild Wild Winter.

woman playing the lead), a TV series starring Sally Field, and at least one parody (Jonathan Demme's *Gidget Goes To Hell*).

■ In the east, meanwhile, thousands of college students on Easter vacation would head south to Ft. Lauderdale for some fun in the sun. The streets of this small Florida beach town would overflow with boisterous students drinking, staggering around, shouting, singing, throwing up, trying to overturn cars or taking their clothes off in public. Ten or twelve occupants to a motel room was not uncommon, and sex—or at least the desire for it—was rampant. As usual, the news media proclaimed outrage at the unrestrained antics of these drunken youths.

■ In 1960 MGM decided to capitalize on this annual Florida pilgrimage with *Where The Boys Are,* the story of four female students (played by Connie Francis, Paula Prentiss, Yvette Mimieux, and Dolores Hart) who head south during spring break to meet boys and have fun. Some do, some don't, and Connie Francis sings a few tunes.

■ *WTBA* wasn't a musical, but it seemed like one. It had a happy-go-lucky air that many people found appealing. Paula Prentiss and Jim Hutton were so popular in this film that they—as a kind of lowbrow Myrna Loy and William Powell—were teamed again in *Bachelor In Paradise, The Love Machine, The Horizontal Lieutenant* and *Looking For Love.*

■ However, it took American-International Pictures (AIP) to do it *right.* In 1963 AIP hired pop idol Frankie Avalon and former Mouseketeer Annette Funicello to play Frankie and Dee Dee in *Beach Party,* the story of a breezy young couple whose entire life is spent on the beach. With them was the rest of their gang: Deadhead, Animal, Candy, Donna, Johnny, and others. Together they would twist their lives away, existing in a world of perpetual summer.

■ Into every life a little rain must fall, and in the lives of the Beach Party kids it appears in the form of Erich Von Zipper and his gang of backdated motorcycle hoods, "The Rats" (and their girlfriend auxiliary, "The Mice.") The Rats do everything in their power to disrupt the lives of the beach people, but they aren't very successful; The Rats are a bunch of morons, and their fearless leader, Erich Von Zipper, is a monument to ineptitude.

■ Von Zipper (as played by Harvey Lembeck) is an inspired invention. With his black leather jacket, motorcycle (with trophy tied to the handlebars), and tough-thug way of talking, Von Zipper effectively parodied the rebellious style of the fifties—a style the surfers totally rejected. Von Zipper was *The Wild One* gone to seed: Marlon Brando played as a stuttering cretin. The most memorable moments in the Beach Party films can be attributed to Von Zipper and his cronies, with lines like "*You*—stupid," and "Uh-oh, the Boss gave himself the finger." The character of Von Zipper appeared in no less than seven of the Beach Party movies, outlasting Frankie, Annette, and the whole surfing crew.

■ After the initial success of *Beach Party,* Hollywood scrambled to imitate this new breed of film. In 1964 no less than *seven* films were released, all dealing with the joys of partying in the sand. Three, produced by AIP, were sequels to *Beach Party.* In *Pajama Party* Frankie Avalon was replaced by another ex-Disney star, Tommy Kirk, who played Go-Go, a Martian sent to spy on earthlings in advance of a future invasion. (Strangely, Kirk would play an almost identical character in another film, *Mars Needs Women.*) 1964 also saw the release of the first Beach Party horror film, *Horror At Party Beach*—a logical synthesis, since the two genres appealed to largely the same crowd.

■ Along with AIP's films came a host of imitators and also-rans. For surfing, the best of the bunch was *Ride The Wild Surf,* filmed in Hawaii at Waiamea Bay where waves occasionally reach heights of 100 feet. For sheer zaniness, though, *Ride The Wild Surf* couldn't compare with the AIP films. When the characters weren't surfing, the action stopped cold.

■ United Artists attempted to join the fun with an uneven film starring James Darren and Bob Denver, entitled *For Those Who Think Young.* Aside from Denver's clever hodaddy routine and the initial screen appearance of Nancy Sinatra, the film has little to offer.

■ Director Lennie Weinrib attempted to recreate the ambience of AIP films with his film *Beach Ball,* a movie about an all-guy band pretending to be an all-girl band. By using pop stars in guest appearances, Weintraub felt he could improve on the Beach Party formula. Whether *Beach Ball* is an improvement is arguable, but the film does provide an opportunity to see some now-established stars in their formative stages, including a young and nervous-looking Diana Ross and the Supremes.

■ Producer-Director Maury Dexter tried to infuse the beach genre with drama and relevance—almost a contradiction in terms. The result was films like *Surf Party* and *Wild on the Beach,* and though they're worth seeing, they lack the pop-giddiness of their predecessors.

■ Action in the AIP films was, to put it mildly, wacky. Scripts were like something out of *Mad* magazine, bordering on the edge of surrealism. For example, dancer Candy Johnson has the power to knock men over just by shaking her hips. Erich Von Zipper learns the secret of "The Tibetan Finger Technique" and constantly puts himself—accidentally—into a state of suspended animation. Frankie Avalon often turns to the camera and addresses the audience concerning events in the film. A derelict sitting in the corner of a local coffeehouse turns out to be none other than Vincent Price, exclaiming, "Where's my pendulum? I feel like swinging!"

■ None of this seems to bother the beach kids. As long as the sun keeps shining, the music keeps playing, and the supply of Dr. Pepper doesn't run out, they're happy. The only thing bothering Annette is Frankie's bohemian outlook and resistance to marriage. The ensuing problems form the backbone of the beach-film plots. The issue of marriage is never resolved, but they do manage to sing a few songs about their dilemma.

■ Most of the singing is done by Frankie and Annette, either as a duo or separately. The rest of the singing chores were mostly handled by Donna Loren, truly the forgotten star of the Beach Party movies. Her happy-go-lucky air epitomizes the spirit of these films. Her singing was not so bad, either; firmer and less breathy than Annette's. Donna achieved some popularity during the mid-sixties, appearing regularly on TV shows such as *Hullaballoo* and *Where the Action Is.* Unfortunately AIP wasn't interested in promoting her career, and aside from singing one or two songs in most of the Beach Party movies, Donna did little more than stand in the background and smile on cue.

■ Most of the AIP Beach films were directed by William Asher, a fine low-budget director who is best known for *I Love Lucy.* The rest were directed by a diverse line-up of people, including horror director Mario Bava (*Dr. Goldfoot and the Girlbombs*), sleaze filmmaker Stephanie Rothman (*It's a Bikini World*), classic 'B' filmmaker Norman Taurog (*Dr. Goldfoot and the Bikini Machine*), pedestrian hack Don Weis (*Pajama Party* and *The Ghost in the Invisible Bikini*), and Don Knott's favorite director, Alan Rafkin (*Ski Party*). It is Asher's films, however, that remain the most lively and engaging of the lot.

■ By 1967 Beach films had just about died out; surfing no longer held the magic for the younger generation it once had. The times were changing; the ultra-clean look was a thing of the past, replaced by the shaggy and the unkempt; colors went from bright to black-light and Day-Glo; stripes and plaids changed to paisleys and wild patterns; the trebly sound of the surf guitar was replaced with wah-wah and fuzztone. The action moved from the beach to smoky dance halls with loud bands and light-shows on the walls. Surfing had been replaced by pot and LSD. ■

LSD FILMS

BY JIM MORTON

Drugs have long been a favorite topic of exploitation films. They allow the filmmaker to include the seamiest kinds of sex and violence, while maintaining a facade of moral righteousness and social concern. Drug movies date back to the silent film era, when cocaine was still a new thrill and opium was smoked in the hidden dens of Chinatown. An early example is Douglas Fairbanks' *The Mystery of the Leaping Fish,* which depicted both drugs in use—and with little retribution.

■ Regardless of the drug involved, the plots of most of these films follow a general pattern: young Dick and Jane are nagged by their "friends" to try a certain drug that is "the rage." Being "good kids," Dick and Jane resist at first but eventually yield to peer pressure, resulting in the total des-truction of their lives. The classic example of this plot is *Reefer Madness.*

■ Long before it became popular, LSD was mentioned in William Castle's 1959 film, *The Tingler,* which starred Vincent Price as a doctor who discovered that every time a person gets frightened, a centipede-like creature begins to grow along the spine. The only way to subdue this creature is by screaming. In the film, Price attempts to experience "The Tingler" firsthand by injecting himself with LSD. Price's bravado performance while under the influence stands out as the first acid freak-out in cinema history.

■ In the mid-sixties, when the world at large discovered the joys of LSD, people said they saw monsters, flew to the moon and touched the hand of God. Filmmakers attempting to recreate these images came up with a wildly creative new movie style that could be termed "garage surrealism." Fish-

Feminist singer Holly Near "grooves out" with Jordan Christopher and friends in **Angel, Angel, Down We Go.**

eye lenses, painted women, op-art patterns and multiple exposures became *de rigueur* for any film illustrating the effects of acid.

■ Once the drug became a household word, there was no stopping filmmakers from exploring its possibilities. In *The Acid Eaters,* a gang of office workers shed their establishment guises every weekend and hit the road in search of cheap thrills. Their quest is finally fulfilled in the form of a fifty-foot tower of LSD! *Turn On, Tune In, Drop Out* was Timothy Leary's how-to guide for trippers seeking maximum spiritual enlightenment. And Ben Van Meter's *Acid Mantra; Or Rebirth of a Nation* showed what happens when you give a stoned hippie a movie camera.

■ The hilarious *Hallucination Generation* starred George Montgomery as a boozy guru of a flock of thrill-seekers. The film was shot in black and white, but director Edward Mann heightened the effectiveness of the "trip" sequences by filming them *in color.*

■ *The Weird World of LSD* also examined—purportedly—the dangers of LSD, but lacked funds for much in the way of special effects. In one scene, a man hallucinating that he's flying on the wings of a great bird is shown lying on a couch, grimacing madly, as a crude drawing of a chicken is superimposed over the scene!

■ The mind-altering potential of LSD provoked much speculation: what secret depravities hidden in the libido might be released? In *Alice in Acidland,* a young woman discovers the joys of lesbian sex after taking the drug. In *Wanda (The*

Sadistic Hypnotist), lesbians again get the treatment, this time as sadomasochistic leather freaks who have the tables turned on them after being forced to take the drug.

■ No-budget filmmaker Andy Milligan managed to include practically every sexual activity imaginable in *Depraved!*— climaxing the film with a girl, high on LSD, leaping from a window (a favorite pastime of girls on acid). In the '70s, John Waters paid homage to this singular type of suicide in his parody, *The Diane Linkletter Story.*

■ The best "trip" movie is also the best known: Roger Corman's classic *The Trip.* Written by Jack Nicholson and starring Peter Fonda, Bruce Dern and Dennis Hopper (acidheads all), *The Trip* chronicled the adventures of a young director of TV commercials who, feeling that his life has no meaning, takes a hefty dose of LSD and spends the rest of the film hallucinating his brain away. Corman, to better understand the subject, actually took acid before making the film. Along with *2001: A Space Odyssey, The Trip* became required viewing for anyone into LSD.

■ With the advent of acid came the hippie movement, centering upon a small neighborhood in San Francisco called the Haight-Ashbury, next to Golden Gate Park. Hippies advocated long hair, exploring inner space, a return to nature, and—most important to exploitation filmmakers—free love. Porno filmmakers wasted no time in exploring *this* aspect. The first "docudrama" on the Haight-Ashbury was titled *The Evil Pleasure,* a rarely seen sexploitationer that takes a "mondo" look at some kinky aspects of hippie living. *Blonde*

149

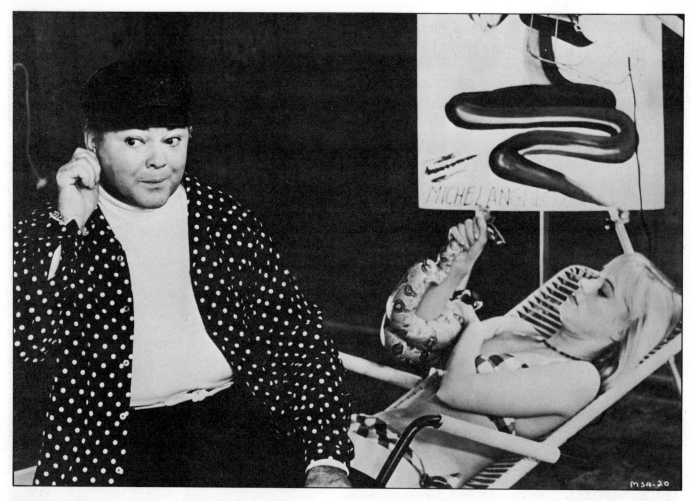

Scene from **Movie Star, American Style, or, LSD, I Hate You.**

on a Bum Trip casts a similar (but kinkier) glance at New York City's hippie community in the East Village. Along the same lines, *Wild Hippy Orgy* purported to show what *really* went on in those Hashbury crash pads. Produced by a group called "Pot Heads' Experimental Films," *Wild Hippy Orgy* was double-billed with an even wilder feature titled *Psychedelicsex Kicks,* which featured nude body-painting, love-making in a balloon-filled room and a woman of Russ Meyerian proportions making lewd gestures with a python. Together, these films ran a total of eighty-one minutes; "epic" they weren't.

■ Occasionally revived at midnight cinemas is *The Hippie Temptation,* a made-for-TV one-hour documentary on the Haight-Ashbury, showing interviews with key founding figures, a concert with light show, a visit to the Psychedelic Shop (the first hippie store in the world, selling the *I Ching,* yarrow sticks, incense, love beads, and books on meditation, the tarot, palmistry, astrology, etc.), a visit to a crash pad, and other archetypal hippie phenomena.

■ *Psych-Out,* produced by Dick Clark and directed by Richard Rush (*Hell's Angels on Wheels, The Stunt Man*), starred Susan Strasberg as a deaf runaway searching for her hippie brother in San Francisco. Arriving in the Haight during the "Summer of Love," she enlists the help of a ponytailed Jack Nicholson to find her missing brother, played by—in his usual weird way—Bruce Dern. With music by Strawberry Alarm Clock and The Seeds, *Psych-Out* is the definitive fable of the Hippie Movement.

■ Reports of people freaking out after being given the drug unawares began to crop up in the news. Filmmakers leaped to exploit the situation. Now no one was safe from the

substance. "It could be *your* son or daughter!" the headlines screamed. "It could even be you!" In *The Dean's Wife,* a man commits suicide after being slipped the drug and confronted with his wife's nymphomania. In *Wild in the Streets,* the entire U.S. Congress unknowingly gets stoned. LSD is used in *The Big Cube* to put Lana Turner out of commission. And in Otto Preminger's strangest film, *Skidoo,* we get to see the effects of acid on Groucho Marx and Jackie Gleason.

■ All sorts of horrible acts, from robbery to murder, were attributed to LSD. The rarely shown *Mantis in Lace* (aka *Lila*) is the story of a topless dancer who turns on and becomes a mutilation murderer. In *Satan's Sadists,* motorcycle thugs dose unwitting girls and then rape them. Russ Meyer—always attuned to the times—joined in the fun by including the LSD-induced crack-up of "Z-Man" in the celebrated *Beyond the Valley of the Dolls.*

■ The '70s saw a decline in the use of psychedelics. Ingredients like strychnine and speed often turned up in hallucinogens, making each trip a new and dangerous experience. The electric madness of the '60s was replaced with a blander, more "mellow" attitude. But acid had one good film left in it: Jeff Lieberman's *Blue Sunshine,* released in 1976. It detailed the misadventures of a group of ex-druggies, now respected members of the community, who suffer from a 10-year delayed reaction to a bad batch of LSD which turns them into psychopathic killers who lose their hair along with their minds.

■ LSD and psychedelic music—often called "paisley"—are currently enjoying a speckled resurgence in popularity. Whether this will lead to any new films remains to be seen . . . . ■

150

WOMEN IN PRISON FILMS

BY JIM MORTON

The appeal of Women in Prison films (hereafter referred to as WIP films) is difficult to explain. Films dealing with men behind bars are uniformly grim and depressing, yet the same stories with women replacing the male roles are much more amusing. The appeal is not merely sexist; women enjoy them as much as men do. In most films women are presented in more genteel surroundings exhibiting "ladylike" behavior, while in WIP films women are hard, mean and take no shit from anybody. Perhaps in this "breaking of the rules" lies the beauty of these films.

■ The WIP film, in its current form, began shortly after World War II. While the men were away in Europe learning about violence (and sex), the women of America were busy working, assembling hand grenades and building planes. When the war ended, America's values and perceptions would never again be the same.

■ Women no longer submitted to the role of housewife, mother, inferior being. Meanwhile, men had discovered that the bawdy, good-natured sexuality of the French was infinitely preferable to the puritanical guilt/shame prevalent in the States. This shift in attitude is well-chronicled in the movies of the times; especially *film noir*. The vivacious "good girls" of the silver screen were fading, replaced with more adventuresome role models. Goodbye Clara Bow; hello Lauren Bacall.

■ *Caged* (1950) is the movie that founded the WIP genre, providing archetypes and a primary theme. Eleanor Parker plays a timid woman whose involvement with a robbery was passive and unaware. Once in jail she quickly learns that only the strong survive. In spite of attempts by the warden (Agnes Moorehead) to keep jail from corrupting her, by the end of the film Ms. Parker is as callous as the rest of the women in the pen.

■ *Caged* was successful both critically and financially; Eleanor Parker and Hope Emerson received Oscar nominations for their performances. But the film was not perceived for what it was: the first of a new kind of movie. To most people it was just another crime-drama. But the exploitational aspects were not lost on Bryan Foy, producer of dozens of exploitation films.

■ In 1955 Foy released *Women's Prison;* the critics didn't like it but it did well at the box office. The film tells the story of a cruel warden (spectacularly played by Ida Lupino) whose sadistic practices provoke a riot. Outstanding performances by Jan Sterling and Cleo Moore continually spark tension, but Ida Lupino's role as the sadistic warden remains

Prison Matron Stella Stevens attempts to maintain order in Chained Heat.

the definitive performance for all WIP films to follow. Sixteen years later, Ms. Lupino reprised her role in Bernie Kowalski's made-for-TV movie, *Women in Chains.*

■ The most popular type of WIP films during the fifties were the ones dealing with teenagers. As each year more and more ended up in juvenile hall, kids readily identified with films about them. The same year *Caged* was released, United Artists released *So Young, So Bad;* the story of four girls incarcerated in a "corrective home for girls." More films were to follow; among them: *Girls in Prison* and *Girl's Town.*

■ By the start of the sixties filmmakers appeared to be running out of ideas for WIP films. In 1962 *Caged* was remade as *House of Women.* This remake was entertaining, but inferior to the original.

■ By 1965, the genre had been taken over by sexploitation films. The emphasis no longer was on legitimate penal institutions but on *covert* ones; most commonly white-slavery rings. In films like *Olga's Girls* and *House of 1,000 Dolls,* women are forced into slavery in prison-like surroundings.

■ During the latter part of the sixties, the majority of all WIP films were coming from Europe. Jess Franco, known for his prolific output and deviant sensibility, joined the ranks of WIP filmmakers with titles like *99 Women, Wanda the Wicked Warden* and *Barbed Wire Dolls.*

■ By the end of the sixties the archetypal roles of the WIP films had been established, i.e.: The Queen Bee: dominant female prisoner who lords it over the others. The New Fish: usually the lead actress, in jail for the first time. The Sadistic Warden: more often than not the one who proves to be the root of all evil and unrest in the prison. The Hooker with the Heart of Gold: a street-smart dame who knows the ropes and befriends the New Fish, for better or worse. The Dyke Guard: sometimes named "Ruby"; no WIP film would be complete without one.

■ In 1971, director Jack Hill took most of these elements with him when he went to the Philippines to film the first WIP film made by Roger Corman's New World Pictures. *The Big Doll House* concerned the misadventures of several women held prisoner in a steamy jungle penal colony. Eventually the women escape, but cannot evade their ill-fated destinies. The film cost $125,000, and grossed millions. Corman followed with *Women in Cages,* which did even better. Over the next ten years New World continued producing WIP films, releasing such classics as *The Hot Box, The Big Bird Cage, The Big Bust-Out, Caged Heat* and *Terminal Island.* Most of these films were made in the Philippines, and in Roger Corman fashion interspersed social commentary between the sex and violence.

■ However, one of the best Philippines-WIP films was not a New World picture at all. *Sweet Sugar* was released by Dimension Pictures and directed by Michael Levesque, who shows a certain talent for low-budget filmmaking. The title character of the film is a young woman busted on a marijuana frame-up. Rather than go to prison, she agrees to work in the cane fields. Sugar soon discovers the men in charge of the cane fields are every bit as brutal and sadistic as those in the prisons. As in most WIP films the women are tough; in spite of the male guards' repeated attempts to break them, the women never kowtow. If anything, they get stronger.

■ Societal anarchy pervades the WIP films. If the prison establishment symbolizes government (which it has to, for these films to make any sense at all), then the message of the films usually favors revolution and social upheaval.

■ The level of corruption varies from film to film. In *Caged Heat,* the entire system is rotten. The warden (intensely portrayed by Barbara Steele) is a crippled woman, full of anger and sexual repression. We catch bits of information that indicate she wasn't always wheelchair-bound, but director Jonathan Demme never gives us enough to arouse sympathy. As in all of Demme's films, the focus is on the quirky personalities of the social misfits.

■ More sympathetic to "the system" is *Concrete Jungle,* directed by Tom DeSimone. In it, a young woman (Tracy Bregman) is set up by her boyfriend to take the rap for a coke bust. When the authorities try convincing her to incriminate him, at first she refuses, but eventually she agrees to help them. This was DeSimone's second WIP film; his first, *Prison Girls,* was filmed in 3-D and chronicles what happens to five female convicts while on a two-day furlough from jail. This film is softcore sexploitation at its worst. Tom DeSimone went on to direct several porno features, mostly gay, before venturing into the world of R ratings.

■ Although WIP films continue to hold their own at the box office, there hasn't been a glut of them as with other genres, partly because their market is smaller, and because they're relatively costly to make. It's easier to film vacuous teenagers being slaughtered in the woods—all you need is a knife, a few bad actors and two gallons of stage blood. To make a prison film you need *sets* (although most WIP films suffer from such minimal set design they look like *Noh* plays).

■ Most of the genres discussed in this book are either dead (e.g. LSD or Beach Party movies), or have degenerated into inferior forms (like sexploitation and gore films). Happily, WIP films are still going strong. Recent pictures such as *Chained Heat, Hellhole,* and *Concentration Camp For Girls* are as enjoyable as their older counterparts. In *Chained Heat,* Linda Blair plays the "new fish" in a prison where the warden (played by ever-slimy John Vernon) makes videotapes of himself fucking the prisoners in his hot tub. *Hellhole* follows a slightly less traditional path by changing the setting to a mental institution, where the chief doctor (Mary Woronov) conducts secret experiments on patients, attempting to perfect the world's first chemical lobotomy. *Concentration Camp For Girls* is a Hong Kong production featuring guards wearing *both* Nazi and US uniforms, plenty of torture and lots of bruised skin.

■ Whatever their faults, WIP films are remarkable for being consistently unusual entertainment. They show no signs of fading and hopefully will continue to be made well into the future. ■

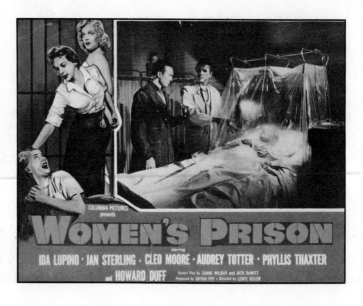

MONDO FILMS

The year was 1963. Across the country, movie theater screens began to throb with insects, blood, natives, transvestites, strippers, and various distressed animals. A new world opened up to film-going audiences, unlike any they'd previously known. Some elements of this strange new world were:

· living insect jewelry
· meals of cooked insects
· a town populated by the distorted look-alike descendants of Rudolph Valentino
· an annual celebration in which men smash in a garage door using their heads
· religious fanatics washing a stairway with their tongues
· a chicken who smokes cigarettes

■ If such subject matter seems too farfetched to be credible, it's probably because the people, places and things just described are all real. *Mondo Cane* brought to neighborhood theaters around the world a huge variety of unusual information disguised as entertainment.

■ *Mondo Cane's* documentation of strange behavior—bizarre customs, rituals and pastimes—was hugely successful, spawning a deluge of sequels and copies that comprise the "Mondo" genre. By way of introduction, what follows is a sampling of representative themes characteristic of the genre:

■ *Unusual rituals* are a prominent feature of nearly all the *Mondo* films. Movie footage from a small town in Italy documents people who fill a garage with food and drink for an annual feast. Part of the celebration calls for the men of the town to smash through the garage doors using their heads as battering rams. Some begin to bleed from the ears and mouth, go into convulsions, and have to be carried off. Eventually the door is smashed in and the anxious villagers rush inside to eat until they're sick.

■ In a more solemn ceremony, a crowd of churchgoing women wash down the parish steps using their tongues. As the cleanup progresses, their tongues become raw and the steps are covered with streaks of blood. Although the performers of this task are undoubtedly *sincere,* it's difficult to imagine how they possibly think that covering something with saliva and blood could be a cleansing process.

■ Another area often given generous coverage is the world of *animals*. A visit to a pet cemetery can be both touching and ridiculous; pet tombstones that humans weep over can soon be matter-of-factly peed upon by visiting dogs. In another part of the world we are shown a restaurant in which patrons select the dog that will provide them their next meal. Elsewhere, snakes are picked from cages, skinned alive and sold (still twitching) to housewives. Still elsewhere, well-dressed sophisticates order expensive plates of fried insects. Tying in with the bugs-for-the-rich theme is footage of enor-

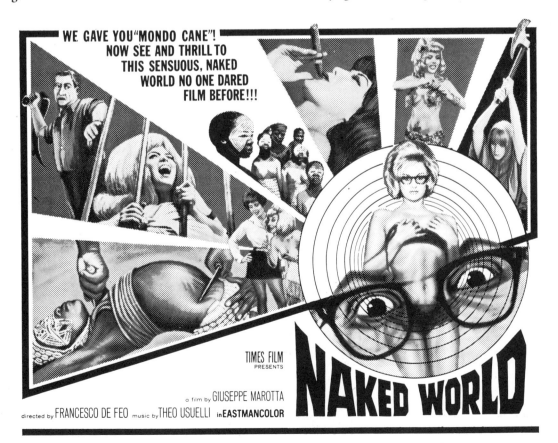

WE GAVE YOU "MONDO CANE"! NOW SEE AND THRILL TO THIS SENSUOUS, NAKED WORLD NO ONE DARED FILM BEFORE!!!

TIMES FILM PRESENTS

NAKED WORLD

a film by GIUSEPPE MAROTTA
directed by FRANCESCO DE FEO music by THEO USUELLI in EASTMANCOLOR

mous beetles with jewels glued on their backs, crawling about on elegant women as a sort of living accessory. Très chic!

■ If these films return again and again to the animal kingdom, it's because there's apparently no limit to the indignities animals can be subjected to at the hands of man. Geese are force-fed quantities of grain far in excess of their total body weight to produce pâté. Chicks are dyed different colors to make cute holiday surprises for children, but after being sealed in plastic eggs and sent through the mails, the surprise may not always be a pleasant one.

■ Of course, not all the coverage of animals involves abuse by humans; some depicts the opposite. One hilarious scene shows the famous "run of the bull" in Pamplona, Spain, where people see how close they can actually get to a rampaging bull. Many spectators do get safely away, but the real fun is watching those who don't. It's a black-humor experience to watch a man openly flirting with death: one moment he's doing a silly dance to attract the bull's attention; the next moment he's helpless in utter horror as the bull's horns rip into him, toss him up and slam him to the ground!

■ Another show of bravery, also involving a bull, makes the Pamplona run look tame in comparison. Intended to demonstrate the readiness of noble young bullfighters to unflinchingly face death, this ritual often fulfills that potential. A single-file line of 6 or 8 matadors slowly approaches the bull to see just how close they can get before retreat is necessary. As a rule, by the time it's necessary, retreat is out of the question—the bull smashes into the line of matadors and slams them to the ground like so many dominos. The first man in line is invariably a casualty. Presumably, the matador's

willingness to put himself directly in the path of almost certain agony denotes a high degree of courage, not to mention a great sense of honor. Whether this courage and honor are much comfort to a man hospitalized with severe internal injuries is open to question.

■ Modern art—long a source of irritation to the general public—shows up repeatedly in the Mondo movies. Legend has it that French artist Yves Klein bribed Jacopetti and Prosperi to include him in their *Mondo* documentary. Not that bribing was necessary, as his use of paint-covered nude women as living brushes was already controversial in the art world.

■ Another featured French artist's output was primarily old automobiles crushed down into cubes. For the general public, finding out what such "artworks" sold for was probably far more distressing than footage of animals being skinned alive, or natives bludgeoning each other to death.

■ The rituals and lifestyles of *primitive cultures* receive extensive coverage in nearly all the *Mondo* films. One shows a tribe which abstains from meat for one year, while fattening hogs for an all-out annual feast in which the animals are bludgeoned, butchered and devoured in one day-long spree. Elsewhere the camera focuses on members of a cargo cult sitting along the edge of a dirt runway they've created, gazing toward the sky and awaiting the cargo plane they think will carry them to the next life.

■ However, the footage most favored by Mondo filmmakers is that depicting the more brutal side of primitive life. Scenes showing unusual games in which participants inflict and receive painful wounds provide a highly emotional viewing experience. In one "match," two natives smash each other

Young women vie for the title of "Miss Spaghetti" in Night Women. This rarely screened film by Claude Lelouch was banned in France when first released.

Scene from Mondo Pazzo.

over the head with logs, each taking turns until one drops unconscious. Another competition involves natives throwing huge rocks at one another. Each stands perfectly still as a sizable stone smashes into him and bounces off, apparently with no ill effect. This particular "game" appears to have even less point than the previous one, although it no doubt teaches the natives something basic about the nature of pain. Natives of New Guinea dive hundreds of feet with only a vine tied to their ankles to break their fall, but sometimes they break their necks instead. In many of the sports and games devised by primitive cultures, those who lose the game may also lose their life . . .

■ Most Mondo films have limited their documentation to strange behavior and unusual customs. Such was the case with *Mondo Macabro, Mondo Nudo, Mondo Infame, Mondo Pazzo, Mondo Bolordo, Ecco, Taboos of the World, Secret Pains, Go Go Go World,* and of course the original *Mondo Cane.* Other Mondo films focus on areas that are especially topical or of special exploitation value; *Mondo Teeno* and *Mondo Mod* explore the odd rites of teenagers. *Mondo Hollywood* was also released as *Hippie Hollywood: the Acid Blasting Freaks,* and boasted an appearance by Bobby Beausoleil, an actor and musician best known for his association with Charles Manson. One very specific Mondo documentary focused solely on the Manson family; it was appropriately titled *Manson.*

■ Not suprisingly, the most popular theme is sex. *Mondo Oscentia, Mondo Rocco, Hollywood's World of Flesh, Hollywood Blue, Mondo Daytona,* and *Mondo Exotica* are all films that purport to explore changing mores. The exploitation circuit saw a deluge of sex films containing "Mondo" in the title, although *Mondo Keyhole, Mundo Depravados,*

Mondo Topless and a rash of others have no connection with the genuine documentaries except a title bearing the word *Mondo,* a word which has come to imply bizarre behavior.

■ While many Mondo films present genuine documentation, the authenticity of others is questionable (though no less fascinating). *Mondo Cane* is comprised of nearly all genuine material, but its sequel, *Mondo Cane 2,* is only partially authentic, with an abundance of patently false scenes added for comic effect.

■ Later films such as *Mondo Bizarro* are almost entirely fake, with only a few real scenes scattered throughout in a vain attempt to provide credibility. Filmed in and around Los Angeles, *Mondo Bizarro* gives us a close-up look at Frederick's of Hollywood, teens who flock to Laguna Beach each Easter to live it up, a "crazy" artist who photographs a topless model while doing a frenzied dance himself, a Nazi play, a sex slave auction, a bizarre voodoo sacrifice ritual, a "special" massage in Tokyo, a man eating glass in a posh restaurant, and more. *Mondo Bizarro* was put together by Cresse and R.L. Frost (who were responsible for *Love Camp Seven*). Frost also shot additional footage for *Witchcraft '70,* a Mondo film which focuses on the occult, purporting to document the widespread existence of practicing witches. At the time of its release it was rumored to contain hidden camera footage of the Manson group (actually, it contains film of another "hippie" family). Whether the bulk of the film is authentic or not is hard to say, but with R. L. Frost in tow it's doubtful.

■ Even *Mondo Cane,* for all its credibility, contains scenes that are suspect. One sequence about the effect of DDT on eggshells shows turtles making their trek from the sea to lay eggs in the sand. For emotional impact, the sequence ends with a confused turtle who cannot find the ocean and some-

155

how ends up on her back. Unable to right herself, the turtle struggles helplessly, and the camera marks her progress from death throes to carcass to skeleton. How the turtle got on her back is cause for speculation—more than likely through a bit of creative intervention, not unlike the Pulitzer Prize-winning photographer who always carried a child's doll in his car to toss down in the foreground of his "documentation" of disaster scenes.

■ One of the first movies ever made, *In the Land of the Headhunters,* is an obviously fake documentary with a contrived plot. Fake documentaries actually flourished in the early days of film; some might even be considered true forerunners of the *Mondo* genre. The jungles of Africa were (and still are) a source of great mystery and speculation, usually involving native girls and gorillas. *Dangerous Journey,* a 1944 documentary, actually depicted bizarre savage rituals and ceremonies, but was surpassed in sensationalism by *Ingagi.* Produced by Congo Pictures Ltd, *Ingagi* spliced old documentary footage of Africa and South America to suspicious-looking footage of a tribe of completely naked "ape-women" sacrificing a black woman to a gorilla.

■ Unfortunately, official investigation forced the film to be withdrawn from the market, after it was discovered that the nude ape-women were actually actresses in black face, and that the locale was a California zoo, not the Congo. The lurid mixture of sex and ritual death would have been acceptable—even educational—had it indeed been documented at some faraway place, but California was a bit too close to home. Not that anyone who saw the film ever doubted it was a sham; the narrator, a Sir Hubert Winslow of London, had no trace whatsoever of a British accent. Although only on the circuit for about a month, *Ingagi* was the talk of the town wherever it played, consistently breaking house attendance records and often doubling them. Of course, what packed the houses wasn't the drive to be accurately informed, it was the desire to see a group of naked women murder someone (whether it was real or not didn't matter).

■ Exploitation pioneer Kroger Babb exhibited a pre-"Mondo" film in the forties when he came across footage of a tribe in the Congo that, among other things, cut the throats of cows and drank the blood as it oozed out. Another choice scene shows the members of the tribe rubbing themselves with animal excrement for protection against evil spirits. Babb saw potential in the footage, re-edited it, and gave it the exotic title *Karimoja.* The theaters bulged with audiences hungering for a glimpse of sensational goings-on, and they got what they paid for, to the extent that some viewers even threw up.

■ Although *Mondo Cane* didn't match *Karimoja* on the nausea meter, its early ad campaign implied the promise of a truly sickening spectacle by offering the audience free *Mal de Mer* pills (Dramamine), in case the film should prove to be too much. Needless to say, most audiences were far more fascinated than nauseated. In fact, at the time of its release, *Mondo Cane* was so popular that its theme song, "More," became one of the most popular songs of 1963, gaining the film an Academy Award.

■ Embodying a unique and profitable concept, *Mondo Cane* soon became widely and blatantly ripped-off, giving rise to an entire genre. For years anything with "Mondo" in the title was hot box office; the mere term guaranteed a built-in audience. Unfortunately, the golden age of *Mondo* films peaked in the sixties, a decade which saw the release of more than 20 such films. The seventies was a far less prosperous time for the genre—with the falling away of old taboos, behavior that had once seemed outlandish now seemed conventional. A good example is *Mondo America,* one of the few *Mondo* films released in the mid-seventies. True to its title, *Mondo America* explores various aspects of life in America: from a dildo factory to a Vegas cathouse and then down to the waterfront to watch a suicide's corpse being pulled from the icy waters of the San Francisco Bay. Though *Mondo America* proved quite successful and was fairly interesting, it lacked the spark of its predecessors. Sadly, most of the other *Mondo* films of the '70s received such poor distribution that only a handful of people ever got to see them. Films such as *Catastrophe, Days of Fury,* and *Mondo Magic* are already all but forgotten.

■ For awhile it appeared that the *Mondo* breed of film had outlived its shock value and was on the brink of extinction. All of that changed with the release of *Faces of Death.* Narrated by a doctor, aptly named "Francis B. Gross," *Faces of Death* presents all kinds of death, both human and animal. Although much of the footage is obviously faked, many people found the film so shocking that it was removed from the shelves of dozens of video stores around the country. A sequel titled *Faces of Death Part Two* continues Dr. Gross' study of death with the same combination of exploitation and edification. Another film that explores death in a similar manner is *The End,* which has yet to be released in this country. The primary outlet for these movies is the Far East, yet most of the films are made by Italians. In Hong Kong and Japan people queue up to catch the latest installment in the black comedy portrayed by the human race. *Violence USA* shows the rest of the world how we in the States treat each other. *Man Man Man* takes a particularly cynical view of human nature, with scenes of executions, whale-slaughters and the Viet Nam War.

■ *Faces of Death* was the first in a resurgence of the genre, in which even more blatant forms of abuse to both animals and humans are depicted. *The Great Hunting 1984* has been (allegedly) banned from the U.S. due to its violent nature. Scenes depicting the slaughter of an entire herd of elephants in three minutes, or goats thrown into water to be eaten alive by sharks, don't exactly recapture the humor of the early Jacopetti and Prosperi films. But then again, they aren't meant to. Grainy, supposedly real Super-8 footage of a white hunter shooting Amazon Indians like fish in a barrel from his seat in a low-flying aircraft is not exactly amusing. The new breed of *Mondo* films are gorier and more explicit, no doubt keeping pace with changing times.

■ An exception might be the recent film, *Dances Sacred and Profane,* which documents roving photographer Charles Gatewood as he visits contemporary American subcults and unusual rituals—a Miss Nude America contest, the Hellfire Club in NYC, etc. The most memorable footage features a real-life piercing master, Fakir Musafar, enacting a genuine Sioux Indian "Sundance" ceremony, complete with steel hooks through chest muscles. The Fakir also stages the Hindu rite known as Kavandi Bearing, in which some 80 spears are stabbed into his back through an awkward frame which he then carries up a steep mountainside.

■ The transvestites that seemed funny or shocking back in '63 are now part of the scenery in most size cities. Even the sex change operation in 1984's *Shocking Asia* wouldn't raise many eyebrows, were it not for the technique demonstrated. Careful sex-change surgery is fairly routine, but actually seeing power drills clearing the way for vaginal implants is considerably less common. So in this sense, there are still exotic sights left to be seen ... exotic because of their unfamiliarity.

■ There are countless other worlds existing concurrently on this planet. So long as humans insist on adhering to strictly codified values and beliefs, there will be other sets of values and beliefs that are incomprehensible (and therefore of interest). Also, there will always be those who (for whatever reason) exhibit behavior different from one's own established norms. Given such circumstances, it's likely that *Mondo* movies will remain a permanent part of the world of cinema, playing the curious dual role of documenting *and* feeding the public's appetite for unusual behavior. ■

SANTO FILMS

BY JIM MORTON

Mexico's history is a litany of atrocities—forced Catholicism, repression, guilt, cultural schizophrenia and an obsession with death that borders on necrophilia. Not surprisingly, when the Mexican movie industry sets out to make a horror movie, the results are so singularly "Mexican" they baffle stateside viewers.

■ Not content merely to ape American horror movies, Mexico has created its own gallery of monsters. Instead of an Egyptian mummy, Mexico created The Aztec Mummy, an ugly-looking creature capable of assuming any form it pleases. While the vampires appear as standard variants of Lugosi's Dracula, they often have powers never bestowed upon Hollywood bloodsuckers. In *The World of the Vampires* the Count is able to turn a man into a werewolf simply by playing the organ!

■ One creature unique to Mexico is *La Llorona,* the crying ghost. *La Llorona* is the spirit of a woman doomed to search forever for her lost children. In Mexico it is believed you can hear her in the *arroyos* at night; searching and piteously crying. Some say the sound of her crying can drive men mad, but this claim has never been scientifically documented. *La Llorona,* on her own, is slim material for a movie, but (like their North American counterparts) the Mexican film industry is not above tampering with a legend if the need arises.

■ Of all the variations in the horror genre, the most uniquely Mexican is the Horror-Wrestling movie. In these, various popular wrestlers take on the forces of evil and pin them to the mat, figuratively and literally. Wrestling in Mexico (called *Lucha Libre*) is not very different from wrestling in the States—there are heroes and villains and the audience always knows who to root for. The wrestlers always wear masks and each wrestler has a mask uniquely his own.

■ One of the first wrestlers to enter the world of Mexican cinema was Wolf Ruvinskis. He plays a character called Neutron who wears a black mask with lightning bolts on it. Like all the wrestling superheroes, he battles evil both human and supernatural.

■ Neutron proved so popular that many similar films, featuring other wrestlers, soon followed. Among the wrestlers to join the cinematic ranks were Blue Demon, a supernatural fellow who often teams up with other wrestlers to help combat evil, and Mil Mascaras (now wrestling in the States), who wears a vividly ornamented mask which he removes at the start of each match, only to reveal an even more impressive mask beneath.

■ But the undisputed champion of filmic Mexican superheros is Santo, who wears a silver mask and drives around in a little white Aston-Martin. When not in the ring protecting his title from would-be usurpers, he is helping the local police commissioner solve crimes. Santo works out of his own laboratory, a Batmanesque-place filled with impressive futuristic machines.

■ Santo was born in Turlancingo, a small town in Hidalgo, Mexico, on September 13, 1915. His real name is Rodolfo Guzman Huerta. Rodolfo started his wrestling career under the name "Constantino," but first gained attention as "Hombre Rojo," a bad guy—one of the ones you're supposed to boo. For a short while he wrestled as "El Murcielago Enmas-

carado II," but when the original El Murcielago Enmascarado protested the use of his title, Rodolfo had to find a new name. He chose "El Santo."

■ El Santo wore a silver mask. When fighting masked opponents the rule was: whoever lost would have to take off his mask and shave his head. El Santo never lost. He successfully defended his title from 1942 until the late fifties when—feeling he was losing his touch—he retired from the ring and went into movies.

■ Santo was an odd sort of character; his mask made him look more like a burn victim than a superhero. There were other wrestlers making movies who also had intriguing masks, sometimes better builds, as well as interesting stories. But Santo always had unpredictable timing, unlikely plot elements, and most important—a charisma hard to define; among the Mexican audience he was the most popular of the wrestling superheroes. More of his films were translated into English than anyone else's.

■ During the seventies and early eighties, Santo toured Mexico as part of an entertainment review. During a show in February, 1984, he complained of chest pains and died of a heart attack shortly afterwards. ■

Santo and friend.

¡LA VIDA DEL SANTO!

ED WOOD JR.
BY JIM MORTON

Eccentric and individualistic, Edward D. Wood, Jr. was a man born to film. In the face of studio indifference, lack of funds and few Hollywood connections, Wood made movies—almost all black-and-white. Among them, a western (*Crossroads Avenger*); a crime melodrama (*Jailbait*, aka *Hidden Face*); two sexploitation films (*Glen or Glenda* and *The Sinister Urge*); and a few low-budget science fiction efforts (*Bride of the Monster* aka *Bride of the Atom*, *Plan Nine From Outer Space* and *Night of the Ghouls*). Even after the market for low-budget quickies dissipated, Wood continued his filmmaking career in the porno field with films like *Take it Out in Trade* and *Necromania*. Lesser men, if forced to make movies under the conditions Wood faced, would have thrown up their hands in defeat.

■ His best-known film, *Plan Nine From Outer Space* (1959), has been dubbed "the worst movie ever made" by many critics. Yet *Plan Nine* is one of the few motion pictures from the fifties regularly appearing at repertory theaters. If there is a "worst film ever made" it is one that is *boring*—a sin Ed Wood, Jr. is rarely guilty of. Some people point out the flubs and continuity errors in his films, yet these same people are likely to become angry when you point out the numerous flubs in such favorites as *E.T.* and *Star Wars*.

■ Wood's most personal film is *Glen or Glenda*—really two films in one. The first is the story of a man who enjoys wearing his fiancé's clothing. He is faced with the problem of telling her about his obsession before they are married; then she must choose between her love for him and her revulsion toward such deviant behavior. The second part of the film concerns a man for whom cross-dressing is not enough—he wants to *be* a woman. Through the miracle of surgery he gets his wish. The two stories are tied together by a psychologist (played by Bela Lugosi) who throughout the film explains the difference between a transvestite and a transsexual. Lugosi's role has long baffled critics; he seems to represent a negative voice as most of his statements are in conflict with the tone of the film. Sometimes he is referred to as "The Devil," but a more accurate title might be "The Moral Majority."

■ The film was released under several titles: *I Led Two Lives; I Changed My Sex; He or She: The Transvestite*. Additionally, at least two versions exist: one print released as *I Changed My Sex* contains a sequence in which a woman does a strip-tease and then is tied up and raped by the devil.

■ If the first half of *Glen or Glenda* seems unusually passionate, it is because Wood *was* a transvestite. He often wore women's jumpsuits and was obsessed with cashmere sweaters. A Marine during World War II, Wood claimed to be

Tor Johnson returns from the dead in Ed Wood's most famous film, Plan Nine from Outer Space.

wearing a bra and panties under his uniform during a landing in the Pacific. In *Watts . . . The Difference* (an erotic novel written by him) Wood describes in vivid detail the joys of cross-dressing and apparel fetishism:

■ Angie started taking her clothes off, at first, slowly, but as his moaning gyrations on the studio couch increased, so did her movements. She couldn't help but permit some of his sexual heat to filter through her. She stepped out of her panties which she tossed to a chair with her other things, and assumed what she thought was an appropriately sexy pose in front of him. She lowered her left breast to an inch above his searching lips. Suddenly with a savage lunge and a girlish squeal from his throat, he took her breast into his mouth for the briefest of an instant, then tearing his own clothes from his body, he flew across the room. There was nothing left to his shorts or his shirt by the time he got through with them. But in the moment the last of his male attire slipped away, so did his speed. With every care, with caressing joy, he put on Angie's clothes. He saved the sweater for last and took a great length of time in letting it slip down over his head. Then he moved to his desk and pushed a hidden button. A great wall mirror came into being from a hidden panel. He took a blonde wig from his desk and carefully adjusted it with the mirror for his guide. Then he took a long time adjusting the sweater over the skirt until it was to his liking. He turned back to Angie, only after he was sure the nylon stockings were straight. The only thing he couldn't get into were Angie's shoes, but he had a remedy for that also. Behind the mirror he had a well-stocked wardrobe from which he selected a pair and put them on. It was apparent from that point on he wanted to be admired for his female self. "I'm called Ginger," he said.

■ When it came time to cast the part of the transvestite in the film, Wood not surprisingly ended up playing the role himself, using the pseudonym, "Daniel Davis."

■ *Glen or Glenda* might never have been made were it not for George Jorgensen, who made headlines in the early '50s by taking part in a series of hormone experiments, culminating in a visit to Denmark to undergo a sex-change operation. Changing his name to Christine Jorgensen, George became the most notorious transsexual of all time. The resulting furor over "The Christine Jorgensen Story" provided Wood with the perfect opportunity to tell the world it's all right for men to wear women's clothing, if that's what makes them happy.

■ However, the film for which Wood is best remembered is *Plan Nine from Outer Space.* Like all his movies, it was made on a budget that barely paid for film and equipment. In order to complete the movie, Ed Wood cut corners wherever and whenever he could; e.g., hubcaps and paper plates became flying saucers! Sometimes his cost-cutting borders on Dada, as when two men dressed as pilots sit in front of an almost-bare wall and pretend they are in the cockpit of a plane!

■ Wood's lead actor, Bela Lugosi, died a few days after shooting began. Determined to continue, Wood replaced Lugosi with a friend (a chiropractor), assuming that as long as the man kept a cape over his face no one would notice it wasn't Bela. Unfortunately, *everyone* noticed—the fact that the chiropractor was a full head taller than Lugosi might have had something to do with it . . .

■ Wood was also a prolific writer (his novels include *It Takes One to Know One* and *Killer in Drag)* and scriptwriter. He wrote all of his own screenplays, plus some for other directors. In this capacity he is without peer. If his dialogue is sometimes laughable, it is because in reality people are rarely as candid as they are in his scripts. When the spaceman in *Plan Nine* exclaims, "You see? You see? Your stupid little minds! Stupid! Stupid!" we laugh, but at the same time not without agreeing with the spaceman's sentiments.

■ In *The Violent Years* (1956), although credit must be given to William M. Morgan (or Franz Eichorn) for direction, it is Wood's dialogue that grabs you. A girl gang led by a spoiled rich girl terrorizes a small community "just for kicks." At the beginning, each member walks by a blackboard on which are written the words "Good Citizenship," "Self Restraint," "Politeness" and "Loyalty." The girls sneer at the sentiments as a narrator intones: "This is the story of violence. A violence born of the uncontrolled passions of adolescent youth, and nurtured by this generation of parents . . . those who, in their own smug little world of selfish interests and confused ideas of parental supervision, refuse to believe today's glaring headlines."

■ In 1961 Wood made his last feature film, *The Sinister Urge* (otherwise known as *The Young and the Immoral* or *Hellborn.)* Ostensibly an attack on pornography (the plot: a psycho kills porno models), the film was really just a way of getting racy material past the bluenoses in charge of the country's morals. As the demand for B-movies evaporated—usurped by television—Wood found it increasingly difficult to obtain financing, and turned to the emerging sexploitation market.

■ *Orgy of the Dead,* made in 1965, was written but not directed by Wood, and starred his old friend Criswell *in color.* Criswell was a true character, every bit as fascinating as Ed Wood. He had previously starred in *Plan Nine,* but was better known as a TV prophet and author of the book *Criswell Predicts.* Among his prophecies: that by the eighties there would be cities entirely composed of homosexuals; that the U.S. Government would give all of New Mexico back to the Indians; that an interplanetary convention would be held in Las Vegas. In *Orgy of the Dead* Criswell plays the Master of the Dead whose job was to mete out punishment to sinners once they have passed over to the great beyond.

■ As the sexploitation market shifted toward more explicit depiction, Wood followed. His first effort toward true pornography was *Take it Out in Trade,* an innocuous film that barely qualifies as hardcore. More down and dirty was his next feature, *Necromania* (aka *Necromancy),* a supposedly hardcore porn film in which Wood appeared as a wizard. He made a few more pornos, but the exact number is unknown; most were shot in 8mm and used as loops or sold through magazine ads. It remains for some diligent researcher to unearth the full extent of Ed Wood's filmic and written achievement.

■ In 1978, on the eve of a rebirth of interest in his films, Ed Wood, Jr. died of a heart attack in Hollywood. ■

SEXPLOITATION FILMS
BY JIM MORTON

Sex and skin have always been a part of cinema. Explicit porn films date from the beginning of the movies; now they are reissued as historical curiosities on videocassette. It's safe to say that the history of cinema is one with the history of sex in cinema.

■ When the nickelodeon, precursor of the movies, was invented (you turned a crank and serial photographs simulating continuity of movement flicked by), the public flocked to see them. Soon "concerned citizens" were voicing outrage at the inevitable introduction of latently sexual content—in 1894, a peep show featuring a belly dancer named "Fatima"

so shocked people that white bars were painted across the film to protect the public from viewing something they might enjoy. The effect is somewhat like watching a belly dancer performing behind a picket fence.

■ By 1908, along with the proliferation of movie theaters across America came the censor boards. Soon every major city had watchdogs objecting to movies on the grounds of "no social or moral values." The basic argument was: it is "wrong" to glorify and celebrate that which is immoral and illegal. Quick to agree, exploitation producers cloaked their products in a mantle of false piety, and the "square-up reel" was born.

Scene from Mundo Depravados.

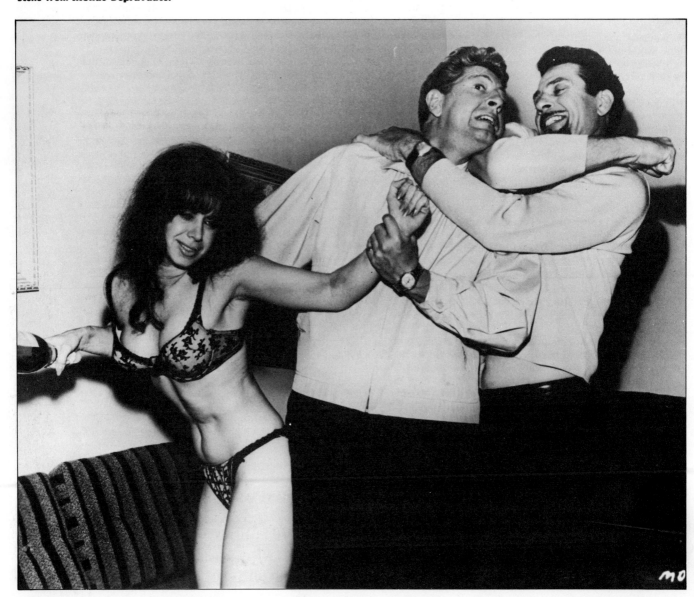

■ This term referred to the final reel of a film in which the "good" people are rewarded while the "bad" people go to Hell, so to speak. Of course, the preceding reels are filled with every variety of vice and corruption. "This is what will happen to you if you follow the Road to Ruin!" the ads shouted. People lined up around the block to see the outcome of a life of sin.

■ Besides sex and drugs, the most popular early exploitation theme was white slavery. Sparked by Universal's 1913 hit, *Traffic in Souls,* films like *China Slaver, The Unguarded Girls* and *The White Slave* vividly portrayed dangers lying in wait for the carefree single young woman. An outrageous example of white slavery exploitation is *Trapped by Mormons,* in which Mormons are depicted as kidnapping fiends who lure young woman into their polygamous harems. On grounds of libel the Mormon Church succeeded in getting the film withdrawn from circulation.

■ During the initial decades of filmmaking, independent producers were little more than a minor nuisance to legal authorities, the real culprit being Hollywood. Following the invention of the movie camera, the inventors, Edison and cohorts, had set up a monopolistic trust on the East Coast, the Motion Pictures Patents Company, which made illegal the making and exhibition of films by anyone other than their members and affiliates! If they heard of anyone making or exhibiting a film who was not affiliated with them, reportedly they would send in goons to destroy the equipment and film. Consequently scores of early filmmakers moved as far away as possible—to the Los Angeles area, which was conveniently accessible to Mexico in case flight to avoid prosecution was required, and began making their "illegal" films. Thus was Hollywood born.

■ Early films by beginning companies like Universal and Columbia often featured gorgeous actresses in skimpy outfits and questionable situations. A frequently used plot involved a young girl going to Hollywood, being "discovered," and enjoying a fabulous career as a movie actress. In reality a few girls did go to Hollywood, perhaps got a bit part in a movie (but little else), then turned to prostitution to support themselves. When arrested by the police they might list their occupation as "actress," and the newspapers—always eager for a cheap thrill—would proclaim: "Four actresses busted in bawdy house raid." America began receiving a very unflattering view of what was going on in Hollywood.

■ The press discovered that the "wild" life of famous motion picture stars (e.g. Theda Bara and Rudolph Valentino) sold newspapers. Sensational copy—more suggestive than substantial—became the daily bill of fare, and straitlaced citizens began complaining that *something* had to be done about the movie world, lest it corrupt *all* good Americans.

■ The turning point came in 1921, during a party at the St. Francis Hotel in San Francisco. Popular comedian Roscoe "Fatty" Arbuckle took a young actress named Virginia Rappe up to his hotel room where she died of a ruptured spleen. Weird rumors began to fly—Arbuckle was accused of introducing a coke bottle into the girl, or of forcing ice into her vagina, and other related atrocities. Eventually he was found not guilty by *three* different juries, but too late to save his career—he never appeared in another major movie.

■ With that the national press turned its full scandalmongering attention on movieland, and everyone became fair game. Hollywood reporters became obsessed with tracking down any little bit of filth they could sniff. Popular celebrities (e.g., Mary Pickford, "America's Sweetheart" who scandalized the nation by divorcing Owen Moore so she could quickly marry Douglas Fairbanks; director William Dean Taylor—killed possibly by a drug dealer) were accused of everything from debauchery to trafficking in drugs. The nouveau-riche motion picture industry began to fear that the *government* would step in and impose laws on them; at all costs they wanted to protect and control their golden egg. Quickly the

Burlesque stripper, "Justa Dream." Note phony black lace inked in to obscure Justa's ample charms.

"Motion Picture Producers and Distributors Association of America" was formed, appointing as its President former Postmaster General Will Hays in 1931.

■ Hays is often portrayed as an intolerant bluenose, but in truth he was not—he was a nothing man. A political stooge, he was chosen for his ability to run an organization without rocking the boat. The fact that he looked like a hick from the sticks didn't hurt. His image was one of "jes' plain folks" who knew what the public wanted.

■ One of the first acts of The Hays Commission was to start Central Casting, a talent-screening agency for would-be actors and actresses which in effect made it impossible for all but a select number of people to "get a break" in motion pictures. Films about young women going to Hollywood and finding fortune and fame were replaced by films about young women going to Hollywood and finding tragedy and despair. The party was over; Hollywood closed its doors for good.

■ Nevertheless, the public clamor for an end to sin in the cinema continued. Billy Sunday, a popular evangelist at the time, led a crusade against Hollywood that the movie industry *had* to pay attention to. Hays wasted no time in drafting up a stringent production code for the movie industry to follow (e.g., brutal killing shall not be presented in detail; the technique of murder shall not be presented in a way that inspires imitation; illegal drug traffic must never be presented; seduction or rape should never be shown by explicit method; sex perversion or any inference of it is forbidden; white slavery shall not be treated; miscegenation is forbidden; children's sex organs are never to be exposed; complete nudity is never permitted. Repellent subjects included: actual hangings or electrocutions; "third-degree" methods; brutality and possible gruesomeness; branding of people or animals; apparent cruelty to children or animals; and surgical operations.) Hays also created a bureau, The Office of the Motion Picture Production Code, to see that the rules were obeyed. The man he chose as head was Joseph Breen. The Breen Office is what

A pagan girl in Barry Mahon's *Pagan Island*.

most people meant when they referred to the "Hays Commission."

■ The Hays Commission restrained Hollywood's depiction of sin, but it didn't stop independent filmmakers from places like Chicago, Florida, New Jersey, New York, and Texas. The thirties and forties were golden years for exploitation. Because most theaters preferred to abide by the restrictions imposed by Hays, independent producers often ended up screening their films in tents, strategically placed just outside city limits. Without intending to, the Hays Commission gave independent producers something money couldn't buy: the exclusive ability to offer the public that which was *verboten* in Hollywood.

■ This was the heyday of "The Forty Thieves"—a loosely-knit gang of independent producers. Many of these exploitation filmmakers had a "carny" background (and a "carny" philosophy—usually they thought of themselves as quite roguish). Often an independent producer would send a road agent out with a print of a movie (sometimes the only print in existence) who would travel from town to town, showing the movie anywhere he could, on the so-called "road-show circuits." In the case of the smaller independents, the producer-director-distributor (one person) would travel around the country showing his latest creation. These men were considered by most to be only a cut above snake-oil merchants and grifters.

■ Independent producers usually exploited sex by pretending to warn of its evils. Another favorite approach was to present a fake documentary film, in which it was acceptable to show bare breasts—as long as they weren't white. Consequently several movies were made purporting to depict native life in darkest Africa. Usually they were shot somewhere just north of San Diego, with the African "natives" appearing in a remarkable variety of shades. Often a man in a gorilla suit makes an appearance, stealing the tribe's comeliest maiden. There were several such films, all with similar plot lines. Among them: *Bowanga! Bowanga!* (1938), *Ingagi,* (1930) and *Love Life of a Gorilla* (1937).

■ When movie houses refused to show films like *The Naked Truth* (a sex education film) and *Tomorrow's Children* (about the sterilization of a family regarded as degenerates), distributors found other venues. As impromptu movie theaters burlesque houses were a favorite choice; occasionally even bars were enlisted.

■ During this period the term "square-up reel" took on a new, opposite meaning. Road agents, always at odds with the law, carried two versions of their films—one tame and one sizzling. If the police showed up, the agent made sure the tame version was projected. If the police left early, the agent would end with a reel filled with nudity and depravity. This reel became known as the square-up reel; partly because it "squared things up" with the audience, and partly as a code to throw the authorities off the track.

■ In the early fifties public attitudes began to shift. Both Hollywood and independent filmmakers began to push the limits of the Production Code to see how much they could get away with. The censors' efforts to crack down just made them look more ridiculous, as when Otto Preminger's *The Moon Is Blue* (1953) was refused approval because the words "virgin" and "seduced" were used in it. Preminger released the film anyway as "Adults Only," and perhaps because of this billing the film made handsome profits. Peo-

162

ple who expected to see something lewd were disappointed—even by the standards of the day, *The Moon Is Blue* is deadeningly chaste.

■ For awhile the term "Adults Only" took on a patina of respectability. Exploitationists dusted off old prints of their films and presented them again. *Tell Your Children,* a campy anti-drug film from the thirties, was re-released as *Reefer Madness.* A 1934 film titled *Children of Loneliness* was exhibited in 1953 as *The Third Sex.* The film tells the story of a woman who, after a frightening childhood encounter with a man, grows up to be a lesbian. Exploitation pioneer Kroger Babb put his "birth of a baby" classic, *Mom and Dad,* back into circulation with profitable results.

■ The downfall of the Hays code had other causes, central being the widespread change in sexual attitudes that followed World War II. After living in Europe, many American soldiers discovered their puritanical outlooks were by no means universal. On the home front, women had been working at jobs previously considered "man's work," all the while broadening their concepts of identity. The old attitudes regarding virginity, sex roles, and even technical basics such as the "French" kiss, oral sex, foreplay, and the orgasm (words scarcely in the common vocabulary) would never be the same.

■ The fifties also spawned another blow to the Hays Code, the "burlesque" films, which are little more than documentaries of their predecessors, the *real* burlesque shows. The camera remains static, and little is attempted to make the films interesting or even watchable. Besides the strip-tease acts, the films often featured many up-and-coming (or down-and-going) comedians. For example, in *Dance Hall Racket* a young Lenny Bruce appears, slapping the dancers and insulting the audience. Burlesque films are important because they helped spawn the more daring Nudist Films, which eventually led to everything.

■ Actually, the nudist films of the fifties were a revival of the documentaries of the nudist craze which originally started in the early thirties and quickly spread world-wide. In 1932, a film entitled *This Nude World* examined nudist camps in France, Germany and the U.S. with a sympathetic eye. The following year producer Bryan Foy released *Elysia,* which also dealt with the joys of nudism. Like their predecessors two generations earlier, the fifties' nudist films also used an educational approach to "get away with" displaying all that skin.

■ For the most part, nudist films are among the most boring movies ever made. These accounts of what supposedly goes on behind the gates of the world's nudist colonies consist of little more than endless games of volleyball. Any activity that could possibly be construed as sexual is debarred. Rarely do people touch each other, and they *never* kiss or hug. While the burlesque films are cinematically dull, the nudies are just plain vapid, offering little more than endless shots of nude people having "fun in the sun."

■ If the nudies are important at all, it is for legal reasons. After a lengthy 1957 court case involving *Garden of Eden*—a *particularly* boring nudist film—it was decided that nudity, on its own, has no erotic content and therefore is not obscene.

■ For filmmakers, the next step was to combine the two genres of burlesque and nudie films. The resultant light-comedic farces were called "nudie-cutie" films. The first one was directed by Russ Meyer: *The Immoral Mr. Teas* (1959).

■ Made on a budget of $24,000 scraped together by Meyer and burlesque house owner Pete DeCenzie, *The Immoral Mr. Teas* is the tale of a man who, after undergoing anaesthesia, develops the power to see all women stark naked, no matter what they're wearing or doing. Teas (played by an old army buddy of Meyer, Bill Teas) is at first delighted by his new power, but eventually it wears thin as it complicates his life more and more.

■ *The Immoral Mr. Teas* broke box office records everywhere. For more than two years it ran continuously in Hollywood. In New York it was so heavily cut that Meyer had to film a three-reel short subject called *This Is My Body* to fill out the bill. Maryland banned the film completely. Numerous legal battles ensued, but Meyer and DeCenzie were making enough money to cover any court costs. The legal rulings on *The Immoral Mr. Teas* varied from state to state and city to city, but enough legal ground was won to open the way for hundreds more nudie-cutie films.

■ Out of the woodwork came dozens of aspiring skinpix producers. From Chicago came *The Adventures of Lucky Pierre* (1961), directed by Herschell Gordon Lewis and produced by the dean of sexploitation, David Friedman. The film cost $45,000 and was one of the more expensive films in the genre. Bob Cresse—who did for sadomasochism what Russ Meyer did for bosoms—produced *Once Upon a Knight* (1961). Jack Harris, after raking in the dough for his previous smash hit, *The Blob,* added a new twist to the field with *Paradisio* (1962), the first adult film made in 3-D. Numerous other lesser-knowns were churned out.

■ By 1963 the novelty of nudie-cutie films had worn out. As their box office sank, producers and filmmakers sought something new. Chicago's David Friedman hit on a solution: If we can't include more sex, we'll add violence. Friedman went down to Florida with his partner, H. G. Lewis, and on a budget that wouldn't pay for film stock today created the gore classic *Blood Feast.* The story of an Egyptian caterer who practices the ancient bloody rites of Ishtar in his spare time, *Blood Feast* was gorier than any movie previously made. The duo made two more movies together (*Two Thousand Maniacs!* and *Color Me Blood Red*) before parting ways. Lewis continued making gore films, while Friedman further explored the combination of sex and violence.

■ From 1964 to 1970 a flood of sex-and-violence films hit the grindhouses of America. The films were referred to by the trade papers as "ghoulies," "roughies" and "kinkies," depending on the ratio of sex to violence. *Lorna* was considered a "roughie" because people get treated "rough" in it. *Blood Feast* is a "ghoulie" for obvious reasons. *Love Camp Seven* is a good example of a "kinky"—it depicts perversions.

■ During this period Friedman's talents as a producer came to the fore, but there were others of similar ability. Bob Cresse teamed up with director R. L. Frost to make a number of sadistic masterpieces, including the infamous *Love Camp Seven* (1968); husband and wife team Mike and Roberta Findlay became Julian Marsh and Anna Riva and brought out the *Flesh* trilogy (*The Touch of Her Flesh. The Curse of Her Flesh* and *The Kiss of Her Flesh*), three rarely-seen but often-talked-about movies of hitherto unparalleled depravity. Joseph Mawra's *Olga* movies (*Olga's Girls, Olga's Massage Parlor* and *White Slaves of Chinatown*) were so violent and sleazy they alienated even diehard S/M fans.

■ As the nudie-cuties lost their audience, even Russ Meyer felt the pinch. His happy little bounce movies began to *lose* money. As others had done, he solved the problem by adding violence. For Meyer it was the last piece to the puzzle; the films he created during this turbulent era of sexual frustration and violent eroticism are among his best. Considered the first of the roughies, *Lorna* (1964) depicted the story of a sexually frustrated housewife who encounters an equally pent-up escaped convict.

■ Nudist and nudie-cutie films, by themselves, were not the sole forces liberalizing America's censorship laws. While Russ Meyer was introducing the subject to Middle America, experimental filmmakers were using sex—sometimes very graphic sex—as part of their art. Filmmaker Kenneth Anger shocked the art world, college campuses and the censors with his fetishistic films illustrating homosexuality, leather and drug fantasies. George Kuchar used seedy images associated with low budget cinema to poke fun at the sexual mores of the time. Andy Warhol managed to shock even cosmopolitan New Yorkers with films like *Blue Movie* and *Blow Job*. Whether these efforts were any more artistic than exploitation films of the same period could be debated, but experimental films coming from the prestigious "art world" added a new point of view to the question of censorship and helped considerably to erode the facade of an antiquated morality.

■ Foreign films also did their part to strip away U.S. inhibitions, appealing to both the "art film" cinéastes and the raincoat crowd. Roger Vadim's *And God Created Woman*, besides introducing millions to Brigitte Bardot, also introduced a vision of a more sophisticated, less-guilty sexual lifestyle. *I, A Woman,* a blockbuster hit which played for years, was instrumental in spreading the idea that a woman's sexual pleasure was also her right. The early films of Ingmar Bergman (e.g., *Summer with Monika, The Virgin Spring*) shocked American audiences with their display of brutal lust and shameless sensuality, although they had the usual retribution endings. Roberto Rossellini's early Italian neo-realist films (e.g., *Open City*) showed women walking around the house in their slips with bruises showing on their legs, etc—hitherto not a common sight. Later, films like *I am Curious, Yellow* (1968), and its sequel, *I am Curious, Blue* were instrumental in getting hardcore films out into the open—the films reportedly depicted actual sexual intercourse, even though most of the film is devoted to the characters having serious discussions about politics. The "Curious" films played for years.

■ The end of World War Two saw an increased use of the 16mm film format, but mostly in industrial and educational applications. In the sixties, the previously expensive 16mm movie cameras began turning up in pawnshops; at the same time they became significantly cheaper through mass production. Filmmaking took a new turn—hundreds of people gained access to a medium previously restricted to a privileged few. The generation that grew up with the movies could now make their own, and they wasted no time exploring (and exploiting) this new gift. Experimental and stag films flourished.

■ At the end of sixties Alex DeRenzy of San Francisco released his notorious classic, *Censorship in Denmark: A New Approach*. DeRenzy went to Denmark and filmed *Sex 69,* a trade show devoted to the business of sex. Included in his movie are scenes inside a porno movie club, where he filmed a hardcore movie directly from the screen as it was being shown. In this way he could defend the material by explaining he was not making a porno film—he was making an objective documentary *about* porno films.

■ DeRenzy followed the successful *Censorship in Denmark* with an even more daring experiment: *A History of the Blue Movie*. Starting with *A Free Ride,* circa 1915, *Blue Movie* is a brilliant compilation of classic stag clips, among them stripper Candy Barr's less-than-enthusiastic introduction to oral sex in *Smart Aleck,* and a film titled *The Nun's Story,* which is considered to be the first stag film with a cum shot.

■ *A History of the Blue Movie* was a big hit and spawned several imitations. One of the best was *Hollywood Blue,* produced by the Phil Spector of pornography, Bill Osco. Osco's film was not nearly so interesting or complete as DeRenzy's, but it does include *Apple Knockers and Coke Bottle,* a film that supposedly featured a young Marilyn Monroe (it wasn't).

■ During the seventies stag films came out of the Elks Clubs and into the theaters. Daring filmmakers like DeRenzy and Osco found supporters among the post-hippie young generation and the members of the Sexual Freedom League. In San Francisco (later to become a major porn movie production center), the Sutter Street Cinema and the Mitchell Brothers Theater drew socially "hip" people to their opening parties, playing their part in introducing the middle-class to explicit

SAVAGE!

FROM SHOCKING START TO SURPRISING END...

Two desperate men and one helpless girl, with a woman's only weapon of defense... *SEX!*

"The WICKED GO TO HELL!"

Introducing the baby-faced Venus
MARINA VLADY
"Miss Body" of 1960!

"I want the truth— who's the squealer?"

"If you knew what he tried last night—you'd kill him!"

"I warn you — be good or I'll kill you!"

sex films. America was in the final throes of the post-World War Two sexual revolution. "If it feels good, do it!" was the catch-phrase of the day. The ultimate blow to censorship came in 1972 with the release of Gerard Damiano's *Deep Throat*.

■ *Deep Throat* tells the story of a young woman whose clitoris is in her throat, making fellatio her preferred activity. She goes to a doctor who "treats" her, then she has sex with a few other men, etc. The negligible plot accounts for about two minutes; the rest of the movie is non-stop sucking and fucking. As a movie *Deep Throat* is not cinematically outstanding; there were other films before it just as graphic and obscene (e.g., Bill Osco's *Mona*). But *Deep Throat* became important as a legal issue when the authorities in New York pounced on it, making it the most talked-about movie of the year. While the courts battled over the legal ramifications, people everywhere were lined up to see it. Audiences no longer were composed of old men in raincoats; *couples—* some in dinner jackets and minks—showed up for the film. *Porno chic* was born.

■ The law came down hard on *Deep Throat*. The theater that first exhibited it in New York was fined $3 million, the judge calling the film "a feast of carrion and squalor." (Later, the verdict was overturned.) Despite legal battles in cities all over the country, *Deep Throat* was a hit, and no amount of moralistic outrage seemed to be able to stop hardcore films

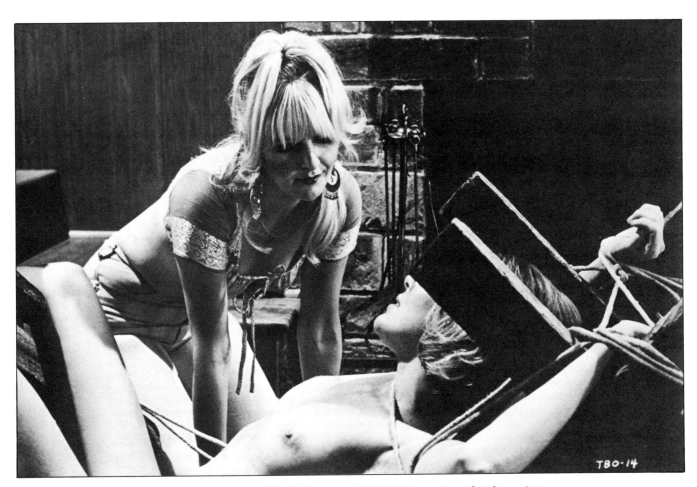

Bondage and sadism; common themes in the sex films of the sixties as exemplified in this scene from **The Bizarre Ones**.

from being made or shown.

■ The advent of explicit pornography in theaters was the death knell for sexploitation. Filmmakers who had previously invented unusual plots and situations to showcase their non-anatomically-graphic sex· found it harder and harder to find a market for their talents. Some, like David Friedman, reluctantly accepted the inevitability of hardcore's supremacy in the sex film market. Others, like Joe Sarno and Doris Wishman, rejected it and continued making movies of a less explicit nature, with genuine plots and characterizations. But by 1977 the market for softcore films had virtually disappeared in America.

■ Curiously, a small number of softcore films were very commercially successful during the seventies. Filmed in Europe with exceptionally pretty actresses, lavish sets, plots, dialogue, continuity, suspense, and even some eroticism), these films may be categorized as softcore Euro-chic. They include *The Story of O* (starring Corinne Clery) and *Emmanuelle* (starring Sylvia Kristel). These films were made by Just Jaeckin, who in his filmic approach curiously appears to be imitating Radley Metzger, who in *his* movies was imitating French new wave filmmaking—art imitating art imitating life . . .

■ There is no true continuum from early exploitation films to modern hardcore porn. Exploitation films, no matter how explicit, were always intended to be shown in theaters. Hardcore, on the other hand, was spawned by the "smokers"—those crude and nasty little films reserved for late-night showings at Elks' clubs, firehouses, and fraternity parties. Like a spermacious juggernaut, the hardcore film burst into daylight, derailing a sizable portion of the exploitation train.

■ The problem with hardcore films is their plotlessness, all activity being generally centered upon a succession of interchangeable anatomical close-ups. In fact the identical close-ups are often used in many different films. Talk (as well as ideas) is minimized or banalized; any art and discipline normally associated with "acting" is simply *non de rigueur*.

■ Some of the better hardcore films of the past decades include *The Opening of Misty Beethoven, Pretty Peaches, Night Dreams, Randy the Electric Lady, Devil in Miss Jones,* and *Take Off (The Picture of Dorian Gray* retold in a porno film). There may possibly be a few more worthwhile experiences, but it remains for other intrepid souls to chart through this territory.

■ With the rise of the home video market, the porno theater may soon be as obsolete as the nickelodeon. Already most porno "theaters" are merely large-screen video projection rooms, or are subdivided into small 25-cent video booths. Perhaps with the advent of home video and the increase of *couples* watching the movies (women may insist on the restoration of genuine entertainment values), there will be a shift away from endless movements of limbs and organs back to more plot-oriented films. ■

EDUCATIONAL FILMS

BY JIM MORTON

Over the past decade film historians have focused a great deal of attention on genres—and on actors and directors, as well—who have, in the past, gone unheralded. Exploitation, sexploitation, 'B' and 'Z' movies are all examined and reviewed in fanzines, newsletters and film books. Gore and porno movies show up regularly at repertory theatres. And directors such as Russ Meyer, Herschell Gordon Lewis and Roger Corman are no longer viewed as anonymous hacks. Even the antics of The Three Stooges have taken on a patina of respectability. Yet in spite of all the attention now given to previously overlooked films, there is still one genre that remains ignored: The Educational Film.

■ Most of us sat through them in high school, if not in grade school as well. On the days when the science teacher didn't feel like teaching class, we would be treated to Dr. Frank Baxter discussing the inner workings of the heart in *Hemo the Magnificent,* or one of the other wonderful films by Bell Laboratories. And few ever forgot the gory films shown in drivers' education classes at high schools across the U.S.A.

■ Because educational films were never regarded as important (either artistically or historically), little has been done to preserve or examine them. These films rarely have any credits, so finding out who did what can be a near-impossible task. Too bad, because some of the best filmmakers around have made educational and industrial films. Among them, Russ Meyer, Herschell Gordon Lewis, Frank Capra and Edgar G. Ulmer.

■ Basically educational films fall into two categories: *instructional films* and *fear films.* Each type has its strength. Through (often inadvertently) demonstrating now-outmoded social mores and behavior, instructional films are more likely to develop into good camp, eliciting nostalgia or ridicule. Fear films offer a better barometer of what's "wrong" with society. Any person who has gone through America's public school system has been exposed to plenty of both types of films.

■ The instructional film, most often shown in grade school, is the more common of the two. Into this category falls the *industrial film*—made by large corporations to improve their public image. Often it attempts to impart a sense of drama and wonder to drab subjects such as wool and soy beans, usually starting with a boy engaging in some everyday activity (eating breakfast, turning on the lights, etc.) when an off-screen voice says to him, "Say, have you ever thought about where that comes from?" Or, "Have you ever stopped to ask how that works?" The narrator proceeds to explain where milk for the child's breakfast comes from or how we get electricity into our homes. Often the boy will, by some miraculous transport, end up at the dairy or the power plant, or he will travel through time and learn the whole story of electricity or pasteurization.

■ During the early days of television, instructional films were a staple of prime-time programming, but the rapid rise of Made-for-TV programs forced them out. At present the only time one airs is in the wee hours of morning, when the late-late show falls short of its slot and one is inserted to fill out the hour. As you slowly nod off, a voice asks: "Have you ever wondered where that bread you're eating comes from? Why, it comes from *wheat;* America's most important food source." Or: "It's important that we all learn to conserve water. Thoughtless water use is harmful to us all. Let's see why!" Often these odd little pieces prove to be better than the movies that preceded them.

■ Unfortunately, a good many instructional films are boring; most of us retain memories of these. But some instructional films get better with age, especially those dealing with social and sexual attitudes, like *Dating: Do's and Don'ts,* or *Good Grooming for Girls.*

■ Fear films take a different tack—instead of trying to teach, they attempt to instill fear, warning of the consequences of *not obeying.* In the right (or wrong) hands, an educational film can instill a fear of *anything.* They are predominantly shown in high school, where teaching often takes on a "you'd better do as I say, *or else"* tone. Nearly all safety and drivers' ed films fall into this category.

■ While the instructional films attempt to appeal to our minds, fear films aim straight for the viscera. You do not learn anything *from* them; you respond *to* them. They are intended to indoctrinate, not educate. A classic example of a fear film

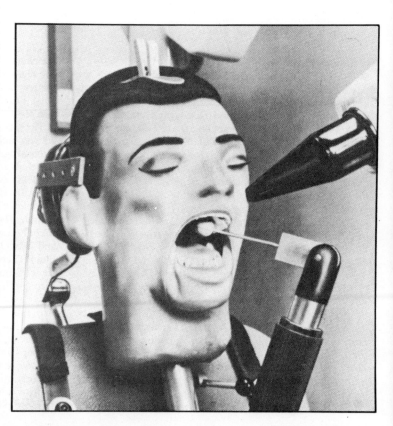

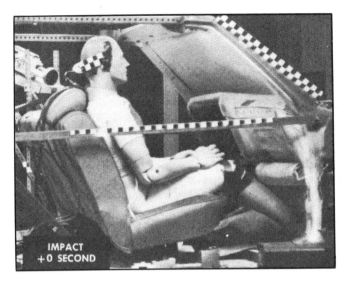

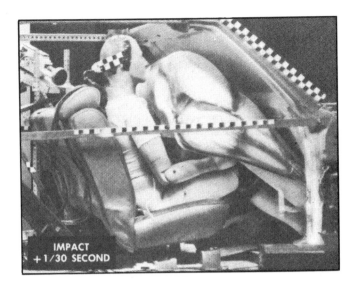

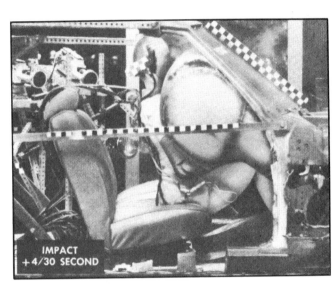

aimed at grade school children is *Lunchroom Manners.* In it, a boy named Phil sees a puppet show featuring a slovenly character called "Mr. Bungle." Afterward a narrator follows Phil to the lunchroom, explaining to the audience the thoughts going through Phil's head. "Phil would like to cut ahead of his classmates," the narrator intones. "But he doesn't want to be a Mr. Bungle."[!]

■ Walt Disney Studios produced many fear films aimed at grade school children. With the help of Jiminy Cricket, Goofy and Donald Duck, Disney kept the kids entertained while warning of the dangers of playing with matches, or forgetting to look both ways before crossing the street. Disney raised the fear film to a level of fine art. Who else could take a mundane concept like *Insects as Carriers of Disease* and turn it into a mini-epic in which the forces of Nazism and Communism are repelled by good hygiene and health care?

■ In terms of paranoia taken to the point of obsession, fear films reached their peak during the fifties, when the American government went all out to persuade the public of the dangers of communism. Titles like *Communism At Our Back Door* and *Communist Blueprint for Conquest* provided indoctrination, not education. The best—and most outrageous—example was *Red Nightmare.* It told the story

of a man who woke up one day to discover what it was like to live under a communist government. The film was introduced by Jack Webb, playing a reactionary version of Rod Serling. Made in deadly earnest, thirty years later it stands as a camp-political classic. The film was recently resurrected by Rhino Video, with its title changed to *The Commies are Coming! The Commies are Coming!*

■ Out of all the types of fear films, the ones seen most often are, of course, drivers' education movies. For many young people, they were the first really gory films seen. *The Educational Film Locator* says it best in their description of gore classic *Signal 30:* "You are there when the blackened and brittle, mangled and bleeding bodies of what once were living, breathing and laughing human beings are pried from their motorized coffins." Many a high school cheerleader lost her lunch at the sight of this movie and others like *Red Asphalt* and *Mechanized Death.*

■ Most highway safety films are little more than a catalog of catastrophies—*Red Asphalt* made no attempt to tell a story or construct a plot. In *Wheels of Tragedy,* the filmmakers took real accidents and used actors to reinact the events leading up to them, switching to the grisly realities for the aftermath. In one of the film's most memorable scenes, a

167

black man loses his head (literally) while arguing with his passenger instead of watching the road.

■ Another common approach is to follow the last few days or hours of someone's life, ending the film with a horrible accident. Although seldom as grisly as the "catalog of death" approach, the film nevertheless can be quite unsettling. In the classic *The Last Date,* a carefree young woman ignores her better judgment and goes for "a quick, fifteen-minute spin" with the local hot-rodder (played by a young and unctuous Dick York). The woman survives, but her face is so horribly disfigured she smashes her mirror to avoid seeing her reflection.

■ During the late sixties, the shock-treatment approach to drivers' education came under fire. A more *instructional* approach was sought (and found) in the crash test footage shot by researchers at Stanford University, who rigged cars with anthropometric dummies and sent them on collision courses with walls, other cars, etc. Cameras were placed both inside and outside of the cars. The resulting footage, while far less gory than the "you are there" films, is nevertheless mesmerizing. For example *Safetybelt for Susie* starts with a happy family on a trip to an amusement park, and ends with endless shots of dummies hurtling in slow motion through windshields and into steering wheels.

■ Equally illustrative of anatomical misadventures were *industrial safety films.* The format was usually the same: a worker ignores the rules and pays for it with a horrible accident. These films were relentless; people lost limbs and lives with great regularity. A favorite film among woodshop students was *Safety in the Shop.* Made in 1944, this may be the first gore film ever made. Within five seconds of the beginning a man loses the tips of his fingers in a planing saw. Later a fellow is impaled on a board because his co-worker didn't follow proper safety procedures.

■ The neglected genre of *eye safety films* contains some of the most traumatic footage ever presented. *Straight Talk on Eye Safety* may not sound too thrilling, but don't let that fool you. *You Bet Your Eyes* and *Don't Push Your Luck* are just two of numerous films developed to promote eye safety in industry, pointing out specific eye hazards in shops and plants. *To Live in Darkness* (1947) is a US Navy film with dramatized incidents showing how three plant workers lost their sight through carelessness. *How Much Are Your Eyes Worth?* (1975) shows an eye operation—inspiring most viewers to shudder and look away; the promo for the film suggests a preview before showing to a group, to allow for "viewing preparation"!

■ In between the "let's all visit the farm or factory" films shown in the primary grades, and the "if you ignore this message you will die" approach used in high school, are the middle grades. In Junior High School, when kids' bodies race to maturity before their minds, the hygiene films are shown.

■ For the boys, the content of *hygiene films* is usually restricted to what constitutes cleanliness and good grooming. Meanwhile, across the hall, the girls are finding out why some of them are beginning to leak blood.

■ Menstruation takes on almost mystical proportions in junior high. Girls are shown films, given booklets and free samples of feminine products, and are thus initiated into the secret society of womanhood. They are given knowledge never intended for male eyes. The booklets, secreted away in the backs of dresser drawers, are often discovered by snoopy older brothers who show them to their friends.

■ It's unfortunate that boys are not shown the menstruation films; the stigma surrounding menstruation might be negated, and certain taboos created by male ignorance might disappear. Guys should be given a chance to see classic films like *Growing Girls,* a 1957 film about a girl's initial reaction to her body's changes; *Molly Grows Up* (1953), which manages to tie menstruation to the importance of a happy home life, and *The Story of Menstruation,* a 1943 animated film made by Walt Disney for the Kimberly-Clark Company.

■ The middle grades are also the years students are introduced to *drug films.* The intent is to discourage youthful experimentation, but the effect is often quite opposite. Many youngsters who saw the infamous anti-drug film, *LSD-25,* consequently tried the substance. The intent of *Curious Alice* was to warn about the dangers of various drugs, but most viewers found their curiosity *aroused* by Alice's "psychedelic" journey. As a result, the film is rarely shown and has been removed from virtually all eduational film catalogs.

■ In America, *sex-education films* are generally shown all the way through high school, with the usual audience reaction one of nervous laughter. Older sex-ed films get the strongest laughs, partly because they are unavoidably campier (because of changes in fashion) and partly because sexual mores have changed so radically since the 1950s. One such unintentional comedy is *Invader,* a crudely animated historical overview of venereal disease. A narrator elicits laughs with lines like: "When Columbus came back from America, he brought back more than trinkets and jewelry; he brought back *The Clap!*" Small wonder that these films have had little effect on curbing adolescent sexual activity.

■ The United States Military is a good source for some of the most extreme exploitational films ever made, perhaps in unconscious counterpoint to the rigid, retrograde military mentality. In one film a young sailor takes LSD and is attacked by a giant caterpillar. In another, Jack Webb narrates the story of a soldier who discovers the girl he is about to marry is a commie spy. But the films best remembered focus on combat first-aid. These films are as gory—if not gorier—than the most gruesome highway safety films. Few could ever forget a film like *Sucking Chest Wounds.*

■ But of all films shown to men in the military, the most infamous was *Sexual Hygiene.* After World War One the top brass became aware of a pressing need to educate young men to the dangers of venereal disease—our boys returning to the States often brought back nasty cases of syphilis and the clap. Hollywood director John Ford was summoned. His film chronicled the misadventures of a greenhorn soldier who, after an evening at the local brothel (his first fling), acquires a severe case of syphilis. The film then graphically illustrates what can happen if the disease is allowed to progress to the advanced stages. It probably never stopped any soldiers from engaging in illicit sex, but they almost certainly enjoyed it less.

■ At some point, educators began concluding that as a film's *entertainment* value increased, its *instructional* value diminished, especially in the case of fear-type educational films. If people laugh at a movie meant to shock them, then something is wrong. So when educational films began to be perceived as "camp," they were taken out of circulation, or like *Red Asphalt,* remade in more contemporary terms. As a consequence, "outdated" educational films by the thousands were tossed into institutional and industrial wastebaskets, with little or nothing done to save them. Of course, solely from the standpoint of entertainment these films should have been preserved. A film like *Invader* may fail at its original purpose of convincing kids of the dangers of gonorrhea, but it's far more amusing than nine out of ten recent comedies.

■ However, finally there is *some* increased interest in educational films. One Bay Area cable channel regularly shows them as filler between rock videos. The makers of *The Atomic Cafe* created a popular movie simply by splicing together previously existing short films (about the atom bomb) in a clever fashion, establishing an editorial viewpoint through careful editing. Reportedly they plan to release a similarly structured compilation based on "dating" films of the forties and fifties. If efforts like these continue, perhaps in the future there will exist widespread awareness of these neglected films, giving us the opportunity to view them in their original form—not on videocassette, but on the big screen. ■

INDUSTRIAL JEOPARDY FILMS

BY RICHARD PRELINGER

For every one of the 50,000 features made since the introduction of sound on film, six "factual" films were produced. They were made for industrial, advertising or educational purposes, and junked as soon as the products or ideas they promoted grew old. No part of American culture and industry was untouched by these films, but almost all of them are now lost. Few are remembered, except by their producers.

■ It isn't surprising, then, that factual films often look into territory largely untouched by mainstream filmmaking. Almost all were produced to weed out the unusual or anomalous, to free consumers and students from mental obstacles standing in the way of the sale or the diploma. Extensive series of films exist (the "Mental Mechanisms" series; the "Industrial Arts" series; the "Discussion Problems in Group Living" series; the "Direct Mass Selling" series) all created to systematize human knowledge and experience with a high degree of efficiency. One of the richest veins of experience, treated in depth by factual films, is *jeopardy.*

■ Although gore and other exploitation genres flirt with jeopardy in all its forms, factual films *systematically* explore morality, shock, accidents, danger, death and the afterlife. Dramatic films overflow with premonitions of (and sometimes disguised wishes for) danger; some of the best show the awful consequences. Factual films seek to *rationalize* and *organize* an infinite number of dangers, a world filled with jeopardy, into orderly categories.

■ As with other private jokes, this pretense doesn't last long. With the first title card in *Play It Safe* (1954), telling us the film was produced by the Peninsular Grinding Wheel Company, we can imagine dangers far more disturbing and anarchic than the bland title suggests. *When You Are A Pedestrian* (1948) starts immediately with an accident, happening so fast it's almost invisible, followed by pre-war stills of dead children on morgue tables, automobiles crushed by streetcars, etc. *Anatomy Of An Accident* (1962) takes us into suburbia, guided on our Technicolor trip by a dead man whose wife and children (not to mention the auctioneer who is liquidating his favorite armchair) cannot see or hear him.

■ Like most genres, jeopardy films follow well-traveled paths. The categories most prevalent follow.

■ **SHOCK FILMS.** These are the famous films most of us have seen. Some, like *Signal 30, Red Asphalt* and *Wheels Of Tragedy* are mentioned elsewhere in this book. They're not confined to the highway. Industrial safety situations, where films play to a highly distracted audience, have encouraged the use of "shock" imagery as an attention-getting device. Films such as *It's Up to You* (1960), showing extreme close-ups of Eddie Briggs' eye surgery under a cynical narration ("Now, Eddie's not getting an anaesthetic here") vie for supremacy with the military V.D. training films, too many to be named, which feature numerous close-ups of male genitalia in the late stages of syphilis and gonorrhea.

■ "Shock" imagery often works through substitution, doubling, models, or schematics. Atomic tests in *Survival Town, USA* (also known as *Doomtown, USA*), newsreels and Civil Defense films (1955 and later) used dummies in *real* dwellings and automobiles to show the effects of atomic weapons.

■ *Safety Belt for Susie* (1962), produced at a time when seat belts weren't yet legally mandated as standard equipment in American cars, aims to show the importance of belting children into their seats. It tells the story of Nancy, a toddler who won't go anywhere without her life-size doll, Susie. A subtly-woven storyline shows Nancy bringing her doll to the amusement park, as the girl and doll are about to be separated for a week. Nancy's parents, on the way to pick her up at her grandparents, sit Susie in the back seat of the car. Naturally, they experience an accident on the road, but escape with minor scratches. The doll, however, is seriously injured ("Suppose it had been Nancy!"). The film then shifts to documentary footage of crash tests shot at UCLA in the late fifties, showing what happens to dolls driving without seat belts. Skillful slow-motion photography, in which dolls' white shoes smash against fisheye lenses mounted within automobiles as they collapse, dramatizes the seriousness of the seatbelt situation while complying with the taboo (which not all factual filmmakers observe) against infanticide.

■ In *When You Are A Pedestrian,* model people and cars on primitive feltboards show conceptually gory accidents in an elegant (though naive) way. The model cars simply bowl down the model pedestrians and leave them lying across the dotted chalk lines. The expense of filming potentially distasteful accidents is simply avoided.

■ **DO'S AND DON'TS FILMS** (or "Goofus and Gallant" films, after the famous characters in *Highlights for Children* magazine) work with time-honored images of good and bad, right path vs. wrong path, reward and tragedy. *Take Your Choice,* filmed in the early 1960s in Detroit's Mumford High School, counterposes the pleasures of sports and outdoor activities against an empty future spent sitting in a room with dark glasses, all to convince students to wear their safety glasses in chemistry lab. *Let's Be Safe At Home* (1948), a brilliant, little-known film produced on an extremely slim budget, shows various children's activities through *double-exposure* (the film is actually wound back within the camera and re-exposed). A boy, hailed by a friend who is standing on the front lawn with his pet rat, stands poised at the top of the stairs, ready to run down (or walk safely), as the case may be. His "ghost" remains on the landing while his other image somersaults down, receiving grave injuries. Later, two boys play with their father's gun; the pair freeze and watch their "ghosts" play a deadly game in which one boy is wounded and falls to the floor. (In the "safe" version, the bullet simply hits the wall, making a small, neat hole.)

■ Sometimes the images are innocuous and danger is simply *suggested,* as in *Safety In Winter* (1952) where the narrator intones, "It's not *nice* to throw snowballs with rocks or iceballs inside of them."

■ **PARABLES AND EXAMPLES.** We are led to identify with stories of ordinary victims who have been led into jeopardy, usually by their own missteps or carelessness. These films number in the thousands, and are perhaps best exemplified by the portentous *Days Of Our Years* (1955), produced for the Union Pacific Railroad. Using the standard device of a trilogy, each episode more heartbreaking than the preceding one, the film argues that people are responsible for abridging their own happiness and shortening their own lives.

■ A minister ("My parish is in a railroad town") walks through what appear to be the outskirts of Los Angeles (the set for many hundreds of safety pictures), recounting stories of wasted lives. Joe, a young railroad worker, waits to marry his girlfriend Mary, a waitress in a luncheonette. As he shaves his neck in the morning he thinks about her. He stops by the restaurant to give her a good-morning kiss. Staring at her reflection in the toaster, she fantasizes about their dream wedding and life together. The toast pops up rudely, and the day is on. Joe performs his job (as road electrical foreman) with dangerous speed. In a hurry to get back to Mary, he flips his truck, breaking his neck. Though Joe lives, there is no dream wedding, and in fact Mary has to stand on her toes in the empty church to kiss him, since his neck brace prevents him from bending down.

■ "Not all trips to the hospital are unhappy ones," says the narrator, as a young welder brings his wife in labor to the emergency room. The doctors send him back to work, where he awaits a telephone call. Receiving his call, he proceeds to pass out cigars in the shop. "One can forgive Frank for passing out cigars on company time," says the narrator. Last cigar in hand, Frank slaps a welder on the back who, startled, wheels around, accidentally blinding him! (The effect is shown by a melting frame of film.) Cut to the yard, where Frank sits on the stoop wearing Roy Orbison-like sunglasses, groping around the crib for his child. "There is nothing more to say; he has said it all a million times. Frank has never seen his son."

■ In an early film, *Bicycling With Complete Safety* (1938), reckless riding carries heavy penalties. Willie, riding and eating popcorn at the same time, wipes out. Flanking his hospital bed, his parents wonder where they'll get the money to pay his medical bills. They finally decide their Christmas savings will have to go to the hospital, "and Willie knows what that means."

■ **HEAVEN.** Finally, of course, almost everyone ends up in heaven. In most jeopardy films, though, heaven isn't usually paradise, but instead a place of judgment. In the wartime film *X Marks The Spot* (1944), Joe Doakes, a reckless driver in life, rises from a huge white "X" (magically appearing in the intersection where he meets his death) through the clouds to a supernatural traffic court, where his "guardian angel"

pleads his case with an unseen judge. His advocate is not successful, and Joe is sentenced to time in purgatory as a guardian angel for other careless drivers.

■ *Safe As You Think* (1950) shows a bureaucratic heaven, all fitted out in art deco, where armies of clerks compile statistics on fatalities and injuries on earth. The walls, covered with totalizers and meters, look like a network newsroom on election night. A bricklayer, about to be killed by a breaking rope, is taken to heaven (again by an advocate who wishes to plead for his life) but the plea for intercession is not heeded, and he must take his punishment.

■ Outside these more or less established genres, jeopardy strikes in many unpredictable ways. *Explosion: Danger Lurks* (1949), produced by the Watts Regulator Company, brings hundreds of engineers and executives into a New England meadow to witness hot-water heater explosions. Pressures within ordinary hot-water heaters sometimes rise to millions of pounds per square inch, and these heaters shoot hundreds of feet in the air. As in *Doomtown USA,* many small buildings are destroyed.

■ *Safety In The Kitchen* (1969) shows the threat that ordinary kitchen utensils and primitive elements (fire, water) pose to a housewife's well-being. At the exact moment she contemplates an unsafe act (carrying a pot of boiling water, cutting the wrong way with a knife, plugging in a wet electric cord), the screen breaks into a kaleidoscopic pattern that whiplashes in and out, shocking the eye. Warned, presumably, by this optical effect, the actress never makes a mistake, and the web of safety *isn't* broken.

■ Although jeopardy is an important ingredient in medical, veterinary, mortuary and agricultural films, accident and chance take second place to experimentation. As more is known about these obscure films, though, significant examples may emerge.

■ The importance of films of jeopardy is proportionate to their naivete. Major breaks in the continuity of life (injuries, accidents) and major social problems (50,000 traffic deaths a year in the USA) are depicted by cinematically-primitive "mom and pop" producers. There is little attempt to obscure the economic interests that lie behind so many of these films. They usually avoid philosophizing, or in trying to do so turn common sense and logic on their head. Attempting to make sense out of mere chance, they illuminate that area where repressed violence collides with the expressed wish for safety, security and order. ■

ESSAYS

YOUNG PLAYTHINGS

ESSAY BY COLETTE COLEMAN

Young Playthings is an obscure masterpiece relegated by its softcore format to late-night viewing on cable TV's "Escapade" or the "Playboy" channel. Ironically deceptive, the titillating title lures the audience with the prospect of a libidinous romp. But this unique sex film penetrates other realms. Seducing the mind as well as the senses, it conforms externally, yet transcends the limitations of its genre. Flesh fondling is not the supreme concern. Rather, sexual experimentation is presented as healthy and indispensable to the underlying goal, which is the rejection of conformist mores, and liberation from socially conditioned sexual attitudes.

■ Radically different from contemporary films of its type, *Young Playthings* treats women not as exploited objects, but as central characters seeking their own sexual identity. Women are neither subservient to men, nor dominated. They are not depicted as vapid sex kittens, victims of Sado-Masochists, nor fetter-bound slaves of Disciplinarians. Psychological motivation is of paramount interest; Jungian symbols abound, replacing the vocabulary and humorously transforming the apparatuses common to most "hump" movies. Cognizant of eternal links with universal ancient rites of passage, Joe Sarno presents the hero's journey and utilizes fairy tales as devices for dealing with sexual confusion.

■ Written, directed, and edited in 1972, *Young Playthings* was shot in Sweden featuring amateurs and an English script. Sarno draws upon a legend familiar to modern Swedish society despite its nineteenth century origin. As the titles run, a quintet of rigidly joined wooden toy soldiers marches briskly across the screen, evoking at once connotations of battle and memories of childhood play with soldiers like these. Thus in the first seconds of the film Sarno presents a visual image which symbolizes and presages a fundamental concern: here are playthings marching mechanically to an ingrained tune. The drum corps precedes troops in battle. Appropriately these drummers announce a campaign replete with warrior-lover imagery.

■ The five soldiers in the preamble foreshadow their human counterparts. Jana is a traveling businessman in a minor supporting role. He initiates little action, appearing primarily as a foil for the two women he loves. Gunilla, his wife, patiently endures his prolonged absences, unaware of his secret liaison with Nora, her oldest, closest friend.

■ Gunilla's sweet demeanor projects an aura of innocence and purity emphasized cinematically by numerous shots in which she holds a spray of luminous white flowers. Yet Gunilla is no simpleton. By means of an eloquent iconographic device, Sarno hints at her quest for understanding; Gunilla is often depicted gazing at her reflection in a mirror. Her self-perusal is motivated not by vanity, but by an inquisitive, self-examining nature.

■ Nora is single, extroverted, and sexually adventurous. But she tires of her duplicity and confesses to Jana her feelings of guilt. Jana loves both women and is unable to choose. Nora suggests a ménage à trois, but Jana questions his wife's amenability. Nora assures him that she will overcome Gunilla's reticence and devises a scheme. Jana is to depart on a fictitious business trip, and in his absence Nora will persuade

Gunilla to share an apartment where she will ready Gunilla for the threesome.

■ It is in the new apartment house that Gunilla and Nora encounter Britt, a mysterious loner who earns her living collecting broken discarded playthings which she restores and sells to collectors. While seeming detached and reclusive, Britt is strangely charismatic. She first appears before Nora and Gunilla at the base of a flight of stairs on the threshold of her slightly ajar door. Such sudden appearances at crossroads by strange creatures recall the classic role of the psychopomp in hero journey myths. Heralds signaling the call to adventure, they beckon the vacillating explorer, offer encouragement, and act as guides in the quest for knowledge.

■ Cinematic clues reflect Britt's function. Her chthonic nature is suggested by her focused, confined space. Vertical and up-and-down shots of corridors leading to Britt's room suggest both the aspiration for a higher goal, and the need to delve deep within.

■ Another ambiguous character plays a major role in the story although she is never seen. We do not know for certain if she exists. Britt's sister Julia is depicted only briefly (in a portrait with her sister) as a clown in Columbine make-up. A poet, Julia composed and narrated stories which Britt has recorded and uses in her pantomimes. According to Britt, Julia ran away with a man, nearly breaking her heart. When Julia tried to return, Britt refused, and Julia went mad. The Orphic or Dionysian reference is obvious; Julia is the unseen voice, Britt the silent interpreter of Julia's fantasies. Julia is perhaps Britt's alter-ego, symbolizing the irrational side of human nature.

■ Britt is a mentor with her own circle of adherents. Analagous to the restoration of broken antiques and toys is her rescue and resuscitation of society's casualties. She invites Gunilla to view her toys, and performs for her a pantomime of one of Julia's poems replete with stage, costume, make-up, and narration. Gunilla is mesmerized and soon convinces her friend Nora to take part.

■ Henceforth, the plot focus centers on the fairy tales enacted in Britt's room. These fantasy episodes are contrasted with outdoor scenes in real time. The dichotomous juxtaposition of fantasy and reality gradually diminishes. What is normally perceived in the outside world as acceptable and real proves duplicitous and hollow in Britt and Julia's contrived theatrical realm. Society's conventions foster disguise and mutation of the true self. Under Britt's direction, comprehension emerges through make-believe, replacing accumulated bourgeois mores.

■ Shortly, Nora and Gunilla become players in Britt's repertory and eventually meet her other followers. The initial plot device standard in many porn films, the seduction and cajoling of an "innocent" (Gunilla) into a ménage à trois, introduces the theme of initiation, here expanded to include an entire group under Britt's spell. Britt presides as mistress of ceremonies over a sort of mythological sexual encounter group. Providing fantasies for her pupils to play out, she makes learning fun.

■ In these episodes Britt engenders a return to a childlike openness. Through make-believe, the players are transported

172

Young Playthings.

to another dimension, cleansed of the fears, attitudes, and defenses accumulated in adult life. Donning costume and disguise, becoming diverse characters, they shed the masks they have clung to. The choice of archetypal figures from antiquity in Western culture engenders the transportation of the group (through similar experience) to a sublimated state.

■ Each successive make-believe session takes place in an epoch chronologically more remote. The temporal regression towards the idyllic Golden Age parallels the psychological transformation of the group members as they uncover and adopt an instinctual awareness (much like a newborn's), untainted by modern accretions of sexually repressive attitudes and conformist obeisance to society's dictums. Additionally, each parable features a character with whom the various personalities can identify, and offers pertinent instruction to each. References to Orphic, Dionysian, and Hermetic mysteries and doctrines pervade the pantomime sequences.

■ The first pantomime concerns the story of a captain who abandons his regiment for a white maiden he adores from afar. Britt applies androgynous features with theatrical white-face. Donning a tri-corn captain's hat and flowing cape over her nude form, she plays the role of the captain in front of a crudely executed backdrop (reminiscent of a carnival set) encrusted with stars and moon. Gunilla only observes this scenario, but actively participates in the next.

■ Gunilla plays the white maiden (symbol of the soul). In this, there are two recurring motifs, the abandonment of a regimented milieu, and the theme of disguise. The soldier gazes longingly at the white maiden, but is too timid to approach. Sensing this, she assumes the role of a bandit in a conqueror mode. Union is effected through role reversal. The two women disguised as a man and a woman now kiss and fondle each other erotically. (Ironically, Nora's calculated attempts to seduce Gunilla have brought about the erotic friendship with Britt. Her sexual antics with a new lover sent Gunilla, lonely, embarrassed and excited, running down the stairs. At the landing she encountered Britt and accepted her invitation to see her toys.)

■ The soldier's abandonment of milieu and the white maiden's transformation into a bandit prefigure the antics of Britt's group of followers. They also abandon their stations in life. Respectable professionals become pick-pockets and thieves in order to participate in Britt's games. All disguise themselves and reject their no longer relevant affiliations and responsibilities in favor of livelihoods compatible with their new-found quest for freedom. The release of the self for these people is predicated on the rejection of socially inherited, unconditionally accepted mores.

■ The ensuing scene in Britt's little theater features Nora and Gunilla as the Red and Blue Duchesses. From the nineteenth-century setting of the Captain's tale, we journey to the Medieval period. The wood nymph Pan teaches the Red Duchess to dance. The Blue Duchess (Nora) considers herself a superior dancer and wonders how her rival has learned to dance so well. When she learns of Pan's part, she begs to be taught. The two duchesses cavort with Pan and we are told that those who have tasted the honey of the nymph's tongue thirst ever after for its sweetness and dance to the tune of its pipe.

■ The pipe certainly connotes Orphic mysteries. Pan in Classical myths was a goat herder, human to the loins, with goat legs, ears, and loins. He was associated with forests, caves and lonely places, and made flocks fertile. He was also the son of Hermes, the messenger of the gods. Hermes in medieval times was the mystagogue and psychopomp of the Alchemists. These connotations in mind, it is plain that Britt, as Pan, imparts sexual wisdom.

■ In the tale of the Peach and Plum Queens and their daughters, Britt plays Puck, whose namesake is the famous trickster from Shakespeare's "Midsummer Night's Dream." Puck wants to play with the Peach and Plum princesses. But they are timid, and their mothers are present. Puck knows that queens like to ride, so he produces a strange horse with no heads, two rumps and two dildoes on its back. The queens mount the horse and gallop in endless circles of delight, as the two princesses and Puck make love. Puck tires and flees into the forest; the two princesses wander in search of a strange horse.

■ The horse symbolism, mounting and riding, is sexually explicit. Further, horses provide transport to another place. One controls the direction of the horse; here, the horse takes control. The queens abandon their regal decorum, and surrendering, achieve pleasure. The strange horse recalls the Centaurs, a tribe of wild beast-like monsters usually thought of as being half-human and half-horse. They live in woods or mountains, and for the Greeks, represent wild life, animal desires, and barbarism, although the most famous centaur, Chiron, was the mentor of divine children.

■ There are intriguing associations with other horse divinities in antiquity. The dualist personas of Britt and Julia, Nora and Gunilla, and the Plum and Peach princesses and queens recall Castor and Pollux, who lived half of the time in Olympus and the other half below the earth. (Compare the descent to Britt's room, a chthonic image—delving into the subconscious.) Castor and Pollux had a cult in Lacadaemon where they were symbolized by the "do-kang"—two upright pieces of wood connected by two crossbeams. They are often identified with the constellation Gemini and are called "riders on white steeds." Their Greek counterparts, the Dioscuri, were connnected with the Phrygian Cabiri, who promoted fertility and protected sailors. Phallic rites connected their worship with the more familiar cults of Hermes, Demeter, and Dionysus.

■ The Hermetic reference is reiterated in the story of a sorceress whose attempts to unlock the mysteries of the universe are interrupted by the warriors of two rival queens. The sorceress gives them a magic potion which causes them to be drawn amorously together, thus ending the rivalry between the kingdoms.

■ Jana has now joined Nora and Gunilla in their vacation flat. The trio spend days and nights in sexual exploration. Nora and Gunilla ask for and receive Britt's permission to introduce Jana to the group. In the midst of one evening's fantasy, Julia's taped voice orders the players to place Britt on a vibrating dildo surmounting a wooden horse: "Show her no mercy. Put her on the horse. If you hesitate, she will destroy you all as she destroyed me." The tape runs out and the players stare in silence as Britt rocks savagely on the contraption. Nora begins to laugh; hesitantly the others follow suit. Gunilla is at first shocked, but eventually joins the others in their mirth.

■ The following day, we learn that Britt is very ill. She claims that her insane sister Julia has escaped from a mental institution and is pursuing her. All the players except Gunilla search the city frantically for Julia. Nora demands why Gunilla abstains and Gunilla replies: "There is no Julia."

■ "You think Britt is insane."

■ "I think Julia is a character that Britt has created."

■ Nora asks why she doesn't just pack up and leave, and Gunilla responds that she can't tear herself away: "I am as hung-up as the rest."

■ But Gunilla senses an irrational undercurrent. She tells Nora that she and Jana will not be joining in the evening fantasy, but are leaving instead. Nora rushes to inform Britt, who silently hands her a knife. Nora returns to her flat, and as Gunilla rushes up apologetically, stabs her. Gunilla screams and collapses.

■ Nora returns to Britt and recounts the deed. Britt announces a change in the evening's exercises, playing instead, "The Saga of the Red Witch and the Scarlett Countess." The tale concerns a "tree of sexual fulfillment" which a terrified princess tries to destroy. Her enraged friend then kills her. The taped voice orders the players to thrust the scarlet princess (Nora) on a vibrating dildo. The voice drones: "eternal torment . . . eternal pleasure . . . eternal torment . . . eternal torment, eternal pleasure, eternal torment for the woman who killed her friend. Drive her out of her mind so that she will forever be an inmate of our group."

■ Nora faces the same predicament which she found so amusing when Britt was the victim. But Britt's pleasure-torment was martyr-like; she became ill the next day, having taken on the burdens of the group. Her enforced orgasm resembled the Dionysian frenzy of a Maenad; she herself demonstrates a lesson she has been trying to impart: one must relinquish control, accept role reversal, undergo conflict, even be victimized, in order to learn. The captain is united with his white maiden only when he abandons his regiment and she exchanges her demure persona for that of an outlaw. The sorceress resumes her lofty pursuits only after transforming two warring factions into amorous allies. The Plum and Peach Queens experience pleasure when they are oblivious to regal status and dignity. Britt's followers gladly

Nora and Gunilla in Young Playthings.

give up their respectable lives in exchange for the pleasurable pursuit of knowledge. Nora is punished because she has shown herself to have changed little since joining the group. She is still a pseudo-sophisticate who thinks she is liberated. Ever mindful of her own gratification, most recently she has shown herself still obsessive. Her punishment is apt.

■ While Nora endures her pleasure-torment, Jana cradles his stricken wife. Picking up the knife, he discovers that it, too, is a toy. Britt has released Gunilla from her circle because Gunilla is the least innocent of all; she understands the duality in nature, the relation between pleasure and torment, reality and make-believe, the rational and the irrational. ■

WIZARD OF GORE

ESSAY BY MARK SPAINHOWER

"*I am Montag, master of illusion . . . defier of the laws of Reason. A magician, if you will . . . but then, what is a magician? A person who tears asunder your rules of Logic? And crumbles your world of Reality? So that you can go home and say, 'Oh, what a clever trickster he is! What a sly deceiver!'—and go to sleep in the security of your own 'real' world . . . what is 'Real?' Are you* certain *you know what reality is? How do you know that, at this second, you aren't asleep in your bed, dreaming that you are here in this theater? I know . . . it all seems* too real *. . . well, haven't you ever had a dream that seemed so very real . . . till you woke up? Then again, how do you know that you ever really* did *wake up? In fact, perhaps when you had thought that you were waking up, you had actually just begun to dream? You see what I mean, don't you . . . ? All your life, your past, your rules of what* can *and* cannot *be . . . may* all *be part of one long dream from which you are about to awake, and discover the world* as it really is . . . !"

—THE WIZARD OF GORE

■ The act of viewing a movie enlists the individual into a symbiotic relationship with the film itself, founded on the audience's willing suspension of disbelief. A "good" movie is identified with verisimilitude—if we do not "believe," then the movie was "bad." "Bad" movies are commonly qualified by one or more of the following components: 1) a conceptual or actual element which conflicts with the belief parameters of its audience, 2) a noticeable lack of funds, and 3) "bad" acting. What different groups or individuals believe to be "true" always varies widely, but all film audiences *want to believe* in the movie they've come to see. When an audience is presented with a film outside the boundaries of their "logic," the symbiosis between the film and the audience dissolves.

■ *The Wizard of Gore* defies the notions of logic, reason, and restraint with carefree (or careless) abandon, stopping at nothing to trap our attention. The camp elements cannot be ignored, but the careful viewer will realize this is one of the most intellectually provocative films ever to emerge from the depths of gore cinema. Complex notions of Time, Space and Logic are presented in the midst of some of the wildest flaunting of cinematic "good taste" ever to appear on the screen.

■ Viewers expecting potent metaphysical themes to be presented in a subdued, restrained manner would be better off elsewhere. Of Lewis's films, *The Wizard of Gore* is easily the most outlandish in premise, if not in execution. To synopsize the story, Montag is a magician whose ghastly specialty is the violent dismemberment of female volunteers from the audience—sawing one in half with a chainsaw, hammering a railroad spike through the skull of another, blasting through another's midsection with an industrial punch press, and forcing two more to swallow wicked-looking swords. Leaving the stage apparently intact, his volunteers always suffer delayed reactions shortly after leaving the theater—Montag's illusions become fatal realities.

■ In the audience is Sherry Carson, hostess of the daytime TV show, "Housewives' Coffeebreak," and her sports writer-boyfriend, Jack. Sherry is amazed by Montag's illusions, while

Jack remains skeptical and unimpressed. After leaving the theater still arguing, they come across a crowd gathering around a restaurant—a woman has just collapsed in a booth, intestines spilling out onto the floor. The corpse's dangling hand brushes against Sherry, staining her hand with its blood.

■ Later, Sherry returns to the theater hoping to persuade Montag to appear on her show. At first he haughtily refuses, but when he sees the bloodstain mysteriously reappear on her hand, he relents. Attracted by the latest newspaper headline: "Psycho Murder in Restaurant," Jack recognizes the victim as the woman Montag sawed in half with his chainsaw, and goes to the police with his suspicions. The police, typically unimaginative and conservative, are of no help whatsoever in preventing Montag's subsequent volunteers from meeting similar fates. (In the meantime, Montag has been stealing the corpses of his victims, for unexplained reasons, and dumping them down what looks like a laundry chute [!] located in a deserted cemetery.)

■ When at last Montag appears on Sherry's TV show, he hypnotizes not only those in the studio but *everyone* viewing the show (". . . but first, let us link our minds," he intones ominously, looking straight into the camera). Wisely, Jack has averted his gaze—thus escaping being hypnotized. Frozen in trance, all the audience within transmitter range sport the bloody stigmata on their hands. Montag's final illusion is revealed to be the immolation of his entire audience, and he proceeds to lead Sherry, the studio crew, and all viewers to their deaths in a flaming furnace. At the last instant Jack bursts in and pushes Montag into the flames, thus breaking his evil spell.

■ As the film ends, Jack and Sherry are wondering just how Montag could have performed his heinous deeds. Suddenly Jack peels off his mask, revealing himself to be Montag in disguise, and tears into Sherry with his bare hands. She, however, laughs in his face and announces to him that he was *her* illusion all along, and transports him back to the film's beginning, fating him to "start his little charade all over again . . ." *Fin.*

■ In Montag's performances throughout the film, heady theoretical phrases such as "tearing asunder the rules of logic" and "crumbling the world of *reality*" are bewilderingly substantiated by extreme gore atrocities. The actors (as well as their dialogue) are amateurish, often to the point of hilarity; an exuberant hamminess shared by the cast predates the flamboyant emoting of John Waters' players (Lewis was one of Waters' major influences/inspirations).

■ Montag's character is particularly droll. Given to punctuating his performances with cheerfully morbid patter ("Isn't there one lady among you who is considerate enough to satisfy her fellow human beings' lust for blood?"), he often plays the jokester. When displaying his chainsaw, he remarks, "You were expecting a *mere* handsaw? And a covered wooden casket? Oh, no . . . that's the *old-fashioned* way of sawing people in half. Today, magicians are mechanized, too!" Later, his predilection for updated industrial technology is further evidenced by his unconventional application of the punch press.

■ The film's notions of plot and continuity are remarkable—blatant non-sequiturs abound. Montag's motivation for these grisly murders is never explored, nor is the source of his powers revealed. The significance of the bloody stigmata appearing on everybody's hands during the mass TV hypnosis remains a mystery. The grave-robbing forays seem to exist for no reason at all. The list goes on, but such trivial considerations are far beside this movie's point—or as Montag himself puts it, "What makes you think *you* know what *reality* is?" Part of *The Wizard of Gore's* unique charm is *precisely* that element of chaos: "Never explain, never complain" seems to adequately summarize Lewis' philosophy of plot.

■ When aiming for his audience's reactionary jugular, Lewis is deadly accurate. As the progenitor of the blitzkrieg-gore approach, he was singularly aware that movies need not be expensive or have "serious" content; his films succeeded by sheer imaginative force and by breaking taboos of decency and propriety—people paid money simply to see them broken.

■ *The Wizard of Gore* is singular for consciously acknowledging the idea of *Gore As Entertainment*. Indeed, the entire plot revolves around the concept of people paying their money to passively observe a maniac subjecting young women to spectacular tortures. (When an interviewer once grilled him on the misogynistic aspects of his films, Lewis snorted that he would just as readily have killed off males as females, had he believed an audience existed for such films.)

■ The implications are obvious as Montag matter-of-factly comments: "Torture and terror have always fascinated mankind ... perhaps what made your predecessors see the sadism of the Inquisition and the gore of the gladiators is the same thing that makes *you* stare at bloody highway accidents ... and *thrill* to the terror of Death in the bullring ..." Montag, like Lewis, is consummately obliging of his audience's desires.

■ The average moviegoer will certainly be mortified by *The Wizard of Gore's* extreme sadism, as well as the "seedy" quality which pervades all of Lewis' films. Absent are the sophisticated latex prosthetics of Tom Savini or Dick Smith, which, while technically virtuosic, appear merely slick and facile next to the crude and vicious carnage of the animal-innard school which Lewis himself pioneered to hideous extremes. In this film, Montag displays a special fondness for mangling the victims' organs with bare fingernails, gleefully kneading them as though dough before the appreciative eyes of the audience.

■ His illusions are shown in a series of jump-cuts, alternating between two distinctly separate realities—the scene of the victim placidly enduring assault as though in trance, juxtaposed with the sight of the victim becoming gore. Particularly eerie is the aftermath of the sword-swallowing scene, where the two victims stand calm and erect on either side of Montag, sword handles protruding from open mouths, intercut with scenes where they dangle from their bonds like broken puppets, crumpled and bloody, while Montag takes his triumphant bows between them.

■ The film's conceptual dénouement takes place in the final scenes where Jack peels off his face in front of Sherry's horrified eyes, revealing himself to be Montag before he proceeds to disembowel her with bare hands. Sherry's reaction, however, is to brush her guts off her chest and laugh in his face—as startling an event for Montag as it is for the audience. She tauntingly informs him that she, too, is a "dealer in illusion." Then the hostess of "Housewives's Coffeebreak" transports herself and Montag back to the film's beginning, dooming him to repeat endlessly his cycle of illusion and murder, while in the audience Sherry remarks to Jack as the film closes, "You know what I think? I think he's a phony!" The turn of the screw is complete: Reality and Illusion have finally become an indistinguishable blur, even to their very manipulators. A radical concept, indeed ...

■ On a multitude of levels this film constantly challenges its audience to examine what is "true" or "real," forcing them to acknowledge (reluctantly or otherwise) that these supposed truths are *merely human truths*—therefore subjective. We as humans are capable only of perceiving dimly what brilliant chaos extends beyond our puny laws and sciences. As John Barrymore cunningly remarks in *Svengali*, "You would do well to remember that there are more things in heaven and earth than are dreamed of in your philosophy ..." The assertion of sophisticated, abstract concepts in such a consummately crude film will doubtless provoke derision in that intellectual "elite" which accepts themes of metaphysical content only when clothed in genteel surroundings.

■ In all its shoddy glory, *The Wizard of Gore* serves as an *unusual* reminder that the mysteries of the cosmos extend themselves as readily into the gutter as they do to the stars, implying a vast realm of similar film experiences antithetical to the promoters and consumers of mass media "Reality" and "Illusion." Regardless of whatever intentions he had, in *The Wizard of Gore* Lewis succeeding in creating a total effect of demented cosmic anarchy. *The Wizard of Gore* is a film which is *truly* perverse, and in all the best possible definitions of that word. ■

GOD TOLD ME TO

ESSAY BY MARGARET CRANE

One clue connects a series of killings: the killers all confess, "God told me to . . ." In the film written and directed by Larry Cohen, police detective Peter Nicholas (Tony Lo Bianco) discovers God to be the wrathful diety of the Old Testament transplanted to contemporary Manhattan. This is the God who calls the powerful to his side while he slaughters the masses in the streets. His messiah is a hippie named Bernard Phillips whose mother immaculately conceived by the divine light of a spaceship. When this God looks down on the world, run for cover.

■ Peter Nicholas, the good cop, becomes a visionary hero as his investigation reveals that both he and Bernard are divine beings, the children of virgin mothers and extraterrestrials. The New York locations, urban sounds and vivid true-to-life characters fade into a mythic landscape as Peter and Bernard compete in an epic struggle for power.

■ *God Told Me To* appropriates the structure of detective films, but this is no formula movie. Larry Cohen alters the formula, depicting disorder as a catalyst to expand the hero's role toward its archetypal fulfillment as the bearer of change. The hero's work, according to Joseph Campbell, is to journey into the unknown and there slay the tyrant, ogre or corrupted god, and so liberate the earth from the domination of the old order.

■ The iconoclastic universe of *GTMT* condemns dogma and organized religion, posing the question: If God and religion are ideas conceived by man, what would happen if these concepts took form and turned against their creators? All hell breaks loose when the malevolent manifestation of the Christian "God" combines with the notion of UFOs and "gods from outer space." The film takes the position: *you made it up, now you have to live with it.*

■ In myths, heroes appear when society is in decline. The killings in the film create a crisis which tests the validity of authoritarian figures and institutions. Religion, law enforcement and the social microcosm of the family are all revealed as corrupt. God—the ultimate authority figure—is stained with blood. The police, rendered ineffectual by their conceptual conservatism, futilely attempt to impose order by suppressing information. A father exercises his "divine right" over his family, and in a testimonial to blind faith describes how he shot his wife and children. When asked why he did it, Dad concludes (smiling beatifically), "Because He gives me so much and asks for so little."

■ Whose side is God on, anyway? Consistent with history, God's elect in *GTMT* are a small group of wealthy and powerful men, seemingly representing the "New Right" and fundamentalist government politicians. In an impressive board room, they await exalted positions in the new millennium. One of the powerful expresses concern over the fate of the dying masses. Another sums up the inequity of a religion based on guilt when he replies, "The only way He has ever communicated is through fear." It appears ill-advised to trust those who believe they have a direct line to God.

■ "I love chaos. Out of chaos comes reason, and out of reason, science." So says the science editor of a New York tabloid before he breaks the suppressed story of the killings. The disintegrating city is observed from above as aerial shots convey the presence of a hostile God overlooking his flock. A happy throng at the Saint Patrick's Day parade is reduced to a terrified mob when a marching policeman opens fire on the crowd, causing mass hysteria.

■ Screaming crowds are common elements in films. They are generally portrayed negatively as the result of terror (crowds fleeing hostile ants or hostile armies). Viewed through the anarchistic vision of *GTMT*, chaos becomes life-affirming and mob scenes are elevated to exhilarating spectacles. When the journalist glorifies chaos, he articulates the perspective of classic mythology in which chaos is an indispensable element of the world cycle, destroying the old order. Chaos is an essential aspect of the eternal round of destruction and regeneration.

■ Religious imagery appears grotesque in contrast to scenes of mayhem. A bloody crucified Christ looms over Peter as he prays. At a street fair he kneels before a neon altar which is significant as a pretty, glowing theater marquee. Peter is a devout Catholic, but the symbols of his faith appear either sinister or meaningless. Although separated from his mystic reclusive wife, Martha (Sandy Dennis), he returns to her often to express his devout nature. Her suburban home is an oppressive cloister filled with religious relics. Beneath a print of a suffering Jesus, she consoles him, "You really believe, but where is the joy?" Spiritual decline, empty symbols and rising violence define the parameters of the known world.

■ Peter's investigation leads him closer to Bernard. Witnesses describe seeing a hippie with "no face" talking with the killers before the murders. One of the killers' mothers states, "Anybody who walks barefoot around New York has got to have something wrong with him."

■ When Peter enters Bernard's mother's apartment building, Mrs. Phillips appears, knife in hand. They struggle on the dark stairs and she falls, gagging as she dies on the word "God." From this point on, interiors become dreamscapes and hallways passages to enlightenment. Peter descends in an elevator to confront Bernard Phillips in an infernal boiler room. His adversary appears wreathed in flames, the simultaneous incarnation of Christ and Satan.

■ Now on a quest for his own identity, Peter follows a labyrinth twisting through New York, leading to his mother (Sylvia Sydney) who gave him up for adoption. She enlightens him as to the secret of his virgin birth. At this point he renounces his religion and realizes his power before the labyrinth leads him back to Bernard.

■ The stairs of an abandoned building lead Peter to his long-sought confrontation with Bernard, who confirms what Peter suspects . . . they are of the same origin, but different. Peter is superior, not only as the new avatar, but genetically as well. Bernard explains, "In me, all that is you became recessive." He exposes a multisexual orifice on his side (a sexualization of Christ's wound) and invites Peter to mate with him. Peter's refusal, an affirmation of *his* power, signifies Bernard's death. The vanquished messiah assumes a gesture of benediction as flames envelop him and walls collapse. The destiny implicit in the myth is fulfilled . . . making way for a new millenium.

■ When the press asks Peter why he killed Bernard, Peter

177

answers, "He told me to."

■ The film (but not most videotapes) ends with a concluding line stating that Peter was sentenced to a mental institution. The ending is left ambiguous: will the new messiah be dismissed as a crazy killer, or will he orchestrate the dawn of a new age? In a mythic sense, the film ends appropriately open-ended. *GTMT* is an unfinished chapter in a larger system which celebrates transformation, but also poses a warning: today's hero becomes tomorrow's tyrant. There will always be a new order waiting in the wings to overthrow the old.

■ The message of the film is greater than the fate of its hero. Larry Cohen utilizes the mythic possibilities of film to its fullest. The hero's journey into the realm of darkness corresponds to an individual's process of psychic growth. *God Told Me To* explores and explodes the major delusions underlying our culture's religious beliefs; it is an exorcism of hypocrisy. ■

BLAST OF SILENCE

ESSAY BY PRAX GORE

Blast of Silence is another exceptional film disguised as a low-budget gangster movie. It looks cheap; it sounds cheap; it's great.

■ The plot is straightforward: Frankie Bono, independent hit man, is hired to knock off a crime boss. He contracts with a fat friend to buy a gun with silencer. He trails his mark. He runs into and falls for some skirt he knew from his orphanage days. The fat gun supplier wants more dough, so Frankie offs him. Then he knocks off the target. When he goes to collect his fee, he gets gunned down by men hired by his employers. This may all may sound somewhat familiar. The plot, however, is only a vehicle for fleshing out the character of the paranoid, existential, post-adolescent-loner Frankie Bono.

■ The first indication that this is not an ordinary crime thriller comes with the opening shot and voice-over. A tiny spot of light in the middle of a black movie screen grows until it becomes the opening of a tunnel into Grand Central Station. The voice-over (which sounds like Lionel Stander, although no one is given credit) begins,

You were born with hate and anger built in. Took a slap in the backside to blast out the scream. Then you knew you were alive. 8 lbs, 5 oz. Baby Boy Frankie Bono. Father doing well. Later you learned to hold back the screams and let out the hate and anger in other ways.

■ This voice-over is constantly informing us (and Frankie) what is going on. Rather than revealing privileged insights, it appears to be Frankie's trained, conscious image of himself talking, reminding him how tough he is, and nagging him when he gets soft.

■ Eventually the film becomes a somewhat schizophrenic experience as this disembodied voice increasingly grows stronger than Frankie, whose own voice is high, soft, nasal, and badly recorded. Toward the end Frankie almost disappears—the high-contrast grainy photography reinforcing the decline of his character.

■ The voice frequently stresses Frankie's need to be alone, and in fact the only real tension in the film occurs when he talks to the girl ("you're making a fool of yourself, buddy"), or making contact with other humans ("watch out, they might trip you up"). This tension is an inversion of normal movie conventions which dictate that you're supposed to get nervous when the character is committing a crime, and relax when he's socializing. When Frankie's doing a crime, he's ice cold.

■ Sometimes the voice is simply an emotional barometer, as when it alerts Frankie, "You're nervous, your hands are hot," or "You're comfortable, your hands are cold."

■ Even though the most memorable stylization of the film is the constant narration, there are exceptionally visual scenes such as when Frankie is dancing in the living room with the girl he used to know. She is relaxed, gazing at the ceiling (toward the distant romantic horizon or back to fond old memories?) when out of nowhere he tries to rape her. Then there's the scene when (with great difficulty) he kills the fat guy, initially employing a fire axe . . .

■ There's also a memorable scene in a cocktail lounge where we see Frankie's prey and girlfriend sitting at a table (he's greasy-looking; she's a gold-digger). Laughing, she gives him a big kiss. Then a live black jazz band appears with a singer who plays congas, singing about how he's "dressed in black a-all the ti-ime"—a plaintive tune furnishing a subtext appropriately reflecting Frankie's thoughts. Then the singer goes "over the top" relating the saga of "trying to find (his) baby in this torrid, torrid, town."—one of the most uninhibited performances ever captured on film.

■ In another classic scene Frankie is walking through Harlem, the camera tracking alongside him. As he walks, the people hanging out on the street stare sullenly back at the camera, refusing to be faceless extras. This documentary sequence makes Frankie seem unimportant, while these unknown "real people" steal the scene, generating *genuine,* uncomfortable emotional tension.

■ The ending, filmed in a horrific wind and rain storm at an isolated summer cottage landing, ranks as one of the bleakest, even among *noir* films. This low-budget masterpiece involving exceptional locations, casting, narration and filming is credited to "Allen Baron" (screenplay, director and star). The modern composer Meyer Kupferman composed and conducted the score. None of the other names in the credits were recognizable. ■

DAUGHTER OF HORROR

ESSAY BY JIM MORTON

"You ... you out there. Do you know what horror is? Smug, confident, secure because you're sane. Do you know what madness is, or how it strikes? Have you seen the demons that surge through the corridors of the crazed mind? Do you know that in the world of the insane you will find a kind of truth more terrifying than fiction? A truth that will shock you!"

■ So begins John Parker's strange 1953 classic, *Daughter of Horror*. Originally filmed MOS (without sound), *Daughter of Horror* is augmented by a music soundtrack and a narration by Ed McMahon. With its long shadows and lonely figures, the film's visual style resembles that of the painter De Chirico.

■ The movie begins in the hotel room of a young woman suffering from recurring nightmares. Awaking from one, she gets out of bed, walks to her dresser, takes out a switchblade and pockets it. On her way out she sees police talking to her neighbors, and though we can't hear what they're saying, it's apparent that a drunken man has just beaten his wife.

■ The young woman ventures out into the darkened city streets—probably Venice, California. The location, along with the *noir* cinematography, gives the film a visual similarity to Orson Welles' *Touch of Evil*. Responsible for the film's moody look is William Thompson, an excellent cinematographer whose work includes the films of Ed Wood, Jr.

■ The woman buys a newspaper from a dwarf which proclaims: MYSTERIOUS STABBING. Smiling, she throws the paper away, but it begins to roll along the ground after her. She runs down an alley and the paper lands on her feet; a slash of light illuminates the headline: MYSTERIOUS STABBING. This time the guilt is explicit.

■ These scenes reveal genuine directorial finesse. Unfortunately John Parker, possibly stung by critical reaction (or lack of it), abandoned filmmaking. *Daughter of Horror* is his only known picture.

■ Next the woman encounters several winos in the alley. One tries to force her to take a drink, but she resists. Suddenly a police car pulls up; a plainclothes cop emerges and begins to beat the man. The woman looks on, laughing gleefully.

■ Wandering away from the brutal scene, she encounters a greased Lothario who stops to buy a carnation from a flower girl, pins it to his lapel, and then converses with the Daughter of Horror. Because the film is silent we cannot hear what he's saying, but it's obvious he's attempting to persuade her of something. Eventually she nods and smiles, seemingly in acceptance. They stop to light cigarettes and a newspaper brushes against her feet: MYSTERIOUS STABBING. She kicks the newspaper away; it tumbles into the street and is run over by a car. The car stops. From the backseat a fat man peers at them.

■ The Lothario walks over to the car and, after talking to the fat man and accepting some money, beckons the woman over. She gets in the car; he doesn't. The woman and the fat man (played by stock heavy Bruno Ve Sota) spend the evening traveling from club to club.

■ While driving through the city, the woman fades into a memory of the past. A faceless figure—presumably the narrator/"demon" who possesses her soul—leads her through a graveyard and shows her scenes from her childhood, some of them most bizarre and imaginative.

■ The woman re-lives the night she murdered her father who had just killed her mother. The tableau is set in a cemetery, with living room and bedroom furniture arranged amidst the tombstones. Her father (resembling the policeman who came to her aid in the alley) is an abusive lush. Her mother, clad only in a black slip and lying on a couch next to a tombstone marked "Mother," is eating chocolates from a box. She appears low-class and amoral. When the father gets home, his attempts at sex with his wife are repulsed. Then he notices a cigar butt in an ashtray. Incensed by his wife's cavalier attitude and the apparent evidence of her infidelity, he shoots her dead. As he stares at the body his daughter comes up from behind and stabs him to death.

■ The scene in which the woman is being led through the cemetery will be recognized by many, for *Daughter of Horror* is the movie the teens are watching just before *The Blob* invades the theater. Seeing this scene years later in the *original* context can produce a strange *deja vu*.

■ The woman snaps out of her reverie in time to leave the car and follow the fat man to his upstairs apartment. Inside, the man sets her aside temporarily for a bite to eat. She watches in disgust as he stuffs his face with food, greedily pulling meat from chicken bones with his teeth. For sheer prandial grossness, only *Le Grande Bouffe* can match this scene.

■ After finishing his meal the fat man tries making a pass at the woman; she rebuffs him. He pulls a wad of bills from his

Daughter of Horror.

pocket and approaches her again. This time the woman smiles, but when he tries to kiss her she pulls her knife and stabs him. He stumbles backwards through a window and falls six stories, his money trailing behind him like confetti in the air.

■ Shocked at her deed, the woman runs down the stairs to the street. Near the body of her victim she pauses to cry. "Guilty!" the narrator scolds, "Mad with guilt and the demon that has taken possession of your soul."

■ Suddenly she realizes she has lost her pendant—the fat man grabbed it as he fell, and now it lies clutched in his lifeless hand. Vainly she tries to pry the pendant loose from his rigid fingers. Pulling her switchblade out once more, she severs the man's hand. At this point she appears to be surrounded by people watching her, but the people have no faces. The narrator informs us they are the "ghouls of insanity," real only to the Daughter of Horror.

■ The police appear and begin to chase her, shining a spot-light on her as she runs. Suddenly she encounters the flower girl and by an impulse places the dismembered hand in the basket (much to the girl's horror), then continues flight.

■ Finding herself trapped in an alley, she ducks into a doorway behind which a jazz band is practicing. Immediately a man bolts the door behind her to keep the police from entering. He provides her with a satin gown and they enter a basement nightclub, where Shorty Rogers and His Musical Giants—an actual band—play bebop before an audience of hipsters and lowlifes. This scene provides a rare glimpse into the jazz underworld that thrived in the early fifties. Later—due largely to the efforts of Jack Kerouac—these hipsters became known as the "beat generation," or "beatniks."

■ The woman begins dancing to Shorty's music, and an air of normalcy resumes. All too soon a police officer arrives. Sauntering around the club, accepting payoffs from various patrons, he at first ignores her; but slowly, slowly he works his way to the front of the stage, where she stands.

■ At the window another policeman kneels beside the fat man, who—very much alive again—points at the woman with his bloody stump. The people in the club look at the fat man, then turn and point at the woman. The policeman holds up a pair of handcuffs, the fat man laughs and the people surround her. She looks down and sees the pendant around her neck. As the theme song reappears, mingling with the jazz of Shorty Rogers, a montage of faces spin in and out of her vision—her mother, her father, the fat man and the Lothario—all of them laughing. The pendant spins before her eyes and giant waves crash down upon her as she runs.

■ The movie ends where it began, with the woman arising from her bed. "Only a dream," the narrator tells us. "Or was it?" She notices a gold chain hanging from her dresser drawer and opens it. Inside, still clutching the pendant, is the fat man's hand. Again and again we hear her scream as the camera pulls away from the hotel and out of her life.

■ *Daughter of Horror* was first released in 1955 under the title *Dementia*. Critical response was underwhelming, and the film quickly disappeared. It resurfaced briefly in 1956, again without much notice. During the seventies the film gained stature among horror fans as one of the strangest movies ever made, with many considering it an overlooked classic. Unquestionably it deserves far more attention than it has received to date.

■ One of the most memorable aspects of the movie is its haunting, repetitive score. The theme song, written by George Antheil and sung by Marni Nixon, is repeated in variations throughout the movie. The only time we don't hear it is when Shorty Rogers plays; even then, Shorty doesn't play long before the theme music comes swelling back, ascending through his jazz in a mad cacophony. Composer Antheil—who first gained fame for his unorthodox scoring of Fernand Leger's *Ballet Mécanique*—was obviously influenced by Miklos Rozsa's *Spellbound*. The singer, Marni Nixon, rose to prominence by dubbing vocal parts for many actresses appearing in musicals, among them Natalie Wood in *West Side Story* and Deborah Kerr in *The King and I*.

■ *Daughter of Horror* is not an easy film to analyze. Its depictions of murder, resurrection and dismemberment—all common elements in horror films—are presented as the hallucinations of an insane mind. Despite the *noir* cinematography and depictions of pimps, payoffs, and venal police, *Daughter of Horror* is not a crime movie. The original title, *Dementia,* probably reflects the film's essence most accurately. In a conventional horror film the terror comes from the outside, with the central figure a victim in a world gone mad. In Parker's film the horror originates from the inside, as an aberrant mind turns upon itself.

■ For three decades ignorant critics and a somnolent public kept *Daughter of Horror* in obscurity. Now, looking at the movie so many years later, we can only wonder at what prevented them from seeing it as the remarkable film it is. ■

Daughter of Horror.

180

SPIDER BABY

ESSAY BY JIM MORTON

Despite late-night TV and local revival theaters, each year obscure films are lost—some irretrievably. Only an arbitrary fraction achieve the cult status necessary for survival.

■ If any film ever deserved cult status, it is Jack Hill's unique *Spider Baby,* which defies classification. Limited distribution and bad marketing, including misleading title changes to *The Liver Eaters* (no livers are eaten) and *Cannibal Orgy* (there is no orgy, cannibal or otherwise) contributed to the film's neglect. Fortunately it was rereleased on videocassette, but is still seldom seen on the big screen.

■ *Spider Baby* was released in 1968, but was made in 1964 or earlier in Los Angeles. The film opens with Lon Chaney, Jr. "singing" about vampires and werewolves, neither of which has anything to do with the film. But the song, with its eerie accompaniment, does set the mood.

■ The film tells of Merrye's Syndrome, a rare disease affecting only members of the Merrye family. This illness causes its victims to regress mentally to a pre-infantile state of savagery and cannibalism. In the large family mansion, the only survivors are the children of Titus W. Merrye: Elizabeth, who dresses like a little girl and wears her hair in pigtails; Virginia, who fancies herself a spider and likes to eat insects; and

Ralph, who, being the oldest, is the most regressed—a six-foot toddler. The children are watched over by Bruno, the family chauffeur, who made an oath to Titus Merrye to take care of the children forever.

■ Two distant cousins of Titus W. Merrye, Peter and Emily Howe, arrive with their lawyer and his secretary. The Howes plan to claim the Merrye inheritance, including the mansion, for themselves. It's obvious this is all Emily's idea, Peter being a soft-spoken, likable fellow who seems only along for the ride.

■ At times *Spider Baby* is like a television sitcom directed by Luis Buñuel. In one scene the interlopers are served a dinner prepared by Bruno and the children. The main course consists of a "rabbit" caught by Ralph (it's really a cat, and for the guests only; Bruno and the children are vegetarians); mushrooms picked by Virginia ("She has an uncanny knack for picking only the non-poisonous varieties"); and a slimy black stew only Virginia will eat ("Oh, no, sir!" Bruno warns Peter, "You wouldn't want any of *that!"*). When Ralph grabs the "rabbit" and begins gnawing on it, Peter asks if Ralph isn't also a vegetarian. "Oh yes," Bruno replies with unfathomable logic, "but Ralph is allowed to eat anything he catches."

■ This remark is typical of *Spider Baby.* All the characters—

Spider Baby.

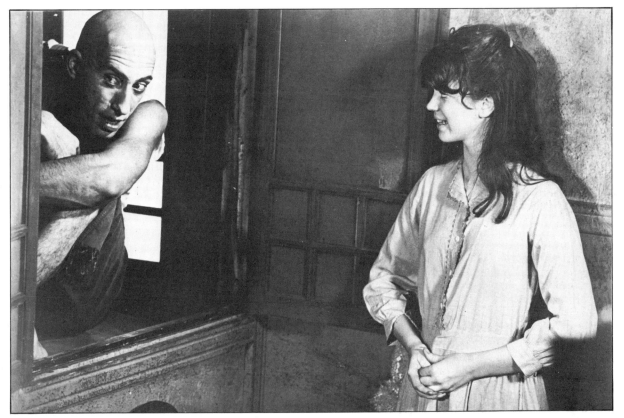

even the "normal" ones—are odd, yet unaware that others consider them odd. Only Bruno seems cognizant of the conflicting realities held by the "children" and the intruders.

■ Part of *Spider Baby's* appeal is due to near-perfect casting. Lon Chaney, Jr.—whose acting was usually somewhat substandard—is brilliant as Bruno, giving the character just the right qualities of compassion and desperation. Carol Ohmart, once touted as Hollywood's hottest new sex symbol, seethes like a frustrated dominatrix. Jill Banner's performance as Virginia, the Spider Baby, is perfect; her character evokes just the right amount of sex, naivete, and menace. Beverly Washburn as Elizabeth is only slightly less effective. Sid Haig, who has since become a successful Hollywood character actor, is almost unrecognizable as the bald cretin, Ralph. Quinn Redeker, another character actor who specializes in nervous nerds, gives the movie great comic moments. The only weak characterization is Karl Schanzer, who, as Schlocker the lawyer, appears too young for the bloated, self-important role he portrays.

■ *Spider Baby's* visual impact may be attributed to Alfred Taylor, who gave this black comedy the chiaroscuro look of *film noir;* the shadows are deep and the lighting melodramatic. Except for a day-for-night chase scene, his cinematography is faultless. Throughout there are clever touches; when Elizabeth announces she has devised a plan for dealing with unwanted visitors, her face literally glows with malevolence.

■ As in most horror movies, the monsters (in this case, the children) are damned from the start; we know the kids are going to die. But death, when it comes, has no sting. It is met by the children with naive anticipation, and by Bruno with a shrug. The shrug sums up the prevailing philosophical attitude of *Spider Baby*—as Bruno says near the beginning of the film, "Nothing is *very* bad."

■ Jack Hill, who wrote and directed the film, made dozens of movies for Roger Corman and other Hollywood producers and worked with some of the industry's most talented actors. However, none of his other works is as unusual as *Spider Baby.* Probably because the film did so poorly at the box office, Hill never made anything remotely like it again.

■ Categorizing this oddity is no easy task; *Spider Baby* is a horror-comedy, but lacks the buffoonery and dumb jokes that most comedies rely on. It has been referred to as a black comedy, but as such it lacks the cynicism and sophistication of typical *humour noir.* It is macabre and grotesque, but in an offbeat, fun-loving way. In offering bizarre situations and weird ethical dilemmas the film rebuffs the simplistic response. Contradictory emotions abound.

■ With the increased exposure that video distribution affords, *Spider Baby* will perhaps receive the attention that has long been its due. If not, the film remains one of the best examples of extreme, idiosyncratic cinema both witty and macabre. ■

GEORGE ROMERO

ESSAY BY MARK SPAINHOWER

George Romero's infamous trilogy of "Dead" films—*Night of the Living Dead, Dawn of the Dead* and *Day of the Dead*—have provoked not just visceral response but serious critical debate, and for good reason. Not only are these movies capable of inflicting dizzying levels of tension and paranoia, they all carry a heavy freight of potent psychological elements and tribal, group-behavioral and political concepts.

■ The films in this "survivalist" series—which span 17 years between them—share the common themes of *territorial defense, self-defense,* and *the invader within.* Each movie depicts the efforts of small groups of humanity to secure their lives and environments against hostile armies of animated, flesh-eating corpses.

■ Ever-present is the tense awareness that each living body is a potential zombie; hence the continual foreboding that boarded-up windows, camouflaged elevator shafts and underground military fortresses are ultimately futile gestures against a ravenous, inexorable enemy capable of surfacing *under your very skin* ... Romero's masterful handling of pacing and action, combined with his ironic wit and profound sensitivity for the mechanics of fear and paranoia, have earned for these three movies a unique stature in the annals of horror cinema.

■ In the first film, *Night of the Living Dead* (1968), Romero communicates raw paranoia untarnished by sentiment, projecting a vision of pure nihilism—all at the expense of the horrified audience's sensibilities. For sheer, unrelenting ter-

ror the film remains unparalleled; even though two decades have passed, its nightmare imagery retains the ability to appall an audience.

■ The movie begins with Barbara and Johnny, a sister and brother who've driven to an isolated Pennsylvania cemetery to place a cross on their grandfather's grave. As the skies darken, Johnny remembers how as a child Barbara had been afraid of the cemetery, and begins to tease her: "They're coming to get you!" Noticing a man staggering toward them, he cries, "Look! Here comes one of them now!" Appropriately enough, the stranger suddenly attacks her. Johnny rushes to her aid, is immediately killed, and the attacker pursues her to a farmhouse where she locks herself in, only to find the building deserted and the phone out of order.

■ In the meantime, other blank-eyed strangers have joined Barbara's attacker outside in ominously circling the building. At the top of a flight of stairs she stumbles on a half-eaten corpse; screaming with terror she flees outside straight into the glare of a truck's headlights. Ben, a young black man, gets out and pushes her back inside the farmhouse, locking the door. Desperately he asks, *Does she live here? Is there a key to the gas pump in front? How many of those "things" are out there?*—but Barbara has retreated into catatonia, shocked out of her wits.

■ Ben proceeds to board up the windows and doors of the entire house (discovering a rifle and ammunition in his search for tools), and informs her that the phenomenon seems to be happening everywhere—people are being attacked and killed for no apparent reason by people who seem to be in a trance. Suddenly, a door to the cellar swings open—five other people have been hiding downstairs as well: the Cooper family (Harry, Helen and their injured daughter, Karen) and two teenage lovers, Tom and Judy.

■ Immediately a conflict arises: Harry scoffs at the makeshift barricades, insisting that "the cellar is the only safe place," while Ben maintains that by remaining upstairs, they're better able to anticipate and forestall attackers. Finally Ben declares, "You go be the boss in the cellar—*I'm* boss up here," thus splitting the group into two factions.

■ The full horror of the situation is revealed when the group finds a television and learns that all over the country bodies of newly dead are coming back to life, killing and eating the flesh of any victims they can find. Outside, the zombies gain in number while their prey desperately barricade the house against imminent siege.

■ In the cellar they discover the keys to the gas pump outside. Tom and Ben volunteer to fill Ben's truck with gas while Harry throws Molotov cocktails from the upstairs window as a diversionary tactic. As they unboard the doors, Judy suddenly bolts, crying, "I'm going with them!"

■ The three drive to the pump, fending off ghouls with torches and gunfire. Unfortunately, gas splashing onto the truck is ignited by a clumsily-dropped torch—incinerating Tom and Judy. This abortive escape attempt provides a cannibalistic feast for the living dead in a scene so disturbing it continues to be regularly excised from televised screenings.

■ Ben manages to make his way back to the house, only to find himself locked out by the cowardly Harry. Breaking his way in, Ben secures the door and then vengefully beats Harry into submission ... The power fails, and the siege begins again in earnest, with the zombies now *inside.* As boarded-up windows begin to splinter, Ben lays down his rifle to bolster the rapidly disintegrating barrier. Seeing his chance, Harry grabs the rifle and tells Ben, "You want to stay up here—you can." Ben grabs the gun away and shoots Harry, who tumbles downstairs into the cellar.

■ The zombies' attack is gaining in force and vehemence. Finally all hell breaks loose as the makeshift fortress of Barbara, Helen and Ben crumbles under the zombie onslaught; our shock and dismay deepen as the living are methodically destroyed one by one. The once-dead Johnny returns for his sister Barbara, dragging her into the frenzied melee of ghouls; Helen is butchered with a garden spade by her now-zombie daughter; and Ben, the final survivor, is mistaken for a zombie by a posse of redneck gunmen who blow his brains out. The nihilism is complete: the dead have "won."

■ Some critics have pointed out the film's psychological and thematic inheritance from '50s "Invasion" films, e.g. *Invaders from Mars, Invasion of the Body Snatchers, Invisible Invaders,* et al. Others have tied in the *EC* horror comics of the same period. Just as these cultural relics illuminate the Cold War climate of that era, *Night's* cinematic images of invasion, paranoia, cannibalism, matri- and sororicide, etc, as as well as subtextual levels of inarticulate racism, were widely discussed as metaphors for the turbulent and unprecedented social upheavals of the mid-sixties. Meanwhile other, more predictably outraged critics (such as Roger Ebert, whose disparaging polemic appeared in the June, 1969 *Reader's Digest*) saw nothing but gore, gore, gore.

■ A moral ambiguity suffuses the film: while the gore is indeed hideous, it lacks actual *sadism.* Far from being gratuitous, the carnage is simply *there,* a byproduct of opposing biological imperatives ...

■ Romero wields violence with swift determination, accelerating the film's inexorable pace to a plateau of panic when the escape attempt (itself a marvelously executed and choreographed sequence) ends in the incineration of the teenage lovers, whose unlikely status as victims is the first intimation that something *unspeakable* was in the offing.

Coolly and dispassionately Romero's camera reveals carnage in a grainy aura of apocalyptic, dreamy horror, economically sketched ...

■ Throughout the trilogy Romero maintains a radical purity of vision, declining traditional reliance on romantic entanglements, "happy" endings, pseudo-scientific "explanations" or any other of the cinematic cliches so common to films of this genre. There are no "explanations," just as there are no "solutions," Begrudging hints at a connection between the zombie phenomenon and a recently returned space mission are dropped, but the subject of cause-and-effect is bypassed. Instead, Romero concentrates on action and atmosphere, graphically delineating what horror can actually *mean,* and here it means your worst fears, the most terrifying and insane events imaginable—being stabbed, roasted alive, devoured, etc. Here, horror need not explain itself to exist; existence itself is sufficient justification.

■ Romero made the film for $114,000 and peddled it to various distributors—some of whom offered to release it only if it were seriously censored and reshot with a "happy" ending. Happily, Romero declined. The film was released in 1968 and has been in circulation ever since. As part of the Museum of Modern Art's permanent collection, *Night of the Living Dead* immediately set new standards for the aesthetics of horror.

■ Originally a student filmmaker who directed TV commercials and industrial films before forming his first production company, Latent Image, Romero remains a *regional* filmmaker, preferring to pursue his obsessions in the relative obscurity of Pittsburgh, far away from Hollywood.

■ Romero's subsequent films include two curious forays outside the gore genre (*There's Always Vanilla,* a 1972 comedy, and *Hungry Wives,* a 1973 tale of suburban witchcraft—both box-office failures). In 1973 he returned to the themes of paranoia and invasion with *The Crazies.* Similar to *Night,* the plot concerns bungled Army nerve gas experiments which turn the inhabitants of a rural Pennsylvania community into homicidal maniacs—"Why are all the good people dying?" was the question posed by posters for the film. *The Crazies,* too, failed at the box office.

■ *Martin* (1976) was a considerably more provocative departure from the "Invasion" format. Set in the suburban/industrial wastelands of Braddock, Pennsylvania, the story centers on Martin, an alienated young man (interestingly portrayed by John Amplas) with a disturbing penchant for murdering young women and drinking their blood. The film attains a surprising ambience of murky, perverse eroticism. While not a box office smash, *Martin* enjoyed an extended run as a midnight feature, and received much critical acclaim.

■ *Martin* also marked the beginning of Romero's association with Tom Savini, who invented some of the most eye-popping gore effects ever to splatter across a screen.

■ *Night* is completely resolute: it is difficult to imagine an ending more ironic or a sequel capable of surpassing its bleak message. Romero wisely let up on the acute claustrophobia and introduced elements of darkest humor with *Dawn of the Dead* (1978).

■ The most visually luxurious of Romero's films, *Dawn* expands the investigation of territoriality to unexpectedly satiric extremes by confining the action within a suburban shopping mall. Here the four "heroes" (two renegade SWAT cops—one white, one black; and a helicopter pilot and his girlfriend) establish their terrain against the ever-advancing zombies, who have significantly increased in number.

■ Once secured, the four proceed to surround themselves in bourgeois material splendor. Idly ransacking the various stores, inspired as much out of boredom as greed, the heroes while away the long hours alternately mowing down the zombies and enacting a hilariously morbid satire on an ultimate consumer fantasy: goods for the taking.

183

■ Their American dream of material largesse is interrupted by the abrupt intrusion of a tribe of bikers who proceed to loot stores and trash zombies right and left, spraying them with seltzer bottles and tossing cream pies in their uncomprehending faces ... before they, too, are overcome. The gore is even more explicit than in *Night* (thanks to Savini), yet somehow absurd—this movie has some of the *funniest* gore around. While not quite upbeat, the ending of *Dawn* is not as depressingly nihilistic as *Night*—Romero does allow his two survivors (the black cop and the woman—easily the most sympathetic of the four) to escape intact.

■ In the trilogy, especially noteworthy are racial implications—not only does each movie features a *black* hero, but black characters (as well as women) are shown to be intelligent, resourceful, *effective* human beings—as opposed to the sniveling Harry Cooper in *Night*, or the white cop in *Dawn* whose gung-ho attitude ultimately gets him killed. This type of social comment is not usually associated with the gore genre.

■ Romero's political consciousness is most acidly expressed in *Day of the Dead* (1985), the saddest, most cynical of the three films. Isolated in the dismal cinderblock gloom of a vast underground military installation, only a handful of the living remain, miserable and barely sane (no shopping sprees for this unlucky group). Above ground the zombies have triumphed, inhabiting entire cities and outnumbering the living by some 400,000 to one. Within the cavernous installation, internal power struggles pit a civilian scientific team researching zombie-control against macho military personnel there to guard them. In his most merciless depiction of the primitive gunman-mentality to date, Romero brings us Captain Rhodes, a notably despicable redneck defender of law and order.

■ Yet a third faction exists, removed from the idiotic clash of ideologies by their situation and common sense: a radio officer and a black helicopter pilot who dream of a place where a normal life can be resumed. They favor the total abandonment of scientific or military methods of dealing with the zombies. By far the most reasonable and sympathetic of *Day's* characters (with the exception of a female scientific researcher, mentioned below), their markedly apolitical sensibilities are emphasized by their environment. While the rest of the personnel huddle in depressingly sterile, prison-like quarters, these two have transformed their part of the cave into an oasis of human warmth (complete with backdrops depicting tropical splendor)—the only emotionally cheering space within the entire cavern. Yet their arguments are unheeded, and the futile experiments of the scientists continue.

■ Noteworthy in *Day* is the development of three separate groups: the zombies, whom Romero has grown progressively more sympathetic toward; the military gunmen, whom Romero disparages; and media personalities, who have ultimately disappeared. As a former video technician, Romero displays a knowingly wicked flair for depicting TV at its most surreal—witness the cornball commentators and unbelievably bizarre interviews in *Night,* or the bellowing, fatuous experts and officials televised in *Dawn* (at one memorable point, a grotesque, one-eyed, overweight commentator hysterically insists that the populace nourish itself on the flesh of the zombies—an idea which suggests a remarkably efficient food chain).

■ At the end of the trilogy we find one lone, playful Dr. Frankenstein tinkering with the "dumbfucks," using behavior-modification techniques and performing quaint surgical experiments on the rotting housewives and construction workers, in an attempt to domesticate the savage dead ... The result is "Bub," the Friendly Zombie (well, almost). Not only can Bub play a tape deck, thumb through a Stephen King paperback, and salute his commanding officer, he's quite a good shot with a pistol, too ...

■ Initially portrayed as murderous machines, the zombies become progressively more droll with each sequel as the police/military become more vicious. *Day* brings us Romero's most caustic depiction of military "intelligence" to date, in the deeply unattractive person of Captain Rhodes, who commands an equally bestial platoon of subhuman oafs (all of whom get what they so richly deserve).

■ The fascistic Captain Rhodes is hostile to the point of psychosis—at one point threatening to shoot the heroine, a no-nonsense scientist, when she refuses to obey his order to sit down. One assumes his hostility towards her is at least partially due to her gender—for she is easily the strongest member of the scientific team (even her wimpy boyfriend acknowledges at one point, "We all know you're stronger than anyone else. So what—*so fucking what.*"). Rhodes finally murders her two colleagues, including the loveable old doctor (who is caught literally red-handed treating Bub to the remains of the Captain's deceased comrades), and is churlishly discourteous to the very end—screaming "Choke on it!" as the zombies greedily tear him limb from limb. The heroine's mortally-wounded boyfriend has let the zombies into the compound; whether his motives were heroic or merely spiteful is left to the viewer to decide.

■ *Day* ends in much the same manner as *Dawn*—Romero allows his most sympathetic characters to beat a hasty retreat via helicopter to parts unknown. At the film's end we find the heroine, the pilot and the radio officer lounging on a tropical island (reminiscent of the backdrop in their underground haven) ... yet again, the triumph of the zombies is implicit. No one has conquered them, nor won any real victory—the living have managed to survive only tentatively. In the meantime, will the zombies learn how to sail boats?

■ Romero's effect on horror/gore cinema is comprehensive—from the overt plagiarisms of *Zombie, Children Shouldn't Play With Dead Things, Night Of The Comet, Dr. Butcher, Gates of Hell,* et al, to the subtler, more intelligent homage paid by filmmakers such as Wes Craven, David Cronenberg, and even John Waters. Where Herschell Gordon Lewis first charted the perimeters of the newborn territory of gore, Romero's films defined their aesthetic standards, and in the process nearly invented a genre—that of the cannibalistic Living Dead. Regrettably, the *Dead* trilogy is now closed. ■

A-Z DIRECTORY

FILM PERSONALITIES

BY JIM MORTON

The film personalities interviewed in this book represent only a fraction of persons worthy of inclusion. Many outstanding figures are no longer available for interview— some have died, the whereabouts of many are unknown, and at least one has fled the country in fear of his life. Would that we could give every person mentioned here as much space as Herschell Gordon Lewis or Ray Dennis Steckler, but we can't. We can, however, do this much: we can salute them.

AL ADAMSON

Al Adamson's films feature low budgets, acting passable to awful, and dialogue full of non-sequiturs. His first movie was *Psycho A Go-Go!* (Los Angeles, 1965), about a gang of jewel thieves (including a Vietnam vet with a brain implant that makes him crazy) trying to recover the booty they lost. Additional footage featuring John Carradine was added later, and the title changed to *The Fiend with the Electronic Brain*. In 1971 *more* footage was added and the title again changed to *Blood of the Ghastly Horror*. The film also appeared as *The Man with the Synthetic Brain*.
■ In 1969, Adamson teamed up with producer Sam Sherman to form Independent-International Pictures. Their first release was *Satan's Sadists,* about a group of vicious bikers. The film co-starred former dancer Russ Tamblyn as the leader of the gang, and Regina Carrol, Adamson's wife. Released during the height of the biker craze, the film made enough money to finance several more movies.
■ Adamson's best-known film is *Dracula vs. Frankenstein,* the story of a mad scientist operating out of a carnival funhouse. The film stars J. Carrol Naish, Lon Chaney, Jr and features Zandor Vorkov in what is undoubtedly the *worst* Dracula performance by any actor alive or dead (or undead). Like most of Adamson's films, *Dracula* is full of choice dialogue, and also features former *Famous Monsters of Filmland* editor Forrest J. Ackerman in a cameo appearance.
■ Adamson's other films include *Blood of Dracula's Castle, Five Bloody Graves, Horror of the Blood Monsters, The Female Bunch* and *Brain of Blood*.

JOHN AGAR

Leading actor who reached his height of matinee popularity during the fifties, when he starred in dozens of great horror and science fiction films. Among them: *Tarantula, The Mole People, Brain from Planet Arous, Attack of the Puppet People, Invisible Invaders* and *Hand of Death*. Agar got his start in pictures when he received media attention for being the second most-decorated man in World War Two (Audie

Murphy held the top spot). At a Hollywood shindig he met and later married Shirley Temple. They appeared in a few films together, but by 1949 the marriage was falling apart— Agar had developed a bad drinking problem. By 1950 he was no longer sought out for 'A' movies, so he turned to making drive-in fare. During the late sixties he appeared in *Curse of the Swamp Creature* and *Zontar, The Thing from Venus,* made by his friend Larry Buchanan. In 1970 Agar dropped out of acting and became an insurance salesman. Although he appeared in a few films during the seventies—including the atrocious remake of *King Kong*—he never tried to become a full-time actor again.

DARIO ARGENTO

The most talented of the recent crop of Italian horror film directors, Dario Argento knows how to create suspense and deliver one hell of a shock in his slickly designed films. Like his American counterpart, Brian DePalma, he shows a definite Hitchcockian influence. Argento is best known for his strong use of color which in *Suspiria* almost bleeds off the screen. This, combined with a maddening musical score by Italian jazz-rock group *Goblin,* turns the movie into an overwhelming assault on the senses. Argento's innovative color usage seems less striking now than it once was, thanks largely to music videos and modern television commercials.
■ Classic films by him include *The Bird with the Crystal Plumage, Four Flies on Grey Velvet, Cat o' Nine Tails,* and *Deep Red.* Also of major interest is his trilogy about three witches called "The Three Mothers." The first, *Suspiria* tells the story of "The Mother of Sighs." *Inferno* is the story of the "The Mother of Darkness." The third film (yet to be made) will tell the story of "The Mother of Tears."
■ Recently Argento has released *Inferno, Creepers (Phenomena), Unsane (Tenebrae),* and produced Lamberto Bava's *Demons*—L. Bava is the son of Mario Bava. Of his latest efforts the stand-out is easily *Inferno,* which bears a physical resemblance to *Suspiria* but is even more surrealistic—it is one of the closest film interpretations of a dream (or a nightmare) in the history of cinema.

WILLIAM ASHER

Asher directed most of the Beach Party films, including *Beach Party, Bikini Beach, Muscle Beach, Beach Blanket Bingo, How To Stuff A Wild Bikini,* and more. He also directed hundreds of episodes of *I Love Lucy,* and now spends most of his time working in television. Although he has devoted a large part of his career to situation comedies and lighter fare, he is equally adept at suspense. His recent film, *Night Warning* (aka *Butcher, Baker, Nightmare Maker*), is one of the few decent films to emerge from the slasher film glut of the early eighties.

KROGER BABB

Exploitation filmmaker *extrordinaire,* whose showmanship and style remains unequaled. For more information see the David Friedman interview.

starring
FRANKIE AVALON · ANNETTE FUNICELLO
FABIAN · CHILL WILLS

THEY'LL TAKE A CURVE...ANY CURVE!

...The guys who drive faster,
love harder and swing higher
than anyone else
on earth!

FIREBALL 600

FROM
AMERICAN INTERNATIONAL IN
PANAVISION® and COLOR

— also starring —

HARVEY	JULIE					
LEMBECK · PARRISH · *written by* WILLIAM ASHER and LEO TOWNSEND · *directed by* WILLIAM ASHER · *produced by* JAMES H. NICHOLSON and SAMUEL Z. ARKOFF · *co producer* BURT TOPPER

ELIZABETH BATHORY

Hungarian aristocrat who is said to have put over 600 young girls to death because she believed bathing in the blood of virgins would keep her youthful. Her story has inspired several films, including: *Countess Dracula, Daughters of Darkness, The Female Butcher, The Devil's Wedding Night, Immoral Tales* and *La Comtesse Perverse.*

MARIO BAVA

Italian director who started his career as a cinematographer. The first film he directed, *Black Sunday* (starring the queen of mad love, Barbara Steele) was initially panned by American film critics, but later achieved its rightful recognition as a classic horror movie. He followed this with *Black Sabbath;* a trilogy of horror stories hosted by Boris Karloff. Other films by Bava include *Planet of the Vampires,* a stylized science fiction film with supernatural overtones; *Blood and Black Lace,* an early slasher film stylistically similar to the films of Dario Argento; and *Twitch of the Death Nerve* (aka *Bay of Blood*), which was heavily plagiarized by the makers of *Friday the Thirteenth, Part Two.* Like all Italian filmmakers, Bava directed his share of low budget exploitation films. Among them: *Hercules in the Haunted World, Beyond the Door II,* and *Dr. Goldfoot and the Girl Bombs.* In the final analysis, Bava never made a movie as good as *Black Sunday,* his first.

WILLIAM BEAUDINE

Few directors, if any, have made more films than William Beaudine, and few have weathered more criticism. He hit his

stride during the early days of Hollywood when studios were less devoted to big-budget productions and more interested in getting as many films as possible out to the American public. In those days, a western had an immediate audience; if it was a *western,* it could not fail. These took anywhere from two days to two weeks to make. Beaudine dutifully churned them out, rarely lavishing much attention on any of them. His films, along with those of Lambert Hillyer, must account for two-thirds of all the westerns ever made!

■ One of the ways Beaudine kept his costs down (and his speed up) was by avoiding retakes whenever possible. He became so notorious for his refusal to reshoot a scene that he earned the nickname "One-shot" Beaudine. If a boom mike dipped into the frame, if a cowboy started to fall *before* he was shot—oh well. Only the most glaring errors and serious gaffes could induce him to retake a scene.

■ But it was not a western that gained Beaudine his greatest notoriety, it was a film called *Mom and Dad.* First released in 1949 and later in 1955, *Mom and Dad* caused an unprecedented furor. The film is—to a certain extent, anyway—a postwar primer on sexual relationships: in it, a young couple falls in love, has sex, the girl becomes pregnant, the couple weds, and a baby arrives. *In that order.* Purporting to be a plea for adequate sex education, the film indeed does its bit for sex education by showing an actual live birth. At some screenings, men in the audience fainted during the birth scenes. (At that time, few men in America had ever witnessed childbirth; additionally, theaters were under orders to turn off their ventilation during premiere screenings). After someone passed out, promoter Joe Solomon would make sure the press was there when the ambulance rolled up.

Solomon knew the power of the press—*Mom and Dad* was a *hit*. As with *The Exorcist,* people went to it to find out what all the fainting was about.

■ After *Mom and Dad,* Beaudine began to slow down. The heyday of the western was over, and he wasn't much interested in making the teen fare that took over the low-budget field after the war.

■ All but forgotten today, William Beaudine's effect—for better or worse—on low-budget filmmaking, particularly cheap westerns, cannot be underestimated. Curiously, he is one of the few directors in this book who has succeeded in getting a sidewalk star at Hollywood and Vine.

LINDA BLAIR

Out of the current crop of Hollywood actresses, Linda Blair stands out as the premier star of exploitation movies. Her portrayal of the "new fish" in *Chained Heat,* coupled with outstanding performances in *Savage Streets* and *Hell Night,* assure her stature. Other classic appearances include a reprise of her role in *The Exorcist* in John Boorman's screwy sequel, *Exorcist II: The Heretic,* and a television J.D. film called *Born Innocent,* in which she gets raped with a broom handle. Unlike other stars who used exploitation films to further their careers and then denounced them (e.g., Jamie Lee Curtis), Blair continues to give her fans what they want. Her style and appearance are too idiosyncratic for the mainstream market.

DAVID BRADLEY

David Bradley's career started as a director of "tasteful" and pedestrian films like *Treasure Island* and *Peer Gynt;* he also received favorable comments for filming stage productions of *Macbeth* and *Julius Caesar.* But critics quickly turned their backs on him when he switched from Shakespeare productions to exploitation films. He made the shift gradually: first, there was *Talk About a Stranger,* a mildly amusing item about a foreigner who becomes the subject of malicious gossip. The film starred Ronald Reagan's wife, Nancy Davis. Soon after, Bradley made *Dragstrip Riot,* a classic J.D. film that unfortunately was overshadowed by *The Cool and the Crazy,* the film it was released with.

■ In 1964 Bradley made his ultimate film: *They Saved Hitler's Brain;* the title says it all. The shift from *Peer Gynt* to *They Saved Hitler's Brain* is astounding. David Bradley made relatively few movies, but the list of his films betrays either a man of remarkable complexity, or callous indifference . . .

TOD BROWNING

Some might object to including Browning, a successful Hollywood director, in this list. He is best remembered for the original *Dracula* starring Bela Lugosi. However, at the time it was released, *Dracula* was laughed at (there exists eyewitness testimony to back this up). Here Browning gets mentioned for his other classic: *Freaks.* Even today, *Freaks* packs a punch.

S.F. BROWNRIGG

Texas-based director best known for his psycho-killer classic, *Don't Look in the Basement,* about a young nurse who goes to work for a mental hospital unaware that the hospital director is really a patient. Other films include *Keep My Grave Open* and *Poor White Trash II.* The latter film has nothing to do with the original; instead, it tells the story of a Vietnam vet killing hillbillies.

LARRY BUCHANAN

Filmmaker Larry Buchanan grew up in Dallas, Texas. His father, a Texas Ranger, died when Buchanan was four, and the boy spent the rest of his youth in a Baptist institution. As soon as he could, he headed for Hollywood, where he worked both as an actor and assistant director for George Cukor. Returning to Texas, he made *Naughty Dallas,* a film about the popular night spot owned by Lee Harvey Oswald's assasin, Jack Ruby.

■ During the latter half of the sixties, Buchanan was hired by AIP to make eight made-for-television movies—for which he is best remembered. The first, *The Eye Creatures,* is a remake of the Ed L. Cahn sci-fi comedy, *The Invasion of the Saucer Men.* Most of the subsequent AIP-Television films were also remakes of previous AIP films; among them: *Creature of Destruction* (a remake of *The She Creature), Year 2889* (reprising Corman's *The Day the World Ended),* and the unforgettable *Mars Needs Women* (oddly, a serious remake of the teen comedy *Pajama Party).*

■ These films were made on the lowest budgets conceivable. Some of them *(Creature of Destruction, It's Alive!* and *Curse of the Swamp Creature)* used the same rubber monster costume. The most memorable is *Zontar, The Thing from Venus,* a remake of Corman's 1956 classic, *It Conquered the World. Zontar* starred John Agar (in one of his last roles) as a

Scene from **They Saved Hitler's Brain** (aka **Madmen of Mandoras**)

A stripper performs in Jack Ruby's nightclub in the Larry Buchanan film, **Naughty Dallas.**

man trying to stop an alien creature trying to take over the planet.

■ Buchanan is noteworthy for his paranoia. A firm believer in almost any conspiracy theory, he's made several movies purporting to tell the "truth" about subjects that the government (or Hollywood) have hushed-up. Among them: *The Trial of Lee Harvey Oswald, Goodbye Norma Jean* and *Down on Us.* The latter—Buchanan's latest—manages to tie the deaths of Janis Joplin, Jimi Hendrix and Jim Morrison into a weird anti-rock conspiracy plot.

CHERI CAFFARO

Blonde buxom actress noted for her role as Ginger—a female spy who specializes in horizontal espionage. As Ginger, Caffaro appeared in three films: *Ginger; The Abductors* and *Girls are for Loving.* the best is *The Abductors,* about a gang of kidnappers that specializes in training abducted cheerleaders to become bondage slaves for wealthy men. Caffaro brings to the role a tough, slutty charisma.

ED L. CAHN

It wasn't until 1955 that Ed L. Cahn hit his stride. He was hired to direct a low-budget shocker about a gangster who, with the help of a mad scientist, gets even with his enemies by using reanimated corpses to murder them. The film was titled *Creature With the Atom Brain,* and it stands today as a classic example of fifties science fiction. Unforgettable is the scene in which police battle to the death with zombies in front of the scientist's house. The "creatures" in the film wear

189

business suits and ties, and aside from the stitches in their foreheads, appear quite normal. Yet their mundane appearance makes the monsters all the more frightening. Cahn must have realized he was onto something with these grey flannel creatures, since he used them again a few years later in *Invisible Invaders,* the film that inspired George Romero's *Night of the Living Dead.*

■ *Creature With the Atom Brain* was a big success. During the late fifties and early sixties Cahn was one of the most prolific directors in Hollywood, making anywhere from six to ten movies a year! Although he made several westerns, J.D. films and crime dramas, he is best remembered for his horror and science-fiction films. Among them: *The She Creature, Voodoo Woman* (which featured the *She Creature's* body with a different head), *Invasion of the Saucer Men* (a sci-fi teen comedy starring Frank Gorshin), and *It! The Terror from Beyond Space* (the original version of *Alien*).

WILLIAM CAMPBELL

Slimy-looking lead actor who appears in dozens of films; mostly AIP releases. Among his performances: *Cell 2455, Death Row* (in which he plays killer Caryl Chessman), *Blood Bath* (which casts him as a vampire artist), and Francis Ford Coppola's *Dementia 13.*

RENE CARDONA JR. & SR.

American exploitation filmmakers have their Mexican counterparts: the men who make the horror-wrestling films so loathed by Mexican cinéastes and enjoyed by everyone else. Of all these men, none is better at his job than Rene Cardona, Sr.

■ Cardona began his career as an actor but made his greatest impact on world cinema directing movies like *Santo, Wrestling Women vs. the Aztec Mummy, Doctor of Doom, The Brainiac,* and *Night of the Bloody Apes.* His films are fun to watch.

■ Like his father, Rene Cardona, Jr. makes exploitation movies. Unlike his father, however, he has crossed the border with his films, in part by using both Hollywood and Mexican actors. His most successful film to date is *Guyana, Cult of the Damned,* based on the mass suicide of People's Temple members in Guyana. The names have been changed (Jim Jones becomes Jim Johnson), but the story, in a lurid way, is essentially accurate.

■ Lacking most in the films of Rene Cardona, Jr. is the seedy reality displayed in his father's films.

WILLIAM CASTLE

Of all filmmakers in this book, none has exploited his craft as well as William Castle. During the late fifties (when movie attendance was down), William Castle managed to draw people to the box office with a variety of gimmicks: everything from inflatable skeletons to shock-inducing electrically wired theatre seats.

■ William Castle's gimmick mania was born during a stormy

NOT OF THIS EARTH
starring
PAUL BIRCH · BEVERLY GARLAND · MORGAN JONES · A Roger Corman Production · Screenplay by
CHARLES B. GRIFFITH and MARK HANNA · Produced and Directed by ROGER CORMAN · An ALLIED ARTISTS PICTURE

night in Hollywood. Seeing a long line of people waiting patiently in the rain to see *Diabolique*, Castle was struck by an insight. People were waiting in the rain to see the film, he reasoned, because they had *heard* it was scary. Whether it really *was* scary or not was almost beside the point; as long as people were promised the *possibility* of being frightened out of their wits, they would take their place in the ticket line. He contacted Lloyds of London and devised a plan whereby everybody who went to see his film, *Macabre*, was insured for $1,000 against death by fright. Thanks largely to this "fright insurance," the film was a big success.

■ After *Macabre*, Castle never missed an opportunity to add a new slant to his pictures. In *House on Haunted Hill*, theatres were equipped with inflatable skeletons that wheeled out over the audience at the crucial moment. For *Zotz!* thousands of plastic "Zotz" coins, similar to the one in the movie, were handed out. For *13 Ghosts*, everyone entering the theatre was given a pair of "ghostviewers" that allowed you to choose between seeing and not seeing the ghosts (as though anyone would choose *not* to look!).

■ One of Castle's most interesting gimmicks was employed in *Mr. Sardonicus*, the story of a man who, after robbing his father's grave, suffers a strange affliction which turns his face into a horrible, grinning mask. At the end of the film, the audience was allowed to choose whether Sardonicus would live or die. This was done with cards depicting the notorious thumbs signal used by ancient Romans to determine the fate of gladiators. Depending on your whim, you could give Sardonicus a "thumbs up" or "thumbs down" gesture. Audiences almost *never* chose to let the man live, and the film is now exhibited with the "thumbs down" ending.

■ In terms of gimmickry, *The Tingler* is William Castle's *magnum opus*. The film features a host of novelty effects: lights go on during the showing of the film and Vincent Price's voice is heard admonishing people to scream as loudly as they can. The Tingler attacks a movie projectionist and suddenly we are treated to a blank screen while the shadow of the creature marches across it. Although most of the film is in black and white, in one scene we see bright red blood pouring from faucets and a bathtub filled with red blood. But most ambitious was the use of "Percepto," a method of shocking members of the audience by means of tiny motors attached to the bottoms of selected theater seats.

■ As the sixties wore on, Castle's films became less and less gimmicky. He began producing films rather than directing them, gaining a certain amount of mainstream credibility as the producer of *Rosemary's Baby*.

■ His last attempt to add a gimmick to a film was *Bug!*, the story of giant cockroaches that spit fire from their tails. Castle planned to install little brushes beneath the theatre seats, which would, at certain times, brush against the calves of the movie-goers. He nixed the plan when theater owners complained it might cause panics. Besides, Castle figured, most of the theaters showing the film would be providing their own live roaches for free . . . .

ROGER CORMAN

Corman began his career as a screenwriter, but was soon directing more films than almost anyone else in Hollywood, dividing his time and talents between Allied Artists and American International. Working with ten-day shooting schedules on limited funds, Corman was adept at making movies that appealed to youths and critics alike. A common Corman technique was to take a male role and script it for a woman!

■ Although his early output was mostly westerns and crime-dramas, Corman is best known for his horror films, in particular the ones based loosely on stories of Edgar Allan Poe. Some of his best films were scripted by long-time cohort Chuck Griffith, who wrote such favorites as *Little Shop of Horrors*, *Bucket of Blood* and *Wild Angels*.

■ During the seventies Roger Corman abandoned directing and started his own film company, New World Pictures. As a producer he has given several talented directors, such as Michael Pressman and Ron Howard, their first opportunities.

WES CRAVEN

Director who shocked the world with his grimly realistic portrayal of killers in *Last House on the Left*. His next film was the classic *Hills Have Eyes*, about a middle-class family's struggle for survival when their car breaks down in the desert and they're attacked by an inbred barbarian clan. Although talented, Craven is disappointingly uneven. His horror film *Deadly Blessing* could have been a classic, but lacked a needed dimension of outrageousness. Next he made *Swamp Thing*, which right from the beginning held little promise. Surprisingly, Craven turned around and made a classic, *Nightmare on Elm Street*, the story of a dead child-killer who returns in the dreams of teenagers to haunt and kill them for the sins of their parents. Recently, Craven has turned his attention to television, directing several (disappointing) episodes for the new *Twilight Zone* series.

BOB CRESSE

Producer Bob Cresse is responsible for some of the sleaziest films to come out of the sixties. Along with director R. Lee Frost, he gave us such classics as *The Ravagers, Love Camp Seven* and *Mondo Bizarro*. Sadism is a key ingredient; at some point in all of his movies a woman finds herself on the receiving end of a whip. Not one to ask his actors to do something he wouldn't do, Cresse appears in several of his own films and is, happily, just as slimy as his scripts. And what he lacks in acting talent he makes up for with enthusiasm.

■ In *Love Camp Seven* Cresse plays the commandant of a Nazi concentration camp for women used as brothel whores for *SS* soldiers. That some of the men who play Nazis are Jewish adds a strange aspect to the affair.

■ At last report, producer Cresse has fled the country after being shot in the stomach.

CRISWELL

Prophet, soothsayer and good friend of Ed Wood, Jr., Criswell appeared in three of Wood's films: *Plan Nine from Outer Space, Night of the Ghouls* (aka *Revenge of the Dead*) and *Orgy of the Dead*. He has published several books of his prophecies and was once a television favorite in the Los Angeles area. Among his predictions: that entire cities will one day be populated by homosexuals; that the laws of gravity will stop working and icebergs will float through the skies, making air travel impossible; and that the entire human race will go "pleasantly insane."

DAVID CRONENBERG

David Cronenberg manages to make films cerebral enough for the loftiest of critics, yet bloody enough for the most jaded gorehounds. His first major film, *They Came From Within* (aka *Shivers*), is about a condominium infested with slug-like parasites that cause wanton sexual behavior. It is one of the few outstanding examples of "venereal horror."

■ All of Cronenberg's horror films are *biological*. In *Rabid*, a young woman (Marilyn Chambers) undergoes experimental skin graft surgery which turns her into a sort of vampiric Typhoid Mary. In *Scanners*, a drug used by pregnant women causes their children to develop acute psychic powers. In *Dead Zone*, Cronenberg's only film based on someone else's story, the protagonist gains precognitive powers after a serious car accident puts him in a coma for five years.

■ Cronenberg is at his best when at his most personal. Before working on *The Brood* Cronenberg went through a nasty divorce; the effects of which show up on screen. Basi-

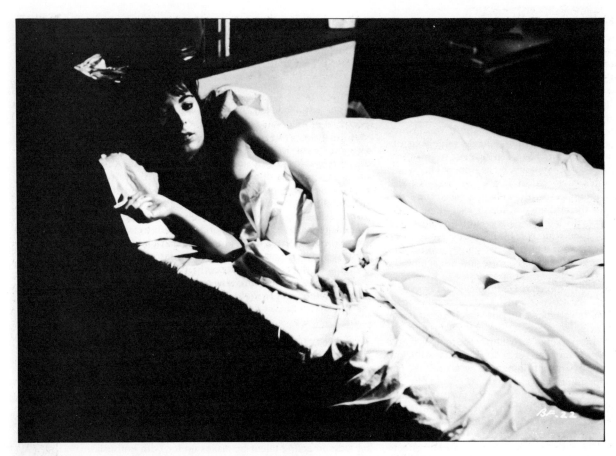

Roberta Findlay appearing as "Anna Riva" in **Body of a Female.**

cally the film is about a man trying to save his daughter from his mad wife, who has the ability to give birth, via exterior womb sacs, to dwarf-like creatures. The creatures, which live only a short time, seek out and bludgeon to death anyone who gets in the woman's way. Eventually the man solves the problem by strangling his wife. After seeing the movie an outraged San Francisco critic compared the experience to that of watching concentration camp documentaries.

■ Even more outrageous is his 1983 release *Videodrome,* the story of a cable TV executive who, while watching pirate videotapes broadcast from a mysterious "snuff film" channel, undergoes a weird biological metamorphosis. During the film we see things as the protagonist sees them; by the end it is impossible to tell where fantasy begins and reality ends. The film did not do well at the box office; Cronenberg's hallucinogenic approach left movie-goers bewildered.

■ Now that David Cronenberg is working in Hollywood, it remains to be seen whether he can sustain his intensity. Reportedly his next project is a film adaptation of William S. Burroughs' pioneering cut-up novel, *Naked Lunch,* to be filmed in some of the actual locations where W.S.B. lived and wrote.

RICHARD CUNHA

The films of Richard Cunha, though few in number, are legendary. As did many low budget filmmakers, Cunha began his career by making industrial films. During the early days of television he worked for Toby Anguish Productions, writing and directing episodes for TV shows. When Anguish decided it was time to retire, Cunha and long-time friend and associate Arthur Jacobs bought Anguish Productions and started their own company, Screencraft Enterprises.

■ Their first film was titled *Giant from the Unknown,* about a very large Spanish Conquistador returned to life by a bolt of lightning. The giant was played by 7' 7" Buddy Baer. Makeup

for the film was handled by Jack Pierce, the man responsible for the makeup in the classic *Frankenstein.* While neither a critical success nor a box office smash, *Giant* did well enough to keep Screencraft Enterprises afloat, convincing Astor Pictures to continue backing the filmmakers.

■ Cunha decided to forge ahead into even more exotic locales. *She Demons* tells the story of a band of shipwrecked people who find themselves on an uncharted island inhabited by beautiful dancers and fugitive Nazis. The Nazis are led by a man who, attempting to restore the face of his beloved wife, performs weird experiments on the dancers, turning them—temporarily—into ugly "she demons." When Irish McCalla (best known for her TV portrayal of *Sheena, Queen of the Jungle*) stumbles onto the island, the Nazi quickly loses interest in his wife and begins making passes at Irish. The situation is resolved when a timely volcano erupts, offering the heroes a chance to escape. Like most truly wonderful films, *She Demons* is a combination of the sublimely ridiculous and the unusually imaginative.

■ After *She Demons,* Screencraft Enterprises was disbanded, Cunha joining forces with Mark Frederic to form Layton Productions. The first film was *Frankenstein's Daughter,* the story of one Oliver Frankenstein, a descendant of the original monster-maker.

■ Cunha's next film is the one for which he is best remembered: *Missile to the Moon.* Astor Pictures approached him with the idea of remaking *Cat Women of the Moon.* Like *Cat Women, Missile to the Moon* was made on a low, *low* budget. To its credit (or lack of same, depending on your perspective), the Cunha film budgeted more for special effects than the original did. The script is somewhat sluggish, but the Gumby-like rock monsters and a description-defying spider puppet make the film a joy to watch.

■ Since 1962 Cunha has eschewed the big screen in favor of the small one, directing hundreds of television commercials.

DAVID DURSTON

David Durston's two films (*I Drink Your Blood* and *Stigma*) seem very different from each other, yet are really quite similar. *I Drink Your Blood* is the story of a group of hippies who come to a small backwoods community, give an old man LSD, and in revenge are fed rabies-infected meat pies. Soon afterward they are reduced to a band of frothing murderers. One of the only ways to fend off the maniacs is by spraying them with water (hydrophobia, get it?).

■ *Stigma* is a different story, but Durston again shows his concern over the effects of contagious disease. In it, a young, black doctor (played by *Miami Vice* star Philip Michael Thomas) takes up practice in a small coastal town where syphilis is rampantly destroying the lives of people. This time Durston heightens the impact by showing a few choice shots of actual V.D. victims. It turns out the cause of the epidemic is none other than the Sheriff's daughter, whose syphilis was congenitally acquired. The last shot shows her fervidly kissing her father, thus reinfecting the source of her disease.

DWAIN ESPER

The father of modern exploitation is Dwain Esper. During the thirties, when the Hays movie code was strictly enforced, Esper circumvented it by showing his films at burlesque shows and road houses instead of movie theaters. By adopting a tone of moral indignation and candid righteousness, he got away with presenting controversial, racy material. His films include *Maniac; Marihuana, Weed with Roots in Hell;* and *How to Undress in Front of Your Husband.* The latter stars Elaine Barrie, wife of John Barrymore. The films all feature glimpses of nudity and displays of moral turpitude.

■ Esper defended his films and supported the movie code as well, reasoning that adults could see adult films and then ascertain whether a film should be seen by children. It is ironic that the very code Dwain Esper defended would eventually cause the deterioration of the adult movie industry.

MICHAEL AND ROBERTA FINDLAY

The most notorious filmmakers in the annals of sexploitation filmmaking are the husband-and-wife team of Michael and Roberta Findlay. Their films include scenes of graphic violence and sadomasochism, as well as some of the most bizarre and imaginative methods of murder ever commited to celluloid. In their early films Roberta Findlay often played the leading role; later, as she took on more technical duties, she moved to smaller parts, and eventually settled into the role of cinematographer. Michael Findlay continued as a director throughout his career. In the early films they used pseudonyms: he was Robert West and Julian Marsh; she was Anna Riva. One of their earliest films was *Satan's Bed*, starring the then-unknown Yoko Ono.

■ Their most notorious work in the sixties was the Flesh Trilogy: *The Touch of Her Flesh, The Curse of Her Flesh* and *The Kiss of Her Flesh*. The films chronicle the exploits of an evil misogynist named Richard Jennings, a man who has a way with murder. In *Touch of Her Flesh* he kills a woman with a poisoned rose: she dances to a frenzied death in the nightclub where she works. In *Kiss of Her Flesh* a pair of earrings is wired for electricity. *The Curse of Her Flesh* features some of the most relentlessly imaginative death scenes ever concocted; in one, a woman dies when Jennings takes her cat, dips its paws in poison and drags the animal across her stomach.

■ Bizarre death scenes became a Findlay trademark. In *A Thousand Pleasures* a man is suffocated by a woman's breast; in *Shriek of the Mutilated* a woman, after being stabbed, drags herself and a toaster across the floor of her apartment. Upon reaching the bathroom the mortally wounded woman plugs in the appliance and throws it into the tub where her hubby is lounging, thus evening the score.

■ But the best-known death scene from a Findlay film occurs at the end of their infamous *Snuff*. Ironically, however, the Findlays had nothing to do with it—the scene, in which an apparently unwilling actress is killed by some "filmmakers," was tacked on later. *Snuff,* originally titled *Slaughter* and based on a script by Michael Findlay that Roberta described as "really awful," was shot in South America MOS (without sound), thereby saving a bundle on sound set-ups and retakes of flubbed lines. Findlay figured he could dub the voices when he got back to New York, and everyone who saw it would then assume it was a foreign film dubbed into English. He was *almost* right.

■ The film he came back with was judged worthless and quickly shelved. But after reading an article in the *New York Times* about the possible existence of a "snuff" movie smuggled into the U.S. from South America, Alan Shackleton of Monarch Releasing Corporation had a brainstorm: with a little reworking, the Findlay film might lend itself to the snuff scenario quite nicely . . . The faked film made a small fortune.

■ Shortly after *Snuff* was released the Findlays split up. Roberta Findlay began her career as a porno director, achieving notoriety when an American film critic announced publicly that her *Angel Number Nine* was directed by a man; the name Roberta Findlay was "obviously a pseudonym." Michael Findlay fared less well. On his way to Europe to demonstrate a new, portable 3-D camera, a helicopter slammed into the roof of the Pan Am building, decapitating him and destroying the camera.

■ Roberta Findlay still lives in New York and continues to work in film, having recently released *Game of Survival* (aka *Tenement*). Preferring privacy to publicity, she generally declines interviews.

COLEMAN FRANCIS

During the forties and fifties this actor-director usually appeared in westerns. In the sixties Francis fulfilled a long cherished ambition—he wrote and directed the immortal *Beast of Yucca Flats,* the story of a Russian scientist who defects to the U. S. with top-secret information. After a high-speed car chase, American and Russian agents shoot it out while the scientist (played by Tor Johnson in his last film appearance) escapes through a nuclear testing site. Exposure to an atomic blast turns the scientist into a monster who likes to kill men and take women back to his cave to drool over. A sheriff's deputy is sent out with orders to "shoot first and ask questions later." Unfortunately the deputy starts shooting at the wrong person, causing much confusion. Eventually all is resolved, with retribution descending from heaven in the form of bullets fired from a police airplane, and the film ends with a particularly poignant scene featuring a dead Tor Johnson and a bunny rabbit.

■ *Beast of Yucca Flats* belongs in that strange sub-genre of The Narrated Horror Movie. Apparently filmed without sound, the film is narrated throughout, with occasional voices obviously dubbed in. The words are sparse and enigmatic; e.g. at one point there is talk of people being "caught up in a web of technology," but what this has to do with the plot is a mystery.

■ Coleman Francis made two more films after *Beast (The Skydivers* and *Night Train to Mundo Fine)* but they were comparatively mundane.

■ By the end of the sixties Francis had fallen on hard times. He appeared in a few Russ Meyer films (*Motor Psycho, Beyond the Valley of the Dolls)* and showed up briefly in Ray Dennis Steckler's *Body Fever* (aka *Super Cool)* before he died.

JESS FRANCO

One of the most prolific and controversial directors working in exploitation today, Jess Franco makes his films quickly and seemingly with little regard to production values. Nevertheless his films have a definite style and flavor. His overuse of the zoom lens is notorious. Multilingual, Franco has made films all over Europe in many different languages. Usually heavily dosed with sex, most of his films are in the horror genre, and several concern the exploits of women in prison. Among his better efforts: *The Awful Dr. Orloff; Jack the Ripper; Venus in Furs; De Sade '70; The Diabolical Dr. Z; Kiss Me, Monster; La Comtesse Perverse* (about Elizabeth Bathory); *Necronomicon; Justine; Vampyros/Lesbos; Night of the Blood Monster;* and *Eugenie ... The Story of Her Journey into Perversion.* Because of their "sexism" and "bad taste," his films are sometimes loathed by even staunch fans of weird films.

R. LEE FROST

Of the many sexploitation directors who started during the sixties, R. Lee Frost is one of the best. He directed several movies and was cameraman on numerous others. Frost had a special knack for showing as much skin as possible without giving the audience the slightest peek at genitalia (a *severe* taboo during that era).

■ During the sixties most of the films Frost worked on were produced and written by Bob Cresse—it's impossible to discuss the career of one without mentioning the other. The team worked well; Cresse had an obvious affinity for sadism and Frost knew how to film it and make it work.

■ Their peak production was the 1968 classic *Love Camp Seven.* Supposedly based on fact, the film told the story of two female Allied spies who allow themselves to be captured by the Nazis. They are taken to a special concentration camp where they're forced to have sex with German officers. There is much degradation and torture, most of it meted out by the camp commandant (played by none other than Cresse). When the movie was released, trailers advertised: "From the people who brought you *Hot Spur* and *Mondo Bizarro* comes another movie of this fine caliber." They weren't kidding!

■ During the seventies, Frost drifted away from the porno film world and now works as an editor at a film laboratory.

ROBERT GAFFNEY

Gaffney made few films, but one of them was the outrageous *Frankenstein Meets the Space Monster,* the story of a robot spaceman named Frankenstein who helps save the world from losing all its women to creatures from another planet.

ED GEIN

In the fifties, this mass murderer who lived on an isolated farm in Wisconsin manufactured various household items and pieces of apparel out of the body parts of his victims, who were mostly passers-by. His curious practices have served as the basis for several movies, among them: *Psycho, Deranged, Three on a Meathook* and *Texas Chainsaw Massacre.* A 20-minute video based on interviews and close-ups of old photographs was filmed, but the definitive documentary has yet to be made.

BERT I. GORDON

Bert Gordon not only writes and directs most of his films, but also creates the majority of his special effects. This in itself is nothing new—Herschell Gordon Lewis went so far as to formulate his *own* brand of stage blood—but Bert Gordon's attempts at special effects, both in scope and imagination, go far beyond those of other low-budget filmmakers. During the fifties, when atomic monsters were all the rage, Gordon convinced his backers he could make movies about giant monsters at negligible cost. And he did so—by extensive use

of rear-screen projection, lots of mattes (a method of placing an object or person, by means of an optical printer, amidst surroundings they're not really part of), and a few postcards.

■ Gordon's first excursion into the realm of brobdingnagia was a rarely shown item titled *Serpent Island.* His lowest-budget production, this film substitutes talk for special effects.

■ His next effort, *King Dinosaur,* is the story of an interplanetary encounter between a giant gila monster and an armadillo. The film was successful, so Gordon decided to tackle even more ambitious material. In *Beginning of the End,* a horde of giant locusts attacks Chicago. In one memorable scene, the insects are shown climbing the side of a building. Upon reaching the top, several of the creatures continue crawling into the sky and out of the frame!

■ Bert Gordon is best remembered for his 1957 classic *The Amazing Colossal Man,* about a man who catches the full blast of an atomic bomb and ends up growing 50 feet tall! The film was so popular it spawned a sequel, *War of the Colossal Beasts.*

■ During the sixties Gordon suffered a dry spell—atomic monsters were "out" and sex was "in." He was never wont to explore *that* subject, a fact that leaves *The Amazing Colossal Man* less of a movie than it might have been! He made a couple of fantasies (*The Boy and the Pirates* and *The Magic*

Movie based on the mass murderer Ed Gein.

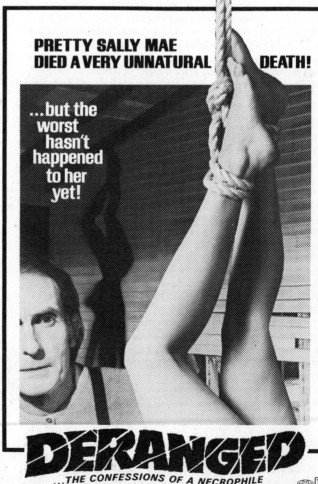

Sword) and a couple of thrillers (*Tormented* and *Picture Mommy Dead)*, but his best effort of the decade was *Village of the Giants,* yet another film about his favorite subject.

■ By the seventies Gordon's films were beginning to look suspiciously alike. *Village of the Giants* is basically an updated version of H.G. Wells' novel, *Food of the Gods.* In 1973 he used the same subject matter again, but this time under the book's title, *Food of the Gods.* In 1977 he remade his locusts movie: *Empire of the Ants* features an army of giant ants which are not only big, but smart.

TOM GRAEFF

Some directors make dozens of movies, but never anything memorable. In 1959 Tom Graeff made only one movie, *Teenagers From Outer Space,* but it's enough to earn him a place in this book. It featured giant lobster shadows and "alien" teenagers in silver jumpsuits and motorcycle helmets.

JOHN A. GRANT

Another one-film wonder, John Grant entered the sexploitation market with *The Sexterminators,* a film about a group of women who take it upon themselves to rid the world of "oversexed" people. In true "roughie" fashion, the movie ends with a castration.

WILLIAM GREFE

Grefe is a director who never quite found his niche. His indifferent morality and slapstick approach to violence were demonstrated in films like *The Hooked Generation* (1968; a tale of drug dealers, ripoffs, and murder which starred William Kerwin) and *Death Curse of Tartu,* (1967; ancient monster seeks revenge for being disturbed), but so far he's never produced a truly wild movie.

JERRY GROSS

Jerry Gross is better known as a producer. He began his career in 1964 with a film titled *Vice Girls, Ltd.* In 1966 he turned out his first attempt at directing: *Girls on a Chain Gang.* Purported to have been shot under extremely adverse conditions in the Deep South, the film was actually made in New Jersey. Next Gross directed *Teenage Mother,* a film title that needs no explanation. By the end of the sixties, Gross had abandoned directing completely in favor of producing. The name Jerry Gross has become associated with low-budget horror oddities such as *I Drink Your Blood* and *The Boogey-man.*

ROBERT GROUND

The technique and style of *The Weird World of LSD* ('67) suggest that Robert Ground is primarily an educational film-maker. The film may be more of a happy accident than an outright *attempt* at deviant cinema.

ARCH HALL, SR.

In 1960, most no-budget independent filmmakers either worked for distributors like AIP and Allied Artists, or went the sexploitation route, establishing shoestring distribution companies to peddle their products. Arch Hall, Sr. formed his

Young Swingers in the Jerry Gross film, Teenage Mother.

distribution company *before* making films. Although he did make one sexploitation film *(Magic Spectacles),* most of his movies are typical sixties drive-in fodder—in other words, *great.*

■ To begin his career Hall wrote, produced and directed *The Choppers* as a showcase for his son, Arch Hall, Jr. The film depicts the activities of a gang of young car thieves. Junior, when he's not stripping cars for parts, takes time out to sing a couple of original songs he wrote, "Kongo Joe" and "Monkey in My Hatband." The film did well, enabling Hall to finance two more films.

■ The first, *Eegah!* was again directed by Hall; this time under the pseudonym "Nicholas Merriwether." He also appears in the movie using the name "William Watters." *Eegah!* tells the story of a teenage caveman found in the desert near Palm Springs. The second film, *Wild Guitar,* is a more subdued tale of a young rock singer's rise to fame and fortune, and the girl who loved him *when.* (Incidentally, this was Ray Dennis Steckler's directing debut.) In both films Arch Hall, Jr. serenades us with several tunes.

■ Although he neither wrote nor directed it, Arch Hall, Sr. also produced an amazing film called *The Sadist* (aka *The Profile of Terror).* Here Junior gave his best performance, playing a demented young man with a vicious hatred of teachers. The film was written and directed by James Landis, and once seen is never forgotten.

■ Arch Hall, Sr. worked with Landis on two more films *(The Nasty Rabbit* and *Deadwood '76),* but in 1966 he stopped producing films. In 1979 he died while teaching a class on

film. Curiously, the ultimate Arch Hall movie is one in which he neither appears nor had anything to do with producing. Titled *The Last Time I Saw Archie,* the film was directed by Jack Webb and chronicles the misadventures of Arch Hall (played by Robert Mitchum) as seen through the eyes of his close friend, screenwriter Bill Bowers (played by Jack Webb). Hall comes off as a likable con man with an inordinate amount of *chutzpah* who succeeds in becoming a governor on the way to the Presidency.

DANIEL HALLER

Starting as an art director at AIP, Daniel Haller is noteworthy for creating the evocative atmosphere in many of Corman's "Poe" films, including *The Pit and the Pendulum* and *The Premature Burial.* The first film he directed was *Die Monster Die!,* about a town full of radiation-deformed people. Based on H.P. Lovecraft's *The Colour Out of Space,* it starred Boris Karloff. Like Corman's Poe films, *Die Monster Die!* is atmospheric to the point of other-worldliness—a dry-ice fog covers the ground in almost every scene.

■ Haller's next effort as a director was *Devil's Angels,* an excellent biker film following the trail blazed by Corman's *The Wild Angels.* But after a few more films of little note, he drifted into television, where he achieved some success directing episodes of *Kojak* and *Ironside.*

VICTOR & EDWARD HALPERIN

These two brothers were early exploitation filmmakers: Vic-

Arch Hall Sr. in **What's Up Front.**

HIDEOUS
BEYOND
BELIEF...
with an
INHUMAN
CRAVING!

AMERICAN INTERNATIONAL'S

QUEEN OF BLOOD
IN PATHÉCOLOR

STARRING
JOHN SAXON
WITH BASIL RATHBONE
JUDI MEREDITH

ALSO STARRING DENNIS HOPPER · Written and Directed by CURTIS HARRINGTON · Produced by GEORGE EDWARDS

tor directed and Edward produced. Their earliest and best known horror film, *White Zombie* (1932), was a successful attempt to cash in on a popular New York play. The star was Bela Lugosi. For its time, *White Zombie* was remarkably lurid, featuring pre-Hays code scanty costumes. A few years later the Halperins tried to squeeze a little more money out of their zombie hit by making a sequel, *Revolt of the Zombies*. The sequel met with less favor. Other horror films by the brothers include *Torture Ship, Supernatural* and *Buried Alive*.

CURTIS HARRINGTON

An unusual filmmaker who began his career making experimental films, Curtis Harrington's initial efforts include *The Fall of the House of Usher, Picnic, Dangerous Houses* and *The Wormwood Star*. His first commercial film was *Night Tide,* an outstanding film fantasy about a lonely sailor who falls in love with a sideshow mermaid. Harrington also gave us *Queen of Blood* (about a hemophiliac Martian vampire), and a "sick" film, *The Killing Kind,* about a psychopathic kid who, while living with his mom, kills people.

RON HAYDOCK

Star and screenwriter for several Ray Dennis Steckler films. Steckler and Haydock first teamed up on *The Deceivers,* a tense drama about the kidnapped girlfriend of a popular rock

star. Halfway through the movie Steckler turned it into a comedy about two bumbling superheros, changing the title to *Rat Pfink and Boo Boo.* A typographical error turned the film into *Rat Pfink a Boo Boo.* In the film, Haydock stars as singer "Lonnie Lord." Haydock was formerly the leader of a rockabilly band called Ron Haydock and the Boppers, so not surprisingly he sings all the songs, many of which were originally released by Haydock's band on 45's from ChaCha Records. Besides helping Steckler, Haydock was an avid horror movie fan, contributing often to the fanzines *Famous Monsters of Filmland* and *Monster Times.* In 1977, while trying to hitchhike back to Los Angeles from Steckler's home in Nevada, he was hit by a car and died.

TOBE HOOPER

The director who shocked everybody with his 1974 classic, *The Texas Chainsaw Massacre.* This film, about a family of cannibalistic killers, set the standard for all future slasher films. What's remarkable is how *funny* it is—although it takes several viewings to truly appreciate the humor. Next Hooper made *Eaten Alive* (aka *Death Trap, Starlight Slaughter,* and *Legend of the Bayou),* a garish tale of a man-eating crocodile. With this film he seems to have taken pains to avoid any resemblance to *Chainsaw; Eaten Alive* is filmed on stage sets with stylized lighting and a chase scene where the victim actually *gets away.* Unfortunately, each successive film (*Salem's Lot, Funhouse, Poltergeist*), is progressively

197

worse; the latest (*Lifeforce*) being the worst yet. Whither to now, Mr. Hooper?

THE ITALIANS

Lumped together here are sometimes marvelous, sometimes inept Italian directors who over the past few years have collectively created dozens of all-too-similar horror movies. They are: Umberto Lenzi, Lucio Fulci, Ruggero Deodato, Sergio Martino, Luigi Cozzi, Antonio Margheritti, and Francesco Martino.

■ The most prolific is Lucio Fulci, who, showing less talent than many of the others, makes up for it in sheer volume. Ruggero Deodato is easily the most bizarre; often his films are extremely sadistic and realistic in their gore. *Cannibal Holocaust* is *the* classic of the cannibal genre (a singularly Italian genre, spawned by Romero's *Dawn of the Dead*). Umberto Lenzi displays a certain amount of technical talent; as does Antonio Margheritti, the "old-timer" of the bunch listed here. Sergio Martino has yet to prove his individuality as a director. Luigi Cozzi is better known to American audiences by the name "Lewis Coates." His version of *Hercules,* starring Lou Ferrigno, is one of the funniest examples of sword-and-sandal cinema.

■ These men are the Italian equivalents of fifties exploitation directors. Before a movie gets made in Italy, the director must answer the question: "What's it like?"—originality being a worthless commodity. However, from time to time these directors manifest a few choice moments of brilliance all their own.

RAY KELLOGG

Ray Kellogg's first film, *The Giant Gila Monster,* is a classic of the atomic monster genre; the story of a boy who sacrifices the thing he loves most (his new hot rod) in order to save his town from destruction.

■ *The Giant Gila Monster* was released on a double bill with another Kellogg film, *The Killer Shrews,* a work that took filmmaking into a realm seldom entered nowadays—the monsters are dogs with fake fangs and carpets strapped to their backs! Such improvisatory genius could not long remain ignored; small wonder John Wayne chose Ray Kellogg to help him direct his outrageous *The Green Berets.*

TOMMY KIRK

Comic actor who started his career with Walt Disney films, appearing in such favorites as *Old Yeller, The Shaggy Dog, The Absent-Minded Professor,* and the standout *Monkey's Uncle* in which he played "scrambled-egghead" Merlin Jones, college whiz-kid. After leaving Disney, he joined Annette Funicello at AIP, appearing in *Pajama Party* where he played a

Martian sent to spy on earth people. Two years later he appeared in a virtual remake entitled *Mars Needs Women!*
■ Without a doubt, Kirk's strangest film of all is *Mother Goose a Go-Go,* the story of a young newlywed who faints every time someone reads to him from Mother Goose. The man's problem is solved after a psychiatrist sprays him with LSD while he is sleeping.

IRVING KLAW

This photographer-publisher made dozens of short films for America's sexual underground during the late forties and early fifties. He started his career as a Manhattan photo store owner, and soon discovered there was a potential gold mine in "girlie" pictures. At first he specialized in pin-up photos, the kind U.S. soldiers used to hang up in their lockers.
■ In the late forties Klaw began emphasizing themes of bondage, with a marked penchant for spike heels and black nylons. Despite his racy themes, Klaw's films apotheosize indifferent cinematography—little, if anything, is attempted in the way of artistic or directorial control. Often the actresses stare past the camera, obviously receiving unheard instructions, and sometimes they laugh when they're trying to look serious. Jump cuts abound.
■ In 1963 Klaw demonstrated, once and for all, his indifference to his art when, threatened with a jail sentence, he burned an entire collection of photographs and negatives. In spite of this indifference (or maybe because of it) Klaw's films are compelling; the actresses (there are no men in his films) appears *genuinely* nonchalant and unpretentious. They seem to be truly enjoying themselves.
■ Although tame by today's standards of anatomical explicitness, Klaw's films are still fun to watch and are treasured by fans of bondage and the bizarre. His effect on the field of exploitation—especially during the sixties, when themes of violence were prevalent—cannot be ignored. Everything from *Barbarella* to *Faster Pussycat, Kill! Kill!* shows the influence of Klaw's little movies and photos. He is best remembered for his photographs of pin-up and bondage star, Betty Page.

BERNARD KOWALSKI

This underrated director made the classic J.D. film *Hot Car Girl,* about the story of a young hoodlum (played by Dick Bakalyan) who ignores the pleas of his squeaky-clean girlfriend to clean up his act. After a drag race in which a cop is killed, the young hood becomes a fugitive from justice, engaging in several robberies before he is gunned down by the police.
■ Kowalski's next film, *The Night of the Blood Beast,* is a favorite among fans of fifties sci-fi/horror movies. His follow-

Typical examples of the photos sold by Irving Klaw.

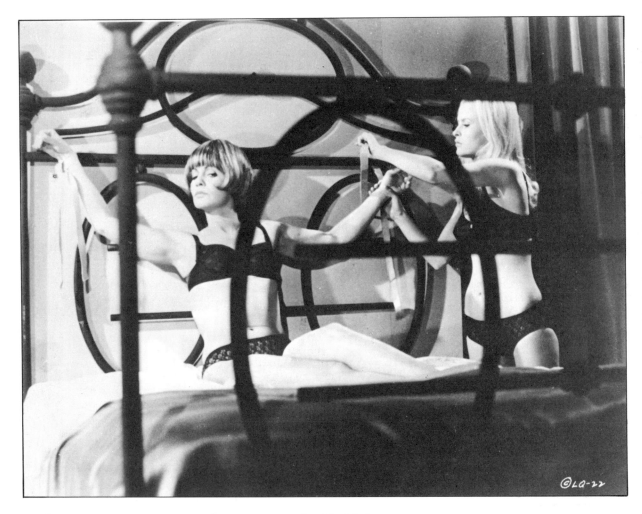

Two couples engage in strange games in Radley Metzger's **The Lickerish Quartet.**

up was the even more incredible, more low-budget *Attack of the Giant Leeches,* which featured Bruno Ve Sota at his slimiest, Yvette Vickers at her sultriest, and a host of poorly-costumed leech monsters. Both films were produced by Roger Corman's brother, Gene.

■ Ironically, Kowalski's career as a movie director is overshadowed by his work in television. Many episodes of *Perry Mason* were directed by him. He also directed episodes of *Banacek* and *Rat Patrol,* and is the executive producer of *Barretta.*

■ Other films by Bernard Kowalski include *Krakatoa, East of Java; Stiletto;* and *Ssssssss,* the story of a scientist who turns his daughter's boyfriends into snakes.

LORNA MAITLAND

A Russ Meyer discovery who, like most Meyer discoveries, has faded into obscurity. Her first film, *Lorna,* the story of a sexually frustrated housewife in rural America, is her best effort. She appeared in two other Russ Meyer films, *Mondo Topless* and *Mudhoney,* as well as two films by Dale Berry, *Hip, Hot and 21* and *Hot Thrills and Warm Chills.*

SCOTT MARLOWE

A moody young actor who made an immediate splash as the heavy in AIP's teens-and-drugs classic, *The Cool and the Crazy.* He had a knack for portraying disturbed young men. Later he would claim this led to an inability to get parts in Hollywood movies. Marlowe's outstanding films include

Blackboard Jungle, Young and Wild, and *Riot in Juvenile Prison.*

CONNIE MASON

The infamous star of Herschell Gordon Lewis' first two gore films, *Blood Feast* and *Two Thousand Maniacs.* Her talent for overacting is unrivaled.'When asked where he found her, Lewis replied, "Under a rock!" Like many exploitation actresses, she began her career as a *Playboy* centerfold—see the June, 1963 issue for details.

JOSEPH P. MAWRA

Of all the sexploitation directors, only H.G. Lewis and Michael Findlay rival Joseph Mawra's talent for screen sadism. Mawra is best remembered for his "Olga" films. Olga, the madame of a brothel, runs a white-slavery ring and indulges in every form of sadism. Unlike most film villains she rarely gets her "just desserts," usually managing to escape scot-free. Mawra's films include: *Olga's Girls, White Slaves of Chinatown, Madame Olga's Massage Parlor, Olga's House of Shame,* and *Chained Girls.*

RADLEY METZGER

Director-producer whose films tread the line between sexploitation and "art." Metzger got his start as a film cutter at Janus Films; he also worked as an editor on independent features including *The Flesh Eaters,* a low-budget horror

Scene from **The Laughing Woman** (Radley Metzger).

movie about amoeba-like parasites that attack a group of island castaways.

■ In the early sixties Metzger formed his own company, Audubon Pictures. At first he was little more than a film broker, buying foreign films and dubbing them into English. The films he released were invariably erotic, and if a film lacked sufficient sexual content, Metzger would add some. For *The Twilight Girls* he added a sex scene starring Georgina Spelvin. For *The Fourth Sex* he added an orgy scene.

■ As a film distributor, Metzger made his biggest splash with *I, a Woman,* a Swedish/Danish coproduction intended for the European sexploitation market. The film, about a nurse who rejects her strict religious upbringing in favor of sexual freedom, made millions and inspired two sequels.

■ During the late sixties Metzger realized his destiny as a director. Because he filmed in Europe utilizing large estates and castles, his movies have an elegant appearance far outshining their budgets. In many stylistic ways his films resemble those of French "New Wave" directors. His films include *Camille 2000,* a futuristic remake of Dumas' *Camille,* and *Therese and Isabelle,* in which a character wanders through an empty schoolyard encountering scenes from her past. In *The Lickerish Quartet*—a standout Metzger movie—the characters find themselves trapped on film, being watched by the people *they* had been watching on film earlier. Thus, the film folds in on itself in a never-ending series of convolutions.

■ During the seventies, when the sex market shifted to hardcore, Metzger adopted the name "Henry Paris" and started making pornography. Like his softcore, his porn films are a cut above those of his peers; *The Opening of Misty Beethoven* is one of few hardcore movies that bear repeat viewing. In *The Punishment of Anne* he treads between hardcore and softcore, with scenes of bondage and discipline so intense they are painful to watch.

■ Currently—after attempting to make a successful "straight" feature, a remake of *The Cat and the Canary*—Metzger continues to direct porno films with his characteristic visual elegance.

DICK MILLER

Character actor in literally hundreds of films, like *The Little Shop of Horrors, Not of This Earth, Sorority Girl* (a J.D. film), and *Carnival Rock*—a 1959 rock 'n' roll remake of *The Blue Angel.* He got his start during the heydey of AIP teenpix, playing characters on both sides of the law. His best role was in Roger Corman's 1959 classic, *Bucket of Blood,* where he played Walter Paisley, a talentless *nebbish* who dreams of someday becoming a famous artist. Paisley's wish comes true after he accidentally discovers that murder can directly inspire the creation of sculpture.

■ Miller is still making movies, often appearing in cameo roles. He has, of late, attained a certain cult status in some horror movie circles.

ANDY MILLIGAN

One of the most controversial directors of all is Staten Island's Andy Milligan, who boasts of never having made a movie for more than $10,000—quite an achievement, considering that most of his 23-plus films are *period pieces* with costumes, etc. (However, he reuses the costumes over and over.) Some critics have dubbed him the "world's absolute worst" director, while others consider him a genius whose singular vision only a few can appreciate. No one is *neutral* on the topic of Andy Milligan.

■ Milligan's films are classic studies in no-budget moviemaking. The key to his money-saving technique is *talk*—Milligan long ago having realized that talk is cheaper to film than action. His films usually feature a brief bit of gore at the beginning (to keep the audience from leaving too quickly), followed by several scenes of conversation (a man and a woman, a man and a man, a woman and a woman, several people, and so on), followed by a bit more gore—low-budget, but always effective.

■ Milligan's filmmaking career began in the early sixties with a film titled *Liz;* producer William Mishkin saw it, had him insert some sex scenes, and retitled it *The Promiscuous Sex.* It did all right, so Mishkin offered him money to film a horror subject titled *The Naked Witch,* which also did well. As in all of his movies, Milligan used his own 16mm camera and did all the photography.

■ It would be three years before Milligan made another film, but once he started, there was no stopping him. In 1967 he released *The Degenerates* and *The Depraved.* The following year he made *The Ghastly Ones; Kiss Me, Kiss Me, Kiss Me; Seeds;* and *Tricks of the Trade.* In 1969 he released *Gutter Trash;* in 1970 *Bloodthirsty Butchers; The Body Beneath; Guru, The Mad Monk;* and *The Torture Dungeon.*

■ Milligan's films usually fall into one of two categories: sex or horror. Sometimes they can be tedious, like *The Rats Are Coming! The Werewolves Are Here!* (1972). But all of his films display his style—summarized by writer Bill Landis as: "period piece settings; sometimes grainy 16mm blowup photography; plots thin yet convoluted; violence ranging from graphic to obviously fake; utilization of horror movie icons like mad priests, vampires, werewolves and hunchbacks; and finally, elements of camp humor." (*Fangoria #20*)

■ With the rising cost of film, it is doubtful anyone will ever again be able to make a movie for less than $10,000, but if anyone can, Andy Milligan can.

WILLIAM MISHKIN

Producer-distributor William Mishkin is legendary for having been one of the first to introduce foreign sex films (called, at the time, "art" films) to the American public. He is also the man who produced most of Andy Milligan's films.

CHESTY MORGAN

An aptly named nightclub entertainer and actress whose breasts measure a full seventy-three inches. She is better known for her posters and photos in "tit" magazines. Two films she stared in, *Deadly Weapons* and *Double Agent 73,* are legendary and incomparable. In *Deadly Weapons* she plays a woman who uses her breasts to kill people—a concept that doesn't take much suspension of disbelief. In *Double Agent 73* she plays a secret agent who has a camera implanted in her left breast. Her assignment: to kill the members of a drug smuggling ring and take their pictures.

K. GORDON MURRAY

Murray is less a producer than a film broker. During the sixties he bought several films from Mexico, dubbed them

(badly) into English and sold them to television. Most Americans got their first glimpse of Santo on television thanks to Murray. Besides the Santo films, he also distributed virtually all the Mexican vampire movies, as well as those featuring the Wrestling Women. Chances are: if it's a dubbed horror film from Mexico, K. Gordon Murray is responsible.

PAUL NASCHY

Virtually unknown in America, Paul Naschy (born Jacinto Molino) is the number one horror film star in Europe. He does his own make-up, creating dozens of characters much like Lon Chaney did; sometimes he is referred to as "The Spanish Lon Chaney." Of his many films, the few that made it to the States are so badly dubbed and edited as to be virtually unwatchable.

■ Naschy also wrote the screenplays for many of his films. His most popular creation is Waldemar Daninsky, a Polish werewolf known in Spain as *El Hombre Lobo.* One of his best films is *Dracula's Great Love,* in which he plays a lovesick vampire who would rather die than spend eternity without the woman he loves. Other standout Naschy films include *La Marca del Hombre Lobo* (released here as *Frankenstein's Bloody Terror*), *La Orgia de los Muertos, El Retorno de Walpurgis, House of Psychotic Women, Night of the Howling Beast* and *El Transexual.*

KITTEN NATIVIDAD

Yet another Russ Meyer find, Kitten appeared in Meyer's *Beneath the Valley of the Ultra-Vixens.* Of all his starlets, Ms. Natividad easily possesses the biggest bust of the bunch, and that's saying a lot! Although no great shakes as an actress, what she lacks in talent she makes up for in enthusiasm. Always fun to watch.

BETTY PAGE

Actress/model who, thanks to the efforts of Irving Klaw, became the archetypal female bondage and domination subject. She appeared in dozens of films for Klaw, none longer than fifteen minutes. Upon watching her old films, one can easily understand her popularity. She was extremely pretty, with a near-perfect figure to match, and she obviously *enjoyed* her work—never losing her spontaneity.

■ Betty Page got her start as a pin-up in the late forties; soon she was very popular. Klaw, whose primary source of income was pin-up photos, was quick to realize her potential in less acceptable erotic forms. Her shiny black hair and expressive eyes lent themselves to Klaw's domination films. Whether playing the role of master or slave, Betty acted out her parts with enthusiasm, and never a frozen expression.

■ Ms. Page's whereabouts today are unknown. She is rumored to have married and moved back to her home state of Tennessee, possibly without comprehending the scope of her influence on the sexploitation industry.

JOHN PARKER

Director John Parker has only one known film to his credit: *Daughter of Horror* which is discussed at length elsewhere in this book. It's too bad critical reaction to his film was so lethal; his talent—which was never again displayed—is indisputable.

JOEL M. REED

Exploitation filmmaker Joel M. Reed makes films that offend the most jaded moviegoers. His most notorious film, *Bloodsucking Freaks* (also known as *The Incredible Torture Show*), managed to draw protesters in *New York City.* When it played in St. Paul, Minnesota, it was billed as a horror movie. Several unsuspecting parents took their thirteen-year-old sons to see it, only to find out it is mostly a sex film.

201

■ *Bloodsucking Freaks* is a mean, sleazy, misogynistic movie with no socially redeeming values. It should not be missed by any fan of deviant cinema. Reed makes his movies on whatever money he can beg, borrow or steal. Considering how low-budget they are, his films—notably *Career Bed, Sex By Advertisement,* and *Night of the Zombies* (1981, starring Jamie Gillis in a non-porn role)—are unusually well-filmed, sound-recorded and edited.

JEAN ROLLIN

French sex/horror film director who specializes in erotic vampire movies. In France he is somewhat of an institution. Over the past fifteen years he has churned out several movies, all with similar themes. Among them: *Levre de Sang, Le Culte du Vampire, Le Frisson des Vampires, Les Femmes Vampires, Vierges et Vampires* and *La Vampire Nue.* Of these films, few have been dubbed into English, and these are rarely screened. Judging from reports, Rollin's films capture just the right balance of sex and blood, eroticism and horror.

JULIAN ROFFMAN

Canadian director who directed only two films: *The Bloody Brood,* about a gang of psychotic, beatnik dope-dealers who feed a delivery boy ground glass just for the fun of watching him die; and *The Mask,* an extraordinary 3-D film about a mask that enables the wearer to see into his own psyche—at the risk of his sanity.

ABEL SALAZAR

The *numero uno* producer of horror films in Mexico is Abel Salazar; it would be difficult to find a horror movie made in Mexico he *didn't* produce. Salazar often appears in them and sometimes writes the screenplays as well. His talent is apparent; the films he is involved in are a cut above the average south-of-the-border product. His films show a strong Universal Pictures influence, but his Mexican outlook gives the movies a special atmosphere. Some titles: *Vampire's Coffin, The Witch's Mirror, The Brainiac* and *Curse of the Crying Woman.*

ERICK SANTAMARIA

Canadian director responsible for a small masterpiece entitled *Decoy for Terror* (also known as *The Playgirl Killer*). The film stars *actor extraordinaire* William Kerwin as an artist whose frustration with models who won't stay still leads to a chilling solution: he puts the models in deep freeze while painting them. The film "features" Neil Sedaka, who only appears in the first half-hour before "leaving for a trip"— but not before he gets a chance to sing a song titled "Waterbug." A classic example of the "Mad Artist" genre; this film is not to be missed!

TURA SATANA

An exotic-looking, half-Japanese woman whose dark beauty and chilly portrayals of strong-willed women have left lasting impressions on anyone who has seen her films. She first apeared in the movies, oddly, as Suzette Wong in Billy Wilder's *Irma La Douce.* But it is her full-throttle performance in *Faster Pussycat, Kill! Kill!* for which she is best known. Her only other screen appearances are in *The Astro-Zombies,* Ted V. Mikels' no-budget tale of cyborgs and espionage; and in *The Doll Squad,* another Mikels film, this one about an all-female team of counter-terrorists. Ms. Satana has retired from films and is currently living in Reno.

JOHN SAXON

Leading actor whose "creepy" good looks are well-suited for roles both as hero and villain. Saxon got his start playing Sandra Dee's beau in the teen film, *The Restless Years.* He followed this with *The Unguarded Moment,* portraying an obsessive young man who attempts to ruin a teacher's career because she spurned his advances. When Hollywood began losing interest in him, Saxon moved to Italy, where he has made literally dozens of films, including *Evil Eye, The Night Caller from Outer Space, Queen of Blood, Cannibals in the Streets, Blood Beach,* and *Tenebrae.*

BARBARA STEELE

Throughout the sixties, Barbara Steele was the undisputed Queen of Horror. Her eerie good looks—with more than a hint of madness in her exceptionally expressive eyes— matched perfectly the Poe-inspired films so popular in those times. She herself admitted, "I love witchcraft, the supernatural, all that's intuitive. I don't like people who are too rational." Her horror career began with Mario Bava's classic *Black Sunday,* in which she plays a beautiful reincarnated vampire. Subsequent roles in *The Horrible Dr. Hichcock, The Pit and the Pendulum, I Lunghi Capelli della Morte,* and *Nightmare Castle* fleshed out her legend as the "acknowledged queen of some of the finest unworldly, eerie films for nearly a decade." Recently she appeared in *Piranha,* David Cronenberg's *They Came From Within,* and *Caged Heat.*

RUSS TAMBLYN

An actor-dancer with impish good looks, Tamblyn was a popular actor during the fifties. He started appearing in films in 1950, at the age of sixteen, but did not receive much attention until 1954 when he appeared in *Seven Brides for Seven Brothers.* Throughout the rest of the fifties Tamblyn appeared in numerous light-hearted films, most notably *West*

Barbara Steele

Tura Satana

Side Story. During the late sixties Tamblyn began experimenting with drugs, and parts in Hollywood became harder and harder to find. After becoming friends with independent filmmaker Al Adamson, he appeared in many of Adamson's best movies, including *Satan's Sadists, Dracula Vs. Frankenstein* and *The Female Bunch.*

WILLIAM C. THOMPSON

Cinematographer whose fine camerawork appears only in the lowest-budget movies. Thompson's *noir* lighting in *Daughter of Horror* is responsible for most of the film's impact. His work for Ed Wood, Jr. is less impressive, but has its moments—can anyone forget Tor Johnson rising from the grave in *Plan Nine From Outer Space?*

DYANNE THORNE

The actress whose performances as Nazi leader Ilsa Koch make *Ilsa, She-Wolf of the S.S.* and *Harem Keeper of the Oil Sheiks* as good as they are. Other films featuring Ms. Thorne in more subdued roles include *Love Me Like I Do* (sexploitation), *The Erotic Adventures of Pinocchio* (she played a fairy godmother), and most recently, *Hellhole,* in which she played a deranged mental patient.

ROGER VADIM

French director who created a furor by introducing America to Brigitte Bardot in *And God Created Woman,* and the opportunity to see *all* of Jane Fonda in the sci-fi comedy, *Barbarella.* Vadim can be tedious—as with *Pretty Maids All in a Row*—but has still given us some great movies. One of his best is the rarely screened *Blood and Roses,* an erotic retelling of Sheridan LeFanu's *Carmilla.* Other standout films include *Les Liaisons Dangereuses, Testament of Orpheus, Of Flesh and Blood* and *Vice and Virtue.*

VAMPIRA

Horror show hostess during the fifties and star of Ed Wood's legendary *Plan Nine From Outer Space.* She also appeared in other films under her real name, Maila Nurmi. During the fifties, Ms. Nurmi spent a lot of time running around with James Dean. After his death, she claimed to be in contact with him. In a published article, she said Dean would call her on the phone even after the wires had been cut. Reaction to her claims was hostile; these days she remains silent on the subject. After her creation of the character *Vampira,* some pale imitations cropped up, but none can hold a candle to the original.

203

BRUNO VE SOTA

Pug-ugly, fat character actor who usually plays heavies because of his menacing, bad looks. His list of credits include some of the best horror movies ever made—a Bruno Ve Sota film festival would be highly entertaining. His films include *Daughter of Horror, The Alligator People, The Undead, Attack of the Giant Leeches, Wasp Woman, Night Tide, Attack of the Mayan Mummy, Creature of the Walking Dead* and *Wild World of Batwoman.*

ANDY WARHOL

Artist/underground filmmaker whose tawdry explorations of New York's "in" crowd (e.g. *Chelsea Girls, Blow Job, My Hustler,* and *Vinyl*) tread the line between exploitation and art. Many Warhol films were done in collaboration with (or were directed by) Paul Morrissey.

HAL WARREN

El Paso fertilizer salesman whose *Manos, The Hands of Fate* is a cult legend. *Manos* portrays what happens to a young couple after they miss a turn in the road and end up at a strange house where they meet "Torgo," a spastic hippie who guards the place when the master is away. After forcing their way in, the couple become frightened by weird goings-on. Eventually "The Master" shows up along with his bevy of wives. There is some talk of other dimensions, a catfight, and Torgo loses his right hand and his job.

■ *Manos, The Hands of Fate* is a joy to watch. It is a true rarity: a film completely devoid of Hollywood influence or conventional filmmaking technique. Jump cuts abound; continuity is non-existent. The editing is *leaden;* it's doubtful if any film ended up on the cutting room floor. If the actors have difficulty remembering their lines, the camera stays on them until they do—no matter how long it takes! Warren was so stingy with his footage that in one scene we catch a glimpse of the clapper as it pulls out of the frame. *Manos, The Hands of Fate* was his first and last attempt at filmmaking.

JERRY WARREN

Producer-director-distributor specializing in ultra-low budget films, including Mexican imports. Unlike fellow importer K. Gordon Murray, Warren eschews dubbing in favor of narration—often radically editing the films he imports to avoid dubbing whenever possible. His films include *Terror of the Bloodhunters, Creature of the Walking Dead, Curse of the Stone Hand* and *The Wild World of Batwoman.* A lawsuit forced him to change the latter title to *She Was a Hippy Vampire.*

ALBERT ZUGSMITH

Zugsmith started his career producing low-budget films, moved to mainstream, and then returned to the world of exploitation. Although better known as a producer, he tried his hand at directing with *College Confidential, Sex Kittens Go to College, Confessions of an Opium Eater,* and others.
■ Zugsmith's first production was the reactionary classic *Invasion, USA* (1952). A group of liberals, drinking in a bar, are hypnotized and shown the danger of their way of thinking, and how easy it would be for the commies to take over the USA. In 1985 the film was remade starring Chuck Norris.
■ During the fifties, Zugsmith worked for Universal-International and Allied Artists, producing some excellent mainstream films such as *Touch of Evil, Slaughter on Tenth Avenue, Written on the Wind* and *Tarnished Angels.*
During the sixties, Zugsmith plunged into sexploitation. In 1965 he worked with Russ Meyer on *Fanny Hill,* not one of Meyer's better efforts. Later he added his own directorial touches to the genre with *The Incredible Sex Revolution, On Her Bed of Roses* and *Movie Star, American Style, Or, LSD, I Hate You!* ■

The hunt for a rapist leads cops into the world of beatniks in The Albert Zugsmith production, The Beat Generation.

MISCELLANEOUS

QUOTATIONS

This is the universe. To the maggots in the cadaver, the cadaver is infinity. And to you: What is **your** world? How do you know what is beyond the beyond?

—Mondo Bizarro

You don't have to know a man to live with him ... but you have to know a man like a brother to kill him.

—Blast of Silence

Total chaos; that's what I like! Out of chaos comes reason. Out of reason, science.

—God Told Me To

I died for you ... Now why shouldn't you return the favor?

—Deathdream

I must experience the greatest act of the human mind: to take another life!

—The Mask

Ever drop a canteloupe from 40 stories?

—Q

MOTHER: I don't see how you can prefer Jerry to Phil when Phil is such a nice boy.
ANGELA: I like Jerry. Phil just isn't my type.
MOTHER: You're fascinated by Jerry because he's different. He isn't like any of the boys you know.
ANGELA: Mother, Jerry's fun—he's exciting. We go places I never dreamed of before.
MOTHER: You're right at the age when you could make a terrible mistake.
ANGELA: And you think Jerry would be a mistake?
MOTHER: Yes, I do. Jerry has no education. He'll

never be able to make a living.
ANGELA: Oh, mother!
MOTHER: If you try to build a life with him, you'll be miserable.
ANGELA: Really, Mother! You're way ahead of me. I just have fun with Jerry, that's all.
(horn honking)
—Incredibly Strange Creatures

Ladies and gentlemen, welcome to violence; the word and the act. While violence cloaks itself in a plethora of disguises, its favorite mantle still remains sex.

—Faster Pussycat, Kill! Kill!

Aren't those crimes horrifying. And yet—so fascinating!

—Daughters of Darkness

Even dying is an act of eroticism.

—They Came From Within

JERRY: Hey, are things that bad you gotta wash your own car?
MADISON: Things are rough all over.
JERRY: Yeah, the world's in a state of depression.
—Incredibly Strange Creatures

Give this man satin undies, a dress, a sweater and a skirt, or even a lounging outfit, and he's the happiest individual in the world. He can work better, play better, and he can be more of a credit to his community and his government because he is happy.

—Glen or Glenda

Going Steady

I've always thought the profession of **butcher** is an honorable one. What would we do without them? They have chosen the profession that is beneficial to us all. They slaughter and chop up their victims so that the rest of us have the wherewithal to live.

—Snuff

The Aztecs identified flayed skin with the new garments of young vegetation . . .

—Q

JERRY: Angie, baby! . . . How's college?
MADISON: Fine. You should try it some time.
JERRY: No, thanks. The world's my college.

—Incredibly Strange Creatures

A man runs. Somebody shoots at him.

—Beast of Yucca Flats

What is real? Are you certain you know what reality is? How do you know at this second you aren't asleep in your bed, dreaming that you are here . . . ?

—The Wizard of Gore

Let a man or woman venture from the well-beaten path of civilization, let him cross the threshold of the limited intellect, and he encounters amazing and wondrous things: the unknown and terrible. If he escapes with his life, he will usually find he left his reason behind him.

—Mesa of Lost Women

How can you run from a dead person, unless you're dead yourself?

—Venus in Furs

Torture and terror have always fascinated mankind. Perhaps, whatever made your predecessors see the sadism of the inquisition and the gore of the gladiators' arena is the same thing that makes you stare at bloody highway accidents and thrill to the terror of death in the bullring. Today, television and films give you the luxury of observing grisly dismemberments and deaths without anyone actually being harmed.
—The Wizard of Gore

The chief enemy of creativity is 'good' taste.
—Pablo Picasso

She was beautiful, even though she was dead.
—Venus in Furs

I was disgusted, but I was fascinated, too . . . I didn't want to watch, but I couldn't help it.
—The Amazing Transplant

You've only dreamed there were women like this, until now. But they're real! Unbelievably real!
—Mondo Topless

Thy form is fair to look upon, but thy heart is filled with carcasses and dead men's bones.
—Lorna

I'm going to awaken you from this earthly nightmare . . . awaken you to the sweet repose of . . . death!
—The Love Butcher

Show me a crime and I can show you a picture that could've caused it.
—The Sinister Urge

This is the age of the non-entity. The glorification of the nobody. As long as they're victims. Look at the virtually non-existant careers of Dorothy Stratton, or Frances Farmer. What makes them worthy of a ten million dollar eulogy on film? Murder, madness,

suicide; that's what stars are made of today.
—Special Effects

After Mr. Edison made these tintypes gallop, it wasn't but two days later that some enterprising guy had his girlfriend take her clothes off and that's how exploitation began.
—David Friedman

You were born with hate and anger built in . . . took a slap on the backside to blast out the scream . . . and then you knew you were alive.
—Blast of Silence

Shared love knows no bounds . . . but it's so degrading!
—Daughters of Darkness

Despite Brett's inquiries about what Martin had seen in the spacecraft, he avoided specific details for fear of disturbing her more than she was. If the truth were known, Martin was more than a little disturbed himself.
—The Creeping Terror

This is a story of violence . . . a violence born of the uncontrolled passions of adolescent youth, and nurtured by this generation of parents—those who, in their own smug little world of selfish interests and confused ideas of parental supervision, refuse to believe today's glaring headlines.
—The Violent Years

You can't get blood out of an illusion.
—The Lickerish Quartet

The tarantulas began to yield amazing results—they grew as large as human beings. They began developing new reasoning powers and I found I had the telepathic power to communicate with them. Then I reversed the process, transplanted the control substance of the insect back into the human body. Doctor, look at this girl—I call her Tarantella . . . If we are successful, I shall have a super-female spider!
—Mesa of Lost Women

No ... No ... You can't do these things! You're tampering with the work of the Creator! You're—evil!

—Mesa of Lost Women

You must remember—blood must be given willingly for the gods to appreciate it.

—Q

—It wouldn't be the first time in history that a monster was mistaken for a god.
—I doubt if New Yorkers would take it as a god.
—Why not, if they come to fear it enough?

—Q

Do you believe the whole world runs by the few laws of the sciences we have been able to discover? There is more; much more. But people are satisfied. They know so much, they think they know it all.

—Martin

Sacrifices to your god are nothing new. Why are you looking at me like I'm the first?

—God Told Me To

The only way the lord has ever successfully disciplined us is through fear. Kill a man and you impress a few people who already believe anyway. Kill a multitude and you can convince a nation.

—God Told Me To

Regrettable ... I was hoping for a colleague, but at least we have another experimental subject ...

—Mesa of Lost Women

—Why can't you get married and have a home of your own?"
—Because I've never found a man I'd want to marry. The ones who'd make good family men are so dumb I couldn't stand them. The ones I like are so worthless I'd starve.

—Mad Youth

Torture! Torture! It pleasures me!

—Orgy of the Dead

Every case history tells the same story. A story that's a tragic pattern of men and women's lives. The cause: marijuana. This harmless looking cigarette is cloaked in many innocent disguises. But light the match, and inhale the smoke, and it becomes an invitation to your own murder. This killer and the man who sells it have no respect for anybody. His victims are any lost souls; it matters not to whom the souls belong. The seller's method of operation, Simple: keep the mind from thinking. The mind thinks; the world becomes a real thing, with troubles and problems without the answers. But he has the answer. Escape! Sell the dreams people want to dream. Keep them from waking up. Because once they do, you're out of business. Of course, the rich can afford to pay more for their dreams. It's a profitable game. And when boredom sets in, heroin, cocaine and opium are always the next steps; at higher prices. If you live that long.

—She Shoulda Said No

I am Criswell! For years I have told the almost unbelievable, related the unreal and showed it to be more than a fact. Now I tell the tale of the threshold people, so astounding that some of you may faint!

—Orgy of the Dead

—Say, uh...where's the kid that was born?
—Oh. Why the baby died. Didn't I tell you?
—No. No one ever tells me nothin' around here.
—We did our best.
—Well, that's alright. One less mouth to feed.

—Tomorrow's Children

Ah, the curiosity of youth. On the road to ruin! May it ever be so adventurous!

—Orgy of the Dead

It is said on clear nights beneath the cold light of the moon, howl the dog and the wolf; and creeping things crawl out of the slime. It is then the ghouls feast in all their radiance.

—Orgy of the Dead

Here you are, folks—the biggest bargain to hit the midway. They'll thrill you. They'll kill you. You'll even ask for more. Twenty beautiful girls. Supple as a serpent; twisting, writhing and twining...The most spectacular show to hit the midway!

—The Incredibly Strange Creatures

Hollywood, California. The man you're looking at is Joe Saxon. He's one of many caught in the web of non-reality. **Non-reality.** This is the reason he is here in Hollywood—land of the stars. Joe's ambition is to be one. A star—a star of motion pictures—that world of make-believe. So far Joe has had very little success, for that road to stardom can be a long and hard grind. Unfortunately, Joe has refused to accept the world of reality and has found himself trapped amongst the monthly payment plans. He's got a new house, a new car, a new TV set, swimming pool. Very impressive to the people here in Hollywood. But unless the monthly payments are kept up, there won't be any TV sets or swimming pools.
Time to call his wife and give her the news of today. This is Joe's wife Liz, former actress turned artist. She gave up the business a long time ago. The insecurity was too much for her, but then she met Joe and love won out. But love can also wear out, and the bills keep coming and the stomach starts to get hungry. But Joe has another hunger—to be a movie star, even if he has to play make-believe all day, just for himself. Joe Saxon ... caught in the world of **non-reality.**

—The Incredibly Strange Creatures

MOVIE POSTERS QUOTES

Her other love is God ... Within the walls of the convent of Monza, our Sister Virginia was violated ... She fell in love like any other woman.

—The Lady of Monza

From penthouse to playgirl: she was a lady ... but wanted to be treated like a tramp.

—The Agony of Love

Sex-starved girls ... forced to use their guns and bodies to satisfy the man who owned them ... he even seduced his own sister!

—The Dirty Dolls

Norma had a way with men ... and they with her!!!

—Norma

From the shadows of their sordid haunts ... they slither like predatory beasts to stalk their prey! Hell is their only address and they offer you a cheap substitute for fulfillment in exchange for your soul! Depraved ... Demented ... Loathsome ... Nameless ... Shameless ... These are the—

—Scum of the Earth!

Mad creatures of the night existing only for sensual sadistic moments of HUMAN SLAUGHTER!

—The Ghastly Ones

Nothing has ever stripped your nerves as screamingly raw as—

—The Gore Gore Girls

If I were to describe in detail what goes on in 'Inga', I'd get arrested.

—Robert Salmagg, WINS Radio

Mondo Bizarro

See the rack-thumb screw-iron maiden torture drugs that make men slaves. Bizarre human sacrifices—today! An authentic catalog of cruelty. Actually filmed in the Dark Corners of This Sick World!

—Sadismo

A thousand thrills crammed into one hundred minutes! Bizarre, barbaric sights never before put on film! Violent beyond belief . . . yet beautiful beyond comparison! Ask your friends—they can't stop talking about it! An incredible orgy of Sights and Sounds!

—Ecco

It's the film that starts where the other MONDO pictures chickened out!

—Taboos of the World

The dead are hungry . . . and they're coming to eat you alive!

—Night of the Zombies

The film that uncovers the lid of small town hate!

1) When you come back from the fields tonight, I'm going to give you the beating of your life!
2) They said I could go off with her to Perkin's Motel and she'd be real cooperative!
3) Nellie—the town's plaything. She passed for white and they loved it!

—Girl on a Chain Gang

Nothing so appalling in the annals of horror! You'll recoil and shudder as you witness the slaughter and mutilation of nubile young girls—in a weird and horrendous ancient rite! (An Admonition: if you are the Parent or Guardian of an impressionable adolescent DO NOT BRING HIM or PERMIT HIM TO SEE THIS MOTION PICTURE.) More grisly than ever in BLOOD COLOR!

—Blood Feast

An entire town bathed in pulsing human blood! Madmen crazed for carnage! Brutal . . . evil . . . ghastly beyond belief! . . . Gruesomely stained in Blood Color!

—2000 Maniacs

FAVORITE FILMS

This list, compiled by Jim Morton and Boyd Rice, represents just a fraction of movies worth seeing. Thousands more await your viewing pleasure!

Abductors, The (1972)
Abominable Dr. Phibes, The (1971)
Acid Eaters, The (1968)
Act of Seeing With One's Own Eyes (1972)
Amazing Transplant, The (1970)
Astro-Zombies, The (1968)
Attack of the Robots (French, 1966)
Atom Age Vampire (1961)
Atomic Cafe (1982)
Baby, The (1974)
Basket Case (1982)
Beast of Yucca Flats (1961)
Beat Generation, The (1959)
Beyond the Valley of the Dolls (1970)
Big Doll House, The (1971)
Black Jesus (1971)
Black Shampoo (1976)
Black Sunday (1961)
Blast of Silence (1961)
Blood Feast (1963)
Blood Mania (1971)
Blood of the Virgin (Mexican)
Bloodsucking Freaks (1978)
Bloodthirsty Butchers (1970)
Blue Sunshine (1978)
Body Fever (1970)
Brain That Wouldn't Die, The (1959)
Brood, The (1979)
The Bubble aka Fantastic Invasion of Planet Earth (1966)
Bucket of Blood (1959)
Cafe Flesh (1982)
Caged! (1950)
Carnival of Souls (1962)
Cat Women of the Moon (1953)
Chained for Life (1950)
Chained Heat (1983)
Cherry, Harry and Raquel (1969)
Child Bride (1941)
Children, The (1980)
Cobra Woman (1944)
Color Me Blood Red (1965)
Cool and the Crazy, The (1958)
Corpse Grinders, The (1971)
Creature with the Atom Brain (1955)
Creeping Terror, The (1964)

Curse of Her Flesh (1968)
Curse of the Doll People (1960)
Curucu, Beast of the Amazon (1956)
D.I., The (w/Jack Webb, 1957)
Damaged Lives (1933)
Daughter of Horror (1955)
Daughter of the Sun (1962)
Daughters of Darkness (1971)
Day the Earth Froze (1959)
Decoy for Terror (1970)
Defilers, The (1965)
Dementia aka Daughter of Horror (1955)
Depraved! (1967)
Deranged (1974)
Devil Doll, The (1963)
Devils, The (1971)
Don't Go In The House (1980)
Double Agent 73 (1974)
Dracula vs. Frankenstein (1969)
Dragnet (1954)
Dragon Zombies Return (1983)
Eaten Alive (1976)
Eegah! (1962)
Eighteen and Anxious (1957)
Endless Love (1981)
Equinox (1967-71)
Eraserhead (1977)
Exorcist II; The Heretic (1977)
Eyes Without A Face (1959)
Faces of Death (1981)
Faces of Death II (1984)
Far Reef, The aka Beyond the Reef (1981)
Faster Pussycat, Kill! Kill! (1965)
Female Butcher (1972)
Female Trouble (1974)
Freaks (1932)
Frozen Dead, The (1967)
Garden of Eden (1954)
Girl Can't Help It!, The (1956)
Glen or Glenda (1953)
God Told Me To aka Demon (1976)
Godzilla (1954)
Gore-Gore Girls, The (1972)
Great Hunting 1984, The
Gruesome Twosome, The (1968)

Gun Crazy (1949)
Guyana—Cult of the Damned (1980)
Having a Wild Weekend (1965)
Hellhole (1984)
Hercules (1983)
High School Confidential (1958)
Honeymoon Killers, The (1970)
Horrible Dr. Hichcock (1962)
Horror of Party Beach, The (1964)
Horrors of the Black Museum (1959)
House of Whipcord (1974)
Human Duplicators (1965)
Hypnotic Eye, The (1959)
I Dismember Mama (1972)
I Drink Your Blood (1971)
I Was a Teenage Frankenstein (1957)
Ilsa; Harem Keeper for the Oil Sheiks (1975)
Ilsa; She-Wolf of the SS (1974)
Immoral Tales (1974)
In the Land of the Headhunters
Incredibly Strange Creatures, The (1964)
Inferno (1980)
Insects as Carriers of Disease (1945)
Invader (1955)
Invasion of the Blood Farmers (1972)
Invitation to Ruin (1956)
It's Alive! (Larry Buchanan, 1968)
It's Alive! (Larry Cohen, 1974)
It Lives Again! (1978)
Jailbait (1955)
Juvenile Jungle (1958)
Kitten with a Whip (1964)
Land without Bread (Bunuel, 1932)
Last Date, The (1950)
Last House on Dead End Street (1977)
Last House on the Left (1972)
Last Prom, The (1954)
Let Me Die a Woman (1932)
Lickerish Quartet, The (1970)
Little Shop of Horrors (1960)
Live Fast, Die Young (1958)
Lorna (1964)
Love Butcher, The (1975)
Love Camp Seven (1968)
Love Me Deadly (1972)

Loved One, The (1965)
LSD-25 (1967)
Macabre (1958)
Mad Love (1935)
Maniac! (1934)
Manitou, The (1978)
Manos, the Hands of Fate (1966)
Mantis in Lace aka Lila (1968)
Marihuana—Weed with Roots in Hell
(1935)
Martin (1977)
Mask, The (1961)
Mechanized Death (1961)
Mesa of Lost Women (1952)
Mr. Rellik (drivers' ed film)
Mr. Sardonicus (1961)
Mom and Dad (1948)
Mondo Balordo (1964)
Mondo Bizarro (1966)
Mondo Cane (1963)
Mondo Hollywood (1967)
Mondo Mod (1967)
Mondo Pazzo (1965)
Mondo Teeno (1967)
Mondo Topless (1967)
Mondo Weirdo (1965)
Monster a Go-Go (1965)
Moonlighting Wives (1966)
Moses the Lawgiver (1975)
Mothra (1962)
Motor Psycho (1965)
Mudhoney (1965)
Mutations (1972)
Night of the Bloody Apes (1968)
Night of the Ghouls (1959)
Night Tide (1961)
Nightmare Alley (1947)
Octaman (1971)
Of Unknown Origin (1984)
Orgy of the Dead (1965)
Peeping Tom (1960)
Pink Flamingos (1974)
Plan Nine From Outer Space (1959)
Point of Terror (1971)
Poor White Trash (1957)
Private Parts (1972)
Psychopath, The (1973)
Punishment of Anne, The
Q (1982)
Rabid (1977)
Rat Pfink a Boo Boo (1966)
Red Asphalt
Reform School Girls (1957)
Repulsion (1965)
Riot on Sunset Strip (1967)
Robot Monster (1953)
Robot vs. the Aztec Mummy, The (1959)
Sadismo (1967)
Sadist, The (1963)
Safety Belt for Susie (1963)
Safety in the Shop (1944)
Salon Kitty aka Madame Kitty (1976)
Santo in the Wax Museum (1963)
Satan's Sadists (1969)
Scorpio Rising (1964)

Russ Tamblyn in Satan's Sadists.

Scream, Baby, Scream (1969)
Sex Hygiene (1942)
Shack Out on 101 (1955)
She Freak, The (1966)
She-Devils on Wheels (1968)
Shock Corridor (1963)
Shock Waves (1977)
Shogun Assassin (1974)
Shriek of the Mutilated (1974)
Signal 30 (1959)
Something Weird (1966)
Special Effects (1984)
Spider Baby (1964)
Star Pilot (Italian, 1966)
Sugar Hill (Blaxploitation, 1974)
Supervixens (1975)
Suspiria (1976)
Swimmer, The (1968)
Taboos of the World (1965)
Teenagers from Outer Space (1959)
Terrified (w/Rod Lauren, 1963)
Texas Chainsaw Massacre (1974)
These are the Damned (1961)
They Came From Within (1975)
They Saved Hitler's Brain (1963)
Thirteen Ghosts (1960)
This Nude World (1932)
Thrill Killers, The (1965)
Thunder Road (1958)
Tingler, The (1959)
Tomorrow's Children (1934)
Trip, The (1967)
Two Thousand Maniacs (1964)
Undead, The (1956)
Undertaker and His Pals, The (1967)
Unseen, The (1981)

Vampire and the Ballerinas, The (1960)
Vampyres, Daughters of Dracula (1975)
Veil of Blood (1973)
Venus in Furs (1970)
Vernon, Florida
Violent Years, The (1956)
Vixen (1968)
Wall of Flesh (1967)
Watts Monster, The aka Dr. Black,
Mr. Hyde (Blaxploitation, 1976)
Werewolves on Wheels (1971)
Wheels of Tragedy (1963)
White Slaves of Chinatown (1964)
Wild Guitar (1962)
Wild in the Streets (1968)
Wild, Wild World of Jayne Mansfield,
The (1968)
Witchcraft Through the Ages (1921)
Wizard of Gore (1970)
Woman Eater, The (1959)
World of the Vampires (1960)
World's Greatest Sinner, The (1962)
Wrestling Women vs. the Aztec
Mummy (1965)
Xanadu (1980)
Young Playthings (1977)
Zontar, The Thing from Venus (1966)
MANSON FILMS
(Films directly based on Manson)
Helter Skelter, 1976
The Hitchikers, 1972
Manson, (documentary, 1975)
Manson Massacre, 1977
Sweet Saviour, (Troy Donahue, 1971)
Snuff, 1976

I N D E X

Hell On Wheels.

SH-63

MASK 12